£3

AN EVIL LOVE

AN
EVIL LOVE

Geoffrey Wansell

HEADLINE

First published in 1996
by HEADLINE BOOK PUBLISHING

10 9 8 7 6 5 4 3 2

British Library Cataloguing in Publication Data

Wansell, Geoffrey, 1945-
   An evil love : the life of Frederick West
   1.West, Fred 2.Murderers - England - Biography
   3.Murder - England
   I.Title
   364.1'523'092

ISBN 0 7472 1760 2 (hbk)
      0 7472 7739 7 (sbk)

Typeset by
Letterpart Limited, Reigate, Surrey

Printed and bound in Great Britain by
Mackays of Chatham PLC, Chatham, Kent

HEADLINE BOOK PUBLISHING
A division of Hodder Headline PLC
338 Euston Road
London NW1 3BH

For every victim of child abuse

Contents

'Man's evil love
Makes the crooked path seem straight.'

Dante, *The Divine Comedy*,
'Purgatory', canto 10

Writing the Biography of Frederick West

A personal preface

This book is a terrible journey through the darkness of one man's mind, and writing it has been an agonising experience. Nothing could have prepared me for what I have read and listened to in the past year. Frederick West took a monstrous pleasure in defacing the beauty of the world. And in doing so, he stole something from each and every one one of us – our innocence. To that extent we are all his victims.

There will be those who say that no book should ever have been written about the life of such a man, that he should simply be consigned to oblivion. It is a view I understand. Indeed there have been times during the past year, sitting in the silence of my room hour after hour, listening to his voice, reading his lies, and threading my way through the maze of excuses he offered for his actions – actions for which there could be no possible excuse – when I too wished I could be rid of him.

But I do not believe we can afford to forget, or ignore, Frederick West. For just as great beauty illuminates the whole of our lives, so great evil reminds us that beauty is to be cherished. To try to push West away, to deny that he existed, is to close our minds not only to the possibility of evil, but also to the redeeming power of good.

Certainly there were days when I sat in front of my word processor with tears running down my cheeks, days when I was unable to type the next word, to utter the next unpalatable truth. Yet, no matter the agony I felt, it was nothing to the agony of those who have lost their daughters, sisters or friends. It was as nothing to the agony of the children, including his own, who suffered at his hands. As the book progressed I became more and more determined to offer those children and young people some explanation of the man who blighted so many lives.

And, as I began to unravel the elements of West's life during the long nights of winter, I came to realise that this was not only a book about a murderer, but that it was also a book about childhood. For it was in childhood that West's own life was shaped, and it was West's abuse of children and young people – his desire to soil their innocence – that first led him along his terrible path.

That understanding, more than any other, sustained me. For it became ever clearer to me that to study the roots of evil is to make a start in preventing its spread. Now in the warmth of summer, having finished the book, I am convinced that if there is a light to be found in the black tunnel of West's life, it is the light which shines to tell us all that we must do everything in our power to protect our children.

I began this journey as a result of a remarkable decision, and a decision not originally taken by me. After Frederick West killed himself on 1 January 1995, the Official Solicitor to the Supreme Court was approached to administer West's estate. He concluded that among his duties 'he had to protect the financial interests of the five minor children', who were all then still in the care of the local authority, and 'to ensure that the best value is obtained for them'. One way for him to do so, he concluded, was to allow an author access to West's many hours of interviews, all of which were West's 'intellectual property', to write a balanced portrait of his life.

I agreed with him. But I only did so after a great deal of heart-searching, because I believed it offered an opportunity to consider evil at first hand, a chance to begin to explain what may have driven this apparently commonplace little man to acts of such extreme depravity. That is how my journey began and how this book came to be written. After West's death, I accepted the Official Solicitor's offer of access to those interviews; as well as to West's ninety-eight page memoir *I Was Loved by an Angel*, written in his prison cell; and to many other papers and statements about his life: more than 15,000 typed pages in all. And, in the early autumn of 1995, I set out to write his biography.

Never before has a biographer been given the chance to listen in quite this way to the innermost thoughts of a serial killer, a man now certainly guaranteed his place in the pantheon of British murderers alongside Jack the Ripper, Dr Crippen, John Christie, the Moors Murderers, Denis Nilsen and the Yorkshire Ripper – even though he was never convicted of a single murder. Writing the book has not only been a challenge, it has also changed my view of life.

When I began I thought, as so many people think, that it is indefensible to describe anyone as evil. There must be good in everyone, it is just a question of finding it. But the further I went along the path of trying to understand Frederick West the more convinced I became that, although there were certainly elements of humanity within him, he nevertheless demanded to be called evil. For West's actions do not lie within the limits of normal human behaviour. They lie far beyond them. And he knew it.

Frederick West was not a madman, not a schizophrenic nor a paranoid, not some solitary loner waiting to pounce on an unsuspecting victim, a man who hid his features beneath a black hood. He was an amiable, deferential family man, the father of at least six children, a baptised and confirmed member of the Church of England, a house owner with a mortgage who took his children for walks in the park on Sundays.

But he was also a man absolutely without conscience. He needed no excuse or explanation to kill. He had no need of alibis like 'medical experiments' or 'being lonely', about 'cleansing the world of wrongdoers', or 'sweeping away evil'. He did not hear voices urging him to act. Nor did he think he was the incarnation of some weird and imagined deity. Frederick West killed for pleasure, to amuse himself and his wife Rosemary. He killed because he enjoyed it.

That is what made the journey to try to offer some explanation of his crimes so difficult. To justify my contention that West demanded to be described as evil meant that I had to convey the full extent of his excesses, to confront the worst that he was capable of. To have pulled back would have been to leave the portrait incomplete, unfinished, the description unjustified.

As a result, I found myself reading and re-reading the *Book of Common Prayer* in the small Anglican church at the foot of my garden, looking at the words that must have been said over the infant Frederick West wrapped in swaddling clothes at his baptism: 'Dost thou, in the name of this Child, renounce the devil and all his works, the vain pomp and glory of the world, with all the covetous desires of the same, and the carnal desires of the flesh, so that thou will not follow or be led by them?'

The more I read those words, and the more I contrasted them with his, the clearer it became to me that Frederick West had wilfully and determinedly set out to disregard every tenet of human behaviour, every commandment of the faith into which he had been confirmed, and taken a positive delight in doing so. He had then taken an almost equal delight in concealing his actions behind the subtlest disguise of all, the familiar. By the time my journey to complete this book had come to its end, Frederick West had become – for me – the face of the devil.

I cannot tell what effect that realisation will have upon me, but I do not regret the decision to embark upon the journey. I must therefore acknowledge, at the very outset, that I could not have begun to try to understand and to explain the life of Frederick West without the help of the Official Solicitor to the Supreme Court, Peter Harris, and his deputy Bill McBryde. Nor could I have continued without the assistance of three members of the solicitors' partnership Taylor Joynson Garrett in London, Paul Mitchell, John Linneker and Niri Shanmuganathan. All of them offered both advice and support, and I am indebted to them all.

I am also very grateful to the Legal Department of Gloucestershire County Council, and particularly Richard Cawdron, for their assistance, as I am to Fred Davies, the county's deputy director of social services and other members of his staff, who helped me to understand the impact that Frederick West had upon his youngest children. Thanks to him I am also able to express my particular gratitude to Louise West, Rosemary West Junior and Lucyanna West, for their willingness to give me their views about their father. Mae and Stephen West also generously gave me theirs.

Indeed Stephen and Mae West's book, *Inside 25 Cromwell Street*, was one I returned to regularly, as I did also to their stepsister Anne Marie West's book, *Out of the Shadows*, which was written with Virginia Hill. Both helped to give me a sense of what life must have been like in that extraordinary cramped semi-detached house in the centre of Gloucester. It was to be some months before I would visit it myself, but when I did so the dankness of it seemed to wrap itself around me like a shroud. One memory, in particular, will never leave me. It is of the tiny window that Frederick West constructed for himself in the cellar, just below the steps up to his front door on the ground floor. He constructed it so that he could hide down there and watch who knocked at his door. I see his eyes at that small window even now.

Frederick West's widow, Rosemary West, has not collaborated with this book. The secrets she knows remain her own. Having sat through every day of her trial on ten counts of murder at Winchester Crown Court in the autumn of 1995, I do not doubt her guilt. Nor do I doubt that her wickedness knows few boundaries. There was no sign of grief or remorse on her face as the evidence against her mounted remorselessly. In its place there was merely a blank, bad-tempered denial, alongside a determined inability to remember or account for any of the awful events in which she played her part.

Speaking of the trial, I must pay tribute to both Brian Leveson QC and Richard Ferguson QC, prosecutor and defender respectively of Rosemary West, for the presentation of their case. At that time my researches were only just beginning, and I had little detailed knowledge of either Frederick or Rosemary West. Their eloquent and lucid explanation of the Wests' story, though delivered from opposite sides, provided me with an indispensable map to the life that I was beginning to try to make sense of. I am indebted to them for their clarity, just as I am to Mr Justice Mantell for his summing up, and to Mike Wicksteed of the Lord Chancellor's Department for allowing me to be present throughout the trial.

I must also thank another group of professionals who have guided me through the complexities of Frederick West's life. Professor David Canter of the University of Liverpool, one of Britain's leading criminal psychologists, has been both enormously kind, and his book *Criminal Shadows* became another indispensable map to guide me through the terrain of West's mind. Dr Eileen Vizard, Fellow of the Royal College of Psychiatrists, and one of this country's principal consultant child and adolescent psychiatrists, helped me to comprehend the complexities of child abuse as they may have applied to West. I am also grateful to Dr Brian Tully, of the Psychologists at Law group, whose insight into interviewing techniques proved invaluable, and to the neuro-linguistic programming consultant, Jane Mathison, who helped me to analyse West's methods of speech. And I must also thank the psychologist Sean MacBlain, who first directed me towards the work of George Kelly, and the concept of the alternative universe.

This book has not been written with the collaboration of the Gloucestershire Constabulary, although the Chief Constable, Dr Tony Butler, has remained unfailingly polite and courteous throughout. Dr Butler explained in a letter to me in May 1996 that a number of 'guiding principles within the Constabulary' had been established in the early days of their investigation, one of which 'is based on the view that it is not appropriate for police officers to comment about individuals except where that is necessary for the investigation and prosecution of the offender'. Dr Butler felt, therefore, that it was 'inappropriate for me or any other member of the Constabulary to pass on some observations about Mr West'.

Though I entirely respect Dr Butler's view, I cannot overlook the fact that Frederick West appeared to have a persistent and continuing acquaintance with individual officers within the Gloucestershire Constabulary. He clearly knew certain officers, indeed he boasted as much in court on one occasion, just as he boasted repeatedly that he was 'raided regular – two or three times a week' at times during his life at Cromwell Street. West existed in the shadowy netherworld occupied by small-time criminals, a world with which some police officers are all too familiar, and in which there may even exist a shared language and attitude to life. Nevertheless it was the persistence of one individual Gloucestershire officer, Detective Constable Hazel Savage, who first encountered Rena West in 1966, probably more than any other single factor, which finally brought Frederick West's murderous career to an end.

There are many other people, however, other than those already mentioned, who have helped me take this dark journey and whose support and advice I have relied upon. Some of them offered that support only on the understanding that I would not identify them, and I must therefore simply offer them my private and heartfelt thanks. But there are some whom I am free to name. Two members of the Bar, James Bullen and David McLaren Webster QC, one still a barrister the other now a judge, helped me to understand some of the intricacies of criminal law, and at the same time provided me with unqualified moral support, for which I am enormously grateful. Frank Longford also encouraged me to think that I was capable of bringing sense to Frederick West's life, as did Jeremy Bullmore, Stephen Fay and David Suchet. I am indebted to them all.

I am also very grateful for the encouragement of some of the writers and journalists who worked on the story of the Wests. In particular I must pay tribute to the work of Howard Sounes, whose book *Fred & Rose* offered the first detailed account of the Wests, and to Andrew O'Hagan, for his book *The Missing*, which drew pointed attention to West's time in Glasgow. Though I cannot name them all, I should also thank each and every writer and reporter who sat alongside me at the trial of Rosemary West for their kindness, in particular Allan Smith of the Press Association, and my fellow authors Brian Masters and Gordon Burn.

I must also thank my agent and first editor, Rivers Scott, whose support, as ever, I have relied upon, and whose counsel has been invaluable, just as I have relied upon the advice of his associate Gloria Ferris. I am very grateful too for the support I have received from Alan Brooke and Headline, as well as for the careful assistance of Alan's associate Celia Kent. Indeed I should thank all the staff at Headline for their unwavering encouragement and enthusiasm.

But most of all I must thank my family, my wife Jan, my son Dan and my daughter Molly. They more than anyone have had to suffer the agonies of my journey through the life of Frederick West, and they have done so without a moment's complaint. I can only apologise to them if sometimes I seemed to have disappeared into another, darker, world.

Not one of the above should be held responsible for my conclusions, however; those are mine alone. Writing the life of Frederick West brought me nightmares: images of faeces and foetuses that, I fear, will never leave my mind, but even they did not deter me. When they recur, the last words of the Lord's Prayer at the beginning of the Anglican Communion – 'Deliver us from evil' – echo in my mind. We can be so delivered, but to do so we cannot afford to turn away from its face.

Geoffrey Wansell
Wiltshire, England
July 1996

Prologue

Arrow of desire

'That one may smile, and smile, and be a villain.'

Shakespeare, *Hamlet*

Half-way between a smirk and a leer, never quite a grin, it was a naughty boy's smile, a smile that hints he's got away with something, but no one is ever quite sure what. It was the smile that Frederick Walter Stephen West hid behind throughout the fifty-three years of his life, his mask against an inquisitive world. Looking back, it was a smile to send a shiver down the spine.

Frederick West was a small, spare man. Five feet six in height, barely ten stone in weight, he would have looked quite at home at a fair-ground, tearing the tickets for the dodgems, winking at the girls as he helped them into their car, then standing on the back as they made their first tentative movements across the rink. West would always have jumped off – just as they started to scream.

His eyes were as sharp as a poacher's. Startlingly blue, darting out from beneath a shock of dark curly hair, they were the eyes of a man who always knew what he wanted, eyes that never missed a movement, particularly from a warm, bloody, furry animal. The Herefordshire countryside that bred him infused every fibre of his body, just as it haunted his voice.

When West moved, it was always quickly. The noose would be around the rabbit's neck before the animal had a chance to move, the pheasant caught by the wire before it could blink. Success was always greeted with an ugly, gurgling snigger, once heard, never forgotten; a dark sound to accompany the sparkle in his eyes.

Never afraid of being dirty, his short strong fingers were forever soiled in offal or manure, clay or mortar, which he would wash off in the cattle trough at the side of the field or the tank waiting to be plumbed into the house on the building site. If there were no hot water, he never craved it. A cold stream from a hosepipe in the garden would do just as well at the end of the day. He would often sit down for supper wearing only underpants or a vest.

1

Frederick West may not have been able to read or write, but that rarely inhibited him. He could talk, and talk he did, incessantly; bragging about his prowess with women, boasting about the size of his motor bike or who he knew 'in the right places', nudging and winking his way through the world, forever ready 'to sort things out', never afraid to 'shoot round' and 'help someone out', anything to keep himself busy.

For West was not a lazy man, any more than he was a stupid one. His intelligence was born in the fields and woods on the very edge of Gloucestershire and Herefordshire, honed in the thickets of the countryside, nurtured in a world in which it was sometimes safer to kill a man than to kill a hare, a delicate skill that he brought to the city of Gloucester, and to the prey there was to be had there.

His hands were large, with the thickened thumbs of a man used to manual labour. He prided himself on being one of the best trench diggers ever to work on a motorway, just as he did on his record as a press operator in the light fabrication shop at Gloucester's Wagon Works. They were the hands of a man who was not afraid of the feel of blood.

Blood did not terrify Frederick Walter Stephen West. He was not afraid of it any more than he was afraid of the sound of a cracking bone. He had grown up with the sharp tooth-edge of violence, the rabbit hit with a pickaxe handle as it runs out from the corn, the pig hanging in the kitchen for its blood to drain away, the chicken caught by a fox leaving its trace of blood in the snow.

When he talked about blood, West would sometimes laugh to himself. But it was not a generous laugh, born of affection and kindness. It was a lascivious, wolfish laugh, the acknowledgement of an illicit pleasure, a laugh that made others uneasy, though they could never quite put their finger on why. It was the laugh of a man who was not afraid to inflict pain.

To a gamekeeper, the laugh made Frederick West seem innocent; that and his endless stream of chatter. The naughty wink, the suggestive story, the knowing leer, all rendered him approachable, unthreatening, an obsequious jack the lad at the end of the public bar with a pint of cider and a bag of crisps. What could be a more effective disguise? West never presented himself red in tooth and claw; he was too careful for that. Instead, he took refuge in the ordinary, the banal. Who could take offence at that? Even a police-woman might be won over.

Women were Frederick West's only hobby. He did not keep pigeons, do the football pools, or dream of Disneyland. Instead, he craved the company of women, vulnerable women, creatures who could be seduced by his relentless, eager talk. His was an unexpected charm, a persistence that never faltered. Women were sexual objects to be conquered, and then displayed as trophies, the only truly worthy prey.

It was no accident that one of Frederick West's nicknames was Freddy the Fox – ''cause nobody can work me out' – for beneath the endless chatter, weaving its spells and fantasies, behind the smirking laugh, tailored to cajole, there lay a ruthless wickedness a wild creature might scent in the air, a ferocious, slippery violence capable of freezing a rabbit on the edge of a corn-field.

Though he would always call it love, lust was the light that illuminated the life of Frederick West. Learned as a child, burnished as an adolescent, and given full rein in adulthood, there was no limit to his priapic desire. To him, it was as natural as the stoat's pursuit of a leveret in the moonlight. There was no shame to be drawn from victory when it came, only pleasure.

It was an evil love, as the world would come to know.

Chapter One

Dark imaginings

'Foul deeds will rise,
Though all the earth o'erwhelm them, to men's eyes.'

Shakespeare, *Hamlet*

It was twenty minutes before two o'clock on the afternoon of Thursday 24 February 1994 when the unmarked police car turned into a narrow street in the centre of the English county town of Gloucester. A light drizzle was falling from the pewter sky, and the plain, flat-fronted houses seemed to huddle together for protection against the wind sweeping up the Severn Estuary from the sea. The lunchtime shoppers, picking their way home past the dustbins and detritus littering the street's pavement, bent into the squall. Then, as the police car drew quietly to a stop outside a flat, sand-coloured semi-detached, the wind abated and the street seemed to hold its breath.

For a moment none of the police-officers moved. They simply sat and stared at the square three-storey house beside them, as if they could not quite believe why they had come to this ordinary-looking abode, in this nondescript street, in this honest English town. But this was no ordinary house. Unlike every other in the street, its entrance was barred by a pair of ornate wrought-iron gates.

With their intricate pattern of whorls and curlicues, the gates looked incongruous amid the rotting sofas and derelict prams cluttering the pavements in this street of bed-sits. They were matched by the sign on the wall beside the ground-floor window, the sign giving the number of the house. It, too, was wrought-iron, every bit as sinuously proud as the gates themselves. It read simply: 25 Cromwell Street. As the five officers pushed open the gates and walked up to the house's green front door, the sign seemed to challenge them.

The officers had come in search of the man who had fashioned those confident wrought-iron gates and flowing iron sign, a son of Gloucester who was about to join another of the city's famous sons,

Richard Crookback, Third of England, among the folklore of his country's villainy. They had come to find Frederick Walter Stephen West.

It was not West, however, but his daughter Mae, who answered the ring on the doorbell on that Thursday lunch-time. Without waiting for an invitation, the four male officers and a single policewoman walked straight past her, across the narrow hallway, and into the ground-floor sitting-room. Frederick West's wife Rosemary, full-figured, dark-haired, and with a pair of large pearl-rimmed glasses planted firmly on her short nose, was sitting on the sofa watching *Neighbours* on television. As the officers came in, she stood up, the belligerence in her face only too clear.

The senior officer, Detective Chief Inspector Terry Moore, handed Mrs West a warrant allowing them to search the garden for the body of her first-born child Heather, who would have been twenty-three, and explained to her that a team of policemen would shortly start to dig up the paved patio behind the house to look for her body. Rosemary West looked back and snapped: 'This is stupid.' Then she walked across to the telephone, as if the whole event were taking place in slow motion, filmed by Quentin Tarantino.

The ringing startled Frederick West. For a moment he could not quite work out what it was. But then he opened the door of his small white van and picked up the mobile phone lying on the seat. It was 1.50 p.m., and he was drinking a mug of tea. 'You'd better get back home,' he heard a voice say. 'Rose says the police are there. They say they're going to dig up the garden, looking for Heather.' The dark, curly-haired man, with such clear blue eyes that they seemed almost out of place against the background of his gypsy's face, merely grinned: 'Well, they'd better bloody well put it back when they've finished.'

At that moment West was barely a dozen miles from his house in Cromwell Street, working alone on the loft of a house in the village of Frampton Mansell. At the most, it would have taken him twenty minutes to drive home, but he made no move whatever to go. West simply clicked off his mobile phone and went back to his tea. The fact that the police were in his house, threatening to dig up his garden, seemed to worry him not at all. There was plenty of time. He had dealt with the police for years. There was nothing to worry about.

Seventy minutes later, shortly before three o'clock on that grey February afternoon, West pulled out on to the main Cirencester to Stroud road, which winds through the valleys of the Cotswolds back towards Gloucester. Just as he did so, the mobile phone rang again: 'Dad, it's Steve. Are you coming home or not?' West paused for a moment, then told his eldest son calmly: 'I'll be home shortly – to sort it out. Tell your mam not to worry.'

He was not home shortly. In fact, he disappeared for two and a

5

half hours. Where did he go? In that space of time, while police-officers sweated and strained to lift the slabs in his garden at Cromwell Street, he could have driven to Bristol Airport, twenty-five miles to the south-west, or to London's Heathrow, a hundred miles to the east. He could have boarded a ship at Bristol docks, or driven to Scotland, as he had done almost thirty years before, to start a new life. Or he could have gone somewhere to dispose of evidence that would have linked him to the deaths of many, many more innocent young women. He never explained, and now one will never know. His son's attempts to speak to him again on his mobile phone never succeeded. Only one thing is certain: it was dark before Frederick West's small white van turned into Cromwell Street just before twenty minutes to six that evening. There was a distinct spring in his step as he walked towards the house that had been his home for twenty-one years, pushed open the wrought-iron gates, strolled up the path, and into his living-room. As the five officers turned to look at him, Frederick West just grinned.

Within an hour, West was on his way to the city's central police station, a little over half a mile away. 'Just remember you've got to bloody well put it back as you found it,' he told the two officers travelling beside him in the back of the car. 'Bloody proud of that garden, I am.'

At ten minutes to eight that evening, Frederick West gave his first official interview to the police. Detective Constable Hazel Savage and Detective Constable Robert Vestey sat opposite him in a first-floor interview room at Gloucester police station and reminded him that he had come there 'voluntarily'. When asked if he wanted the services of a duty solicitor, Fred West replied calmly, 'I won't bother at the moment', and lit a cigarette.

For the next forty-three minutes Frederick West denied any knowledge whatever of his daughter Heather. He could not remember her date of birth or her age, he had 'no idea' where she was. All he did know was that she had left home years before to go away with her 'lesbian friend', a girl who had come to Cromwell Street to collect her. But he remembered the girl very clearly. 'She had a red miniskirt on just about to the bottom of her knickers,' he went on. 'You know, if she bent, it lifted like that – you could see everything.' West winked and took another drag on his cigarette.

'Heather obviously didn't want nothing to do with us, or she'd have been back home,' he told the officers. 'I mean, Stephen left home, Mae left home, but they've all come back.' But he did not worry about her. He had seen her in Birmingham eighteen months before. He had heard from her on the telephone, when she told him she was 'mixed up with drugs', and she had been talking to a newspaper reporter. 'Lots of girls who disappear,' West suggested cheerfully, 'take different names and go into prostitution.' He did not report her as a missing person because as far as he was concerned 'she wasn't missing'.

'Is she under the patio at your home?' he was asked.

'No,' he replied firmly.

There was a long pause until the grey-haired woman detective asked West softly why, if that was the case, there seemed to be 'a family joke' among his children that Heather 'was underneath the patio'. Frederick West's laughter echoed around the stark interview room. 'Oh, for God's sake. I mean, you believe it.' Then he stood up and said: 'I think we better pack it up, Hazel. We're talking rubbish, aren't we? . . . I mean, you're digging me place up. Carry on doing it.'

'Where is she, Fred?'

'You find her and I'll be happy. That's all I can say.'

Just five minutes after Frederick West sat down for his interview at Gloucester police station, his wife Rosemary began her first official conversation with the police – in the bar room that West had created for them on the first floor of Cromwell Street. Unlike her husband, she had refused to go to the police station, opting instead to answer their questions upstairs. Her conversation was recorded on a portable tape machine, and she sat throughout looking stonily at a huge photograph of a sandy beach on the wall opposite her. When Detective Sergeant Terry Onions and Woman Police Constable Debbie Willats reminded her that she wasn't under arrest, she barked back: 'If I'm not under arrest, why are you here?'

Like her husband, Rose West could not remember when Heather had left home. She could not even remember what season of the year it was, though 'it could have been the summer', because the girl was forever 'running away on school trips', and 'having arguments with her teachers'. The belligerence of Rose's manner was softened only by the Devon burr that had lingered in her voice since childhood. Heather had been a 'stubborn girl' who didn't want to do her own washing, or 'move up off the seat'.

'We didn't hit it off that well,' Rose West told the tall, clean-cut detective interviewing her. 'She didn't seem to want to know me that much. She was all her father, not me.'

Then, after about twenty minutes, Rose West echoed her husband's explanation of her daughter's disappearance. 'She was a lesbian as far as I know,' she said, like a bolt out of the blue. When her daughter had been at infants' school, her mother said she had known 'exactly what kind of knickers the women teachers had on'. When the two detectives asked whether she was worried about the daughter she had not seen since 1987, Rose West replied bluntly: 'She obviously doesn't want to know me any more, does she?' The whey-faced, dumpy woman, with the manner of an overwrought parking-meter attendant, growled: 'Ask Fred. He knows all about her . . . I know he had several phone calls off her, but she didn't want to speak to me.'

Detective Sergeant Onions reminded her gently that she was describing her first-born child, whom she had not seen since the age of sixteen. Rose West exploded: 'Thousands of kids go missing. It's only a mystery because you wanted it a mystery . . . If you had any brains at all you could find her. It can't be that bloody difficult.'

'Is there a body?'

'There ain't.'

Shortly before a quarter to nine on that Thursday evening, Detective Sergeant Onions drew the interview to a close: 'You know in your own mind what's happened to her.'

'No, I don't,' Rosemary West snarled back.

The two detectives left number 25 Cromwell Street shortly after their interview with Rosemary West. One uniformed officer remained to keep watch on the garden, sitting on a chair and trying to read a book, while another was stationed outside the front door. As the two climbed into their car the rain was falling steadily. Darkness shrouded the house like a cloak.

At Gloucester police station, Frederick West was interviewed for a second time. Once again he refused the offer of a solicitor, and once again he launched into a rambling series of reminiscences about his last contacts with his daughter Heather, and why he had never reported her as missing. 'She was bringing drugs from somewhere and taking them up to schools, recruiting schoolkids,' he told one officer confidentially, and he did not want to get her into trouble. For more than forty minutes West provided the police with elaborate descriptions of all the places that he had seen or heard from his daughter, and the reasons why she could not be under the patio in his back garden, until, shortly before nine-thirty, he walked out of the interview room and made his way back across the city to his home.

Not long before ten o'clock that evening, Frederick West walked back into the ground-floor sitting-room of his house at Cromwell Street, and there was still a smile on his face. The first thing he did was to re-connect the electricity supply to the meter in the hall: he had been fiddling the electricity meters for years, routing the supply to a faulty meter, and then re-routing it again just before it was due to be read. His son could hardly believe it: 'God knows why, it was all Dad was concerned about.'

West took a shower, then sat in his underpants watching the television news, as he usually did, drinking a cup of tea. Then, shortly afterwards, he and his wife took their two newly acquired dogs, Benji and Oscar, for a walk in the park at the bottom of Cromwell Street. Neither Stephen nor Mae West could ever remember them doing so before.

As they walked down Cromwell Street together, Frederick and Rosemary West were whispering, and they kept up their private conversation for the rest of the night. There were no phone calls, and no visitors, and the only person Frederick West spoke to was the woman who had been his wife for twenty-two years. He told her what he had told her a thousand times during those years: 'I'll sort it out.'

As West put it months later: 'We sat up all night, never went to bed, never even went to sleep all night.'

By the time dawn broke over Cromwell Street, Frederick West had made a decision. He telephoned his boss and told him that he would not be at work that day, then asked his son Stephen to help him clear out his van. While they were doing it, he told him: 'Look, son, look after your mum. I'm going away for a bit.'

West then packed a few belongings, including what he called his 'prison lighter' (a tin of tobacco and cigarette papers), and put them beside the front door. When Detective Constable Hazel Savage returned to Cromwell Street shortly after eleven o'clock on the morning of Friday 25 February 1994, West was ready. As soon as she asked for the address of Rosemary West's elderly mother, West took her to one side and asked to go back to the police station with her. After a thirty-second private conversation with his wife, West picked up the small bag of belongings he had prepared, walked out of the door of Cromwell Street and climbed into the waiting police car.

Without prompting, and as soon as the driver had started the engine, West turned to Detective Constable Hazel Savage and said in his gentle Herefordshire accent: 'I killed her.'

At eleven-thirty that morning, barely thirteen hours after he had left it, Frederick West walked back into Gloucester police station unaided and unhandcuffed. But no sooner had he been asked to empty his pockets than he became unsteady on his feet and had to be helped to sit down on a wooden chair. 'I feel sick and I've got a pain in my head,' he told the officers, who remembered later that his hands 'became very shaky' and that he 'had to be helped to sip from a cup of cool water'.

Shortly before twelve-thirty he was examined by a police doctor, and then allowed into the station's exercise yard for a cigarette with a uniformed constable. For the next eighty minutes, he walked around the yard holding his head and looking into space. When the young constable asked him if he was all right, West simply told him: 'My head hurts and I keep seeing stars.'

The other thing West told the young police-officer was that he had killed his daughter Heather.

Once again it was raining, but digging continued in the garden of Cromwell Street throughout the day. And just before five o'clock that Friday afternoon, Frederick West confessed formally, during a thirty-eight-minute taped interview, how he had killed his daughter Heather. His voice a monotone, he told the police that he had cut up his daughter's body into three sections – 'legs, a head and a body' – and had buried them in 'a hole in the ground' about 'four, five feet' deep with a spade. Then he had put all his daughter's belongings out for the dustmen in St Michael's Square behind his house.

'The thing I'd like to stress, I mean, Rose knew nothing at all . . . She hasn't done anything.'

Shortly after the interview, West and Hazel Savage returned to Cromwell Street. He pointed out the exact spot, half-way down the garden under a line of small fir trees, where he had buried Heather. And later that evening he explained that although he tried to 'revive' his daughter for two or three hours he never considered calling an ambulance or a doctor. All he could think to do was to dismember her body and hide it, 'in case Rose came back from the shops or the children came back from school'.

On the surface it looked as though the police case against Frederick Walter Stephen West was closed. He had confessed. All that was left was to find the body.

Meanwhile, seven miles away at Cheltenham police station, police-officers were once again questioning Rosemary West. Shortly after her husband's first confession they had arrested her on suspicion of the murder of her daughter Heather, and now they wanted to know the details of what she knew. But once again Rosemary West was a distinctly hostile witness. She was prepared to tell them only what her daughter looked like.

'Bit shorter than me, about five foot four,' she told them, 'with really dark hair.' Heather 'liked to be different to everybody else' and was always 'trying to be opposite to everybody else'. Rosemary West could not remember the precise date on which her daughter had left home, although she thought it was in June, and she also could not remember if she had left with anyone. 'Past experience told me at the time,' she said bluntly, 'that once a child does cut you off there's not a lot you're going to do about getting them back or being able to talk to them.'

Detective Sergeant Onions then told her that her husband had confessed to Heather's murder.

'So she's dead. Is that right?' Rosemary West said flatly.

'I'm telling you . . . Fred had confessed to murdering Heather.'

'What?'

'That automatically implicates you.'

'Why does it automatically implicate me?' Rosemary West snapped back.

'Our suspicions are that you are implicated.'

'It's a lie.'

By lunch-time on Saturday 26 February it looked as though Rosemary West might be right. The police had not found anything. There was absolutely nothing to indicate that the body of Heather West was buried beneath the patio of 25 Cromwell Street, Gloucester. Frederick West was interviewed for the sixth time, shortly after one-thirty that afternoon, and when Hazel Savage admitted that her colleagues digging in his garden had found nothing his demeanour changed in an instant.

The grin that had been missing since the previous morning began

10

slowly to spread across his face, and the glint in his blue eyes suddenly seemed to return.

'Did I ask them to go and dig my garden up?' he asked suddenly. 'Let them keep on digging.' And he broke off the interview after just eight minutes.

Less than half an hour later West asked to resume the interview, and this time he repudiated totally everything he had said in the past twenty-four hours. His daughter was not dead.

'Heather's alive and well, right. She's possibly at this moment in Bahrain' working for a drug cartel, he announced. She had a Mercedes, a chauffeur and a new birth certificate. They had even had lunch together recently in Devizes in Wiltshire. 'I have no idea what her name is 'cause I would not let her tell me. She contacts me whenever she's in this country.'

There was a half-smile on his face as he went on: 'Now whether you believe it or not, that's entirely up to you . . . There ain't nothing in my garden. You can dig it for evermore. I've never harmed anybody in my life . . . I do not believe in it, hurting people.'

When he was asked what benefit there had been for him in the admission of his daughter's murder, his smile widened still further. 'The police are out there digging . . . I feel a lot better for it.'

Was Heather West buried in the garden of Cromwell Street?

'No. They can dig there for evermore. Nobody or nothing's under the patio.'

An hour later the police found three human bones in the garden of 25 Cromwell Street. But they did not all belong to Heather Ann West. The twists and turns that were to mark one of the most terrible murder cases in British criminal history had only just begun.

Shortly after half-past four on the Saturday afternoon of 26 February 1994 Frederick Walter Stephen West walked back into the first-floor interview room at Gloucester police station. The first thing he did was to apologise to Hazel Savage.

'I got nothing personal against her at all,' he said, looking down at the floor. He had taken two diazepam pills. 'I don't know what happened.' What had happened was simpler than two pills. West's solicitor, Howard Ogden, had informed him that the police had found human remains in the garden at Cromwell Street. Frederick West could not wriggle or talk his way out of the fact.

'Heather's where I told you she is,' West confessed, his voice once again flat and monotonal, 'and I mean they should have found her anyway by now, because she's there.'

The two officers did not comment and explained that their colleagues had been having difficulty because of the water in the holes they had been digging. The jobbing builder started immediately to tell them that Cromwell Street 'used to be part of the moat round Gloucester', and there was an 'underground spring' in the garden forcing up the water table.

11

Detective Constable Savage listened, and then asked whether there were any other bones in the garden. For the first time in two days of interviews, Frederick West hesitated.

'Well, that's a peculiar question to ask, ain't it,' he said after a long pause. 'Heather is in there, and there ain't no more.'

It was almost two hours before the police returned to question either Frederick or Rosemary West. When they did so, Rosemary West denied any knowledge of her daughter's fate, or her husband's murder. 'He just said she'd left,' she said flatly.

'We just want to get to the bottom of it,' Detective Sergeant Onions told her at Cheltenham police station. 'There's no charades now. What do you know about it all? Or what have you known about it over the last eight years.'

Rosemary West did not pause. 'I don't know anything about it. I was not aware of it.' When the detective asked about her feelings she said: 'Put it this way. He's a dead man if I ever get my hands on him.'

'Are you protecting him?'

'What's the point?' Rosemary West replied flatly. 'Protecting him from what?'

Back in the interview room at Gloucester, Frederick West had recovered his composure. Now he was intent on telling the police the details of his disposal of Heather's body in the garden. As he had done so many times already, West started to digress, offering longer and longer explanations, building detail upon detail of the night he had buried his daughter. 'It was raining. It had been absolutely tipping it down all day, and that bottom was like a swamp with water.'

Finally, after almost twenty minutes, Hazel Savage stopped him in his tracks, and told him that the police had found another bone.

'This is a third femur, a leg bone, Fred. The question is, is there anybody else buried in your garden?'

West did not blink. 'Only Heather.'

DC Savage persisted. He had never told her that Heather was 'scattered all over the garden', and besides, 'Heather didn't have three legs'.

For the second time that afternoon, Frederick West could not find anything to say. The silence in the interview room wrapped itself around him like a blanket, until his solicitor's clerk asked whether he knew where this other thigh bone might have come from.

'Yes. Shirley,' West said softly.

'Shirley who?'

'Robinson, the girl who caused the problem.'

It was the first indication that Frederick West was more than simply a domestic murderer, the first indication that he was capable of killing more than one victim. The next chapter in his extraordinary story was about to unfold.

★   ★   ★

A little over an hour later on that same Saturday evening, West was to admit that there were not one but three bodies in the garden of Cromwell Street. The third victim was 'Shirley's mate' who had 'turned up at Cromwell Street' with a photograph he and Shirley had had taken together, and asking where she was. Like so many other horrifying stories that West was to tell the police in the days and weeks to come, it was a lie.

The death of 'Shirley's mate', like those of Shirley Robinson and Heather West, was infinitely more bizarre and terrifying even than Frederick West's brutal descriptions. They were his particular method of concealing the truth. He would utter the unmentionable, confident that no ordinary man or woman, whether police-officer or not, could imagine that the ugly truth he was telling could possibly be an invention.

In reality they were simply another layer of the lies that he heaped upon lies, another fabrication to conceal the true nature of the horrors that lay beyond. Indeed, Frederick West would not have made this third admission had he not visited his garden the night before and seen the full extent of the police excavation.

When the first sets of remains were discovered he calculated, in his characteristic fashion, that if he admitted to three killings they would probably give up the search, and that his house would be left intact. It was that careful measuring of possibilities, not the onset of remorse, that persuaded him to confess. For no matter what the officers sitting in the tiny interview room in Gloucester police station may have thought, West was still not telling the truth.

The next afternoon West firmly denied there were any other victims. And in an effort to convince the police that they had finally got to the bottom of his crimes, he embarked on a description of precisely how and why he had killed his daughter Heather.

It was a description that was to sicken the hearts of the officers who listened to it, and enough to make Janet Leach, the thirty-eight-year-old woman who had agreed to act as West's impartial 'appropriate adult' during his police interviews 'turn green'. It was also the first clear indication of the depth of his evil love.

On that Friday morning in mid-June 1987, West explained, his wife had gone shopping and Heather West was upstairs when he shouted up to her. She had expected to be leaving home that morning, to take a job at a holiday camp near Weston-super-Mare, but the night before had received a telephone call saying the job had fallen through. Nevertheless, she had assembled all her clothes and personal belongings in a suitcase and a set of plastic carrier-bags, and put them by the front door of 25 Cromwell Street.

'I called her into the hallway,' West told the police on that Sunday afternoon in February 1994, 'and I said to her . . . now what's this about your leaving home . . . You know you're too young. You're a lesbian and there's AIDS and all that. I mean, you're vulnerable for anything.'

13

But Heather 'just stood there and looked at me'.

'I said, "Well, Heather, I'm not going to let you go" and she said, "If you don't fucking let me go I'll give all the kids acid and they'll all jump off the church roof and be dead on the floor".'

The sixteen-year-old girl then tried to get past West, but he grabbed her. 'First of all I went to slap her across the face. Then I suddenly stopped and thought on a previous occasion me and Rose had had an argument and I slapped her across the face and I dislocated her jaw . . . so I mean the last thing on my mind was to hurt Heather in any way.

'But Heather's standing there grinning all over her face, with her hands in her pockets shaking her trousers. So then I grabbed her by the throat and I'm shouting at her in anger really, you know, "How dare you say that about your brothers and sisters?" '

West told the police that he kept his hands on his daughter's throat and she still 'had this grin on her face' until it got to a point where 'I was actually still looking at her but couldn't see her for some reason'.

'Then all of a sudden I spotted she'd gone blue. So I let go of her quick and, of course, she just started to fall backwards on to the washing-machine and slide forward.'

West tried to give his daughter mouth-to-mouth resuscitation. 'I tried, you know, pressing her chest and that to make her breathe again.' But, as he confessed to the police, although he had 'seen it on the telly' he had 'never actually gone to classes or learned how to do this type of thing . . . and there was no way I could get anything out of Heather'.

'She was making funny noises, whether it was coming from her throat or her chest for a little while', and West dragged her into the living-room of Cromwell Street and got some wet cloths to put on his daughter's face. He even 'tried to get a drink of water into her mouth'.

'By this time I'm panicking like anything. I mean, I'm literally a nervous wreck at this stage because of what had happened. I had no intention whatsoever of hurting Heather because I think the world of her.' But West did not call an ambulance, nor did he telephone the police. Instead he took a brass mirror off the living-room wall 'and put it over her mouth' to see if she was breathing, 'and there was nothing on it'.

He then dragged her inert body into the bathroom near the kitchen on the ground floor of Cromwell Street and as he did so 'she wet all over the floor', he told the police. 'I put her in the bath and I ran the cold water on her and I still couldn't get nothing, no life out of her. So I can remember standing there and thinking, how do you know when somebody's dead?'

Heather West was now lying naked in the bath at 25 Cromwell Street. Her father told the police that he had removed the culottes his daughter had been wearing because they were 'soaking wet', and he had previously taken off her blouse in the living-room. Heather had not been wearing a bra or pants. He took his daughter's naked body out of the bath and dried it.

14

Frederick West then told the police that he 'put something round her neck . . . to make sure she was dead'. He thought he had used a pair of tights which had been lying around in the bathroom. 'I didn't want to touch her while she was alive. I mean . . . if I'd have started cutting her leg or her throat or something and she'd have suddenly come alive . . . that's what I was thinking.

'I can still see her. I can see her sat there in the bath,' he told the police.

West went to get a dustbin from the garden. 'I put the dustbin flat . . . tipped on its side on the floor . . . and I folded Heather and tried to slide her in . . . and lift the dustbin back up.'

But the plan did not work. When he lifted the dustbin back on to its base, Heather West's body was sticking out. 'No way you'd get the lid on or nothing. I mean, she was a good foot, two foot above, above the thing, and I mean her legs were even farther up than that.'

'So then I . . . put her back on the floor and pulled the dustbin back off her and then rolled her back into the bath and then I . . . then I did the rest.'

What West then told the police was exactly how he had dismembered his daughter. He began by closing his daughter's eyes before he started. 'If somebody's sat there looking at you, you're not going to use a knife on a person are you?'

Frederick West had intended to use an 'ice knife' but it was not sharp enough, so he threw the knife to one side and found another, sharper knife in the kitchen of Cromwell Street to use in its place.

West cut and twisted off his daughter's head. He described the sound. 'I remember it made a heck of a noise when it was breaking, horrible noise . . . like scrunching . . . I suppose . . . I had my eyes closed. I just couldn't look at her face and do it to her, you know what I mean. I just couldn't look at her . . . how I cut round I've no real idea.'

He then cut off his daughter's legs, cutting her groin with a knife and then twisting her foot until he heard 'one almighty crack and the leg come loose, like'. Then he left his daughter's two legs in the bath, and lifted her 'main body and put it in the bin'. She 'filled the bin shoulder-ways'.

When the police-officers asked him how he felt, West told them: 'I was absolutely dead. I couldn't think of nothing. I mean, I was trembling. I mean, I was absolutely trembling.'

Nevertheless, he was able to put the lid on the dustbin, which now contained his daughter's dismembered body, and 'using it like a steering wheel to roll him out down into the garden . . . Then I spotted this rope hanging out of the tree, so I went down and cut two pieces off it and then tied the handles on the bin.' West rolled the dustbin 'down the garden round to the back of the Wendy house, covered her over with a sheet'.

'Then I went back in the house and washed everything . . . There was no blood anywhere . . . no marks anywhere.' As soon as he had finished, and had cleaned the urine from the living-room floor with a

15

dishcloth from the kitchen sink, West picked up the case and plastic carrier-bags containing all his daughter's belongings, which were sitting in the hall, stuffed everything into black plastic bags and 'put them out for the dustman'.

'Then Rose came back, must have been an hour or more later,' West told the police, and shortly afterwards his other children started coming home from school.

That night, after his children had gone to bed, West told the police he sent his wife out for the evening and set about burying his daughter's body in the back garden. He started digging a hole, after putting polythene around the sides to protect his clothes. He wore wellington boots. But before he got far, he hit water.

'The wind was blowing like anything and the amount of water that was in there. I mean the water was making a noise.' West pushed his daughter's naked and dismembered body into this small hole, about four feet deep, with water at the bottom, with his spade. 'I then back-filled the hole, levelled it out . . . rolled this big piece of plastic out and put it on the top.' He did that 'to cover up the digging'.

Heather West's body had remained in that hole for almost seven years, until the Gloucester police discovered it late on Saturday 26 February 1994, the day before Frederick West's third confession, a confession he was later to retract.

As West was escorted back to his cell beneath the police station on that Saturday afternoon in February 1994, he looked for all the world as though nothing whatever had happened. What the police could not have suspected was that even this horrifying story concealed an even darker, bleaker truth. The two police-officers may have suspected they had spent the last forty-five minutes in the company of evil. What they could not know was how much more there was to know.

To discover that, they would have had to retrace West's steps since childhood. They were to begin that process a few days later, after Hazel Savage suggested to Frederick West: 'Imagine you're writing a book about your life, Fred, and we're the ghostwriters.'

For a moment the tiny gnome of a man looked perplexed, and then the grin returned to his face.

Chapter Two

Unnatural deeds

'It is my belief, Watson, founded upon my experience, that the lowest and vilest alleys of London do not present a more dreadful record of sin than does the smiling and beautiful countryside.'

Sir Arthur Conan Doyle, *The Copper Beeches*

The Herefordshire village of Much Marcle, barely a mile from the Gloucestershire border, is not quite a picture postcard. Straggling and a little disjointed, it meanders across the fields seven miles north-east of the ancient town of Ross-on-Wye rather than nestles round a duck-filled pond. There is no tiny thatched post office, nor black and white framed high street; in their place lies a pub at the crossroads, a cider-making factory and a substantial church. But the poet John Masefield, who was born nearby, described the area as 'paradise', and Elizabeth Barrett Browning, who lived there a century before, celebrated it in her poem 'The Deserted Garden'.

Frederick Walter Stephen West was born and raised in the village, and his father, Walter Stephen West, was born nearby in 1914, the grandson of a wagoner who tended horses for the plough. Educated at the tiny village school, Walter West worked in the Much Marcle fields throughout the seventy-eight years of his life, and raised his family of six children in a cottage there, where one of his sons remains to this day. The shallow valleys of the 'narrow country' between the Severn and the Wye, the Cotswolds and the Malvern Hills, were then, as they remain, lush and fertile, although the great orchards of apples, pears and plums that graced the fields throughout Walter West's childhood have been replaced with grain and dairy cattle.

Much Marcle and Walter West shaped the life of Frederick West more decisively and completely than even he knew. It was Walter West, more than anyone, who taught his son to love the countryside and to obey its laws. Walter West taught him to poach in a land where the gamekeeper saw to it that it was almost 'safer to kill a man

17

than to kill a hare', and to bow the knee in proper 'obeisance' to his betters. In turn, Frederick West worshipped his father and aped his attitude to life. 'My father was a fantastic man,' he told the police in 1994. 'He was the most understanding man you'd ever meet.' His was an influence that was to remain with Frederick West until the last day of his life.

As a young man Walter West worked as a farm labourer at Preston, a mile and a half away from Much Marcle, and it was there that he married for the first time. In 1937, at the age of twenty-three, West took the unusual step of marrying a forty-five-year-old spinster, Gertrude Maddocks, one of twin sisters. It was an unlikely match for a young farm labourer, and one that was not destined to last. Within two years Gertrude West had died in mysterious circumstances, apparently stung by a bee in the garden of their cottage. West reported her death when he found the body. Shortly after his wife's death, Walter West decided to return to the local orphanage a year-old boy that he and his first wife were about to adopt.

Walter West kept his first wife's Bible, with her photograph inside it, for the rest of his life, but there is no denying that it provides an extraordinary parallel with his son's life. The death of Gertrude West in mysterious circumstances, and without any witnesses, after what may have been an argument over an adopted child, set an eerie pattern that was to repeat itself time after time in the life of Frederick West. It was not to be the only parallel.

Just two and a half months after the death of his first wife, Walter West settled upon the young woman who was to become his second wife, and the mother of Frederick West. He had known Daisy Hannah Hill, the sixteen-year-old daughter of a cowherd, since she was a child, and now he set about courting her with a passion that his son would come to emulate. Daisy Hill came from a famous Much Marcle family, sometimes mocked in the village for their simple-mindedness, and she had been 'put to service' in the nearby town of Ledbury, four miles away, as soon as she left school. Living in during the week, she returned home only on Sundays, but she now found herself being courted by the tall farm labourer. There is no doubt she must have been flattered, and seduced, by the attractions of a widower ten years older than herself.

Walter West married Daisy Hill in the Much Marcle village church of St Bartholomew's on 27 January 1940. The bride wore white and carried a bouquet of tulips, while her new husband sported a carnation in the lapel of his only suit, and his own father's pocket watch on a gold chain in his waistcoat pocket. The bridegroom signed the parish register in block capitals, and together he and his new bride posed for a black and white photograph at the church door. The new Mrs West was already pregnant with their first child.

But once again Walter West's family life was to take a mysterious, even macabre, turn. Early in August 1940, almost eight months into her pregnancy, Daisy West was disturbed at home one afternoon by the arrival of a uniformed police constable. He was reportedly enquiring about a road accident nearby. But according to Walter West's version of events, his young and unsophisticated wife had been so upset by the constable's appearance at her door that she had gone into labour that evening, and the child had been born prematurely. There is no doubt that the fragile grip on life of the baby daughter born later that same night, whom the new Mrs West named Violet, lasted only a matter of hours. The child died the following day, 7 August 1940.

The story of the terrifying of Daisy West bears a remarkable similarity to some of the stories that Frederick West later invented to explain the disappearances of his victims. Like the bee-sting that accounted for Gertrude West, it stretches credulity to the limit. For a start, Daisy Hill was brought up in Much Marcle, where the village's uniformed police constable was part of everyday life, so much a part that Frederick West could remember his name from his own childhood. There is also no doubt that Daisy West never again demonstrated any sign whatever of such a frailty; quite the reverse, according to her son Frederick. But equally there is little doubt that Walter West was a powerfully built man with a fierce temper, much taller and stronger than his tiny seventeen-year-old wife. There seems every probability that Walter West violently attacked both his wives.

Family violence was hardly discussed in the villages of Herefordshire in 1941. A husband who beat his wife was nobody's business but the couple's own. Each village kept its secrets, never revealing them to outsiders. Those secrets could be a 'half-witted' child, a girl 'made pregnant' by the squire, a labourer who took his sexual satisfaction from animals, or a husband who beat and abused his wife. They were secrets that were to be kept away from the preying eyes of authority, and if, by chance, the local policeman were to hear of it he could be persuaded to turn a blind eye more often than not.

It was the natural secretiveness of the village that nurtured Walter and Daisy West. The secrets that they kept behind the door of their small cottage were not to be discussed with anyone – except the other members of the family. A wife was there to satisfy her husband in every way he might demand, and there is little doubt that Walter West demanded sexual satisfaction regularly. If he did not receive it, his response was quick and violent. He took the naive young girl he had sought out, and groomed her to fulfil his every expectation in a way that his son was to emulate thirty years later.

The truth of precisely what happened to Daisy West and her first-born child Violet will never be known. But with her death the first strand in the life of Frederick West and his family emerged. It was a family in which violence, and in particular violence towards children, was a natural and accepted part of life. In his turn, Walter West may have been physically beaten by his own father, a sergeant during the First World War, but it seems certain that the cycle of abuse and violence was well established in Walter West's own home by the time Daisy West was pregnant for the second time.

Walter West moved his wife into Bickerton Cottage in Much

Marcle to wait for the birth. Already more than a century old, the tied cottage, like almost every other in the village, lacked electricity and gas, and what water it had came from a well in the garden. Cooking was done on a black range, and there were just two upstairs bedrooms. The garden boasted a few apple trees and a willow in front of the outhouse where Walter West decided to keep the family's chickens and a pig for food. Behind that lay the cesspit into which, every morning and evening, Walter West emptied the bucket that served as their only lavatory.

It was into this world that Daisy West bore her first live child, and first-born son, at eight-thirty in the morning of 29 September 1941. She and her husband named him Frederick Walter Stephen West, and a few weeks later she carried him down to St Bartholomew's to be christened, just as she had been. Whatever the secrets of their life together, Walter and Daisy West maintained the proper dignities the village demanded. They were members of the congregation each Sunday morning, and were determined to ensure that their son should follow their example.

The boy Daisy West always called Freddie was born with curly blond hair and piercing blue eyes. It was to be almost three years before his hair would turn black, and by that time his mother had given birth to a brother, John, just twelve months and three days after his own birth. In the years to come, the two brothers were to become allies against an inquisitive world, sharing their secrets as the years passed.

Whether from remorse at his own actions or not, Walter West took to drink after the death of his first child. 'That was how my mother came to take over the family and everything,' his eldest son was to explain in 1994, and in the next handful of years Daisy West was to emerge as a strong, even violent woman. After John's birth she bore a third son, David, one year later, but the boy suffered from a weak heart and died within a month. By that time she had taken to wearing a wide leather belt around her waist, a match for the one her husband wore around his.

It was Daisy West who engineered the move that brought her new family of two sons to the slightly larger Moorcourt Cottage, tied to Moorcourt Farm, where her husband now worked as a cowman and general labourer. Walter West had to get up at four-thirty every morning and milk the dairy herd twice a day by hand before rolling the churns up to the road to await collection. The three-bedroomed cottage, which had electricity and a view out across open country to Letterbox and Fingerpost Fields, Yewtree Coppice and Stone Redding, lay on the outskirts of Much Marcle at a bend on the Dymock road, and it was here, at the age of barely twenty, that she bore her fourth child, and her first daughter, whom she called Little Daisy.

'And that was it, the old man was back to normal,' as Frederick West was to recall years later. 'He used to take her miles in the pram for walks. I mean, Daisy was his idol.' The daughter that Walter West had always wanted was followed by a third son, Douglas, and then two further daughters, Kathleen – always known as Kitty – and, in 1951, Gwendoline, named after the midwife who helped deliver all the children at home. In barely eleven years, Daisy West had produced eight children, and had grown into a fierce, thickly set dumpling of a woman, with a temper to match her husband's.

Life at Moorcourt Cottage was shepherded by the seasons. From dawn to dusk Walter and Daisy West would work on the farm. In the autumn they would turn out together, to collect apples for the village cider factory, and in the summer harvest she would help wherever she could. As soon as they were old enough to walk, the children would help, whether in the fields or with the pigs, sheep and cows. Daisy West dressed her sons in simple clothes and provided them with just one pair of shoes, a stout pair of hobnail boots, which could be repaired easily. By the time Freddie West got to Much Marcle school in the autumn of 1946, he 'stunk of pig's muck', but that did not seem to bother him in the least. Neither did the taunts of the cleaner, tidier children who shared the school's one classroom with him.

In the evenings Daisy West would put her children to bed early. Freddie and John shared a double bed, while their new young brother Douglas slept in a small single in the room with them; her daughters shared a double bed and another single in Moorcourt Cottage's third and last bedroom. She would usually keep her latest child in bed with her for a time, the baby lying between her and her husband in their own narrow double bed, and Walter West offered not the slightest objection. Once his wife had presented him with a daughter, his interest in and attitude towards his children changed.

Daisy West was a firm, strict disciplinarian. She would beat her children with her belt if she felt they deserved it, and would not hesitate to throw them out into the garden in the winter if they 'got under her feet'. But Freddie was her favourite, 'Mammy's blue-eyed boy', in the words of his brother. For his part Frederick West liked to tease her and then run away. 'We used to have a fir tree by our back door, and we had the top cut out where the electric came through and we made a house up in there. When my mother used to get at us we'd shoot straight up this tree. My mother was a big woman, and she used to say: "You'll come down when you're get hungry." She wouldn't bother with you, but when you came down, she'd have you.'

'Whatever Mother said went,' Frederick West would explain. 'You didn't answer Mother back or she grabbed you and wopped you a bit quick. I mean, sixteen or sixty, didn't matter. She was a pillar of steel. There was no messing. She'd sort anything out. No problem.' West was a little afraid of her. 'Mother was a bit of a neurotic about things. She used to shout a lot really when she was talking to you. She was very dominant, like, and you didn't get a chance to get a word in. She would tell you and that was the story, like.' For her part Daisy West doted on her eldest son, although she also recognised his tendency to lie. 'My mother knew exactly what was going on. You

21

could tell her the biggest lie you ever thought up, my mother would just listen and tell you the truth.'

In contrast, Frederick West idolised his father Walter, following him into the fields whenever he got the chance, helping with the lambing, herding the cows, piling the corn in sheaves for the harvest. 'Me and my father got on great together. There was no doubt about that. He was a massive man, mind, big man, tall, you know, massive hands on him. But he wouldn't hurt a fly,' West was to insist after his father's death. 'He was the most understanding person you'd ever met. You could go to Dad and ask him anything. He was always calm, and he always understood you.'

Though Walter West enjoyed his son's company, he may not have been quite as enamoured of his son as he was of his daughters. Freddie was his wife's favourite, and Walter West had come to believe that she favoured him at his expense. Besides, his eldest son was a scruffy, unkempt child, his curly hair always sticking up like a bramble bush on the top of his head, while Walter West had always taken a pride in his appearance, taking care to shave carefully on a Saturday evening before walking down to the Wallwyn Arms in the village.

Walter West became one of Much Marcle's respected sons. Each May, he helped to organise the annual day-trip to Barry Island on the South Wales coast, the only holiday most of the villagers could afford, and he wanted his son to inherit his mantle. Walter West even hoped that Frederick would take over Moorcourt Cottage in his own right in the years to come. In the village, that was what was expected of the first-born son, that was the tradition to be respected, a tradition that had to be maintained in public. In private it was another matter. There Walter and Daisy West, like every other couple in the village, worked out their own compromise, his violence and his sexual appetite kept under control by his wife.

Sex was one area of his life which Walter West shared with his son. 'My mother was very old-fashioned in her ways about sex and things like that. Dad was different altogether. If it's on offer, take it, son, that was my father's idea. Whatever you enjoy do, only make sure you don't get caught doing it. That was Dad, like.' It was a sexual lesson that his son was never to forget. And it was not the only one. Walter West may also have told him that it was a father's duty to 'break in' his own daughters at an early age. Incest was another of the secrets kept by Much Marcle, and the West family.

'Dad got on with anybody, he didn't judge nobody,' his eldest son remembered. 'If you went to the old man and said, "So-and-so is doing something", he would say, "That's their business, son. What you worrying about? You're not doing it." That was his attitude to life. Just did his own thing . . . He was so placid it was unreal.' It was an attitude that stood Walter West in good stead in Much Marcle in the years just after the Second World War. You kept yourself to yourself, and you kept your own secrets, as well as those of the people around you.

22

Although he joined Much Marcle school at the age of five, what learning Frederick West did was at his father's knee. 'I was thick as two short planks, and I wasn't interested in school at all. All I was interested in was farming.' The boy went lambing with his father – 'learning to blow into a lamb's mouth to give it life' – went hunting with him – 'although I didn't like ripping the fox apart after' – and watched while some of the other village children were 'blooded' with the fox's paw.

Dirty, dishevelled, and always getting into trouble, Frederick West was an outsider at the village school, but it did not concern him. He took his pleasures in the fields with his father, a boy anxious to become a man, impatient with childhood. If ever he was caned for misbehaviour, he would simply complain to his mother, and the now formidable Daisy West would march down to remonstrate at the top of her voice with his teacher. The grin that would come to mark his adult life began gradually to appear as he realised that, no matter what his classmates thought, he could get his own way. If they called him a 'mummy's boy' behind his back, it could not matter less. They would not dare say it to his face.

In return Daisy West expected every one of her children to work in the house, making up the fire in the kitchen, feeding the chickens, chasing the rats away from the sewage pit. They would be given a raw turnip or parsnip for their lunch at school, and on Sundays they would be expected to troop down to church behind their parents, wearing their Sunday best, a dress for the girls, grey flannel shorts and a Fair Isle sweater for the boys. Looking back, Frederick West would insist: 'We were a close-knit family, a very happy family.'

Moorcourt Cottage was full of animals. Walter West had five dogs, 'Lassie, Ben, Brandy, Whisky and Lad, each one had a different job'. There were also the hens for fresh eggs, and, more often than not, a pet pig, which Walter West would slaughter in the autumn, to help feed his family throughout the winter. 'Mother used to get very attached to it, like, 'cause she would give it a pet name like Sally or something.' His son would never forget how his father 'would cut the animal's throat and hang it up for twelve hours to allow the blood to drain out.'

Inside the cottage Frederick West felt safe, cocooned against the world. There was no need for anyone else. 'As the seasons changed you just did the same things, like.' In the spring they would pick wild daffodils from the fields outside their window, to sell at the side of the road. In the summer there was hop-picking in the nearby hop-fields, then the harvest, chasing the rabbits out of the corn and clubbing them with a stick, before taking them home and skinning them for the family table. In the autumn there was apple-picking for the cider factory. But as the light began to fail the family would retreat behind the lath-and-plaster walls of their cottage to endure the winter.

There would still be milking night and morning, and gradually the arrival of the first lambs to chase Walter West and his family out into the fields around them, and to ensure the strength of next year's flock. As he grew older Frederick West went with his father whenever he could, conscious of what was expected of him. By the age of eleven, he was being paid half a crown a week, and he would give his mother two shillings and keep the sixpence for himself.

What went on at Moorcourt Cottage concerned only the West family, and Frederick West preferred it that way. He never lost his temper, and disliked fights, unlike his younger brother John, but most of all he 'hated the fact that everybody knew what was going on in the village all the time'. He especially disliked the postman, who 'always knew what was in every letter he delivered'. There were West family secrets which he wanted to keep, not least about sex.

Frederick Walter Stephen West reached puberty early. His first erections took place shortly after his twelfth birthday, and they could hardly be concealed in the cramped bedrooms of Moorcourt Cottage. Both Walter and Daisy West realised the change that was taking place in their eldest child, and they responded to it as generations of other villagers had done before them in the wilds of the Herefordshire countryside. They took his sexual initiation into their own hands. Just as Walter West had groomed his sixteen-year-old bride to satisfy his own desires, and just as she had realised how she could in turn control him by the skilful use of her own sexuality, so between them Walter and Daisy West groomed their first-born son. Sex became the first important secret of Frederick West's life.

Daisy West almost certainly took her son into her bed one winter night before his thirteenth birthday. The experience was to colour the rest of Frederick West's life. The illicitness, and yet the force of his desire, uncertain at first, then rapidly catching fire, fascinated him. Sex became his only hobby, his consuming passion. It was a passion fanned by his father. For Walter West's sexuality was as powerful as his son's was to become, and he had quenched it both with animals and with young children. West recalled years later that his father had first told him that it was possible to have sex with a sheep by putting its rear legs down the front of your own wellington boots, and he would laugh at the memory of his own first attempts to do so. As Frederick West's own son was to say: 'Dad was obsessed by sex.' It was an obsession that he indulged as often as he could.

Sexuality was a constant strand in the life of every member of the West family, something that could never be ignored or forgotten. Frederick West's incestuous relationship with his mother was almost certainly matched by some sort of sexual relationship with his father. Whether Walter West let him watch while he abused young girls, or whether he encouraged his son to take his place, or whether, in fact, he abused him directly Frederick West was never to reveal. But there is no doubt that his father's example, in the sexual abuse of children, and his own son in particular, led Frederick West to the conviction that 'Everybody does it'.

Frederick West became his parents' able and devoted pupil. Sexuality came to overwhelm his every waking moment, the one

24

reason for his very existence. The cycle of child abuse that was to re-emerge at 25 Cromwell Street in Gloucester two decades later was forged a dozen miles away across the Severn at Moorcourt Cottage, Much Marcle. It was the first evil love that Frederick West fell victim to, the inspiration for each and every one of his subsequent actions.

Not that children were the only focus for Frederick West's rapidly burgeoning sexuality. There were some village girls of his own age prepared for a fumbling experiment in the fields after school on a summer day. But soon those were not enough to satisfy the blue-eyed young man with a gypsy's face and hobnail boots. He wanted sexual intercourse, and he did not want to wait for it. There was no courtship, no affection in his mind when it came to any consideration of sex. It was a matter of animal desire, to be satisfied, extinguished, then explored again. Girls were to satisfy the lust as readily and as simply as the sheep in his father's flock. 'And you kept quiet about it.'

Morality was satisfied by church on Sunday morning, and preparation for confirmation. There was no contradiction in Walter or Daisy West's mind between preparing their son to become a confirmed member of the Church of England and preparing him for sexual life. To be confirmed 'was tradition', he was to explain later, as much a part of the family tradition as buying the eldest son a twelve-bore shotgun 'for rabbiting and crows' for his fourteenth birthday. And in the autumn of 1955 Frederick West was confirmed into the Anglican communion at St Bartholomew's Church, Much Marcle, in the presence of his entire family. After school the next day he went rabbiting with his new shotgun.

In September 1956, to celebrate his fifteenth birthday, Daisy and Walter West took their son to Gloucester and bought him a brown double-breasted suit at Burton's the Tailors, together with his first pair of proper leather shoes. Then they took him to a fish-and-chip shop in the city for his first 'meal out'. Walter West's father had done exactly the same for him in the year that he left school, and it was another tradition to be kept up, a mark that 'the boy' was about to leave school and start work. A worker, even a farm labourer, had to have a suit for Sunday best.

Frederick Walter Stephen West 'couldn't spell or nothing' when he left school in December 1956. He had no need to. What little reading he needed he taught himself in the years to come, 'though writing was always beyond me', but he had little need of either. What pay there was would be delivered in a brown envelope on Friday morning. Active, and growing in strength, West worked long hours in the fields, just as his father did, returning to Moorcourt Cottage at dusk. 'I thought nothing of staying up all night with a cow or a pig or whatever it was', and he 'got used to watching pigs being butchered', just as he accepted that now he was expected to kill the West family's latest pet pig in his fifteenth year. He took the knife to its throat in the kitchen, watching it run round squealing for a moment before dropping to the floor. He helped his mother hang it up to let the blood drain away.

At the age of fifteen, West was being paid ten shillings a week for his work on the farm. He gave five shillings to his mother, kept half a crown for himself, and put the remaining half a crown into a post office savings account. He was saving for a motor bike. On Saturday evenings he and his brother John used to meet some of the other young men from the village 'for five Woodbines and a pint of cider'. In his spare time he would shoot squirrels with his shotgun and sell the tails. And on rare occasions there would be a trip into Ledbury, five miles away, at the foot of the Malvern Hills, but only if there was someone to offer them a lift.

One attraction of Ledbury was the possibility of meeting girls, for by now Frederick West's appetite for sex could not be quenched solely in the privacy of his own home. Together with his brother John, he set out for the small Herefordshire town with increasing regularity, to visit a café and the cinema, or to go to the local youth club. At sixteen, he had learned little sophistication, but he knew instinctively that some girls fell for his direct approach. As John West was to put it later: 'Fred was always a ladies' man. I never stood much of a chance.' But there was no flattery in his manner, or his voice, when he approached a girl in Ledbury; no payment of even the most rudimentary compliment. Instead, his assumption was that girls were 'begging for it' if they were there in the first place.

Four decades later, in the last year of his life, Frederick West made a list of the girls he had seduced in Ledbury and Much Marcle as a young man. He could remember them all, in detail, and took pride in recounting his experiences. At one stage he had even kept a diary of all their names, but 'once you forget a few you lose interest'. Every local girl in Ledbury, if he was to be believed, had had some kind of sexual encounter with him. Not that he was always telling the truth. He took refuge in bragging to conceal his failures, going to elaborate lengths on many occasions to make up 'stories' about the girls he had seduced, the women who could not resist him. Some young women in the area could not stand his ignorant, lascivious bragging, complete with its distinctive brand of innuendo that insisted every girl 'would be much better off with me'.

Frederick West would think nothing of stealing another boy's girl, or of grabbing someone he fancied off the floor at a local dance. If her boyfriend objected, his brother John was expected to step in and defend him, for West did not like getting into a fight, especially with a man. He dressed a little more smartly now, often wearing the double-breasted suit his parents had bought for his fifteenth birthday. 'Girls were impressed by a suit. They didn't see one that often.' It made him a raffish figure in the small country town, the sort of young man that some mothers would warn their daughters against, a man to be kept secret.

Frederick West knew the rules. He taught himself never to use a girl's name when he made love to her. 'I once went and called the wrong one, the wrong name . . . and she whipped her shoe off and smacked me straight in the face with it, and said, "Oh, you've been with that bitch". So I learned from that lesson, like. I never ever used their names.' It was not the only rule he taught himself to abide by. 'You weren't allowed to go home and say that's my girlfriend because you weren't allowed a girlfriend until you was twenty-one; that was the whole village way of life, like. Everything was done hush hush.' That suited him only too well. 'I mean, you couldn't take a girl home when you were thirteen, fourteen, fifteen and say to your parents I'm going with this girl, because you were in big trouble. The first thing lights started flashing in their head that you were having sex and you could have a baby and you'd be a disgrace to the village.'

He learned to conduct his sexual life covertly. 'Whenever opportunities came up with different girls they would, exactly the same as we would, meet you somewhere in the woods, or anywhere quiet in the fields, anywhere. You just went with them, and that was it. You enjoyed yourself that time, and then it was finished until you met them again.'

Not every local girl would succumb at once, but that 'only made me more determined'. Even at the age of sixteen, he did not like to fail, and the more reluctant the girl the more he would talk. It was his way of hypnotising any girl he met, and as the years passed it became his trademark. Frederick West became the braggart, the boaster, the story-teller, the fantasist, but above all the talker, a man never at a loss for words, ready to use language as his defence against a hostile world. Daisy West's 'young Freddie' might be almost illiterate, but 'he talked and talked and talked', in the words of one friend. 'Never stopped for a moment. Telling the girls he had a motor bike "that was being repaired". Telling them that he "was just about to get a job in Hereford". Telling them they were the "prettiest girl he ever met".' West would talk as fast and as quickly as he could in pursuit of his prize, and it was not the only tactic he adopted to seduce young women.

Another trick was even more ingenious. West would offer the girl he fancied an 'engagement ring'. 'No sex, no ring used to be the thing in the old days. So I gave them a ring,' West admitted at the end of his life. 'I started that when I was about sixteen I think. The engagement rings got better, mind, over the years.' At one stage he had collected 'anything up to a hundred' of them. 'I carried engagement rings for special occasions. I mean, I couldn't see the difference, making love with a ring on or a ring off . . . no difference, is there? But it was what they wanted.' It was also what Frederick West wanted. There was nothing to lose, besides: 'They always threw it back at you when it was over.'

As the sixteen-year-old Frederick West's appetite for young girls grew, so his mother grew increasingly more irritated. She may also have been more than a little jealous. Then only thirty-two, Daisy West was, after all, just twice her son's age, and was still his lover. One girl in particular, whose father Daisy herself had had a sexual

27

relationship with as a young girl, irritated her so much that she gave her son 'some stick over it'. And on New Year's Eve 1957 he left Moorcourt Cottage to stay with the girl and her parents, the first time he had ever stayed away from home.

Chapter Three

Foul whisperings

'So bloody, raw, and sudden it was, it resembled an outbreak of family madness which we took pains to conceal, out of shame and pride, and for the sake of those infected.'

Laurie Lee, *Cider with Rosie*

In the early summer of 1957, without warning and without leaving a note for his parents, Frederick West disappeared. 'I got up during the night and just went. I got on me fixed-wheel pushbike and went to Hereford.' The journey took him two days, and he slept in the hedgerows on the way, but quietly he had saved £15 to help him to survive without his parents' help. He had every intention of striking out on his own, not least because he wanted to make enough money to buy a motor cycle. 'And if I said I was going to leave home, there would have been one mass of tears, 'cause we were that close. I couldn't just go to Mum and say I was leaving home.' At sixteen, he was still a little in awe of his mother.

Not that West could write and tell his parents where he was, any more than he could telephone them. Moorcourt Cottage did not have a telephone, and he was still unable to read or write. For the moment the West family would have to wait. He would return home when he was ready and not before. The dark-haired, tousled country boy got a job as a labourer on a Hereford building site, and slept in one of the partially finished houses on the estate each night. He stayed there for almost a month, gradually getting filthier and filthier, as layer upon layer of concrete dust covered his sallow skin. 'I wasn't afraid to do the nastiest jobs, 'cause that way I would be paid more, and I could be sure I would keep the job. Nobody else wanted to do them.' It was another approach to life that he would return to time and time again.

A month after he left Much Marcle, Frederick West returned 'covered in cement'. He had bought his mother and father a watch each as a present, and had decided that he did not want to spend the rest of his life 'carrying a stick and walking behind a cow'. The trip to

Hereford had opened his eyes to the possibilities a larger town might hold. It had also alerted him to the chance to earn more money. 'I still love the country,' West was to say; 'the only reason I've never gone back was because of the wages.' Instead of returning to the fields, West took a job in the village cider factory, Weston's, and started to save even more determinedly for a motor bike. It was a means of escape, escape from what he saw as the 'prying' of the village that seemed always to know everyone's business. Frederick West wanted his anonymity, and he had set his heart on finding it in the town that his parents had taken him to for his fifteenth birthday treat, Gloucester.

In the meantime West returned to his old haunts. 'My favourite place with all my local girlfriends,' he explained, was in Fingerpost Field less than a mile outside Much Marcle, 'watching the badgers come down from the set and drink, and the foxes and all that.' No matter which girl he was with, he would sit with her on a hunting stile at the edge of the field with his back to the wood, and 'look out over the valley, the woods, Much Marcle and all that' on a summer evening. 'You could see the church clock.' It was a field he was to return to time after time after leaving Moorcourt Cottage for good, a field that would eventually hold the remains of the first young woman to die at his hands.

Handsome now, his face stronger and more confident than it had been, and with his hair more carefully combed than when he had been working in the fields, Frederick West began to slip out from beneath the all-pervading influence of his mother and father at Moorcourt Cottage. In the autumn of 1957 Frederick West bought himself his first means of escape from the inquisitive eyes of Much Marcle, a 98-cc Bantam motor bike, registration number RVJ 199. It was to become his one pride and joy, and another means to show off to any young woman who might be impressed by the sight of a motor bike. He took to parking outside the café in Ledbury when he went to the town on Saturdays, 'playing the big man', and then taking trips into Gloucester on Sundays. Another strand in Frederick West's life had been formed, a vehicle that would allow him freedom to roam the countryside in search of his own version of prey.

In the next year West drove throughout Herefordshire and Gloucestershire, discovering a world beyond the fields of Much Marcle, but always returning there at night to sleep and work in the cider factory. He took to wearing an elderly leather jacket and a battered helmet, which was just as well: on his way home one evening in late November 1958, he crashed. Driving back in the dark to Moorcourt Cottage, along the road from Dymock, he ran over a bicycle lying at the roadside. It belonged to a girl he knew, Pat Mann, and West said later that he thought she had stopped to 'drop her knickers' out of sight of the road. Whatever the reason, he careered off the road and smashed into a brick wall.

In the years to come, Frederick West would romanticise the drama of his accident. At one stage he even suggested that he 'was paralysed from the waist down for twelve months', and that he had 'lain in the ditch for eight hours before anyone found me', while 'Pat saved my life, 'cause I was choking myself on me helmet'. Certainly, he was taken unconscious to Ledbury Cottage Hospital, only to be transferred immediately to the larger Hereford Hospital, and a local man ran to Moorcourt Cottage to tell his parents. His brother John later maintained that the family feared 'Fred would not make it through the night', and he did lie unconscious in the John Masefield ward at Hereford Hospital for seven days after the crash.

Years later West would tell his children: 'I woke up on the mortuary slab. If I'd been a minute later I would have been in the fridge.' In fact, he finally regained consciousness with his mother at his bedside; she had taken to sitting there stoically every day. She came back relentlessly after he had begun the mundane task of recovery from his string of serious injuries. The wound to his skull took weeks to heal, although he did not 'have to have a steel plate in it', as he told more than one friend later, while his right leg was so severely broken that he was given metal callipers to support its recovery, and asked to wear a special metal shoe. More wounding to West's pride, however, was that his nose was also broken. It would remain slightly crooked for the rest of his life, just as he would for ever afterwards have a slight but nevertheless discernible limp.

Most important of all, however, the crash seemed not only to coarsen his features but also to affect his personality. The open-faced, blue-eyed boy turned steadily darker, and sourer, in the aftermath of his accident. His brother John noticed that his personality changed, while his sister Daisy felt he became more of a loner than before. Years afterwards, West himself denied that the crash had affected him at all. Instead, he insisted: 'Half the bloody problem of what changed me was John, because he kept stirring the shit for me all the time. He was always top monkey, like, couldn't do anything but he had plenty of talk, and he always reported on everything. If you broke a spade handle and skived off, he would tell the old man "Fred's gone".'

The passionate relationship between the two brothers, just a year apart in age, had grown steadily at Moorcourt Cottage, and it was to last the rest of Frederick West's life. His brother John became friend and ally at one moment, rival and enemy the next. It was a passion that extended into their sexual lives, with one trying to outdo the other when it came to girls. For Fred his brother was 'too forward . . . hand on the bottom . . . kiss 'em before he even knew their name', while for John his brother was always the ladies' man, while he never stood much of a chance. Yet in the years to come they would more often than not find themselves going out together with sisters, or friends, as foursomes, both rivals and allies in the sexual game.

It was the spring of 1959 before Frederick West was strong enough to work again. For a short time he returned to Weston's cider factory, but he did not settle. The restlessness that the motor bike had satisfied remained, though the bike itself was written off. 'I wanted to branch out, leave home, go.' He had lost patience with life as it always had been in Much Marcle. And that summer he packed a small suitcase and set off for Gloucester to find work. But this time he did not choose a building site.

Now almost eighteen, West 'went to the docks and got a job on the ships', first as a deck hand on the waste-boats taking sludge out to the dumping-grounds, and then on the oil-boats that plied down the sixteen-mile channel to the estuary and the sea at the Bristol Channel. It was still hard and dirty work, but there was a sense of an adventure, the taste of a different world, a world of his own. 'I've always been a loner to a certain extent,' he would explain years later. 'I enjoy my own company. I don't like parties and things. I don't like being clammed up to people.' During the next two years Frederick West would work on a variety of ships, first out of Gloucester and then out of Bristol, always a willing deck hand, never afraid of hard work, but also happy to hide himself away on the ships.

When he was not at sea he took a job as a bakery roundsman in Cheltenham: 'You'd have probably a couple of months when you'd be on shore.' It was the first time he visited the small town of Bishop's Cleeve, about three miles north of the city. West did not forget the experience. He boasted later that a woman on his round seduced him. 'She said, "Oh, bring me a brown loaf in." . . . I went back and got it . . . tapped on the door. She said, "Come in" . . . and I walked in and there's a big rug in front of the fire and she's starkers on it . . . Well, I mean I couldn't refuse . . . Anyway, a couple of months went by and she turned up at the van one morning and said: "What about this? I'm pregnant." I jacked the job there and then. I was gone. I didn't finish the round.'

Frederick West took to signing on as crew on the oil-boats under a series of different names, 'So you didn't pay tax or nothing, like. You could put any name up. I very rarely used to use my own name.' The trips carrying waste out of Sharpness were gradually succeeded by longer trips to Portsmouth carrying fertiliser, 'horrible smelly stuff', and then to the Clyde. And early in 1960 he ventured even further. 'I went to Jamaica twice for bananas and stuff.'

Once again the experience was to change his view of the world. 'I couldn't read about this. It was just the pictures I'd seen. So I didn't actually know what sort of life it was. I just wanted to see.' There were other voyages, to Hong Kong and the Pacific. 'It was a great life. Fantastic. You can go round the world and, you know, I mean, you can be who you want to be. I got locked up once in Australia for being drunk and disorderly.' It was not an experience he enjoyed.

But there were always girls. The attraction of a girl in every port had probably played its part in his decision to go to sea in the first place. Years later he would brag, 'I've got three hundred children around the world', although, as ever, there was no way to substantiate the claim. One thing had not changed, however. Frederick West believed any woman was fortunate to meet him. He disliked intensely the prostitutes that frequented the docks of every city that he visited, insisting: 'I wasn't paying for it. I got it for nothing.' He was also afraid of venereal disease. But that did nothing to inhibit his sexual appetite. 'These girls loved it. There was times when I slept with three or four girls twice in the same night, all in the same bed, like. That's what sex is all about – pleasure.'

After every voyage, Fred West would return to Gloucester. He never wanted to be too far from his parents for very long, even though he had taken to living above the Rendezvous café in the nearby town of Newent whenever he was briefly home from the sea. Living there meant he could look up 'all my old girlfriends' without incurring the wrath of his mother. Ashore, he bought himself another motor bike, this time a grey 1000-cc Triumph, not least because of the effect it might have on the local girls. For a time he was even a member of a motor cycle gang in the town. 'We used to just bomb up the street and if there was a load of girls or something in the café, bikes up and in.'

It was not until the end of 1960 that Fred West finally returned to Moorcourt Cottage. His parents had heard rumours that he had been seen locally, but he had deliberately avoided them, preferring to 'duck and dive here and there' when he was home from the sea. But he decided to go home for Christmas. When Daisy West saw her son at the gate that December morning, she walked out to meet him. 'She took off her big thick leather belt with laces on and give me a beating in the gateway, then put it back on and said: "Welcome home, son, we're level",' he remembered. 'All because I called her an old cunt when I went out the gate.'

Life at Moorcourt Cottage had hardly changed, although West's sisters had grown up considerably in the time he had been away at sea. 'Little Daisy' was now sixteen, Kitty was growing quickly, and Gwen was almost ten. Now nineteen, with a motor bike and endless stories about his voyages around the world, Frederick West must have appeared an almost impossibly glamorous figure to his young sisters, who had never travelled further than Hereford in their lives.

Walter West's attitude to young girls had not changed, and neither had his son's fascination with sex. Frederick West slipped back into life at home in Moorcourt Cottage, working in the fields with his father again, though now with the possibility of disappearing to Gloucester or Ledbury whenever he wanted to on his heavy grey motor bike. Then he passed his car driving-test, and he and his brother John between them bought an old Ford Popular. The years spent travelling had brought him an arrogance that it was impossible to ignore. West had become convinced that he could do what he wanted and get away with it.

Three months after his return home, Frederick West was arrested for the first time, for theft. He and a friend had stolen two ladies' cigarette cases and a rolled-gold watch-strap from two separate shops in Ledbury. When they were stopped for questioning by the police, he had the cases in his pocket. A week later, in April 1961, at

Ledbury magistrates' court Frederick West pleaded guilty to two charges of theft and was fined £4. As he walked out of the court he seemed not to care in the slightest that now he had a criminal record. The boy fined along with him remembers him only as 'devil may care'. West simply climbed on to his motor bike and went back to Much Marcle, back to work.

Within three months he was in the hands of the police again, but this time on an infinitely more serious charge: incest. His thirteen-year-old sister was pregnant, and it was alleged that Frederick West had had an intimate sexual relationship with her 'four or possibly five' times since his return home at Christmas. During questioning, he did not for a moment disguise the fact that he had been having sexual relationships with his sister, any more than he disguised the fact that sometimes other girls he approached objected to his sexual advances. West treated the investigating officers exactly as he treated the girls he attempted to seduce. He simply talked and talked, suggesting in a slightly aggrieved, almost puzzled voice, 'Doesn't everyone do it?'

Whatever his attitude to the police, however, West had breached one of the village's greatest taboos. He had been caught. To his father it was the one cardinal sin, and to Daisy West it meant disgrace. No matter how much she liked her 'Freddie', he could not stay under her roof for another night. She arranged for him to go and stay with her sister Violet and her husband at Daisy Cottage in Much Marcle. He could stay there until the trial, which was set to take place at Hereford Assizes in the coming November.

For his part Frederick West showed not the slightest sign of remorse or contrition. He simply stopped working in the fields with his father, and took a job on a building site at Newent, five miles away to the south-east. But the move did nothing to change his attitude. Even before his trial at Hereford, he was in trouble again, this time for stealing materials from the building site he was working on. Charged with 'larceny as a servant', he was found guilty at Newent magistrates' court on 18 October 1961 and fined £20. His excuse was all too familiar: 'Everybody else was doing it.'

The approaching trial for incest did nothing to curtail Frederick West's sexual appetite. Before his arrest by the police, he had started going out with a local fourteen-year-old, whom he had met first at a dance in the Memorial Hall and then at the Rendezvous café in Newent, where she worked as a waitress at the weekends. His brother John had started going out with her sister. On three occasions Fred had even taken the girl home to see his parents, when Daisy West told her that she 'hoped we weren't doing anything we shouldn't'. At that stage they had not become lovers, but Frederick West was not anxious to wait much longer. Shortly after her fifteenth birthday, he started to talk about marrying her and produced an engagement ring, although for once the sweeping gesture did nothing to affect the girl's attitude. Ring or no ring, she was not going to give in. What she did not know was that she was not Frederick West's only girlfriend at

34

the time. Without her knowledge he was also seeing another local girl. 'I used to drop one off and then pop round to the other.'

If one girl was unwilling, West was only too happy to find another, and on one Saturday evening that autumn he attempted to do exactly that at the Ledbury youth club. He made a grab for a girl who had taken his fancy on the first-floor landing of the iron fire-escape stairs at the back of the club. She had gone outside with him, but his plan had backfired when he put his hand up her skirt. Instead of being seduced, she hit him, hard, so hard that he lost his balance and fell backwards over the railings, landing head-first on the ground ten feet beneath him. Just as he had been after his crash three years earlier, he was unconscious. He was taken to Ledbury Cottage Hospital, but once again he was quickly transferred to Hereford, although this time he came round after just twenty-four hours. There was no obvious damage, and certainly no broken bones, although his temper seemed to grow a little shorter. But just as his crash had done, the fall seemed only to prove that he was, in some mysterious way, impregnable against injury. It became another of his jokes, a claim that 'nothing can hurt me – I'll always survive'.

Frederick West wore his brown double-breasted suit to Hereford Assizes on the morning of Wednesday 9 November 1961. His hair was carefully brushed, and his hands, for once, showed not a sign of dirt or grime as he stood quietly in the dock and pleaded not guilty in a confident voice. He listened carefully to the police evidence against him being presented to the jury, but then smiled slowly as he heard his family's general practitioner tell the jury that his motor-cycle accident three years before might mean that he was possibly an epileptic 'given to blackouts'. And the sly confident smile broadened still further as Daisy West gave evidence on her son's behalf. The woman who had berated the teachers at Much Marcle school was not about to see him sent to prison without a fight, no matter what some of the villagers might think. She insisted that he often took the blame for 'things that weren't his fault'.

Neither the medical evidence nor the pleas of his mother were necessary to save Frederick West. When his thirteen-year-old sister entered the witness-box she refused to answer any questions whatever. She was asked by Mr Justice Sachs, the trial judge, if it was her boyfriend or her brother who was responsible for her pregnancy. She shook her head. The judge asked her to speak up, and with her voice barely above a whisper, she said simply 'No' to both questions. The judge then handed her a piece of paper and a pencil and asked the charming round-faced young girl to write down the name of the person who was responsible.

There was a long pause, and she simply looked down. Mr Justice Sachs asked her again to write down the name of the person responsible for her pregnancy, and again there was a lengthy silence. The judge then sent her out of court for a few minutes 'to consider her decision', and retired from the bench to allow her to do so. But when the court re-convened ten minutes later, she still said nothing. She refused utterly to write down the name of any person; instead, she sat silently in the witness-box, her head bowed.

Mr Justice Sachs asked the jury if they 'felt it was safe' to continue to hear the case on the basis of a 'suspicion' that Frederick West was guilty of incest, and received the only reply that he could have expected. After a brief retirement, the jury announced that they did not wish to go on with the case. As the *Hereford Gazette* announced the following Friday morning: 'Farm Worker Not Guilty: Case Stopped at the Assizes.' Incest was another evil love not to be discussed with anyone beyond the family.

The twenty-year-old Frederick Walter Stephen West walked free from Hereford Assizes on that November morning in 1961 convinced in his heart that there was nothing that he could not do, and nothing that he could not get away with. As he boasted years later: 'It hadn't lasted many minutes.' And because the case against him had been dismissed, it did not appear on his criminal record: that still simply showed that he was a petty thief.

Shortly after the trial, Fred West celebrated his victory. He was with the local girl who had refused to be swayed into sex by the offer of an engagement ring. Giving her a lift home through the Herefordshire lanes early one evening in the black Ford Popular, he suddenly stopped at a gate and got out. Not certain what was happening, the fifteen-year-old followed him. West told her that she had to marry him when she was sixteen, but she still steadfastly refused. Suddenly, 'He pushed me back on to the bank and he raped me', she told a court thirty-three years later. Then he 'fell over on to his back on the floor' appearing to be 'unwell'. When he eventually recovered enough to get to his feet, all Frederick West could think of to say to her was 'sorry', and 'not to be frightened', because he 'had blackouts.'

Then, without a moment's further hesitation, West opened the door of the Ford Popular and climbed back behind the wheel. His passenger still needed a lift home, and he saw no reason not to give her one. His experience at Hereford Assizes had taught him a lesson he would never forget. Whatever he did, the young woman who was the object of his desire would not report him to the police, and if she did she would not repeat the accusation in court. The shame was too great.

In that, as in so many other respects, Frederick West was absolutely correct. The fifteen-year-old part-time waitress from the Rendezvous café would not reveal what happened that evening for more than three decades. He could get away with anything.

Chapter Four

A Scottish marriage

'The most violent passions sometimes leave us at rest, but vanity agitates us constantly.'

La Rochefoucauld, *Maxims*

There was now a distinct swagger in Frederick West's limping stride, and the smile in his startling blue eyes grew ever brighter. He was a young blood, a twenty-year-old with a criminal record, someone who had walked free from Hereford Assizes, and he took to carrying a sheath knife in his belt to prove it. Aunt Violet's cottage in Much Marcle was no longer big enough for him. It was time to return to Gloucester, and West announced to his parents that he was going to move back into the city, 'to get bigger money on the building sites'. There was even the possibility of going back to sea.

Shortly after Christmas in 1961, West moved into the flat of a friend above an ice-cream parlour in Wellesley Street, Gloucester, a short walk from the city's cemetery, and went to work at the local power-station as a labourer. But no matter how confident he may have appeared, his private world had not changed. His poacher's instinct when it came to young women had not dimmed. In the dark winter evenings after work, he took to driving out to Newent on his motor cycle, to creep around the garden of the girl he had raped. As it turned out, Frederick West had no need to prowl around the girl's house at night. A few weeks after his first attack on her, she turned up at the flat in Wellesley Street to see her sister, who was now going out with the friend with whom West was sharing.

When West returned to the flat from work late one afternoon, he found the fifteen-year-old he had delivered home to Newent in his Ford Popular waiting there for her sister. Once again, he did not hesitate. 'He pushed his way into the flat, threw me on to the bed and raped me,' as the girl was to remember more than thirty years later. And once again Frederick West did not appear to feel that he had done anything wrong. Quite the reverse: as soon as the attack was over, he suggested that they both sit and wait for the girl's sister

37

to arrive. It was as if the rape had never taken place. And once again, it went unreported.

In the last year of his life, West himself insisted that the girl 'was mad in love with me, mind', and had become 'one of the first big sex symbols for me . . . I had other girls but she was my first serious girlfriend . . . I was going to marry her, live in her house'. He was certainly also convinced that 'we made love three or four times a night, over a couple of years'. The self-delusion and deceit that had begun to form in Frederick West's mind had grown ever stronger. So, too, had his restlessness.

The job at the power-station did not satisfy him for long. He wanted something that would allow him to indulge his appetite for movement, to roam the lanes of Herefordshire and the streets of Gloucester, and discover whatever that might bring by way of girls. He had heard that lorry-drivers were always picking up pretty young hitchhikers, so that was the obvious answer. In the early spring of 1962 West took a job driving a lorry for Ledbury Farmers, a local cooperative, collecting and delivering grain from his old stamping ground at Avonmouth Docks to and from farms throughout Herefordshire. To save money he moved back into Moorcourt Cottage with his family. Several months had passed since Hereford Assizes, and as far as Walter and Daisy West were concerned the incest case was forgotten.

Frederick West had been driving for Ledbury Farmers for only a 'few months' when he stopped in the town centre one afternoon in the autumn of 1962 for a cup of tea and a sandwich at a café 'opposite the hospital . . . I had ten ton of wheat on'. One of the waitresses was a nineteen-year-old girl he knew called Margaret Mackintosh. 'She went to school with me when she was little', and he always called her 'Haggis' because she had spent so much of her life in Scotland. Indeed, she had only recently returned to Herefordshire, after a period of time in a borstal in Greenock on the Clyde. She had been released on parole to her mother's home in Ledbury. Another waitress in the café was a friend of Margaret's from the Greenock borstal, who had just come down from Scotland to join her. Her name was Catherine Costello, but she was known as Rena.

'Margaret was serving, and Rena was on a half-day off,' West recalled in the last months of his life. 'She said, "This is my mate Rena", and Rena looked a fair picture. Fair play, she was a beautiful-looking woman, girl, like. Well, Rena said, "Can I come with you, like?" and she did. I delivered, then picked up another load, then went back to the café and dropped her off.' It was the beginning of a relationship that would eventually lead to the young Scottish woman's death, and the discovery of her dismembered body in a field barely five miles away from that café in Ledbury.

Catherine Bernadette Costello was born on 14 April 1944, the fourth of five sisters, and had spent her childhood in Calder Street, Coatbridge, just outside Glasgow. Her mother Mary left the family home when Catherine was still a child, going to live in Belfast, and by the age of thirteen Cathy, as she was then called, was in a children's home in Port Glasgow. She returned to her father and sisters after a year, but was soon working as a street prostitute in Glasgow itself, and was warned by the police for 'importuning' in November 1960. A month or so later she was sentenced to seventeen months 'borstal training' for attempted burglary. When she first met Margaret Mackintosh she was serving the sentence at Gateside Borstal in Greenock. Well built, but only five feet, three inches in height, she peroxided her hair, turning it straw blonde from mid-brown and usually cut in curls on the top of her head. Strong-willed and naturally rebellious, she had left Glasgow just a few weeks before meeting Frederick West, suspecting that she was pregnant by her pimp. But for the moment, that was something West was unaware of.

The day after their first meeting, West agreed to take Rena Costello with him in the cab of his van for a second time. He drove down to Avonmouth on the Severn to deliver his load of grain, and on the way back stopped in a lay-by. 'Rena told me she was "on the run" from a convent in Glasgow', where she was supposed to be living under the terms of her parole, 'and that she was pregnant'. Rena Costello then, almost certainly, had sex in the lorry's cab with the man who was shortly to become her first husband, and sex in a less inhibited way than he had ever truly experienced before. For his part, once it was over, the ever-helpful Frederick West told her that he had 'learned to do abortions' during his time 'away at sea', and that he could 'help her out'.

One Sunday afternoon a few days later, Margaret Mackintosh, Rena Costello and Frederick West went to Dog Hill, near Much Marcle, and he tried to abort the child Rena Costello was carrying. West may well have used one of the horrifying, extempory tools that he was later to display proudly to friends, including a twelve-inch metal pipe with what resembled a corkscrew attached to the top of it, but whatever the instrument, the abortion attempt failed. West's vanity was pricked. He had failed, and by then he was also besotted with this sexually experienced young Scottish woman. She had already begun to open his eyes to the deviations that sexual intercourse could offer. Frederick West did not hesitate: he asked her to marry him.

For her part, Rena Costello could see the attraction of the tousle-haired young man who seemed to have an insatiable sexual appetite. She was used to satisfying men, and she thought that he was a man she could control. If she accepted the proposal, he could also provide a means of escape from the attentions of the police over her breach of parole, and, if they went back to Glasgow together, perhaps even protection from some of her former associates in prostitution. By the time that the police caught up with her a week or so later, in early October 1962, and a police surgeon had confirmed that she was pregnant, Rena Costello had agreed to his proposal. For Rena Costello, her husband was a way out; for Frederick West, she was the first entry point into a different world, even if he did insist later it: 'was only to get her out of the shit'. She recognised in him something of her own disdain for the law and all it stood for, and he had discovered with her a fierce, unquenchable and deviant sexual energy that his earlier experiments had only hinted at. Frederick West and Rena Costello decided to marry immediately after his twenty-first birthday in November.

'My mother wouldn't come to the wedding, and my father wouldn't have anything to do with it,' West remembered later. 'Mam went mad about it, calling Rena a lot of names, because my mother knew I wasn't going with Rena and she could see she was pregnant.' Daisy West loathed her prospective daughter-in-law on sight, calling her 'filthy and common'. Her son remembered that she 'even cleaned the toilet seat as soon as she'd left the house'. Another reason for Daisy West's dislike of her future daughter-in-law was that she was a Catholic, and there was no prospect, therefore, of a marriage in Much Marcle church. She and the rest of the family were convinced that the only reason Freddie was marrying was because she was pregnant by him, and Frederick West did not trouble to dissuade them. Not every member of the West family took quite such a strong exception to Rena Costello, however. Walter West for one took a shine to the girl whom he would call 'Cath'.

It was hardly a marriage made in heaven. 'I'd be lying if I said I loved her,' West was to say. Five minutes before the ceremony he even offered his brother £5 if he would marry her in his place, 'with a smile on me face'. But John West refused. He was the only member of the West family to attend the brief ceremony on 17 November 1962 at the Ledbury Register Office. Walter and Daisy West had gone apple-picking, although Rena had managed to borrow a blue dress from Fred's sister Daisy for the occasion as she had hardly any clothes of her own. John West and Margaret Mackintosh were the only witnesses. The bridegroom gave his occupation as 'lorry-driver' and his new wife described herself as a 'waitress'. The ceremony was over in a matter of minutes. 'There was no reception. My brother just bought a bottle of Bristol Cream sherry and we stood outside in the street and drank it. Then we went back to work.'

Frederick West wanted his new wife to move into Moorcourt Cottage with him, but Daisy West put her foot down: 'She refused to have her in the house.' So after ten days staying at the tiny flat Rena shared with Margaret Mackintosh above the New Inn at Ledbury, the new Mr and Mrs Frederick West decided to move to Glasgow. John West drove them to Birmingham to catch the train.

Frederick West never revealed precisely what Rena Costello told him about her life in Glasgow before they married, but it seems certain that she promised that he would be well looked after if he went back there with her. She may have suggested that he would profit from her prostitution, even that he could watch whenever he wanted to. In the years to come West would maintain that the father of her unborn child, 'a Pakistani that ran a string of corner shops', had 'offered him a job as her minder' before they left Ledbury.

Whatever the truth, there is no doubt that Frederick and Rena West moved into a tenement flat at 46 Hospital Street in her native Coatbridge in the first week of December 1962, and West started working for someone she knew, 'driving a Vauxhall Cresta . . . with two big fins on the back. There were two big aerials on the back with flags. One Pakistani, one Indian, I think. I thought this was a good life.'

Frederick West gave so many conflicting accounts of his life in Glasgow that it is difficult to piece together exactly what happened during his time there over the next three years. Nevertheless, certain things remained constant. He kept in touch with his parents – though it was Rena who wrote the letters rather than he, as he was still unable to write – and regularly returned to Much Marcle to see them. The influence of his father, and mother, remained at the core of his life, no matter where life took him.

It is also certain that the strain of violence in his father's marriage surfaced quickly in his own. Frederick West started to beat his pregnant wife within a matter of weeks of their marriage, not because he drank – for by now he was 'almost teetotal' – nor because she did, even though 'she could sink a bottle of Johnnie Walker Red Label a day', but because she refused to become his puppet. Rena West was not prepared to stand by and do only what he wanted. As he put it in the last months of his life: 'That was when I realised that I was the bloody keeper of her. I didn't own her.' He demonstrated his frustration by 'bruising' her around the face. 'I was mixed up with these bloody Indians and that. But I got the motor and the money, and I played it through.'

In fact, West was apparently expected to abide by the rules that Rena's lover, and the father of her child, laid down for him. The six feet tall Pakistani, whom West nicknamed 'Billy Boy', reportedly told him: 'I couldn't make love to her, and I had to leave when I was told to leave and not ask questions, and not be caught snooping about. He gave me a list as long as your arm.' On the surface at least, West was prepared to oblige. He thought 'it was better to know nothing with these people . . . 'cause they used to cut your throat first and ask your name afterwards'. Besides, there were other compensations: the Pakistani would tell him 'where I could go where there would be a woman for me. He never charged me, like.'

Rena West had been in Scotland for only eight weeks when she wrote to Walter and Daisy West to tell them that she had 'lost the baby' she had been expecting. Then, barely a month later, she wrote again, this time to tell the Wests that she and her husband had 'adopted' another baby, a half-caste whom they had christened Charmaine. In reality, of course, Rena West had given birth to the child she had been carrying all along; the story about the 'adoption' was one of Frederick West's elaborate fantasies to 'protect' his parents. The little half-caste girl was born on 22 March 1963 at the Alexander Hospital in Coatbridge. But her 'father' was not there to see the birth. Frederick West spent the night of his wife's

41

confinement in bed with one of her four sisters.

The birth of the child did not affect Frederick West. He took no interest in the baby, and for a time even refused to register the birth of the little girl, whom his wife wanted to christen Charmaine Carol Mary (Mary in honour of her own mother). 'The registrar of births threatened to take me to court,' West insisted many years later, because he wouldn't register the child's name as West, and he did so only after repeated threats from the Scottish authorities. The fact that the child was not his own did not endear Charmaine to him.

Meanwhile, Frederick West's sexual demands on her mother increased. He would demand sex at any time of the day, no matter what she was doing or what mood she was in. If she refused he would hit her, repeatedly, taunting her that 'she only liked doing it with other men', though he also seemed to find that arousing. Rena West went back to working for 'Billy Boy', but Fred West soon 'got bored.'

'Rena kept disappearing for a week or a fortnight at a time.' He retaliated by answering an advertisement for drivers for 'Mr Whippy' ice-cream vans, to operate from a depot at Coatbridge. The restless, peripatetic strain in his character had surfaced once again. In the early summer of 1963, in his first weeks on the ice-cream van, Fred and Rena West moved into Glasgow itself, first to Shettleston on the outskirts, and then to a dilapidated tenement flat at 25 Savoy Street, Bridgeton, one of the decayed areas at the city's heart, not far from St Enoch's station.

The birth of Charmaine West did nothing to improve the marriage. West would still beat his wife around the face when he lost his temper, and she would still disappear to her former lover's flat in Coatbridge. Nevertheless, there was also an implicit respect between the now eighteen-year-old Scottish girl and the black-haired young man not quite three years her senior. In spite of the fights and the brutal sexual demands: 'Me and Rena got on well together, because we stuck to our agreement for a long while. She didn't want no children by me. She just wanted to have the one.' Certainly, when he was not working on his ice-cream van on his round in the Shettleston area of Glasgow, West would drive his wife to her clients, leaving one of her sisters, or a friend, to look after Charmaine. 'Whenever these certain blokes walked in I was given £5 to fuck off, and I went.'

Whatever their sexual habits, West and his wife believed in the religious proprieties. Charmaine was baptised and christened as a Catholic at St Mary's in Coatbridge on 6 September 1963, and Rena even tried to convert her husband to Catholicism. 'She wanted me to change and we went and seen about it,' West said later. 'Father Small his name was . . . He asked me for £25. I'll never forget his name. When anybody asks me for money I never forget them.' Frederick West neither paid the £25, nor underwent the training necessary to convert to the Roman Catholic Church.

West was a little in awe of his young wife. Even though he assaulted her with agonising regularity, he knew that she could give as good as she got. 'She knocked me out cold on three occasions,

42

with one blow.' He also noticed that she was now carrying a cut-throat razor in her handbag, a weapon favoured among the Glasgow gangs, as well as another knife. 'You didn't mess with Rena. Nobody did. No matter how big they were, she'd drop 'em. She was a vicious type if she wanted to be.' But Frederick West also acknowledged that his wife 'looked after me. She was never unkind to me in any way. Me and Rena had no bad feelings towards each other at all, because it was accepted the way she lived.'

Rena West also accepted the way her husband lived. She was well aware that his rounds behind the wheel of his Mr Whippy van meant that he met a great many young women, many of them with young children, and many of them bored. His old habits had not died away. Frederick West would park in a side-street, look out for a particular young woman that took his fancy, observe her for a while until he knew her habits, then engage her in conversation and offer her a lift in his ice-cream van. 'I had masses of girlfriends at the time,' he boasted later. 'Hundreds of them.'

That did not prevent him from still being sexually attracted to his wife, however; rather the reverse. There was nothing he liked more than to thumb his nose at her Pakistani lover and pimp. It proved that he was something special, someone who didn't have to pay. She was his wife, after all. One Sunday evening in October 1963 West took her to Barrowland, Glasgow's great dance hall, where Rena got a little drunk and he consumed his now familiar glass of shandy. 'We stopped off half-way home, and I give her one in the back of the car.' By the time Frederick West took his wife and daughter back to Much Marcle for Christmas, Rena West was pregnant with his first child.

Rena was not altogether happy to find herself pregnant only a few months after the birth of Charmaine. It threatened her income as a prostitute, and raised the possibility that she might fatally antagonise her relationship with her Pakistani lover. She may even have suspected that had been in her husband's mind in the first place. In any event, this time she attempted an abortion without her husband's help. 'I think she shoved a knitting-needle up herself,' West said coldly long afterwards. Rena West was taken to Bells Hill Maternity Hospital, where the staff saved the baby. The attempted termination was an action that Frederick West would never forgive. Afraid of his violent reprisals, not sure where else to turn, and by now heavily pregnant, Rena West decided to leave Glasgow for Much Marcle shortly afterwards to visit her husband's sister Daisy.

Her husband paid not the slightest notice. He drove his wife to Much Marcle, then drove back to Glasgow, where he 'spent the rest of the week in bed with one of the beautifulest women in Scotland', a girl he later boasted was 'a mate of the pop singer Lulu'. As far as he knew his wife was going to be away for a fortnight. In fact, conscious that her child was due at any time, she changed her mind and returned to Scotland early, to give birth. It turned out to be a wise decision. On the way back to Glasgow on the train she went into labour. But she did not take a taxi to Bells Hill Hospital; instead, she took it home.

When Rena West walked in she found her husband in bed with the woman he had spent the week with. The memory of it delighted West until his dying day. 'She says: "You two better get out of that bloody bed and let me in." Rena lay on the bed and the baby started coming.' By the time the girl had returned from calling the midwife from a nearby telephone box, West himself had delivered his first child. 'I brought Anna-Marie into the world,' he would announce proudly. It was shortly after nine o'clock in the morning of 6 July 1964.

According to Frederick West, in the months that followed, Rena West 'stayed off her' second daughter 'straight from the word go', because 'she'd only had the child most reluctantly'. But that did not affect him; unlike his attitude to her one-year-old stepsister Charmaine, he doted on his own daughter, whom he christened Anna-Marie Kathleen Daisy (Daisy in honour of his own mother), and whose birth Frederick West registered without a moment's hesitation. And he would think nothing of slapping her stepsister if ever she annoyed him. Rena fought to defend her first-born against his violent attacks, but he would merely smile as he told his wife 'she deserved it'.

West took such a great interest in his new daughter that he made a cot for her out of a wooden orange box, and put it under the counter of his ice-cream van when he went out on his rounds. Like his father before him, Frederick West was hypnotised by his own daughter. Anna-Marie recalled the experience: 'Apparently, I used to sleep for most of the day with the cheerful tune of the ice-cream van for my lullaby.'

Life at 25 Savoy Street returned to its pattern of fights and beatings, bitter arguments and separations followed by reconciliation and sex. 'Me and Rena would always make love after,' West would insist at the end of his life, 'no matter how bad we fell out with each other.' Rena West was 'drinking heavily – a bottle of Scotch a day, mind'. But he encouraged his wife to drink. 'She never got aggressive with drink. She was rather loving actually. It did actually change her nature, take her off her guard, 'cause she was very much on her guard all the time.' On one rare occasion, when West himself was drunk, Rena West tattooed the word 'Rena' on the upper part of his left arm in blue Indian ink in capital letters. 'She wrote her name on my arm so no other woman would be in any doubt who I belonged to,' West told his daughter Anna-Marie many years later. 'He was quite proud of that tattoo,' his daughter would remember; 'proud that she managed to do it without him knowing and that she wanted to put her mark on him.'

It was a marriage of opposites: the country boy and the city girl, the poacher and the prostitute, bound together by a fascination with sex. But there was an intensity in the relationship of Frederick and Rena West that everyone who met them remarked on. It could burn white-hot for weeks at a time before suddenly turning cold, and the sparks of violence in both of them fanned the flames. To the outside world he was a placid, slightly humble man 'eager to please' his customers on the Mr Whippy van, but alone in the privacy of his house with his own wife the obsequious ice-cream salesman became a vicious bully. But Rena West was not a rabbit in the moonlight, freezing at the sight of a fox; she was not afraid of Frederick West.

Not long after Anna-Marie's birth, Rena West again returned to the comparative tranquillity of Much Marcle, taking Anna-Marie with her. The new baby was the first grandchild, as Charmaine had been 'adopted', and she wanted to show her off to Walter and Daisy West. A strange bond began to develop between the tall, silent farm labourer and the short, pretty Scottish girl with an accent that was difficult to understand. Whether Walter West sensed what she might be suffering at her son's hands, or whether he, too, nursed a sexual desire for her is not clear, but whatever the reason, the relationship between Walter West and the girl he always called 'Cath' grew steadily, until it was clear enough to the rest of the family.

Frederick West's fascination with the possibility of sex – with any young women who happened to cross his path – had not dimmed. Out all day touring the streets selling Mr Whippy ice-cream allowed him to indulge his pastime, the search for another sexual conquest, another girl to impress. At the end of his life West would recall that he picked up one girl 'dressed like a tramp' whom he found sitting on a step 'crying her eyes out'. He called her 'absolutely beautiful, but dressed in rags, her hair all matted'. He took her back to Savoy Street, helped her to clean up, and in the weeks to come took her out with him in the van. It was an approach he would use throughout his life, apparently offering help to a young vulnerable girl, but then eventually demanding sex from her in return.

At Christmas West took his family back to Much Marcle, as he always did, and was introduced to his brother John's fiancée. The girl had just been badly burned in an accident when her night-dress had caught fire at home, and West took his brother to see her in hospital in Birmingham, where she had been sent because of the severity of her injuries. His first remark when he saw the young girl lying in the hospital bed was: 'Christ, you're not marrying that, are you?' Even Frederick West himself admitted later: 'It meant that she didn't much care for me.' Rena West told the girl privately that she should be thankful she was engaged to John, not his brother Fred.

In the first weeks of 1965 Frederick and Rena West moved for the third time. They rented a tenement flat at 241 McLellan Street in Kinning Park, one of the longest streets in Glasgow. On the first floor, and larger than Savoy Street, it boasted its own separate lavatory and two bedrooms. The tenement's entrance was the last at the southern end of the street. Beyond it was a set of allotments, small plots of land for hire, on which families could grow vegetables and flowers. West hired an allotment, but barely cultivated the land. Instead, he took advantage of the small shed which came with it, returning there at night whenever he could, more often than not to have sex with a girl he had picked up on his round.

Life went on as it had always done for Rena West. She would be at home in the morning and usually out working in the evening. When she was not working she would sometimes visit the local bookmaker's, Telky's, not far away from the flat in McLellan Street. It was here, one morning that winter, she met the man to whom she was eventually to turn to protect her from her husband's violence, John McLachlan, at the time a bus-driver for Glasgow Corporation, working out of the nearby Possilpark garage. McLachlan was married but liked the young woman who now sported a new beehive haircut. He met her again, shortly afterwards, at the ground-floor flat beneath her own, where they had a drink together. Then, as Andrew O'Hagan reports in his book *The Missing*: 'John remembers seeing a face at the window, a dark face, a head of curly hair, and he opened the door to see who it was. It was Fred. He came charging in and grabbed Rena, and pulled her up the stairs. He was belting her on the way up.'

John McLachlan steadily began to see more and more of Rena West. He would take her for drives to Loch Lomond in his green Ford Zephyr, and he would protect her whenever he could. An amateur boxer, McLachlan remembers having to pull West off his young blonde wife on a number of occasions, 'because he was beating the shit oot a her'. But West took care never to get involved in a fight with McLachlan. Once, when he found the bus-driver kissing his wife in Kinning Park, West pulled out the knife he still carried at his belt and drew it across McLachlan's stomach, but when the Scot hit him again West turned away, unwilling to fight a man, but punching his wife as he dragged her across the park.

Frederick West may not have wanted to be faithful to his wife, and he may have been more than prepared to profit from her earnings as a prostitute, but he was still proprietorial towards her. He did not want 'to be made a fool of'. She in turn resorted to spending more and more time away from the flat, partly with McLachlan, but also looking for company, and for people she could invite to her home. If there were other people present, West could sometimes be deflected from hitting her. She had proved that when her sisters had helped her look after the two girls. So when she did not meet McLachlan at Telky's Rena West would often take refuge in the nearby Victoria café in Scotland Street.

That spring Rena West met two young women at the Victoria café. Isa McNeill and Anna McFall worked together at Livingstone Knitwear on Kilmarnock Road, and had known each other since childhood. Isa was the elder of the two, a brunette of eighteen, brought up a Protestant, while Anna (who always preferred to be called Ann) was just sixteen, and a Catholic. Nevertheless, they were very close friends, and they quickly became Rena West's allies and supporters. The two girls would wheel Anna-Marie in her pram and hold Charmaine's hand as they walked up McLellan Street together, and they would go for walks with Rena when the children got fed up with sitting in the Victoria café.

Isa McNeill was going out with a friend of John McLachlan's called John Trotter, and she and Rena West started going out together in the evenings to the pubs along Paisley Road with their boyfriends. In July 1965 Rena West invited Isa McNeill to come to stay with her at 241 McLellan Street. Ostensibly, she wanted her to work as her 'nanny' and help to look after the children, but the reality was that she hoped Isa might protect her from the excesses of her husband's temper. Isa McNeill had barely lived there a week when she told her friends that Frederick West was like 'Jekyll and Hyde', violent towards his wife and Charmaine, but never to his own daughter, Anna-Marie.

What Isa McNeill did not know until she arrived at McLellan Street was that Frederick West insisted that his daughters should sleep together on the bottom of a pair of bunk beds, and that he had nailed a set of vertical slats across the space between the upper and lower bunks so that they could not get out. As soon as she arrived, West instructed his wife's new 'nanny' that he wanted the two baby girls to 'stay in there' while he was in the flat, and that they should be fed, changed and made to play there. He would sometimes allow his own daughter Anna-Marie out of 'the prison' for a time, but two-year-old Charmaine West was never to be allowed out while he was at home.

Rena West clung increasingly to John McLachlan for support, and their sexual relationship, which had begun that summer, contributed to the breakup of his marriage. Rena West talked about moving in with him, and would confide in him about her husband's obsession with sex, and how he would never get home until three or four in the morning. She would tell him time after time that all she wanted was to be allowed to live in peace with her kids. But, usually, the determined young Scottish woman would return reluctantly to McLellan Street, anxious about her daughters.

Not that her husband was always there. In the past few months Frederick West had taken to spending the entire night away from home, rather than simply the early hours of the morning. One reason was that he was increasingly involved with one of the young women he had picked up on his rounds, a twenty-year-old Scottish girl called Margaret McAvoy. 'She'd walk hundreds of miles just to be with me,' he would boast later, and she had started to 'help on the van at nights when I was busy.' In the autumn of 1965 she became pregnant by West. It was to be one reason why he would decide shortly to leave Glasgow and return to Gloucester and the familiar territory of Much Marcle. But there was another reason: fear.

On the afternoon of 4 November 1965 Frederick West ran over and killed a three-year-old boy in his ice-cream van in a cul-de-sac on the south side of Glasgow. West had got to know the boy in the preceding few months and had even bought him a 'bright-coloured ball . . . about four or five inches' to play with. He had even told him that he would 'have a firework for him' if he came back that afternoon. 'The mother brought the child down and led him across the road,' West would recall. 'When I came into the cul-de-sac he was playing with his ball, and he bounced his ball and it went over the hedge, and he went through the gate. He was round behind the hedge when I came in . . . I used to go in and turn round . . . and wait for the kids to come. I went into the cul-de-sac, looked it was all clear. I came back a matter of two or three foot and there was an almighty bang and I stopped there.'

West had backed his four-ton ice-cream van over the boy. 'I could see the child was lying underneath the van under the back axle.' West said that he had 'passed out' immediately, and someone took him into their house. But he also admitted that 'the father came down. He was going to kill me or summat . . . There was a load of people there fighting to stop him getting to me.' When the police and ambulance arrived, West was taken to hospital. 'I was put under sedatives in Glasgow Royal, and then I discharged myself after a while and I went home.'

In the years to come Frederick West would increasingly embroider his version of the fatal accident with the ice-cream van. But he always insisted that he returned to McLellan Street after discharging himself from hospital, only to find the flat full of a motor cycle gang called the Skulls, 'the wierdest-looking blokes', whose members, he alleged, included John McLachlan and John Trotter. He then found his wife 'starkers' in bed with two of the gang's members, 'with two more sat on the bottom of the bed'. West said he tried to hit one of the men, but 'accidentally' ended up hitting his wife instead, and 'she went out cold', at which point he also fainted. 'The next thing, the gang's disappeared and the police and the ambulance turn up' and the police took him away and 'locked me up'.

In West's subsequent version of events, the police let him go but told him to go back to the hospital. But when he got there he was so upset that he 'assaulted a nurse', which led to his being arrested for a second time, 'and put in Barlinnie prison for the night'. In court the following morning, West insisted, the 'judge' cleared him but advised him to 'get legal advice on my matrimonial problems'. But outside the court 'I runs into the Skulls and Rena, and they tell me I'm a dead man'. In this version West was so terrified that he went to live with Margaret McAvoy, and took a job delivering timber for a timberyard rather than return to the ice-cream van.

It was this version of his being 'hounded out' of Glasgow by a motor cycle gang called the Skulls that Frederick West was eventually to convince himself was the explanation for his return to Gloucestershire. In the final weeks of his life, Frederick West was even to write it down in his own 'book', a version of his life. He wrote the story in his own hand on lined prison paper, poring over it for hours at a time, struggling as he did so to teach himself to write for the first time in his life, and he was working on it in Winson Green prison when he was found hanged in his cell shortly before lunch on Sunday 1 January 1995.

Here is the second page of his book, exactly as he wrote it, describing the events of that November day:

I workd 7 dats a a Week 16 hrs a day as a self employed icecream salesma. I Love Workin With the public you got to kno wow the OTHER 1/2 lives ther ar always sumone Worse of then you. but Disaster hit me. I had a fatal accident and kill a 3 to 4 year old Boy with My icecream Van the Boy was a god customer I see him Ever day. I love him as a son. I had no son at that time. I Wonted a son but that Was no time for one. so I spoil him by giving him presented a Boll and Badge and allway a icecream sunday. the accideent Was on 4 of November at TEN PAST three I had a firework for him. U told him I Wood bring them the day befor so was that Way he ream in to the back of the VAN I did not see him. I was in shock. I Went Backwards over a fence in to a garden sumone tuck me in ther home the police tuck me to hospital I Was Given Drugs and was taken home by the police. I went into my home it was full of yobs.

My wife Rean was in Bad With two of them. One of them went for me so I Went to hit him My Wife went to stop me I hit her in the eye. I did Not Mean to it was a accident. I was arrested and charged Withg Wife Assault and Was put in prison for 24 HRS. I Went to court and Was clard, and told by the Judge to see a Solciitor and sort My Marriage out, as I left the court My Wife and the yobs were out side and I Was told by My Wife if I Went home I Wood be killed.

In another version of events in the city at the end of 1965, however, West maintained that Rena's former lover, the Pakistani 'Billy Boy' had thrown him out of the house when he discovered that Anna-Marie was not a half-caste and could not therefore be his child. 'Rena had pulled the wool over his eyes that her second daughter was his child, just as Charmaine had been.' (West's explanation for the fact that the child was by then almost eighteen months old was that the Pakistani had 'been away at sea all that time'.) The Pakistani, according to this second version of events, 'chucked the baby's clothes into the car' while his wife had come down with Anna-Marie and 'chucked her in through the window to me and said, "Get out before he gets you".'

West gave another, third version of the events in the book he wrote in Winson Green prison in the last months of his life. This version begins with the words 'I Was Loved by an Angel', but the angel to whom Frederick West was referring was not his first wife Rena, nor the newly pregnant Margaret McAvoy. His angel was the sixteen-year-old Glaswegian Anna McFall, who, together with Isa McNeill, had befriended his wife Rena. In this version of events it was, in fact, his 'angel', Anna McFall, who helped him to leave Scotland and to remove his children from his wife.

She sead she Wood help Me get the Girls out and back to England so I gave ana a PHON number the nex day ana Rang Me and sed Rena had gon out with the yobs. so I got the car and Went to my home ana was ther We gopt the first out ana sead you Will have to beet Me up. I sead no way you can say I did. so we agreed that ana Wood tell Rena and the yobs I had.

In this version of events Anna McFall, whom West called Annie, stayed in Glasgow and agreed to tell Rena West that he had punched her in the stomach and had taken her two daughters with him 'to my farther and Mother in Muck Marcle.'

In West's diary he remembers that he 'made a bed in the car' and 'drove all night, arriving at Much Marcle at six o'clock in the morning', just as his parents were getting up. He asked his mother and sister to look after the two girls, so that he could get a job and 'pay them to do it'.

In Scotland, however, the story of Frederick West's return to England is more mundane, and infinitely more believable. Rather than having to escape from the Skulls motor cycle gang and taking his two daughters with him, West simply informed his wife and Isa McNeill, who was still living with them, that he had decided to take them all back to England. He was going to get a job, and in the meantime he was going to give notice to Glasgow Corporation that he no longer wanted the flat in McLellan Street. His decision certainly provoked a heated argument, and led Rena West to tell him he could go on his own. She would decide whether she would join him when he came back.

There are elements of truth in all three of the differing versions of the events in the life of Frederick West and his family in Glasgow in the final weeks of 1965. But there is no doubt whatever that by the middle of December West had arrived back in Much Marcle together with Charmaine and Anna-Marie, but without his wife. He told his parents about his accident with the ice-cream van and the death of the boy, and then asked his mother and sisters if they would look after his two daughters while he went out and got a job to pay them for doing so. But Daisy West refused to accept the little half-caste girl. 'Mother did not like Charmaine.' So Frederick West told his mother: 'You have to have the two girls or none of them.' Daisy West did not hesitate. She would not house either of them.

On 29 December 1965, at Frederick West's instigation, both Charmaine and Anna-Marie West, at the ages of a little over two and a half and just eighteen months, were taken into care by the Herefordshire Children's Department. The two little girls were in 'a deplorable state', and the council found that it had to 'clothe them pretty well from scratch'. With his daughters in care, Frederick West went back to living at home and found the perfect job – at Clenches Field Farm in Longford – picking up hides and skins from a local slaughterhouse.

Chapter Five

'Loved by an Angel'

'Brisk Confidence still best with woman copes: Pique her and soothe her in turn – soon Passion crowns thy hopes.'

Byron, 'Childe Harold's Pilgrimage'

Back in his natural habitat, Frederick West wasted no time in returning to his old ways. There may have been women who fell victim to his seduction in Glasgow, but there he was always just a little out of place. 'When I got back I went round all my old girlfriends', he told the police jauntily almost thirty years later, even 'making love to one on the altar of the church down the road'. But, as ever, West did not restrict himself only to girls whom he knew. Like a predator returning to its hunting-ground, he lost no time in searching for prey. In the first weeks of 1966 two young women found themselves pursued by a dark-haired man who never stopped grinning or talking.

West's methods had not changed. He would tour the area in a car, looking for a young woman whom he would follow until he decided she might be tempted, or physically persuaded, to have sex with him. One sixteen-year-old recalled almost thirty years later that she was stalked by West in Gloucester, and when she ran away he followed her on foot until she managed to escape. 'I didn't know what fear was until then,' she explained. Two nights later West followed her again in his car, and she froze. 'I didn't know what to do. I couldn't move. I couldn't scream.' It was only the arrival of her younger sister that frightened him away. 'She ran up and banged on the car and told him to get lost.'

At about the same time, another young woman accepted a lift from West when she was hitchhiking to Cheltenham to see her boyfriend. During the journey he pulled into a lane and stopped the car. West told the girl to remove her knickers, but she refused. He then exposed himself, but when she tried to get out of the car to run, he hauled her back by throwing his arm around her throat. Afterwards, 'he was charming, pleasant, laughing'. The smile remained on his face when he returned to Moorcourt Cottage. For although both young women reported to the police the attacks on them, no policeman found his way up the road from Dymock towards Much Marcle and the Wests' cottage. There was still nothing, and no one, to stop him. And as far as Frederick West was concerned, every young woman was still 'begging for it', no matter what she said.

West was convinced that he was irresistible to women, and he had no intention whatever of allowing his wife to remain the one woman who could prove him wrong. He was already planning to return to Glasgow to collect her, and thereby bring to an end her affair with McLachlan. The only question was: where were they going to live? West wanted somewhere that the Children's Department would consider suitable enough for them to allow him to reclaim his daughters from care, because he knew that Rena West would not consider joining him in England if she were not reunited with her children. West could not afford a house, but he rapidly came up with an alternative: a caravan. If he could raise £600, he could buy one and put it on a site in Gloucester. The only difficulty was that he did not have £600.

West asked his parents if they would agree to guarantee a hire-purchase agreement that would allow him to buy a new caravan, but Daisy West refused point-blank. Her husband might have been persuaded, but she would not even consider helping him. He had got himself into these difficulties, and he could get himself out. An angry and disappointed Frederick West stormed out of Moorcourt Cottage and went to stay with his eldest sister Daisy, who was now married with her own child. Perhaps she could help, if his parents would not.

A persuasive Frederick West explained his plan to his sister. It was his family's chance to be together again, the children needed their mother, it was their only hope. He even took Daisy to see his children in Hereford in the slaughterhouse lorry. If he could buy a caravan, then Rena could join him from Scotland and the children could come out of care. The persuasion worked. After a little thought, and to his obvious relief, Daisy and her husband Frank agreed to act as guarantors, and West sold the blue Vauxhall Viva he had bought in Scotland in part-exchange for a new caravan in Hereford, the hire-purchase agreement making up the rest. He then arranged to have the caravan delivered to a site at Sandhurst Lane on the outskirts of Gloucester. West did not intend to be too near his mother's enquiring eye, and yet he could not bring himself to remove himself altogether from Much Marcle. Just as it had been five years before, Gloucester was the natural place.

One Saturday afternoon in early February 1966, Frederick West watched as his newly acquired brown and white caravan arrived at the Sandhurst Lane site, barely a mile north-west of the city centre. Sandhurst Lane was right beside one of his old routes from Ledbury, a runnel hidden in the flat-lands of the Vale of Gloucester, alongside the River Severn's burgeoning East Channel. It was as inconspicuous as it was anonymous, the perfect place to hide in.

A few days later West drove the abattoir lorry north to Glasgow to collect his wife. Reluctantly, Rena West agreed to come south with him, on condition that Isa McNeill could come as well. She could help to look after the children and provide moral support. Rena West's affair with John McLachlan had already begun to wane, and she wanted to see her children again. Besides, her friend Isa was not going to be the only friend to rely on. Anna McFall had asked if she could join them and 'start a new life' in the south. The three girls sat in the back of the lorry, the stench of the hides filling their nostrils, as West drove them back to Gloucester.

Life in Glasgow without Isa McNeill or Rena West did not seem all that attractive to the frail young girl. They had become the most important people in her life, after her mother, and she had come to depend on them. Anna McFall's childhood had not been happy. Born on 8 April 1949 in Stobhill Hospital in Glasgow, her father was Thomas McFall, a baths attendant at the Parkhead Baths in the city, as well as a street bookmaker. But McFall was not married to her mother, Jane Hunter. In fact, he had a wife and another family in another part of the city. Brought up in Malcolm Street in Parkhead, and a Catholic, Anna had a brother three years older than she was, who was also called Thomas. But both their parents were alcoholics and refused to take any responsibility for their children, McFall often returning to his other family for months at a time, leaving Jane Hunter to fend for herself.

Both Anna McFall and her elder brother had found themselves in trouble with the police for 'thieving and truancy' from an early age. Thomas McFall junior was rapidly to find himself branded a 'young offender' and to earn the nickname 'Scarface', while his sister hardly fared better. Always known as Ann or Annie rather than Anna, she was eventually placed in care at the Nazareth House children's home and convent in Aberdeen on 1 April 1960 at the age of ten. The care order called for her to remain at Nazareth House until she was fifteen, and she enjoyed her time there, even joining the convent's Girl Guides. But when she left Nazareth House in July 1964, Ann McFall could not bring herself to go back to live with her alcoholic mother. She elected instead to stay with friends around Glasgow, and it was then that she worked with Isa McNeill at Livingstone Knitwear. Some time after that both girls befriended Rena West.

Though she was not living with her, Ann McFall was still trying to look after her alcoholic mother throughout 1965, but nothing she did seemed to make any difference, and it often led to arguments. Frederick West later maintained that Jane Hunter used to 'get men in for Ann – to pay for her drink', and there is no doubt that McFall and her brother Tom seldom managed to persuade their mother to eat more than a slice of toast. Life at McLellan Street with the Wests and their two girls must have seemed infinitely more attractive. Though she tried to conceal it, Ann McFall was looking for someone

54

to love, and someone to look after her. Though she had only hinted at it to her friend Isa McNeill, the person she had chosen was Frederick West.

By the spring of 1966, when they set off for Gloucester in the back of the slaughterhouse lorry, Ann McFall was almost seventeen years of age, five feet, two inches in height, with brown eyes and straight, dark brown hair almost long enough for her to sit on. A slight, vulnerable but attractive girl with a reedy nervous laugh, she wanted nothing more than to find a family that she could call her own, and she was obviously impressed by Frederick West's endless relentless chatter. Her first boyfriend had been just that, a boy, and she was flattered by the attention of a man of twenty-four. As Isa McNeill was to recall, 'she kinda flaunted herself at him'.

They had hardly settled into the caravan on The Willows site, as Sandhurst Lane was known officially, when Isa McNeill and Ann McFall realised that life would be very little different from McLellan Street. Fred and Rena shared the small bedroom at the front of the van, while Isa and Ann were expected to sleep on the U-shaped sofa built into the cramped lounge. Nevertheless, Charmaine and Anna-Marie were returned to their parents by the Herefordshire Children's Department on 23 February, and Frederick West and his wife put them to sleep together in a single bed that pulled out of the wall. The next morning West set off for work shortly after seven, leaving the three women with strict instructions not to take the children far off the caravan site.

Though there were no slats across their bunk beds this time, the two little girls were still supposed to be kept in this new 'prison' unless Frederick West said they could be released. They were his children, and he would decide exactly what was to happen to them. He told his wife, Isa and Ann that he would pop back at odd times during the day to make sure they were there, and took great pleasure in doing so. If they were not where he expected them to be, he would scream at all three women.

Whatever Rena West may have hoped, it did not take long for the regime of beatings and violence to return. The presence of the two other young Scottish women did not inhibit Frederick West in the least. He would return from work, his overalls covered in blood and his black wellington boots smeared with offal, stinking of the slaughterhouse and demanding his supper. If it was not ready immediately, he would hit his wife without warning. Even if it were, he would sometimes smile slowly and then hit her anyway. If Rena West tried to stop him slapping Charmaine for being naughty, he would hit her even harder, and the two Scottish girls would take the children out into the site itself until the beatings stopped.

Within six weeks Rena West had decided she could not stand the situation any longer. Isa McNeill telephoned the Victoria café from the call box at the entrance to the caravan site and left a message for John McLachlan, asking him to phone her back on that number later that evening. When he did so, she asked him to come to collect her and Rena and the children as soon as he could. And she told him to come at a time when Frederick West was sure to be out at work. A few days later McLachlan phoned again, at a pre-arranged time, and told her that he and John Trotter would be down later that week, and asked her to meet them beside the telephone box at the entrance to the caravan site.

But Rena West and Isa McNeill had reckoned without Ann McFall's infatuation with Frederick West. In spite of the beatings, in spite of the abuse of his children, in spite of his boasting about how attractive other women found him, the young Scottish woman had convinced herself that she alone could change him. She was the one woman who could make him happy. When Isa McNeill had confided in her, telling her of the plan for them all to return to Glasgow together, Ann McFall had listened intently. She had then told Frederick West.

When John McLachlan and John Trotter arrived at the entrance to the Sandhurst Lane site on that April morning in 1966, in a borrowed Mini, Rena West and Isa McNeill were ready, and had packed for Charmaine and Anna-Marie. But Ann McFall seemed slower, less enthusiastic than her friends, dragging her heels as the other two women carried their stuff out towards the waiting car. Within a quarter of an hour, the reason became all too clear. Frederick West suddenly appeared, walking calmly on to the site.

An argument broke out at once. Everybody screamed at everybody else. Rena disappeared into the caravan to collect her coat, but Fred West followed her inside and started hitting her. John McLachlan shouted at him to stop, and eventually punched him in the stomach when he came back out of the caravan clutching Charmaine in his arms. But nothing anyone said or did altered West's demeanour. He was not going to see the two girls removed from his care. Isa McNeill accepted the inevitable and set off for the Mini, carrying her suitcase. She was expecting Ann McFall to follow her. But the young Scottish girl just stood at the entrance to the caravan with the twenty-two-month-old Anna-Marie in her arms, shaking her head slowly.

Desperate to reclaim her daughter, Rena West started pulling at Charmaine, trying to prise the child out of her husband's grasp, but the harder she pulled the more firmly Frederick West held on. Not even another punch from McLachlan would persuade him to give her up. Meanwhile, Ann McFall looked on, cradling his other daughter in her arms. When Isa McNeill shouted at her friend to come with them, Ann McFall slowly shook her head. She was going to stay and be the girls' 'nanny', she said quietly.

A uniformed police constable suddenly appeared, riding a bicycle, and the argument came to an abrupt halt. Rena West and Isa McNeill climbed into the back of the Mini, while John McLachlan and John Trotter got into the front. The Mini disappeared down the muddy track between the caravans before the policeman got off his bicycle. Through the rear window, Rena West watched her husband put on his familiar obsequious smile, to explain to the officer that there was nothing to worry about. It was merely a family argument. She cried most of the way back to Glasgow, frantic that Charmaine might be hurt.

In the last weeks of his life, Frederick West wrote his own version of these events, and it paints a slightly different picture. In particular, though there is no evidence to corroborate it, West insisted that Rena had first turned up in Much Marcle with Isa McNeill and 'three of the yobs' in January 1966, while he was still living there with his mother and father, and before he had bought the caravan. The object of the visit, he maintained, was revenge for his taking the children without telling his wife. West insisted that his mother had telephoned him at work to warn him, telling him not to go home, but that he had ignored the advice.

> I went and got a piece of timber about three foot long and went home. Rena and the yobs were asleep in the car. I stopped alongside and said 'Follow me'. My mother was at the door and called to me to get the police, but I went down the road to the church . . . It was a moonlit night . . . There was a lot of shouting . . . I said to Rena to come to me and say what she come down for. So she did. I had the piece of timber in my hand. She said: 'What you going to do with that?' I said: 'Whatever I have to. No one is going to get me.' . . . She said: 'We have come to get you for getting the children out of Glasgow and beating Anna up.' I said I was sorry for what I did to Anna . . . I could not put Anna in danger . . . Rena said: 'Charmaine is my daughter and Anna-Marie is yours.' I said: 'They are sisters and they will stay together.' So we came to an agreement that she would write to me and sort it out. Rena went back to Glasgow. I went home.

In a subsequent interview West even elaborated on that version, suggesting that he 'hammered the shit' out of the yobs, using a knife he had picked up from a rack at the slaughterhouse against their bayonets, and injuring two so badly that he had to deliver them to Ledbury Hospital. 'I finally won, and they went,' he said, although there is no evidence to support his allegation that the fight ever took place. There is also little doubt that West's natural cowardice when it came to violence with men had not deserted him.

Frederick West then agrees, however, that a few weeks later his wife came down 'with Anna', and they went to reclaim their daughters from care. 'Anna got hold of Anna-Marie and was kissing her for about twenty minutes and was looking at me. She loved the girls, I knew that, but why was she looking at me and smiling . . . I felt wonderful and marvellous. I could feel her love. But I said to myself, No, Rena is my wife.'

According to West's version, the experience of life in the caravan with his wife was a disaster. But it had nothing to do with his own violent nature; it was the result of her inability to give up prostitution and drinking. 'Nothing changed. Rena was always out, and came back drunk, if she came at all . . . It went on for about two months. Then Rena took the children back to Glasgow and left Anna with me . . . So I lived in the caravan. Anna slept in the bedroom at the back of the van and I slept in the front.'

Life with Ann McFall was quite different, West wrote. 'Anna was happy and contented and joyful . . . All Anna was me. When I came home Anna was always stood in the doorway. She always made sure she touched me . . . When I looked at her she would always give me a smile. I knew love was in the air.' But 'I was married with a wife and two daughters, three and four years old. My marriage was a disaster, which was putting it mildly, so my daughters was the love of my life. Anna was more of a mother than Rena. I was about to let an angel love me.'

One evening, after West had given Ann McFall 'money to buy new clothes', she would not let him see what she had bought; instead, the young Scottish girl sat combing her hair.

We knew we were in love, but who was going to move first? . . . We kept looking at each other and smiling. I said to Anna, 'Can I comb your hair?' . . . I was combing her hair for two hours. It is now about nine-thirty on a Saturday, so we went out for a walk by the river . . . The moon was up and shining on the water. It was beautiful and romantic. We chatted about the girls. How much she loved Charmaine and Anna-Marie. I said: 'I will bring them back from Glasgow. Rena will not have the girls long. They will get in her way. Rena loves the children and me, but also needs to be free to do her own thing.' . . . We walked home side by side, not saying no more . . . just having our own thoughts.

Back at the caravan, West recalled:

I went in and Anna had made a cup of coffee for me and gone to bed. I said 'good night' to Anna and Anna said 'good night'. My bed was made up by Anna. I undressed and lay on the bed. The moon was shining in the window. My only thoughts were of Anna. It was so peaceful, as if the world had stopped for me to be loved by an angel . . . I had never felt like this before . . . Anna was so beautiful. I had no right to her love.

It was about eighteen months. I had not made love to my wife. She was always too drunk or gone. I was in love with Anna, but was Anna in love with me? It was twelve-thirty now. What I did not know I was minutes away from knowing. Anna's bedroom door opened. Anna stood in the doorway. She had on a black negligé night-dress . . . and said: 'Do you like it?' I said: 'Yes, you are stunning.' Anna said: 'That's not me, that's my night-dress.' I was not sure what she meant by that. Anna moved to the bed. My heart was beating so fast. Anna said: 'I am in love with you and have loved you from the first time I seen you. I loved chatting to you in Glasgow. When I went to bed I said my prayers and asked God for you to love me.'

In spite of the obvious lies, that his children had not gone back to Glasgow, and that he had certainly made love to the pregnant Margaret McAvoy, if not to his wife, in the previous eighteen months, there is perhaps a strain of honesty in part of his account of his seduction by Ann McFall. There is little doubt that he liked to cast himself as a glamorous and romantic figure to the young Scottish girl and that she in turn was prepared to accept the fantasy. He sustained that in the final part of his account of the start of their affair.

I said: 'But I am married.' Anna said: 'Is that what you call it?' I pulled back the bed covering and said 'Get in'. Anna did not move . . . 'You are not looking at me. You are looking at a night-dress. That's not me.' 'Well, remove it then.' Anna said: 'No, that's up to you to do that. From this day on I belong to you. No man will ever touch me or see me as you will.' . . . So I got out of bed and undressed Anna slowly . . . Anna's body felt like silk and a smell of spring flowers . . . I put my arms around Anna and kissed her on the lips. It was wonderful but strange to be kissed by an angel that loved you.

The following morning, according to West's account, 'I got out my guitar and sat on the step of the van. Anna sat by me. I played and sang to Anna . . . "Kiss an angel, good, good morning" . . . From then on I always sang to Anna . . . We always had tears in our eyes, tears of happiness and love. Anna would wipe the tear from my eyes and I would from her eyes.' West did not reveal in his memoir that the next line of the song after 'Kiss the little angel in the morning' was 'And we love her like a devil in the evening'.

Although there is no evidence to suggest that Frederick West ever used any form of contraception in any sexual encounter, he maintained that Ann McFall soon began to pester him to make her pregnant. 'Anna said: "Can I have your baby?" I said: "Not just now. Let's get the girls back and get a house." ' But this did not satisfy the seventeen-year-old girl, who told him soon afterwards: 'All you have to do is to marry me, so I can be Mrs Fred West and the mother of your children and ours.'

In West's version of events in the spring of 1966, he then took a week's holiday and went to Scotland himself to bring his children back to the caravan site, and was even helped to recover them from a brothel by the Govan police, although yet again there is no evidence to corroborate his story. Nevertheless, it is certain that at the beginning of May 1966 Ann McFall was indeed looking after Charmaine and Anna-Marie West at the caravan site on Sandhurst Lane. Their relationship was not, however, exactly as West chose to paint it more than twenty-eight years later.

For no matter what Frederick West cared to suggest in the last months of his life, there is compelling independent evidence that far from he and Ann McFall being wrapped in each other's arms as the perfect loving couple he was later to characterise, they were, in fact, arguing relentlessly. Certainly, by July 1966 the twenty-four-year-old lorry-driver and his seventeen-year-old companion had come to the attention of the Gloucester Children's Department, where an internal memorandum suggested that Ann McFall was being difficult and that Frederick West was anxious for her to leave the caravan as there was not much room. The same memorandum also suggested that although Rena West had left the family home in the caravan, she was planning to return.

In fact, Rena West had spent part of the intervening months living with Isa McNeill in a tiny flat in Arden Street in Maryhill, Glasgow, and had taken a job as a bus conductor at the same depot that McLachlan worked from as a driver. But she had not settled. Her old habits were hard to break, and she rapidly got herself a dubious reputation at the bus depot by offering to have sex with any driver or conductor who was interested. The peroxide-blonde woman, with the strong, vigorous open face, seemed almost to crave some element of her husband's brutality: loathing it at one moment, craving it the next. There was something in her relationship with Frederick West that she could not quite throw off.

By the end of July 1966 Rena West had decided to go back to Fred West. At the age of twenty-two, she even tried to persuade Isa McNeill to go with her again, but her friend was getting married and refused. At the beginning of August Rena West was reunited with her husband and children at Sandhurst Lane. Meanwhile, Gloucester Children's Department reported that Fred West's 'little angel' had returned to Glasgow.

Ann McFall had kept in touch with her mother throughout her time in the south. She had sent postcards, letters and photographs regularly, including one of a large house in which she said she was living, and describing the man who was looking after her as 'tremendous'. Frederick West's own version sustains the same adolescent fantasy, the fantasy of a young man and woman infatuated with one another, an infatuation that could not possibly last.

West's account of his time with McFall in the caravan at The Willows, however, also reveals one of the contradictions in his own character. He recalled, for example, that either he or the slight Scottish girl 'always said prayers with the children. That had come special to us.' Indeed, he maintained to the end of his life that 'she was God's gift to me and my daughters . . . her smiles lit up the heavens'. West also insisted that for two months 'we all had a wonderful life of love and happiness . . . then disaster hit us. Rena and the yobs came down', and to his amazement Rena threw Ann McFall out of the caravan. 'I felt so sorry for Anna. The only thing Anna had done wrong in her life was to fall in love with me.'

At the time, according to West, his daughters preferred Ann McFall to their mother. He insisted that he tried to reassure McFall that his first wife would not be staying for long in Gloucester, but he also warned her that she could be dangerous. 'I never knew what Rena was up to . . . She drank too much and when Rena was drunk she could be violent. Rena always had a open razor and a dagger in her handbag . . . and would use it. So I told Anna to keep away from Rena.'

In fact, West suggested that Ann McFall should stay at a friend's caravan on the site while his wife was back with him. The girl not only did so, but she also found herself a job in a bakery in Court's Road, Gloucester, telling West, 'I am saving up for our baby'. Finally, West maintained that he decided to try to escape from his wife altogether. Taking advantage of one of her trips back to Scotland, on August Bank Holiday Monday in 1966 he seized the opportunity to tow his caravan to another site, one where he hoped his wife would not be able to find him. The site he chose was behind the Flying Machine pub at Brockworth, about six miles away across Gloucester, and was called Watermead. And it was here, according to West, that he finally agreed that Ann McFall could have his child.

'It was time to sort out what we were going to do with our life as man and wife,' he wrote in the last months of his life. 'This was love that was for ever and ever. Anna and I could work together and build a home for our children and us, but I had to slow things down.' He accepted that 'Anna had to have her baby. It was not fair to Anna to have my two children and not have one of her own.' He decided 'to make Anna my life . . . I had to get a divorce from Rena'.

'At least I would be getting married for love,' he wrote. 'Not as I had with Rena to get her out of trouble with the police. Rena had said she would divorce me when I wanted her to, but it was no good trying to sort it out with Rena until she stopped drinking so much.'

In September 1966 West changed jobs, partly in the hope of making it difficult for Rena to find him, leaving the slaughterhouse and turning instead to driving a sewage lorry, emptying septic tanks. At one stage during the summer he had been doing both a night and a day delivery run, leaving his children, wife and 'nanny' for hours at a time on the Sandhurst Lane site. It was then that he had first become friendly with a young local lad called Robin Holt, whom he said he found 'crying' one night on his way home to Sandhurst Lane. West had told Anna McFall that Holt was 'unhappy at home', and started to take the fifteen-year-old boy out with him in the lorry. There is little doubt that the boy was every bit as impressed by Frederick West's bluster and bragging as McFall herself had been.

Only Rena West remained immune to West's vain, chattering charm, a situation that obviously infuriated him. His account of the days at the Sandhurst Lane caravan site are punctuated with references to his first wife's dangerous habits. 'I was always nervous about what Rena was up to and where she was.' She would dress up and go out in the evenings, not returning until 'five-thirty or six' the following morning, when she would be drunk. He suggested repeatedly that she was working as a prostitute in Gloucester at the time, and would regularly be picked up from the caravan site by a man called Rolf with 'a flash car', a man who was to reappear a number of times in his description of events in the years to come.

'Anna was no match for Rena,' West wrote. 'But Anna would have a go; that was what was dangerous. Anna was not hard; she was gentle, kind and pleasant. She was my angel. Rena could be the devil if she wanted to be . . . I did not just love Anna, I worshipped her. If Anna had my baby that would be the answer to all my prayers.'

In late September 1966 Frederick West's plan to evade his wife fell apart. Rena West turned up at the Watermead site, and West went to great pains to disguise his relationship with Ann McFall. Once again he sent McFall to stay with a friend, incidentally a woman who had followed them to Watermead from Sandhurst Lane. In the weeks to come West shuttled between the two Gloucester caravan sites, spending part of the evening with Ann McFall at a smaller caravan at Sandhurst Lane and part with Rena and their two daughters at Watermead. He changed jobs again during this period, swapping grain delivery for emptying septic tanks, and he still regularly took the six-feet-tall, fifteen-year-old Robin Holt out on runs with him.

More important still, whatever his commitments to Rena and Ann McFall, West had also lost none of his appetite for touring the countryside in search of young women. There were more than half a dozen violent sexual assaults on young women in the Gloucester area during the time that West was resident at Sandhurst Lane and Watermead, including one on a fifteen-year-old girl in the city. Many of them were carried out by men whose description fitted Frederick West, but the smiling lorry-driver was never suspected of anything.

Rena West's wildness had not disappeared with her return to England. On 11 October 1966 she stole an iron, some cigarettes and money from another caravan at Watermead, and fled to Scotland in the hope of evading the police. The ruse did not work. She was arrested in Glasgow in mid-November, and a twenty-two-year-old woman police constable, Hazel Savage, who had joined the Gloucester Constabulary just two years previously, was dispatched to collect Rena and bring her back for trial. On the journey back to England, Rena West told the young policewoman how much she disliked her 'cruel' husband, who was always having affairs, and that she had committed the offences to 'spite him'. (Nearly twenty-eight years later, Savage would be one of the five officers who knocked on the front door of 25 Cromwell Street on that Thursday afternoon in February.)

When Rena West stood trial for housebreaking and theft on 29 November 1966, her counsel maintained exactly the same line of argument, saying in his plea for leniency that the offences were 'the actions of a jealous woman', and adding that if she were sent to prison 'her children must go into care'. Frederick West appeared before the court himself, admitting his relationship with Ann McFall, but adding that he intended to pay his wife's fare back to Scotland. The pleas for leniency succeeded. Rena West was placed on probation, but she did not return to look after her children. Instead, she went back to Scotland. A delighted Ann McFall moved back from Sandhurst Lane to Watermead, and life with Frederick West.

In West's version of their next few months together, he and Ann McFall were idyllically happy once again. They often made love on top of a concrete bunker that lay just above the Watermead site, and which West called 'our heaven'. It was there, in early November 1966, that West said he made Ann McFall pregnant. 'Home to Anna was in my arms,' he wrote at the end of his life. 'Anna said: "I am going to have a baby just like you and name him Fred Junior." '

'I was proud of Anna and my daughters,' West was to write. 'The girls liked Dad to cook their dinner, because I would make a face on their plate. I would put the chips as hair, two eggs for the eyes. The nose and mouth was bacon, and beans for a beard.' Then he and Ann McFall would 'put the girls to bed and say prayers with the girls'.

Shortly after her pregnancy was confirmed, West took the slight young woman with a broad Scottish accent to visit his parents in Much Marcle together with his two daughters. He drove them all there in his grain tanker, then went off to make a series of deliveries before coming back to collect them again. When he arrived back, 'Anna was talking to my mother in the front room', and that took him by surprise. 'You had to be special for my mother to let you in there. Rena had never been in the front room. We were never allowed in there.'

His daughters were in the fields outside Moorcourt Cottage, playing with his sister's rabbits, the family's dogs and a goose. 'I had a chat with my father. He could not get over the size of the tanker I was driving.' Ann McFall and his mother 'got on well. That was the first girl I had my mother took to. I felt wonderful about it.' His mother had prepared supper for the family. Afterwards, 'Dad went out and came back with a bottle of home-made wine. We all got a glass full, and the two girls. Then Mother said a toast to Anna being pregnant. Anna looked at me and smiled . . . I smiled back. We both had tears in our eyes.' When he got back to the caravan site in Gloucester that evening, West remembered that he thought, 'Now . . . it was time to start looking for a house or flat with a garden.'

What makes Frederick West's idealised version of his life with Ann McFall so chilling is how far it departs from reality. In December 1966, barely a month after her pregnancy had been diagnosed, she told one social-worker that there was 'now nothing between them' and suggested that the best thing 'was to leave the caravan'. She even told the astonished social-worker that West had planned to 'artificially inseminate' her, but there had been no need. For a time, Ann McFall moved back to Sandhurst Lane. But Frederick West knew that his two daughters were too strong a tie for the young Scot to break. By the middle of January McFall was again back with them at Watermead.

Frederick West practised his talent for manipulating young women on Ann McFall in a way that he had never been allowed to do by his wife Rena. McFall was his pupil, someone who would not question the wisdom of what he said or did, someone who could be moulded into the woman that he wanted. The only drawback was probably that she did not share his wife's appetite for sexual experiment. Rena West's sexual experience, and her willingness to deviate from the conventional forms of sexual intercourse, was one reason why her husband was always prepared to take her back – to the annoyance and anger of Ann McFall.

Rena West's overt sexuality is the hidden theme in West's memoirs of his time with Ann McFall. When he does describe it, he does so with a sense of awe, almost bewilderment, and casts himself in the role of the innocent rather than the fascinated, rapacious voyeur. At one point, for example, he describes going to the Bamboo Club in Bristol with his wife, and her friend Rolf, where they 'had a drink and a dance'.

'Rena and Rolf were at the bar. I walked over to Rena and put my hand on her arm. A man grabbed me and said: "You touch her, you're dead." Rena said, "That's my husband." So he put me down. He was Greek, six foot and four foot across, the biggest man I ever seen. I said to Rena: "Who's he?" She said: "My bodyguard." ' West was clearly enthralled. His wife then led him out of the club on the way to the party that she had announced she was taking him to. 'Rena said: "You will have to be blindfolded." So I said: "All right." . . . We went down some steps and in a basement of a house. Rena took off the blindfold. I could not see, it was so dark. There were flashing lights, red, blue and yellow. It was full of black people and a smell of drugs.'

'There were four small tables in two rooms with what looked like Christmas cakes made with Christmas paper [on them]. Two spot-lights came on. The paper was ripped off. There was young girls in them. They were drugged. They were handed round to drugged and drunken men.' In his prison memoir West maintained that all he wanted was to go back to 'Anna, my angel', although he also admits that 'I got out of there after fourteen hours'.

Though he refused to admit it in his own writings, by this time Frederick West's appetite for deviant sexuality was already formed. It had been shaped in Moorcourt Cottage and refined in the lanes of Gloucestershire. He had learned it peering through the keyholes and windows of Herefordshire cottages, and practised it in the orchards and fields that he worked in alongside his father. He had indulged it by acting as a minder for his prostitute wife among the cobbled alleys and stone closes of Glasgow, and returned to it in his native habitat of Gloucester, where she remained a prostitute. It was an appetite that could never be satisfied, one that demanded constant, relentless gratification; an appetite that craved the illicit, the unsuspecting, an appetite as powerful as a tyrant's taste for blood.

It may well have been an appetite that Frederick West revealed and then demonstrated to Robin Holt, the 'nice-looking' fifteen-year-old that West found 'sat on a gate crying' in the lane that led to The Willows caravan site in Sandhurst Lane in the summer of 1966. He may well have treated him 'like a son', just as he had the three-year-old killed beneath the wheels of his ice-cream van in Glasgow, taking him out with him regularly in his lorry in the evenings. In his own account of those months, West reveals that he introduced the boy to his family, and 'Robin got on well with my sister', just as he welcomed the boy on to the caravan site with Ann McFall.

Late in February 1967 Robin Holt went missing from his home in Gloucester, but was seen shortly afterwards in Much Marcle. Nine days later, on 1 March 1967, the boy's body was found hanged in a disused cow-shed not far from the Sandhurst Lane site. Pornographic magazines were found beside his body, with nooses drawn around the necks of the young women in their pages. At the inquest, the jury returned a verdict of suicide, and so it may well have been, a suicide brought on by guilt at what he had learned at the side of the small bushy-haired man who took him out night after night. Looking back, however, it is a little curious that the boy should choose to kill himself with a method that the man who had all but adopted him would himself choose almost twenty-eight years later.

Perhaps the only person who fully appreciated the darkness at the heart of Frederick West's soul was his wife. She had seen it at first hand, and survived it. She had also sensed how she could control it, with the judicious use of her own sexual experience. It is the only consistent explanation for their intermittent marriage, he at once appalling her with his violence and sexual greed, she nevertheless never quite able to abandon her fixation for the swarthy stoat of a man whom she had first married five years before.

One person whom Frederick West may have confided in was his brother John. The two were still as close as they had been as children, and in the year since his return to Gloucester from Glasgow West had taken to visiting his brother regularly, usually to hold lengthy private conversations with him out of earshot of John's new wife Catherine. West may even have boasted to his brother that he and Rena had developed a technique for befriending young girls in order to tempt them into prostitution, and that together they were supplying the girls for the parties that West described in Bristol.

No one can say for certain where Frederick West's appetite for sexual bondage came from. It is entirely possible that it first appeared in adolescence, during apparently harmless games in the Much Marcle fields. But by the time he had reached maturity, it had come to express itself in a darker form. For West, bondage represented complete control over a sexual partner, whether willing or unwilling, the absolute acceptance that anything was possible, that nothing could or would ever be denied. It may well have been Rena West, then still Rena Costello, the experienced street prostitute from

65

Glasgow, who first excited West to its significance and its potential, but there is little doubt that he rapidly became its devotee and advocate. For bondage allowed Frederick West to reveal his true feelings towards women, a loathing that he could not quite contain, a loathing that was symbolised in the violence implicit in the act of binding a woman until she was entirely powerless.

The victims cannot flee, for they have been rendered powerless; they can only wait and anticipate their fate. Bondage may lie at the heart of the death of Robin Holt, significantly hanging with a noose around his neck, for by then it had become the latest variation in Frederick West's fascination with sex. Holt may have become West's prey, or acted as his accomplice, as Rena had done, but the fact that he died in a form of bondage cannot be ignored. Bondage was to become one of the fingerprints of Frederick West's sexuality, a deviation that he never lost the appetite for. Once captured, the prey was to be kept helpless, to be devoured as and when the predator chooses, in whatever way he chooses.

In his reminiscences at the end of his life, West makes not one single mention of his sexual appetites beyond saying that he would 'make love' to his 'angel' Ann McFall in their 'heaven' behind the Watermead caravan park. His true desires towards her are concealed beneath the sickly words and saccharine sentimentalism of his 'eyes filling with tears'. But, as it was throughout his life, the truth was infinitely more terrifying. He wanted nothing more than utterly to control the pregnant seventeen-year-old Scottish girl, rendering her helpless to refuse him anything he desired.

There must have been an ever-present smile on Frederick West's face as he began slowly to reveal to the pregnant girl exactly what sexual experiments were in his mind. Her letters to her alcoholic mother Jane merely peddled the fantasies that he had so carefully fed her, and her dislike of Rena meant there was no chance she could turn to her. She might argue with him but she could not shake off his hold upon her; her pride would never allow it, not now that she was pregnant.

Ann McFall could not have brought herself to admit to the local authority what was going on, even though she was being visited regularly, because of Charmaine and Anna-Marie. Shortly after her eighteenth birthday in April, however, the Gloucester authorities were indicating their concern in writing. A local official reported that they were 'extremely worried about these children, who are being looked after by Annie McFall, who is expecting Mr West's baby'. But they did not intervene, or suggest that they might take the children into care. Their report merely noted that the caravan 'had become dilapidated'.

Four weeks later Rena West was back at Watermead caravan park, living in the now dilapidated caravan with her husband and looking after her two daughters. When the local authority enquired what had happened to Ann McFall, Frederick West simply told them that she was living in another caravan at the site. It was a technique of cheerfully helpful obeisance that he would perfect in the years to come whenever a local authority officer presented himself at his door. On this occasion it worked as it would work on so many other occasions in the years to come. The local authority official left satisfied that everything was in hand. The fact that Rena West stayed less than a fortnight, and Ann McFall again took her place, did not matter at all. When it found out, the local authority department suggested only that the children 'are now thoroughly confused'. So, too, was the local authority. It was exactly what Frederick West intended.

When Rena West returned to Watermead again in July 1967, Frederick West did exactly as he had done twice before: he moved Ann McFall back to the small caravan he had rented specifically for her at Sandhurst Lane. She complained bitterly, suggesting that she was not going to put up with it, and reminding him that she was nearly seven months' pregnant with his child. But he smoothed her ruffled feathers as he had done so many times in the past, and told her there was nothing to worry about. He would 'sort everything out'. In the meantime it was best to 'keep out of Rena's way'. The explanation was partly true, as it was in so many of his lies, but the reality was also that a move to Sandhurst Lane meant that no one would know precisely what had happened to her.

If Ann McFall were now to disappear, who would be in the least surprised?

Chapter Six

The abortionist

'No one ever suddenly became depraved.'

Juvenal, *Satires*

The sexual frenzy that had swept over Frederick West in adolescence had become an addiction. He could think of nothing else. Women were objects to satisfy his desires, and if they said no they could not really mean it. His wife Rena understood that, and he had tried to explain it to Ann McFall. He had even enticed her into experimenting in bondage in the small rented caravan at Sandhurst Lane. But she was now almost seven months' pregnant, her unborn child inhibiting both her sexuality and her freedom of movement. She was tired, she was fractious, and she was only eighteen years old. But there was nothing that angered Frederick West more than a woman who said no.

Alone in the small caravan in the first days of August 1967, Ann McFall decided to leave Gloucester and Frederick West. Rena was back, and there was her own child to think about. She was not prepared to shuttle back and forth between Watermead and Sandhurst Lane any longer, only stepping into the gap in his life when Rena disappeared. She would pack her bags and return to Glasgow. That was the obvious thing to do. She could stay with her mother for a time – after all, she had kept in touch with her – and there was still her friend Isa McNeill; even if she were married now, she would help. Ann McFall slowly packed her belongings into a small suitcase and prepared to leave Sandhurst Lane, and Gloucester, for ever.

When Frederick West came to visit her that evening, as he usually did after seeing Rena and his daughters at Watermead, Ann McFall told him she was leaving, and he lost his temper completely. The obsequious little man, who made sure to smile at anyone in authority, revealed again the violence that lay beneath the surface. He screamed and shouted at the pregnant girl, throwing things around the caravan, and threatening her with the knife that he always wore at his belt.

Frederick West may even have stabbed and killed Ann McFall in the caravan on that August evening. No one can be absolutely sure. For West went to his grave denying forcefully that he had killed the pregnant young Glaswegian. Time after time he would sob that he had 'nothing whatever to do with her death', repeating it in interview after interview, insisting that someone else had killed her, and inventing endless variations of what had happened. In particular, he repeatedly blamed his wife Rena for Ann's death.

Nevertheless, after insisting in hours of police interviews that he knew nothing whatever about her death, West admitted to his solicitor Howard Ogden in July 1994 that he had actually been present when she died. It was the first occasion on which he accepted that he had been involved. But West's version of the death of Ann McFall, like so many of his other explanations of his actions, contained both fantasy and fiction, as well as a kernel of truth.

'Ann to me was perfect,' he explained in Winson Green prison in July 1994. 'She was prepared to give her life for me . . . But she used to accuse me of thinking of Rena all the time. We had plans for me and Ann to just disappear . . . drift away.' But West did not have the courage to leave his wife and children. 'When I was with Ann I was all for it, but I wasn't, I wasn't, if you know what I mean . . . I didn't know what to do.'

West told his wife that Ann McFall had 'gone and left me', even though he had simply moved her to Sandhurst Lane. One night, he 'got back to Sandhurst, must have been about half-past eleven at night. I parked the lorry in the road . . . and came through the back way straight into the caravan. There's Rolf and Rena in there. Rena's absolutely out of her brains. She hadn't got a clue where she was, what she'd done.'

So, of course, I said, 'Where's Ann?' and Rolf said, 'Come outside'. So we went round the back of the caravan and he said, 'Rena's stabbed Ann – by mistake'.

Now I quite believed that. I don't think that Rena would have done it absolutely deliberate. I think she was so drugged out of her brains and everything else, drink and everything else, that she stabbed Ann.

Anyway I said to Rolf: 'What the bloody hell we going to do?' And he said: 'You ain't got no choice.' And I thought, Fuck me. I knew exactly what he meant.

Whether Rolf was actually there when Rena stabbed Ann, I don't know. Or whether she rung him and he came to her, and bring that case to her. I'd never seen that case . . . It was a massive bloody case. He said: 'We're going to take her and put her on the tip, Gloucester tip.'

By this time 'I am literally brain dead. The mind's just gone. I hadn't got a clue what I was thinking, or saying, or nothing'. None the less

West was capable of saying, according to his version of events: 'No, the only place you can put her is in our special place at Marcle.'

We drove out there, and me and him dug the hole together, and Rena was sat in the car, watching Ann. Then we both walked back up the field, and then him and Rena went down with the car and put Ann in and covered her up, and come back to me. I was sat on the tank beside the gate splashing water on me face. And that was it.

'As far as I know she wasn't touched,' West insisted in his version of events, a version that he embellished and altered repeatedly.

At one stage Rena West had 'gone off for two or three days at the time Ann disappeared', leaving a hugely fat female friend to look after Charmaine and Anna-Marie. Then his wife had 'forged a letter' from Ann McFall telling him that she had 'gone back to Scotland', so that he would not look for her. 'She was a brilliant forger, mind.' Then Rena had gone off and killed her on her own. In another version his father had told him that a neighbour in Much Marcle had seen 'his wife and a man' in a nearby field one night that month.

As ever, the reality was quite different. For although he would deny it until the day of his own death, the murder of Ann McFall carries the unmistakable signature of Frederick West, a signature that was to be found on every other murder that he was to commit in the next twenty-seven years. The death and dismemberment of the girl he called 'a dainty little piece' was to be repeated almost exactly at least eleven more times during the rest of his life.

By West's own admission, the young Scottish woman was in the habit of waiting for him in bed at her caravan every evening wearing 'only a cardigan'. They would make love, and then West would leave to return to his wife at Watermead. He relished the opportunity, but there is no doubt that Rena West had discovered that Ann McFall had not 'gone off' as her husband had told her she had, and was extremely angry. There is also no doubt that Ann McFall was planning to return to Scotland, to give birth to her child in two months' time. Frederick West seized the opportunity to rid himself of a troublesome problem.

On the night of her death in August 1967, West may have argued with his young lover in her caravan at Sandhurst Lane, and it is possible that – as he later suggested – she was 'stabbed through the heart' during a quarrel, although by West himself rather than his wife Rena. But it is far more likely that his sugary words would have worked their charm on her, and she would have welcomed him back into her bed. For in spite of her experiences, Ann McFall was still a young and impressionable girl, the same girl who had written to her mother for months past to tell her about the wonderful man she was going to marry. In her mind, even though she may have threatened that she was going to leave him, there was still hope. She was younger, more attractive than his wife, and she was prepared to agree to experiment sexually. What she could not know was that West had lost patience and decided to kill her. It seems almost certain that Ann, wearing only a blue patterned round-necked cardigan, agreed to make love to Frederick West that night, and died, literally, in bondage.

When her body was eventually discovered, more than a quarter of a century later, her hands were still tied, and a long length of rope was twisted around her arms. Whether West overpowered her and forced her to submit to being tied up, or whether she allowed herself to be tied up willingly as part of her desire to satisfy her lover, no one will ever know. But it is highly likely that she died during the act of intercourse, either strangled by her lover or, more probably, stabbed in the heart immediately after his own orgasm.

Frederick West had already worked out what he was going to do. There was no panic in his actions that night, no sense that he had stepped across a boundary in his life that he would never be able to re-cross. He calmly wrapped her lifeless body in the quilt from the bed they were lying on and carried it out to his lorry. It was an experience that he did not enjoy, and would make sure never to repeat. In future he would never transport a dead body any distance.

West then drove Ann McFall's body to Much Marcle to a place he knew, a place that was quiet, and a place that even if he was seen at no one would ask any questions. He trusted Much Marcle to keep his secrets, just as his father had done. Frederick West had already decided to bury the remains, just as a poacher would have done. His prey had served its purpose. But he was a countryman, and he did not believe in throwing a carcass carelessly away to be discovered by a wandering fox. That was an amateur's mistake, a mistake that any decent gamekeeper would see in an instant. No one would discover a deep, well-dug hole, especially a small one. A patch of earth could conceal a thousand secrets. The countryside, especially his own native countryside, looked after its own. A body was to return to the soil, as it had done for centuries.

West chose the site with infinite care. He wanted the body to be within sight of his home at Moorcourt Cottage in Much Marcle, but he also wanted it to be in Gloucestershire, for that was the county he now identified himself with. He had known since childhood exactly where the county boundary with Herefordshire ran, and he chose a site just on the Gloucestershire side, in Fingerpost Field, where he had worked with his father as a boy.

He also knew that it was August, and the ground would be hard from the summer sun, so West had carefully chosen a place where the ground would be softer, but where the disturbance to the earth would not be noticed, because cattle trod it night and morning as they came to drink. West and his father had constructed a 'concrete ramp which we put in there, years and years ago, and the water builds up just in front of it, and then runs over it, and the cattle get in there and drink'. In the darkness of the night, Frederick West dug a hole in the damp earth where the water ran over into the field, and he did so exactly as he had done countless times in the past to plant a tree or a stake.

With Ann McFall's body hidden just inside the wood at his back, still wrapped in her rose-patterned quilt, West dug a small deep oblong hole, a place to hide remains, not a grave for a human being. It was fifteen inches wide and twenty-eight inches long, and a little over three feet deep, and it took him less than half an hour.

Used to hard physical labour, and to the sight of blood, West then put his experience in the slaughterhouse to good effect. With the body over the hole, West set about dismembering it, allowing the escaping blood to seep into the hole. He used the knife he kept in his belt to cut off the pregnant young woman's legs at the hip, twisting her thighs out of their sockets; then he pushed what remained of her body into the hole, pelvis first, shoving the thigh bones down each side after her. There was no frenzy in his actions; he worked as methodically as a slaughterhouse man would have done, and with exactly the same matter-of-factness. The body passing through his hands was no longer a living being but simply a piece of meat to be stored out of sight.

Ann McFall's body held one fascination for West, however. It contained an unborn child. And, like any predator, he took exceptional interest in a pregnant victim, anxious to root out the foetus, to satisfy a morbid curiosity. West had become fascinated with female anatomy, steadily taking a greater and greater interest in the genital organs, even to the extent of boasting that he could perform abortions, so intimately did he 'understand the workings of the womb'. Frederick West would not have been able to resist the temptation to breach one of the last taboos, and dissect the young Scottish woman's stomach: not least to determine whether she would have given birth to the son that they had discussed so often. When Ann McFall's remains were eventually unearthed in that Gloucestershire field, the unborn child's tiny, barely formed bones were found by her side.

But the remains were more than a fascination; they were also a trophy, proof that Frederick West was no ordinary man. From now on Ann McFall was condemned to remain within his power and control, even within his sight when he went to visit his mother and father. And just as he buried her remains, he buried the few remaining mementoes of her life alongside her. West threw the floral quilt into the narrow hole after her, along with the cardigan she had been wearing, wrapped in two plastic bags that he had in the lorry because there had been so much blood on it. As he swiftly shovelled the damp earth on top of her on that warm August night, the only thing the eighteen-year-old girl was wearing was a small cross-patterned ring that he had given to her. Her unborn child was her only companion.

West also took his own mementoes from Fingerpost Field. Before he interred the young woman's dismembered body, he removed forty-two of Ann McFall's bones. Mostly they were her fingers and toes, as well as some of the bones from her ankle and wrist, but he also took the upper half of the left shin, the slenderest bone in the body, and the right twelfth rib. Part of his reason lay in a desire to eliminate any possibility that she could be identified if, by chance, the body were ever discovered. But there was another, grimmer reason. The bones were the ultimate proof of West's dominance over the inanimate woman in the ground; elements that only he would understand; trophies of his power. Ann McFall's bones carried no fear for the tiny wiry man, as he collected them and washed his arms and chest clean in the field's cattle trough. Frederick West was only too familiar with the smell of blood, just as he was with the bones of a slaughtered calf.

There is not much doubt that there would have been a small, sly grin on his face as he opened the door to his caravan on the Watermead site in the early hours of the morning, pulled off the soiled overalls and climbed into bed with his wife. On his way, he would certainly have kissed his children good night as they slept, for he did so every other night, just as he may well have demanded to make love to her, as he did on almost every other night. Why should this be an exception?

The following morning Frederick West returned to Fingerpost Field. From the cab of his lorry he probably admired his handiwork, noticing that it was impossible to see where the ground had been disturbed in the muddy footprints of the cattle. Then he did as he so often did when he drove the road from Dymock to Much Marcle: he went in search of the man whose approval he wanted more than any other, his father. Almost twenty-seven years later Frederick West would confess: 'I went to my father and told him what had happened. I asked him to go up there with me, 'cause I couldn't go up there on me own. So he walked up there with me, and we're stood there talking.'

'I set myself up round me father,' West explained. 'My old man was great. Me and him got on ace. He was my God, like. Me and him never ever fell out in our life. If I ever had a problem – straight to Dad. When I buried Ann I went straight to Dad. Same thing. I wanted to be my father. I admired all he stood for.' Certainly, Walter West did not condemn his son in the August of 1967. Instead he told him: 'I'm your father. I'm not going to turn you in or nothing. If you can live with it I'll say nothing, leave it.' The family's secrets were still not to be revealed to the outside world. Frederick West went to see his father 'every day for about a month' thereafter, because, as he was to explain many years later, 'you know me, I got to talk about it'.

The other person West certainly talked to was his wife. Rena West may have been horrified by her husband's confession, but it is far more likely that it merely confirmed her worst fears. She knew his appetite for violence, and the cruelty that he was capable of towards women. She had suffered it for five years, and had told John McLachlan about it in Glasgow. She knew that he liked to tie up young girls and sexually abuse them; he had even encouraged her to help him do it. Killing them was simply the next step. Now, just as Walter West agreed to keep the secret, so too did Rena West.

Frederick West may have told his father that Rena was responsible for Ann McFall's death, just as he may well have told his wife that it was an accident. To lie, for him, was as automatic as breathing. Secrets were power. If no one knew everything, no one could harm him. And, as his family knew only too well, Frederick West was not a man to volunteer information. People had to ask, and they had to ask the right question, before he would consider telling them anything. If they did not ask the right questions, then he would simply spin them a story, as he had always done. That way no one could threaten him.

'When that accident happened that Ann got killed,' West would recall at the end of his life, 'it give a sort of grip of Rena for a while.' Rena West's attitude to her husband changed after the death of Ann McFall. 'Rena made me a load of promises . . . That she was going to stay with me, look after the children, never mess about and all that.' One explanation was that she was terrified that the same fate might befall her, or that he might implicate her in the murder, as at the very least a willing accomplice. Whatever the precise explanation, from then on 'She was with me for about twelve months, living on and off, gone, come back, gone, come back'. It was the longest period she had consistently spent with her husband since their marriage.

Rena West was no innocent bystander in the life of Frederick West. By his account she had even used Ann McFall to help her to entice girls into prostitution. 'That's what Ann was used for, to mingle among these girls, in Manchester, Salford, Bristol, Reading, talking to them, starting on the game. That's why Rena came every so often and took her,' West maintained. 'Rena used to get these young girls for these bloody parties. They used to get these young girls from homes – runaways from homes – take 'em to these parties and give 'em a right rough time. And then they used to beat the life out of them, then put them on the game, drugs, whatever.'

West's version of events could be an exaggeration, even a fabrication, but there is no doubt that Rena West knew and exploited her husband's appetite for sex with young and vulnerable women, including Ann McFall. As West was to put it himself, 'Rena would come and stay with me for a while, then she'd piss off. Then Ann would come and stay. Then Rena would come back and just chuck Ann out. She'd say, "Right you, out".' Rena West could not have failed to take an interest in what happened to the girl she would so often 'chuck out'.

No one missed Ann McFall. Though West insisted on more than one occasion that he had reported her missing to the police, the police themselves can find no record that he did so. West cleared out the caravan he had rented for her, telling the Sandhurst Lane site that she had gone back to Glasgow, and her friends in Glasgow assumed that the end of the letters she habitually used to send meant only that she had sorted out a new life for herself in England. Her father was already dead himself when she disappeared from Sandhurst Lane, and her mother was to die of malnutrition barely eighteen months later. Her daughter did not return for the funeral, but no one took much notice. By then there was no one to grieve, or search, for the dainty girl with a 'braw Scots accent'.

With Rena West now more settled at Watermead than she had ever been, Frederick West went back to work, confident that his secret was safe within his two families. And so it was, even though his mother Daisy West discovered within a few days that her son had killed Ann McFall. Walter West himself must have told her one night at Moorcourt Cottage, but no matter how great the shock, the family's loyalty to each other held. In Daisy West's eyes, her Freddie was still the blue-eyed boy he had been as a child; she would not disclose anything he might have done to anyone outside the family. She had not even done so during the incest case against him six years before.

Daisy West kept the secret to herself, until one evening later in the month she broke down and cried at the kitchen table, telling her confidant: 'Freddie's killed the girl and buried her in Kempley Woods.' But she went no further, and no one pressed her to. In spite of the accusation, neither she nor her husband, nor any other member of the West family, discussed the matter with the police or with anyone else. And none of them went to search the fields near Kempley Woods for the body.

Frederick West did, however, take the precaution of leaving Watermead caravan site. It was already scheduled for conversion to a housing estate, and builders had begun work on part of the site early in 1967. Now the development was to press ahead, and West seized the opportunity to leave without arousing any suspicion. But he did not return to Sandhurst Lane in Gloucester. Instead, for the first time since leaving Much Marcle, he moved to somewhere else altogether. To Bishop's Cleeve, almost ten miles away, and just over three miles north of the neighbouring town of Cheltenham. It was one of the biggest geographical moves West had ever made, almost as large as his move into Gloucester from Much Marcle. To a man used to treading familiar paths, retracing his steps whenever he could, Bishop's Cleeve was a significant distance away from his favourite stamping-grounds. But he had worked there before, as a bakery roundsman.

This time West rented a permanent caravan, rather than transporting his own, taking number 17 on the Lake House site off Stoke Road at the edge of Bishop's Cleeve. Like most of the others on the site, the caravan looked like one of the prefabs put up at the end of the war to accommodate some of the returning troops. It had no wheels, stood on a firm concrete base, and had a small garden. A little over twenty feet long, with two bedrooms, a lounge and small dining area, it also boasted an indoor bathroom and lavatory. West moved his wife and their two daughters in during the first week of October 1967, and subsequently he got a job as a labourer at

Oldacres, a flour and animal feed manufacturer in Bishop's Cleeve. Not that his job was his only interest. At West's encouragement, Rena went back to prostitution at Bishop's Cleeve, sometimes using the caravan at Lake House as her base, and he took some delight in suggesting to any likely young woman whom he came across that she 'could make a fortune' on the streets of Cheltenham. 'Women are sitting on a fortune,' he would say with a smirk. 'Thing is, they don't always know it.' Within a few weeks Frederick West had turned up at his parents' cottage in Much Marcle with another young woman who was not his wife, but no one made the slightest comment. This time the girl was short and blonde, with hair rather shorter than Ann McFall's, but once again she was fifteen or sixteen years old, and Frederick West had the familiar sly grin on his face.

The deceit that characterised West's attitude to women extended into every other area of his life. Everyone, man or woman, was to be taken advantage of, if an opportunity presented itself. The rules were there to be bent, the law to be evaded. All that was necessary to get away with it was a fast tongue and the ability to keep moving. West was certainly not above deceiving his own family. The hire-purchase agreement which he had taken out for his caravan on Sandhurst Lane at the beginning of 1966 had been guaranteed by his brother-in-law but, typically, Frederick West had 'forgotten' to keep up the payments, and the company had started to pursue him. It proved no easy task, for every time the company searched for him at Sandhurst Lane, the neighbours would insist he was at Watermead, but every time the company arrived there he was, of course, at Sandhurst Lane. In desperation, the hire-purchase company began to pursue West's sister and her husband. But when they asked him, West insisted he had been paying, showing a set of receipts, which later turned out to be false. Eventually, the company repossessed the caravan, which was one reason for his decision to rent one at Bishop's Cleeve, but West's disregard for the truth, and the law, never left him.

Now almost twenty-seven, West had become a character worthy of Dickens, an apparently humble man only too adept at concealing his true desires, and intentions, behind an obsequious grin and a careful ordinariness. He would brag that he could 'help any woman out', if they had a problem, and insinuate that he knew more about sex than their boyfriends did. At the Lake House site he would invite local girls to see his 'pictures', locking the door quickly behind them as they climbed into the caravan after peering out to see if anyone had watched them go in. More often than not the 'pictures' showed his wife in sexually explicit poses. West took care to make sure that the curtains were always drawn.

There were plenty of opportunities for West to find a replacement for Ann McFall, to groom another young woman to become his sexual apprentice. Just as he had done in Ledbury five years before, he spent his spare time in the Gloucester cafés, talking to the young waitresses, impressing them with his experience, enticing them to take a trip with him in his newly purchased green van. One café West visited regularly was the Pop-In in Southgate Street, only a few yards from the city's docks and quays alongside the Sharpness Canal. The café attracted motor cycle gangs, and West was more than willing to brag about his 1000-cc Triumph and the accident that led to him 'waking up on a mortuary slab'. He also liked to try to beat its one-armed bandit. 'I was a bit addicted to that actually at one time.' One of the young waitresses at the Pop-In was a short, slim girl of fifteen, whose straight shoulder-length blonde hair was usually parted in the middle. Her name was Mary Bastholm.

Shortly after seven o'clock in the evening of Saturday 6 January 1968, Mary Bastholm disappeared. She was last seen standing at a bus stop in Bristol Road in Gloucester, not far from the café and the youth club she attended at Quedgeley. The night she went missing she was on her way to visit her boyfriend, who lived about five miles away, and was carrying a white plastic carrier-bag with a Monopoly set in it, presumably to play that evening. She never reached her boyfriend's home. Indeed, she was never seen again. Mary Bastholm simply disappeared off the face of the earth on that January night in 1968.

No one can say for certain that Mary Bastholm went out with Frederick West. He denied repeatedly before his death that he had been in any way involved in her disappearance, although he did recall that he and Rena, together with the children, had been stopped at a police check-point during the search for the missing girl. Rena was driving a 'blue Beetle', he remembered, that 'she'd driven down in from Scotland'. West insisted that he 'didn't have a vehicle at that time', even though his family remember him arriving at Much Marcle in an old green van. Indeed, Rena West taught his sister Gwen to drive in the van a few months later.

West must certainly have seen Mary Bastholm at the Pop-In. He was even employed there for a short time on some straightforward building work. It is almost certain that Mary knew Ann McFall, and that she was the slim blonde girl he took to Much Marcle not long after McFall's disappearance. Shortly before his death, West hinted both to his son and to his first solicitor that he was responsible for her disappearance, but gave little more away. Although he made a habit of picking up young waitresses, and had even married one, there is nothing to prove conclusively that he had abducted and killed the young blonde waitress. Rena West may have met Mary Bastholm on a visit to Lake House to see West's pictures, or she may have been with her husband when he offered the fifteen-year-old a lift at the bus stop on Bristol Road on that Saturday evening in 1968. But she, too, is not alive to tell us.

The hunt for Mary Bastholm was extensive and relentless. Gloucester police sought the assistance of Scotland Yard. Volunteers searched local waste land. There was even a television appeal, which Walter and Daisy West would have seen on their set at Much Marcle. But no trace of the girl, her clothing, or her bag with its Monopoly set was ever found. She disappeared into thin air, never to be seen or heard from again, one of the many mysteries that haunt the life of Frederick Walter Stephen West.

There is absolutely no doubt, however, that the disappearance of Mary Bastholm bears every hallmark of the actions of Frederick West. She was young, impressionable, attractive and a little naive. To her West would have seemed a worldly figure, prepared to treat her like a woman rather than a child, intriguing her with his discussions of a sexuality that she had yet to experience fully. It was a lure that he would return to time after time throughout his life, and it would always serve him well. Ugly though the thought may be, it is impossible to avoid the conclusion that he raped and killed the young Gloucester girl and buried her, as he had buried Ann McFall, in a place that he knew well. The fields and woods of Gloucestershire within sight of Moorcourt Cottage may hold many secrets still. The fact that West was not prepared to divulge them only underlines how little he was ever prepared to give away – until he was ready to.

Daisy West may well have suspected as much. For while the police hunt for Mary Bastholm was at its height, she was taken to Hereford Hospital suffering from a suspected heart-attack. The woman who had burst into tears just five months before with the words 'Freddie's killed the girl and buried her in Kempley Woods' may well have wondered whether the same fate had overtaken the slim blonde girl the police were looking for on television. Two days later, on 6 February 1968, Daisy West died at the age of forty-four, after another sudden heart-attack.

One person who did not shed a single tear at her funeral three days later was Daisy West's eldest son. 'I thought I got to be brave here. It's not good me bawling me eyes out with them,' Frederick West insisted later. But as he stood in the churchyard of St Bartholomew's, in the shade of one of the oldest yew trees in England, Frederick West whispered to his wife, who was standing beside him: 'We should sell her clothes.' The rest of the West family were horrified.

Chapter Seven

The sorcerer's apprentice

'My companion must be of the same species, and have the same defects.'

Mary Shelley, *Frankenstein*

The murder of Ann McFall in the summer of 1967 was arguably the single most significant moment in Frederick West's life so far, the moment at which he crossed his own personal Rubicon. Before her killing he was a violent man with violent emotions. After it, he was not only a murderer but a murderer who could never turn back, a man who had discovered the irresistible sexual excitement it aroused in him. In West's mind the killing gave him a sense of power – power over women, women who had formerly had power over him, women who had despised him. In one sense her death was his revenge on the whole sex.

In the years since Much Marcle, Frederick West's life had become a quest for an innocent young woman to share his world. And Ann McFall had been the first to suggest that she might actually fulfil his dream, thereby satisfying the hidden fantasy that was now driving him. She was an innocent, someone whom he could turn into a compliant, endlessly admiring companion. His first wife, Rena Costello, could never have been that companion. She was more experienced in the ways of the world, and the sexual world in particular, than he was, and that inhibited him. By contrast, Ann McFall had been his first blank canvas, the first young woman whom he could groom in his own likeness, and mould into his own perfect partner. The fact that she had then let him down, failing to satisfy his most extreme demands and then threatening to leave him, was a tragedy for which her death was the only solution. If he could not have her no one else would. His creation was to be destroyed, and the process started again.

That is why West's prison memoir, *I Was Loved by an Angel*, is of far greater significance than may at first appear. For West's insistence that 'Ana' was the only person who ever truly loved him is, in some degree, a reflection that she was the first woman whom he ever truly loved, the one woman who satisfied his distorted vision of what love really meant. Frederick West loved his 'angel', but once she betrayed him he was capable of killing her, and systematically abusing and destroying what remained of her body. In the murder of Ann McFall Frederick West was both her lover and her torturer, tragic at one moment, exultant at the next. And the act of sexual union was the obvious moment to kill, the snuffing out of her life mirroring West's own orgasm as certainly as if he had been a villain in his own Jacobean tragedy.

Like Mary Shelley's creature, created by Victor Frankenstein, West was also a creature in pursuit of his own version of love. As a child he had struggled to develop a loving relationship with his mother, and had been rewarded with abuse rather than affection. He had resented it, and had nursed that resentment deep within him, concealed from the preying eyes of every woman thereafter. Tragically for her, Ann McFall had failed to live up to West's dream of a perfect mate – the dream that he was giving voice to in *I Was Loved by an Angel* – the dream that had come to preoccupy his mind. She had betrayed his inner fantasy, but nevertheless she had been a willing accomplice, an apprentice to learn the trade of sexual excitement and exploitation at his shoulder. Rena West had first demonstrated to him how exciting that could be, and how valuable in encouraging young women to trust him, but West had always been a little afraid of her, in awe that she knew more than he. Now, with Ann McFall dead, he wanted another innocent to school in his own version of love.

Ann McFall's death made it inevitable that he would continue the search for his perfect mate, as Victor Frankenstein's creature had done, and so West's pursuit of his own version of love became the hidden narrative that he would live by, the explanation he gave himself for his own behaviour. It is conceivable that West believed, for a moment, that the young waitress Mary Bastholm might have been a candidate to replace Ann McFall, only to discover that she was not willing to participate in his sexual experiments. As a result, West may have forced her into a sexual union and killed her, while she, too, was a bound and helpless victim.

But even when West believed that he might have found someone who came close to his ideal mate, as Ann McFall had done, his search for another was not abandoned in case the first were to be found wanting. West could never allow himself to trust a woman completely. They were always likely to betray him at the last moment, just as his mother had done when she asked him to leave Moorcourt Cottage in 1961. The memory of the incest case fuelled his private anger against a society that did not approve of what he, and his father, saw as perfectly acceptable behaviour, their own version of family love. The memory rankled still.

West's rambling prison memoir *I Was Loved by an Angel* demonstrates precisely how far he could conceal the hidden nature of his desire, even from himself. His sentimental narrative displays at one level the explanation that he was presenting to himself, and to the world at large, for his actions, but disguises at another level the far darker story of a man determined to express and experience his own bizarre and perverted version of love.

The memoir also reveals the method that Frederick West depended on throughout his life when he was cornered. The rambling digressions, the lengthy descriptions of the stunningly mundane, the endless repetition, all would appear time after time in his interviews with the police, and with anyone in authority. West used this smokescreen of minor detail and irrelevant description to befuddle anyone attempting to analyse his motives. Lie set against lie, half-truth portrayed as truth – these were the methods he used to escape from trouble. For Frederick West talk was camouflage, a disguise that allowed him to creep closer to his victim.

Movement was another way of concealing his intentions. In the past West had depended on motor cycles, cars, vans and lorries as a means of escaping attention and freeing himself from the prying eyes of neighbours. But shortly before his mother's funeral in the first week of February 1968, and not long after he had moved Rena, Charmaine and Anna-Marie to the Lake House caravan site in Bishop's Cleeve, West was obliged to stop driving his grain lorry ''cause there was nowhere to park a lorry at Lake House'. Instead, he got a job in the packing department of Oldacres, working on a bagging machine. It meant that he could walk to work, but it also meant that, for the moment, his freedom of movement was curtailed.

For a time, therefore, Frederick West contented himself with inviting girls to his caravan at Lake House rather than driving around in search of them. He would talk to girls in the village, offering to help with odd jobs, 'making himself useful', and would use exactly the same excuse that he had used in Scotland to tempt them back to the caravan. West told any likely candidate who presented herself that he was looking for someone to help him to take care of the two girls, Charmaine and Anna-Marie, now aged five and four.

Rena West, meanwhile, had taken a job near Tewkesbury, as a waitress in a mobile canteen for the workers on the M5 motorway, then under construction nearby. Not that West had encouraged her to give up prostitution: far from it. It brought in regular money, and he enjoyed arranging her sexual appointments, and watching surreptitiously if the chance presented itself. Besides there was always the chance that if he could find a 'nanny', the girl might be 'persuaded' to work as a prostitute with his wife.

One experience that made a lasting impression on Frederick West was a party to which Rena took him and where he stayed for several hours despite claiming in his prison memoir that 'All I wanted to do was to get back to Ana'. There is evidence that the party itself involved the deliberate humiliation and abuse of young women, some of whom were 'sold' to the organisers and forced to attend. One friend of West's recalled many years later that West had told him that he had seen a man stub out a lighted cigarette on a young woman's breast that night. The twin attractions of sexual excitement and financial gain that such a party offered almost certainly proved difficult for Frederick West to ignore.

Certainly, West would repeatedly ask the men he worked with at Oldacres whether they were interested in sex, and where he could meet girls. The older girls at Bishop's Cleeve school soon began to talk about him among themselves, discussing what went on when they went up to Lake House after school and he ushered them into the caravan with its curtains drawn. There were tales of photographic sessions, and of the offer of abortions, of how much money a girl could make 'on the streets of Cheltenham' if she were willing. One girl at the time remembers that West was given the nickname 'Weird Freddie'.

Rena West also set out to find clients for herself, and even started to call herself by the 'working name' of Mandy James. 'When Rena left the caravan one time,' Frederick West recalled later, 'I cleaned it all out, and I found all her letters underneath an old fireplace.' His wife had taken an advertisement in the local newspaper saying: 'Young, attractive lady looking for employment. Anything considered . . .' 'She got loads of letters. People actually offering real jobs. But a load of them were from actual men. Prostituting. And she had quite a round going on.'

Rena West came and went increasingly throughout their year together at Lake House in 1968. Their familiar pattern of argument, violence, departure and then reconciliation, which had been set in Scotland, continued, with West wheedling and encouraging at one moment, vicious and jealous at another, oscillating between a fascinated, lascivious delight in his wife's sexual conquests and brutal retribution for her success. But this was not a face he showed to the young women he enticed into his caravan at Lake House. To them, as to outsiders in general, he was, on first acquaintance at least, the affable, engaging 'friend' that no one could possibly be afraid of, even if he were a little preoccupied with sex. The nudging innuendo, the smirking suggestion that he had employed with such success on the ice-cream van in Glasgow still stood him in good stead. 'He could be very, very persuasive,' one young woman remembered from that time. He took photographs of the girls – or rather, more often than not, of their vaginas – with a new black and white Polaroid camera he had stolen. West's fascination with the female anatomy had not disappeared.

Frederick West's life was lived on the periphery of the law. Chances were there to be taken, and usually they came off. If sometimes they did not, there was nothing lost; he just kept on doing what he fancied. In the early summer of 1968 West was arrested for stealing a cheque and using it to buy a record-player for the caravan, and on 10 June 1968 he was convicted at Cheltenham magistrates' court on one count of theft and another of obtaining goods by deception. He was fined £10 on each count, £20 in total, but it served only to encourage him. He vowed never to pay for anything unless he had to, and kept the vow throughout the rest of his life.

Now that Daisy West was dead, West took to taking his wife Rena and their two daughters to Moorcourt Cottage more regularly, and the young Scottish woman's relationship with Walter West deepened still further. 'Cath', as Walter West always called her, got on increasingly well with the rest of his family. In the summer of 1968 she even taught West's youngest sister Gwen to drive in an elderly green van. Indeed, the young Scottish woman, who by this time had taken to abandoning her yellow peroxide dye from time to time and allowing her hair to return to its natural brown, seemed more content with her husband than ever before. Even though Frederick West had claimed at first that his marriage to Rena 'wasn't a wedding anyway . . . it was a convenience thing to cover the rules of me getting paid and that', their relationship had now endured for more than five and a half years.

Indeed, in spite of Frederick West's violence towards his wife, he insisted in the last weeks of his life: 'We didn't get upset with each other over anything . . . Me and Rena, when we were at home, we used to go for long walks round the fields and that was our spot. It was an oak tree, and it sprayed out like an umbrella – it wasn't very big. There was a hunting stile by the side of it. We used to sit up on this style and just look out over the valley, the woods, Much Marcle and all that. You could see the church clock. It was so peaceful, we loved it, and we used to make love there – regular. Whenever we had problems. When I was trying to persuade her to come back to the kids and all that, we used to go up there.' The tree and the stile were in Letterbox Field, only a few hundred yards from the site of Ann McFall's body.

Rena West's job on the mobile motorway canteen gave her plenty of opportunity to extend her activities as a prostitute, and for a time her husband joined her there, not only to help her to gather more clients but also to work as a trench digger for Costain's, the motorway construction firm, and to drive one of the road-building machines. The hyperactive Fred West became known as 'the best trench digger on the M5, a man who would keep on digging when everyone else had stopped', and he himself was more than happy: 'We were in a few bob then. Things were going well.'

His appetite for sexual abduction had not deserted him, however, and neither had his ability to escape detection. A thirteen-year-old girl would recall almost thirty years later how, in the late summer of 1968, West had tried to grab her but she had managed to get away. Once again, however, he eluded detection. She reported the details of the attack to the police, but he was never even questioned. Nor is she likely to have been his only intended victim that year. For West still could not control his desire for conquest, and there were always unsuspecting young girls to be found by the roadside.

'Then Rena got pally with one the big boys on the motorway, and she pissed off with him and left me again,' West would recall. It meant that he found himself on the dole, which he despised. As a result he became more determined than ever to persuade a local girl to look after his two daughters when they got home from school so that he could go out to work. It did not prove a particularly difficult task. The attraction of looking after a five-year-old and a six-year-old to the thirteen and fourteen-year-old girls West habitually targeted, in return for cash, and with the suggestion that they might earn even more, or 'learn something about sex', proved irresistible.

In spite of the fact that Rena West had left Lake House for lengthy periods at the end of 1968 and into 1969, Frederick West never approached the local authority with the suggestion that perhaps his daughters should be taken voluntarily into care. With the help of a variety of schoolgirls, as well as a 'fat girlfriend of Rena's' who had come down from Scotland, he managed to maintain the outward appearance that his daughters were being well looked after. If the truth were different, the local Bishop's Cleeve schoolgirls he enticed to help him were not going to tell anyone – especially not after he had made sure that they were compromised by their own actions in making love to him. And it was while Frederick West was employing this system, and Rena West was away, that he encountered the girl who was to become his true apprentice.

Rosemary Pauline Letts was, in her mother's words, 'a babyish' fifteen-year-old who had just left Bishop's Cleeve comprehensive school when she met Frederick West. She almost certainly knew who he was, not least because so many of her contemporaries at school had made the illicit pilgrimage to his caravan at 17 Lake House. Indeed, he may have encouraged one of her friends to orchestrate their first – apparently chance – meeting, so exactly did she fit the pattern he always looked for in young women. This naive, unworldly girl, dressed in old-fashioned clothes, would have been only too susceptible to his particular form of flattery. What Frederick West did not know was exactly how perfect a target Rosemary Letts would turn out to be, or how alike they were.

Frederick West was twelve years of age and working in the fields alongside his father when Rosemary Letts was born in a maternity hospital on the North Devon coast near Westward Ho! on 29 November 1953. A small, brown-eyed baby, with olive skin, brown hair and an eager smile, she was the fifth child and fourth daughter of William and Daisy Letts of Northam. Indeed, though it may not have seemed so on the surface, her parents had much in common with Walter and Daisy West of Much Marcle, Herefordshire. Like Frederick West's own mother, Daisy Letts had been in service when she met her husband, and she, too, had been at the start of her marriage as reserved as Daisy West had been at the start of hers. And like her counterpart in Herefordshire, she had rapidly discovered the violence that lay at the heart of her husband's character. But, though William Letts was not as large and intimidating a man as Walter West, he was capable of even more extreme violence.

Married in April 1942 in Ilford, Essex, not far from Daisy's parents' home, the twenty-one-year-old Bill Letts and his twenty-four-year-old wife returned to the Letts' family home in Devon immediately after the wedding, where he worked as a radio engineer. Their first child, Patricia, was born a year later, while they were still living with Daisy's parents-in-law, and a second daughter arrived eighteen months after that, just as William Letts was about to be called up to join the Royal Navy as a radio operator. He was to remain in the Navy for the next seven years, serving at one stage on the aircraft-carrier *Ark Royal*, and volunteering to stay on after the end of the war in 1945. Indeed, it was not until after the birth of his third child, another daughter, Glenys, and the family had been given their own council house in Northam, that William Letts finally decided that the time had come to retire from the sea. He was still only thirty.

Bill Letts did not find it easy to fit into the family that he now suddenly found himself a member of. His three daughters were noisy, boisterous and untidy, and that offended his obsessive desire for neatness and order. And life in Northam rapidly became intolerable, not least because he found it difficult to keep a job when he found one. The martinet's manner that he had depended on in the Navy was out of place among the high-hedged lanes, the holiday cottages and the caravans lined up overlooking the North Devon beaches. When his first son, Andrew, was born in 1952, Letts was briefly working as a television repair man, but his unbending attitude did not endear him to customers and he quickly lost the job. Letts took out his resentment on his family.

The Letts household rapidly became not so much a family home as a prison with only one sadistic jailer, William Letts. Letts would punish any infringement of his rules, or orders, with violence. If his wife disobeyed him he would hit her repeatedly; if the children did not perform their household chores on time and to his exact standards they would suffer the same fate. He thrashed them, throwing one daughter down the stairs, banging the head of another against a brick wall. If their mother protested she would be beaten again. As a result the children were taken on long walks across the sand by their mother to keep them out of their father's way, to protect them from his temper. But, as Daisy Letts admitted many years later: 'We lived under terror for years. We literally suffered hell behind locked doors.' Though Bill Letts had never admitted it to his wife and family, he was a diagnosed schizophrenic, prone to violent mood swings, persecution mania and aggression.

By the beginning of 1953 Daisy Letts was suffering from anxiety and depression, and a psychiatrist recommended a course of electro-convulsive therapy (ECT). At her husband's insistence she went on to be given six treatments. It was while these violent electric shocks were being administered to her shaved skull that her fourth daughter, whom they were to christen Rosemary, was conceived. The foetus grew to its full term in the womb while the shocks were still being administered to her anxious and depressed mother. And, by the time

85

she was two years of age, Rosemary Letts was regarded by her father as 'thick as two short planks'. She would sit rocking from side to side for hours at a time, staring into space.

Rosemary Letts was to spend a good deal of her time as a child lost in her own world of make-believe. She would delight in her dolls and pet hamsters, but remain reserved when it came to her elder brothers and sisters. But the arrival of first one and then another younger brother, Graham and Gordon, provided the focus she came to depend on. The developing young girl kept herself a child by looking after children, making her younger brothers her own live dolls, happy in the knowledge that they at least looked up to her. The 'slow' baby grew into a 'babyish' child, dressed to suit her father's old-fashioned rules, then an uncertain teenager, uncomfortable in the company of anyone except her own family.

Bill Letts had another unique inheritance to offer his 'slow' daughter, however, another of the secrets which she was to keep. Hardly had her elder sisters left home and thereby escaped his tyranny than the man who would suddenly take it into his head to scrub the carpets, or steam-clean a room, was to turn his attention to the sexual possibilities of his fourth daughter. The example of parental love that Rosemary Letts was to receive at her father's knee was every bit as distorted as that offered to Frederick West by his own father. The male love that she saw as a child was brutal, irrational and perverted, but she learned to cope with it and to turn it to her advantage. Rosemary Letts may have been babyish, but she was not a fool.

At school, Rosemary Letts struggled to make sense of the rudiments of reading, writing and arithmetic, although eventually she did learn both to read and write. She took refuge in playing with her younger brothers, and any other small children who might take an interest in her, thereby following her father's example, for he, too, took what some people in the village saw as an unhealthy interest in other people's children. He secretly groomed her in an interest in his own sexual desires, and she, in response, learned quickly that satisfying her father's demands meant a happier life. And so it did. He forgave her for her slowness, stupidity or misdemeanours for which he would brutally punish his other children. It did not take long for her to understand that this gave her power.

The gossip about Bill Letts finally drove him to leave Northam, and in 1960, at the age of thirty-nine, he moved his family across the county to Plymouth, where he found work in the Naval Dockyards at Devonport. The change of scene did nothing to soften his vicious temper. His wife's depression, already manifest, became more serious, and within two years Bill Letts decided that the family should move again, this time to Stratford-upon-Avon, where he had been offered a job in a children's home. But shortly after starting there he was evidently found unsuitable, and he moved on again, this time to a job with Smith's Industries near Cheltenham. The Letts family moved with him to a semi-detached house on the company's estate in the nearby village of Bishop's Cleeve. The year was 1964, and Rosemary Letts was almost eleven.

In other respects the family's circumstances remained much as before. Bill Letts's finances improved, but not his temper, which he lost with increasing violence and agonising regularity, beating his children when the mood took him, and threatening his wife with a knife. He would turn off the electricity, insult the neighbours, lock his children out in the street if they were late home, and insist that his wife clean meticulously every inch of their semi-detached house. And he set out to make his fourth daughter his sexual puppet. He would remain a man she both feared and manipulated throughout the rest of his life.

Rosemary Letts learned her father's lesson well. At Bishop's Cleeve school, around the corner from her parents' home at 96 Tobyfield Road, she soon began to show the same aggressiveness as her father, hitting anyone who annoyed her or who threatened her beloved younger brothers. By the age of thirteen, she was also the dominant force in the lives of all her brothers and sisters. Her father went out early in the morning to Smith's Industries, not returning from his job as an electronics engineer until after six; her mother had taken a cleaning job starting at half-past three in the afternoons lasting into the evenings, which meant that she hardly saw her husband during the week. The eldest son Andrew was now working, and Rosemary was left in charge of her two younger brothers, Graham and Gordon.

All the Letts children were given household chores to do by their father before he left for work, but when they returned from school it was Rosemary Letts who saw that they were carried out. Taking her lead from him, she was also discovering and exploring the strength of her own sexuality. She took to walking around the three-bedroomed house naked when her parents were out, and bathing her brothers while she was alone in charge of them. Rosemary Letts would dry the two younger boys with infinite care as they stood naked in front of her on the bathmat, preparing them to sleep in the double bed which she shared with them both. It was not long before she started masturbating her brother Graham when she was in bed with him, finally tempting him into intercourse by straddling him.

Rosemary Letts did not restrict her sexual interest to her brother. She also revealed it in Bishop's Cleeve, though not to her contemporaries at school. By the age of fourteen, Bill Letts's daughter had focused her sexual energy on older men, flirting with them whenever she got a chance. Indeed, one of the men she may well have flirted with outside the shops in the centre of the village was Frederick West, by then settled at Lake House. By her own admission, she was to lose her virginity at fourteen, and within a matter of weeks of her fifteenth birthday in November 1968 she was to be raped by a stranger after he offered her a lift home from a Christmas party, an attack she did not report to the police.

By the first weeks of 1969 Daisy Letts could stand life at home

87

with her husband no longer. She took her fifteen-year-old daughter Rosemary and her two younger sons Graham and Gordon to live with their elder sister Glenys, who had recently married a motor mechanic, Jim Tyler, in Cheltenham. Glenys ran a mobile snack-bar on Cirencester Road, while her husband worked in the town, but she was in the final stages of pregnancy, and asked her younger sister to stand in for her. Rosemary Letts agreed, and each morning Jim Tyler dropped her and the mobile snack-bar off at the roadside in a lay-by at Seven Kings, undertaking to return to collect them in the evening. And just as it did for Rena West only a few miles away, the mobile canteen provided Rosemary Letts with every opportunity to explore her by now promiscuous sexual appetite. Jim Tyler would often return to the snack-bar during the day to find his young sister-in-law climbing out of the cab of a lorry looking distinctly flushed and with her clothes dishevelled.

Removed from her father, Rosemary Letts embarked on a sexual relationship with an older man of thirty, who was a friend of her sister's, and she left home briefly to live with him in Cheltenham, working as a trainee seamstress while she did so. The affair continued until the police discovered it, and she was warned to stay away from the man. That did not deter her. At first she would creep back to see him late at night, but eventually the relationship came to an end. Soon afterwards she went back to live with her sister Glenys. News of her affair with a man twice her age created something of a local scandal in Bishop's Cleeve, and the gossip it had stirred up had its effect on her mother. Shortly after Rosemary's return, Daisy Letts took her two younger sons and moved out of Glenys Tyler's house without telling her daughter where she was going.

Rosemary Letts was alone, vulnerable and still only fifteen years of age. Inevitably, she turned back to the only person she believed truly loved her: her father. She moved back to Tobyfield Road to share his house, and this time there was no one else there to inhibit them. He went out each day to his job at Smith's and his daughter took a job herself, at a baker's shop in Cheltenham. She would start each morning at seven o'clock, and sometimes Bill Letts would collect her from the shop in his car, but as she often did not finish until after nine o'clock in the evening, more often than not she would wait for the bus to take her the four miles or so from the city to Bishop's Cleeve.

It was while she was waiting for the bus that Rosemary Letts was raped for a second time. In her version of the events, a man approached her at the bus stop and started 'chatting me up', but she 'resisted his advances'. He would not be put off, and started grabbing her, at which point, she later insisted, she 'ran away'. She did not run towards the city centre, however, or to a nearby house to bang on the door. Instead, she ran 'towards the park' in Cheltenham. The man caught her at the entrance to the park, 'smashed the padlock off the gate' and dragged her down by the lake under some trees, where 'he raped me'. But once again Rosemary Letts neglected to report the attack to the police, or indeed to anyone else. She simply returned home to her father, and resolved 'to catch the bus in future from the main depot in Cheltenham'.

In fact, it is just possible that the man who raped Rosemary Letts in Pittville Park when she was fifteen, after standing beside her at a bus stop, was Frederick Walter Stephen West. And it is also possible that the violence of his attack stirred up such intense feelings within her that from that moment on she would be for ever in his grasp. It may just have been at that moment that West first identified a woman who shared his perverse sexual tastes, and who took as much delight in them as he did.

Whatever the truth, it was while she was again waiting for a bus, in the summer of 1969, that Frederick West first acknowledged that he approached Rosemary Letts. It was certainly not the first time he had seen her or heard about her. He knew her reputation in Bishop's Cleeve. She and her father were a topic of conversation in the village, and she was among the girls from her school whom he would invite into his caravan. He would also know of her reputation for being 'babyish' and keen on children. At that particular moment, West would later recall, 'Rena had disappeared again', and he was 'on the dole – trying to find someone to help me look after the kids'.

'I first met Rose at the Cheltenham bus station,' West explained in the last years of his life. 'She was going on the same bus as me to Bishop's Cleeve.' The small, grimy man, wearing the inevitable overalls, had probably been waiting for her for some time, and he sat in the seat beside her without waiting to be asked. 'I made a date with her there and then on the bus,' he recalled. That was not how Rosemary Letts remembered it. In her version of the events, she refused West's invitation to go out with him, and did so again a few days later when he approached her again at the same bus stop. But, eventually, she agreed when he came into the baker's shop she was working at and shouted across to her: 'The Swallow – eight o'clock.'

'You could see the pub from her house,' West explained later. 'That's the reason I chose it.' According to his version of events on that summer evening in 1969, he met Rosemary Letts outside the Swallow in Bishop's Cleeve, but he did not take her inside for a drink. Instead, he took her 'on home' to his caravan at Lake House. 'There was a girl staying there,' he explained, 'staying in the caravan, but she was on drugs and I couldn't allow her near the children. But Rose refused to come in the van because the girl was there. She knew her. They went to school together.' A disappointed West walked part of the way back to Tobyfield Road, according to his recollection, before returning to his caravan, waking up the sleeping girl and telling her that he was 'taking her back to her mother' the next morning.

Again, Rosemary Letts had a different version of events. According to her account, West not only bought her a drink in the Swallow, but he also produced 'a fur coat and a lace dress' as presents for her. 'I wanted him to take it back because I had no intention of getting

89

involved with this man,' she explained more than a quarter of a century later. 'But he insisted I took it, and I said there was no way I could take it home because my parents would not agree to it. So he took it and kept it in the caravan he lived in.'

Whichever version is true, there is no doubt that both Frederick West and Rosemary Letts agree that she started looking after Charmaine and Anna-Marie very shortly after that first meeting. 'The next day I came home,' West insisted, 'Rose had been down and stripped the caravan – cleared it completely out. Loads of girls had been staying there. But Rose puts all the girls' clothes and that. She put it all in a big tea-chest and said: "Dump that." ' West did nothing of the kind. He gave the clothes, which included 'knickers, bras, pants, God knows what' – which he had been keeping as trophies of his sexual prowess – to another girl he knew. 'There was loads of Rena's clothes as well, 'cause Rena never wore the same clothes twice. She never washed a pair of knickers in her life. When she took a pair off, she's put a brand-new pair on.' Within a matter of days Rosemary Letts had become Frederick West's newest partner.

West was now supporting himself partly from augmenting his income by stealing whatever he could, whenever he could, as ever determined to avoid paying for anything at every opportunity. 'I would steal sand off the side of the road,' he would admit cheerfully later, 'and load it into my van.' In June 1969 he was convicted of four motoring offences, including stealing a tax disc for the white camper-van with a blue stripe on its side which he was then driving. In August he was caught again, this time for straightforward theft. On the first occasion the Cheltenham magistrates fined him £22 and required him to pay £12 in road-fund duty, while on the second they fined him £50 and gave him a six-month prison sentence 'suspended for two years'. He made no effort to pay either of these fines.

In the late summer of 1969, just as Daisy Letts was deciding to return to Tobyfield Road with her two youngest sons to live with her husband again, Rena West reappeared at Lake House. Unabashed, Frederick West introduced her to the fifteen-year-old girl who had been 'babysitting for him'. This would not have deceived the twenty-five-year-old Scottish woman, who would have known exactly what West had been doing with the babyish Rosemary Letts, and now probably joined in. This would have had the added advantage of protecting her from the violence – the beatings, the abuse – to which he had so often subjected her. While he had a new young woman as a plaything, her husband would be more amenable, less vicious, than during those periods when she had to deal with him on her own.

There was another benefit too. Rena West did not intend to remain at Lake House for long, and she knew that the bait that her husband had used to lure Rosemary Letts into a sexual relationship with him was her two daughters, Charmaine and Anna-Marie. It meant that she could come and go as she pleased. There is little doubt that Rena West was only too pleased to see another 'nanny' looking after her girls as Ann McFall had done. Even a quarter of a century later

Rosemary Letts would insist 'I loved them straight away. I felt sorry for them because they never had their mother around to look after them'. What Rena West did not know was Rosemary Letts's ambition to replace her – completely.

For his part Frederick West sensed how excited Rosemary Letts was at the prospect both of looking after the two children and of enlarging her sexual repertoire. By now she was a voluptuous young woman, with the generous breasts that West always sought, prepared to join him in any experiment he suggested. 'Rena got on well with Rose,' West maintained in the last year of his life. 'But I don't think Rose liked Rena that much. Rose wanted her out, and, of course, when Rena disappeared, Rose stepped in a bit quick.'

In the third week of October 1969, when Rena West duly left her husband again, Rosemary Letts was there to 'look after the children'. By now Frederick West had persuaded her to give up her job at the baker's shop and to act as the children's full-time nanny. He had agreed to pay her enough to give her mother the £3 a week she expected to receive, but had suggested it would be best if she said nothing about the arrangement. Instead, she pretended to leave every morning for Cheltenham as she had been doing, a deception which appealed to her and seemed to satisfy her parents.

At first all went well, but four weeks later, on 18 November, West was arrested for the non-payment of the two sets of fines imposed on him earlier in the year. Knowing that the Gloucestershire Children's Department would not consent to Charmaine and Anna-Marie remaining in the care of a fifteen-year-old girl, he asked for them to be placed in care for the three days of his prison sentence. But when he was released, he found that the local authority had contacted his wife, who had returned to Bishop's Cleeve and the caravan at Lake House. Their official 'reconciliation' was not destined to last. Three days after his release from prison, Rena West left him again, and her two daughters were returned to care, first with foster-parents and then at a children's home not far away in Whitminster. It was to prove a wise decision, as, in early December 1969, Rena West was arrested for soliciting in Gloucester.

But even though Charmaine and Anna-Marie were now in care, and therefore not there to be looked after, Rosemary Letts was still a daily visitor to West's 'scruffy' caravan at Lake House. For her parents' benefit she was still pretending to go to Cheltenham, but by now she was living openly with West. To celebrate her sixteenth birthday in November, Frederick West maintained that he bought her 'a fur coat – it was only imitation, mind, not the real McCoy – and a white lace dress and underslip, and bra and pants to take her out . . . 'cause she only wore school uniform all the time'.

Early in January, however, when Frederick West took her to the Swallow in Bishop's Cleeve for a drink one evening, he encountered 'her father standing there, with his crash-helmet on, and a big coat, wanting to fight me. I couldn't do nothing. So anyway he hit me on the jaw and I walked away, and he took Rose home, and shouted down the road "I'm gonna burn you alive in the caravan tonight" or summat like that.' West ignored him.

The following evening West went round to Tobyfield Road. 'Rose came to the door and nearly passed out with fright when she seen me stood there. I said: "Can I see your parents and let's talk this over?" But they wouldn't come out.' Two days later the meeting did take place, but it was not a success. Letts already sensed that his daughter's relationship with this dirty-looking twenty-eight-year-old man with thick, bushy hair and sideburns was not platonic, and the thought enraged him. The more West boasted about the 'hotel and caravan site' that he owned in Scotland, the more incensed Letts became, and as West left his house he instructed his daughter that she was never to see this 'dirty gypsy' again. To make sure, he locked his daughter into the bedroom he had given her after his wife had returned, telling her that she would not be allowed to leave the house until she agreed to do as he said.

'I wasn't welcome in the family at all, by anybody, not from the beginning,' Frederick West recalled later. 'Rose had been banned from seeing me, by her parents. So I never seen Rose all over Christmas.' At the time he was working on a 'big sandpit' at Bishop's Cleeve, driving a lorry on the site, transporting sand. 'It was snowing when I went to work after Christmas. The foreman said: "There's a young lady at the cabin to see you." It was Rose. She was stood outside the hut this morning. She said: "We've got to do something, 'cause Mum and Dad's going to get a court order on me." She said: "The only answer to it is . . . for you to get me pregnant." And I said: "Is that what you really want?" And she said: "Yes." '

It was indeed what she desired. West had touched a nerve in the young Rosemary Letts, a nerve that would never cease to vibrate through her body. Though she was not a virgin when they met, the sexuality that he introduced her to, sometimes with his wife's assistance, had fanned a flame that would never be extinguished. Even before she knew she was pregnant by him, she wrote to West to confirm how much she loved him, and yet also to underline how afraid she still was of her father. 'Last night made me realise we are two people, not two soft chairs to be sat on . . . I love you, Fred, but if anything goes wrong it will be the end of both of us for good. We will have to go somewhere far away where nobody will know us. I will always love you. Rose.'

Rosemary Letts suggested that she could meet West that Sunday afternoon by the boating-lake in Pittville Park, Cheltenham. 'I will have to get Lynda to say I'm going with her . . . Keep saying your prayers and remember I'll always love you.' Within a fortnight she knew that she was pregnant with Frederick West's child, just as Ann McFall had been almost exactly three years before. But Rosemary Letts was not to suffer the same fate.

Chapter Eight

The ugly duckling

'And the Devil did grin, for his darling sin
Is pride that apes humility.'

Samuel Taylor Coleridge, 'The Devil's Thoughts'

William Letts underestimated his daughter's stubbornness and guile. Used to being obeyed without question, and to her willing participation in his sexual life, he did not believe that she would disobey him. He thought she would see sense. Although he kept her locked in her bedroom at Tobyfield Road for the first weeks of 1970, he failed to realise that she would soon find ways to escape. The sixteen-year-old Rosemary Letts did so frequently, sneaking across Bishop's Cleeve to visit Frederick West at Lake House, and relishing the secrecy and deception these exploits involved. The beating her father had administered when he had first discovered her affair with Frederick West had failed in its effect. She was flattered to be the subject of this older man's attentions, and also more than a little pleased to have made her father jealous. Above all, she was also utterly delighted to be pregnant. The childish girl who liked to play with babies was about to have a baby of her own.

Rosemary Letts was fascinated by the world she had found herself being drawn into. The unbridled sexuality that oozed from her every encounter with West thrilled her and left her wanting to discover more and more about their sexual possibilities together. What is more, she knew that Rena West had been prepared to do almost anything to satisfy his appetite for sexual experiment, and she did not intend to be outdone. If Rena was a prostitute, she would be one too. If Rena was prepared to be tied up and whipped during intercourse, so would she be. If Rena was prepared to encourage young girls into the caravan for Frederick West to abuse, so would she. If Rena West's pimp was Rolf, so he would be hers. If Frederick West wanted to make her his sexual slave, so would she be. Rosemary Letts knew how to do that: her father had been a good teacher.

Rosemary Letts was not, however, Frederick West's only sexual partner. The Full Moon pub in the High Street in Cheltenham attracted crowds of young people, and West liked to sit in a corner of the bar and engage whomever he could in conversation. At twenty-nine, dressed in worn jeans, and with his hair as dark and unkempt as ever, he was an unlikely figure among the teenage hippies who made up the pub's regular clientele. But Frederick West's extravagant fantasies about his life, woven in an endless, unselfconscious stream, made him an object of some curiosity, which he turned to his advantage. West was looking for female companionship, especially the companionship of young women who might need a home for the night, and he was prepared to go to almost any lengths to find it. On one evening at the Full Moon, West ran into Terry Crick, a young man who had lived at the Watermead caravan site at Brockworth with him in 1965. Crick was hitchhiking with his girlfriend, and West offered them both a bed for the night at Lake House.

Terry Crick could not have bargained for what he was to discover at West's caravan in the two nights that followed. Indeed, a quarter of a century later, when he was aged forty-eight, the memory was to drive him to commit suicide. But when he first accepted the invitation, Crick explained many years later, West just seemed 'like a very nice bloke. I thought it would be fun'. It turned out to be a nightmare. Frederick West's caravan had grown even gloomier in the weeks since Charmaine and Anna-Marie had been taken into care. Now there were tools, piles of old clothes and strange pieces of metal strewn around the small rooms in place of children's toys.

The atmosphere was dismal, made even more so when West started to boast about his skill as an abortionist. If they ever 'got into trouble', he told Crick and his girlfriend, he could sort it out for them, and he produced what he called his 'tools' to prove it. Crick would remember many years later that one was a steel rod about a foot long with 'something that looked like a corkscrew' attached to the top of it. West then produced a set of black and white Polaroid pictures of what he said were the 'vaginas of the girls' he had operated on, and went on to inform Crick and his girlfriend that if 'things went wrong' during one of his operations, he would 'sort the girls out once and for all'. The next morning West even took Crick to a 'large wooden shed' with a 'dirt floor' on the caravan site, and showed him a set of oxy-acetylene bottles and equipment.

For all that, the pair stayed that night and the next. One reason may have been that the Full Moon had a reputation at the time as a 'drug pub', and West made no secret of his interest in drugs, or of his approval of them. If young people wanted to take them, he was only too happy to play the willing host, the non-judgemental adult prepared to accept the vagaries of young people experimenting with their lives. If he did not take drugs himself, no more than he now ever drank more than a glass or two of shandy, that should not put them off. Frederick West liked the company of young people who were prepared to allow themselves to lose control. Once they had done so, they were at his mercy. It was his latest new technique, a new addition to his repertoire of seduction, and one that he would refine in the years to come.

On their second night in the caravan, Crick and his girlfriend were introduced to Rosemary Letts. Terry Crick remembered more than two decades later how they lay awake that night listening to West and his newly pregnant sixteen-year-old girlfriend talking, making love and giggling. Towards the end of his life, Crick became convinced that during that night he had heard Frederick West and Rosemary Letts plan to commit murder, although he did not report the events to the police at the time. Instead, Crick and his girlfriend simply left West's caravan the next morning. Terry Crick was never to return, although his girlfriend was to do so, one of the many young women who fell under Frederick West's seductive spell, but not one of the young women who paid for that with their lives.

When William Letts discovered that he had been mistaken, and his daughter had given him the slip, he called on the local authority for help. In early February 1970, repeating his claim that Frederick West had been having sex with his daughter when she was still under-age, he applied for an injunction to keep West away from her. West ignored the order, and a few weeks later Letts followed it up by insisting that his daughter be taken into care. Frederick West himself explained later: 'The reason she was put into care was she was expecting my baby, and they wanted to force her to have an abortion. It wasn't until Rose was pregnant that all the trouble started. There was no hassle before, 'cause I never met 'em and didn't know 'em.' Letts was convinced that this would make his daughter see sense at last, and at first it seemed as though it had. After three weeks in a home for troubled teenagers in Cheltenham, Rosemary Letts announced that she was now prepared to have the abortion. 'I came home on the Wednesday,' she would remember later, and was 'due to have the abortion on the following Monday.'

Rosemary Letts never had the abortion. She never planned to. She had simply hatched a plan to escape with the man she loved, Frederick West. On the Saturday before she was due to go to the clinic, she made an excuse to go into Cheltenham and met West, who was then working as a tyre-fitter at Cotswold Tyres. Together they agreed that instead of climbing into the ambulance that was coming to collect her on the following Monday morning, she would run across the road and climb into his van instead. But that plan, too, never came into effect. On the Sunday evening Bill Letts gave her an ultimatum: 'My father told me that I could stay at home as long as I went to work and earned money, and had an abortion, and had no boyfriends. Or I was told I could go off with this Fred West and never see my family again.' Letts also told her that if she chose the second option, and he saw them together in the street, 'he would knife us'.

Rosemary Letts left home, and Bishop's Cleeve. She chose to have her child, and to take on Frederick West's two children. 'I wanted them to have parents and a better home life, and I wanted my baby,' she maintained later. Frederick West was delighted. He was under no illusions about why Bill Letts had made his daughter's life so difficult. He sensed the sexual abuse in the Letts family as surely as he recognised it in his own. 'Why her father wanted to get rid of the baby and get her back home was 'cause he'd lost her, sort of thing, when her was with me.'

His delight was short-lived. Just as Rosemary Letts decided to leave home, Rena West reappeared. She had turned up at Cotswold Tyres and announced that she had come back to him. They could take the children out of care. West could hardly refuse, and no sooner had she settled back into Lake House than Charmaine and Anna-Marie were reclaimed from the Parkland's Children's Home. But then Rena 'did the dirtiest trick she's ever done on me in her whole life'. After collecting the two girls, 'We took 'em home, put them to bed. I got up the next morning and Rena had scarpered. So I had to put them back again.'

By now the local authority was beginning to lose patience, and it insisted that West should find a 'permanent home' for his family. If he failed to do so, it would take his two daughters into care formally, rather than simply offering them voluntary foster-homes when he ran into temporary difficulties. It was one reason why Frederick West had been keen for Rosemary Letts to join him, 'so I could get the girls back'. But even before her father's ultimatum, West had told the local authority that his brother Douglas would be moving into a small flat in Clarence Road, Cheltenham, with his wife to live with him and provide a permanent home for the children. It was another of his plausible lies, another invention to keep the prying eyes of authority at bay, but Frederick West calculated that the arrival of Rosemary Letts would fill the gap before the local Children's Department discovered the truth. Or at least, he could lie to make it appear that way.

It was with his customary sly subservience that West rang the local authority in the last days of February 1970 to tell it that 'their mother had returned again' to live with him and Rosemary Letts, and therefore there was no reason for his two children to remain with the two separate sets of foster-parents they had been with for the past week. The ruse worked because, like so many of his lies, it was partly true. The Children's Department had no particular reason not to believe him. As far as it could see, West was the single stable element in the lives of the two little girls in the Department's temporary care, and he was doing everything in his power to help. What the Department did not do, it would appear, was to check the living-conditions that West was intending to provide for his children. There is no evidence that the local authority ever went to see the single room that he and the two women were supposed to be living in with Charmaine and Anna-Marie at 9 Clarence Road. As Rosemary Letts was later to recall: 'It was a real pit. We were all in this little room together . . . There was just a tiny sink in the corner. It was hopeless.'

In fact the ménage was to last only a few days. When Bill Letts

96

discovered where his daughter was, he informed the police rather than the local authority, and insisted formally that Frederick West had been having sex with his daughter while she had been under the age of sixteen, thereby breaking the law. At the police's insistence, the local authority intervened and placed the two children back in a foster-home. But yet again Bill Letts was to be thwarted. When a police surgeon examined Rosemary Letts, he discovered that she could not have conceived before her sixteenth birthday, as her pregnancy was not sufficiently advanced. As a result West was interviewed only briefly, and not detained. In the circumstances the local authority decided it could not hold on to the children.

The experience of being interviewed had convinced West that he had to do something. Partly annoyed by his wife Rena, who had insisted on visiting her daughters while they were being fostered 'and only taking Charmaine out . . . not Anna-Marie. I mean, Anna-Marie was a complete failure as far as she was concerned, never should have happened', and partly furious with Bill Letts for subjecting him to the police interview, Frederick West decided to disappear. Without telling his wife or Letts, West arranged to collect his two daughters on the morning of Good Friday, 27 March 1970. But he did not take them back to 9 Clarence Road. Frederick West and Rosemary Letts had decided to start their life together in the city that he had always loved: Gloucester.

In the first week of April 1970 they moved into a one-bedroomed flat at number 10 Midland Road, on the east side of the city's central park. Filled with once-respectable Victorian villas, the area was to be their home for the next quarter of a century. Down at heel, with bags of rubbish littering the pavements, it was a long way from the days when the villas might have housed a local solicitor's clerk. Now each house was broken up into flats, the houses' once-proud front gardens often obscured by paving-slabs, the rear all too often overgrown with nettles. The area reflected something of Gloucester itself – itinerant, shifting, perched at a crossroads, a city that was somehow doomed to be a meeting of railway lines and canals that took its inhabitants in other directions. Its population always seemed to be wondering where to set off for next, be it the River Severn, the Cotwolds or the West Country.

Rosemary Letts refused to stay in the new flat for more than a fortnight. 'It was the first experience Rose had ever had of coloured people, and she didn't enjoy it,' West recalled, and he arranged for them all to move to 4 Park End Road. Then two months later they were back in Midland Road, though at number 25. The flat was on the ground floor of a substantial square villa, with a bedroom, living-room and small kitchen. There were two other flats in the house, on the first and second floor, and a basement, which, when they moved in, was occupied by an elderly Polish gentleman: 'But it was uninhabitable, really, and he moved out.' There was also a small unkempt garden at the rear, where an elderly coal cellar was attached to the house.

Frederick West was still working at Cotswold Tyres, but spending more time each evening working for the owner of the flat, a Polish immigrant called Frank Zygmunt, who was encouraging West to learn about the building trade. The harder West worked, the more work Zygmunt gave him and the more grateful he became. The faster Zygmunt could make habitable some of the run-down houses he had been buying up in the area, the sooner he would be able to rent them out. Zygmunt came to rely increasingly on the willing Frederick West.

Charmaine West was now a bright, energetic seven-year-old, and in September 1970 she joined the nearby St James's School, while Anna-Marie West, now six and more subdued than her elder stepsister, remained at the Hatherley Infants' School that she and Charmaine had attended earlier that summer. Each afternoon they would return home to the increasingly pregnant sixteen-year-old girl who was now acting as their mother. Charmaine was the prettier of the two girls, her soft brown skin setting off a sparkling childish smile, while her sister was coarser featured, with her father's broad nose and wide-set eyes.

In spite of their time in foster-homes, they were lively, interested children, obviously only too happy to be back with their father again. But Charmaine made little secret of the fact that she preferred her mother Rena to Rosemary Letts. 'For a start Charmaine hated Rose and told her so,' Anna-Marie was to write a quarter of a century later. 'She never missed a chance to remind Rose about our real mother.' West was well aware of the animosity, but he did nothing to soften it. If anything, he seemed instead rather to encourage it. Nevertheless, from their first weeks together West had instructed his two daughters to call Rosemary Letts 'Mum', even though they were reluctant to do so, just as he told them to call their mother Rena 'Aunty' on the few occasions that she came to stay with them. Neither child wanted to obey him, but both knew just how vicious his temper could prove to be in private. Charmaine, in particular, suffered the same coldness from Frederick West that she had in Glasgow. She was not his child, and never had been. 'He always favoured Anna-Marie,' was how one of her mother's sisters described it.

Rena West was not there to protect her first-born daughter, although she had not forgotten her. On one of her many trips back to Scotland in 1969, Rena West had formed a new relationship, and had taken her new boyfriend to meet one of her sisters that Christmas. Now, as 1970 progressed, she told her family that she was considering taking both her daughters to Saudi Arabia with her in the near future, as her new boyfriend was getting a job there. She was going to make an exploratory trip, and then go down to collect them as soon as she had decided what to do for the best. One thing was abundantly clear. Rena West did not want to leave Charmaine with her husband for very long, because she had always been worried about his attitude towards the bright-eyed little girl with skin the colour of light chocolate.

But it was not Frederick West who disciplined the 'lovely' little half-caste girl who had just come out of care. He had handed over the task to the pregnant sixteen-year-old girl who had become his willing pupil. West had told her firmly that Charmaine was 'about old enough for the strap now', and the childish young girl with long dark hair and wide brown eyes had lost no time in putting his wishes into practice. Rosemary Letts preferred a wooden spoon to the leather strap West remembered from his own childhood, but in every other respect he approved of her violent, often brutal, punishments. The violence that had been part of life at Tobyfield Road now surfaced in Midland Road, with the encouragement of the man who had replaced her father as the one significant male in her life. When she administered her punishments Frederick West would never complain, only ever advising her not to hit them 'where it would show'. And, as her pregnancy wore on that summer, so her temper shortened still further.

But Frederick West did not only expect Rosemary Letts to look after the children; he also expected her to take over from Rena West and trade as a prostitute. In his mind there was no reason not to continue with a system that had worked perfectly well in the past. West suggested that she start working the bus garage, just as Rena had done in Glasgow. For her part, Rosemary Letts was quite prepared to go along with the plan. She even gave herself the same professional name that his wife Rena had used, Mandy. Meanwhile, West took a job as a milkman, delivering for Model Dairies in the early mornings before going on to his other job as a tyre-fitter. The milk-float presented him with a chance to see what 'opportunities' might present themselves during his rounds, and West was still an incorrigible thief, taking whatever he could, whenever the opportunity presented itself.

One night in late September 1970 Bill and Daisy Letts turned up without warning at Midland Road, having discovered from one of her sisters where their daughter was living. 'There was a knock on the door, and Rose went to the door. She was very near due to have her baby,' West recalled. 'Rose come back to me and she looked as white as a sheet . . . and she said, "Mum and Dad's at the door." ' West went to the front door himself, and said: 'Look, I've got nothing against you whatsoever, but give me any trouble and I'll give you more trouble than you brought me.' Then, after consulting their daughter, West invited them in. 'We got on quite well . . . It was only a matter of days before Rose fell into labour, and her mother and father said they would have the children . . . Charmaine and Anna-Marie, while she was in hospital.' Someone to look after his daughters was not the only advantage Frederick West may have seen in a reconciliation with the Lettses. He may also have sensed a way in which he could draw Bill Letts into his own plans, knowing his lust for his own daughter, and aware that the knowledge gave him a hold over him. 'He was bloody everlasting there after that,' West would remark in the last months of his life.

On 17 October 1970 Rosemary Letts, who now called herself Mrs Rose West, gave birth at Gloucester Royal Hospital to the child she had conceived shortly after her sixteenth birthday. She and West decided to christen the dark-haired, blue-eyed baby girl Heather Ann. But the child had been at home in Midland Road for only two weeks when West was arrested for 'swapping' a vehicle excise disc from one of Frank Zygmunt's vans to his own, and changing the details. Two weeks later he was arrested again, this time for the theft of four tyres from his employers at Cotswold Tyres. Not surprisingly, West was dismissed as a tyre-fitter, and he went to work for Frank Zygmunt every day, after he had finished his milk round, still apparently convinced that he could get away with anything. In this he was to be proved wrong.

His new daughter was barely seven weeks old when Frederick West was fined £50 and sentenced to three months' imprisonment at Gloucester magistrates' court for the theft of the tyres and the road fund disc. In turn, that conviction breached the suspended sentence he had been given the previous August in Cheltenham for the theft of some fencing, which brought him a further six months' imprisonment. On the afternoon of 4 December 1970 Frederick West left court for Gloucester Prison, barely a mile away from his house, and the first night of a nine-month sentence. But his problems did not end there. On 31 December he returned to court again to receive a further one-month sentence for another theft, which brought his total sentence to ten months. Frederick West was to spend the next six months and three weeks in prison, first in Gloucester and then at Leyhill Open Prison. Meanwhile, Rosemary Letts was left alone in Midland Road with Charmaine, Anna-Marie and her new baby daughter Heather. She was just seventeen.

In Leyhill Open Prison at Wotton-Under-Edge in Gloucestershire, twenty-one miles from his home, Frederick West acted exactly as he had trained himself to do in the presence of anyone in authority. Prisoner Number 401317 calmly settled into life there from 27 January until 24 June 1971 aware that he was not entitled to either 'home leave' or 'outside work'. Even had he been able to, West would have been reluctant to abscond. He would not have been anxious to risk the possibility of a return to the Victorian prison at Gloucester with its locked cell doors, rather than the more relaxed atmosphere of Leyhill, where the prisoners could walk around the grounds between five and nine o'clock each evening if it was light. He passed his time by making elaborate models out of matchsticks, including one of a gypsy caravan.

Frederick West was nothing if not a model prisoner at Leyhill. Without fail he called the prison officers 'sir' at every opportunity, and presented himself to them, as he did to the world at large, as a meek, humble man who was 'only too anxious to please' and ever prepared to 'help out'. It was the approach that West had perfected with the local authority Children's Department over the past four years of his 'asking for their help' in finding 'a temporary home' for

Charmaine and Anna-Marie. West would never argue or use bad language in the presence of a prison officer, or anyone from the Children's Department, just as he would take particular care to treat every policeman or policewoman with whom he came into contact with an almost obsequious humility. To the outside world he made sure that he seemed no more than an insignificant petty thief with a taste for slightly smutty jokes.

But within the privacy of his own home Frederick West was quite a different person. In her first months in Gloucester, Rosemary Letts had been subjected to the same violence and rapacious sexual demands that Rena West had been forced to put up with seven years before in Glasgow. But, unlike Rena West, Rosemary Letts had found the experience intensely exciting. It had steadily begun to bind her ever more tightly to the dark, brooding man she now shared her life with. She had increasingly sought to excite him herself, vying to outdo his imagination with her own sexual experiments. And now, even though he was incarcerated twenty-one miles away in Leyhill Prison, she saw no reason to stop. Rosemary Letts took great pride in recounting her sexual experiences to Frederick West in hushed whispers during her afternoon visits every four weeks. They would huddle together, their new baby on her lap, giggling like children while Charmaine and Anna-Marie amused themselves nearby. Frederick West and Rosemary Letts had begun to forge the unique and secret bond that would bind them together for ever, insulating them from an inquisitive world.

So even though West was temporarily no longer resident at 25 Midland Road, it was his personality that was the dominant force there, he who shaped how the family lived. It was his encouragement that led Rosemary Letts to beat Charmaine with a wooden spoon, and his enthusiasm that led her to continue working as a prostitute while he was away. West did not only do so to increase her sexual enjoyment, however; he did so for a more practical reason. Frederick West had organised a system of sexual barter for some of the goods and services Rosemary Letts would need while he was away. He almost certainly offered her to his landlord, for example, in exchange for the payment of rent, as well as to other people whom he believed might be useful in looking after her. For her part, Rosemary Letts was only too happy to agree to the arrangement. Sex fascinated her. When Bill Letts appeared to try to persuade her to leave Midland Road and return to Bishop's Cleeve with him, she had no difficulty in turning him down.

Even though he was in prison, Frederick West ruthlessly exploited his young partner's interest in sex, instinctively recognising that her brutalising experiences with her own father had coarsened her attitude to intercourse. 'Making love to your father, you don't have a chat-up, I shouldn't think,' he confided towards the end of his life. 'So she lost that part of her life. Rose didn't want foreplay; she wanted rough sex.' West put her appetite to his use. And he could not have had a more willing pupil.

But West not only called on his landlord to take advantage of his wife; he also asked Rena's pimp, Rolf, to provide her with clients. In fact, towards the end of his life West suggested that the pimp had taken an interest in Rose after being introduced to her by Rena West. Indeed, his wife was the other person whose help he called upon while he was in prison. His daughter Charmaine had told him that Rosemary Letts had 'tied up and gagged' her and Anna-Marie while he was in Leyhill. And even though the seventeen-year-old had told him, 'It was only play', West nevertheless 'got Rena to keep an eye on Rose and the kids while I was in prison'. Another reason for doing so was that he wanted the two women to compete for his attentions. It confirmed his power over both of them.

Rena West and Rosemary Letts were in constant contact while West was in Leyhill Prison, just as they had been before his sentence. Towards the end of his life West remembered that all three of them had briefly stayed at 9 Clarence Road in Cheltenham, and explained that he had also seen his wife just before being sent to prison, when Rena had returned from Reading to 'work for some Irish blokes in Gloucester – prostituting'. Although Rosemary Letts was to deny it repeatedly during her trial, there is no doubt that she was only too well aware of Rena West's activities – and of her ambition to return to Frederick West's protection.

'Rose used to come down and see me in prison regular,' he recalled, 'and she told me that Rena was seeing the girls at school.' West relished the idea that the two women were competing for him, just as he knew that Rena's visits to her children, and particularly to Charmaine, would not endear her to Rosemary Letts: ''Cause this was giving Charmaine ammunition to use on Rose . . . Charmaine used to say to Rose: "I'm going with my mammie shortly, so I'm not taking no orders off you." '

The possibility that his lively stepdaughter might annoy the young woman who was just nine and a half years older than she was suited Frederick West. It was another means of control over both his wife and Rosemary Letts. If Charmaine felt the rough edge of Rosemary Letts's tongue, or the back of her hand, West was perfectly happy. He even told his wife so, and on 4 May 1971 Rosemary Letts acknowledged it in a letter she sent to West in Leyhill Prison. Headed 'From Now Until Forever', her letter explained: 'Darling, about Char. I think she likes to be handled rough. But darling, why do I have to be the one to do it.' She went on: 'I would keep her for her own sake, if it wasn't for the rest of the children. You can see Char coming out in Anna now. And I hate it.' The letter was signed: 'Well, Love, keep happy, Longing for the 18th. Your ever worshipping wife, Rose.'

During her visit on 18 May, when Rosemary Letts took both Charmaine and Anna-Marie with her to Leyhill, Frederick West discussed with her the possibility that the elder child might leave them. In a letter to her dated that day, West wrote: 'Let me know about Char, yes or no. I say yes, but it is up to you darling, and then we can have our son, ha ha, darling and we will keep our own darling.' Significantly, he concluded: 'I love you and Anna and Heather forever my darling.'

The power West wielded over the 'babyish' young woman who was now calling herself his wife was clear in another letter Rosemary Letts sent to Frederick West a little later. Once again headed 'From Now Until Forever' it explained: 'I know you love me darling. It just seems queer that anyone should think so much of me.' Dated 22 May 1971, the letter concluded: 'Sending all my love & heart your worshipping wife, Rose. PS Love, I've got the wireless on and its playing some lovely romantic music. Oh! How I wish you were here beside me. Still remembering your love & warmth, Rose.' It was decorated with a heart and a set of crosses for kisses.

Rosemary Letts had become confident enough to tell West that the one person not welcome in her life was Charmaine. On one of her visits to Leyhill, she clearly told him that she would be quite happy to see Charmaine West disappear. West confirmed it in a letter he wrote that day: 'So you say yes to Char, that good. I will see to it when I get out, but don't tell her for you know what she is like and you can have our son as soon as I come out.' For her, the child was a potent reminder of the woman she wanted to replace. For West, Charmaine was simply a tool with which to extend his power over Rosemary.

Exactly as he had planned it should, Rosemary Letts's dislike of Charmaine West developed into loathing during his period in Leyhill Prison. It meant that years later Frederick West could pretend that the dislike was all hers, suggesting that 'we were going to let Charmaine go off with Rena . . . 'cause what I wanted to do was to just come home, grab the kids, get another place, and forget about it. But Rose didn't fucking want that because Charmaine was giving Rose a hard time.' At her trial for the murder of Charmaine West, Rosemary West admitted herself that the eight-year-old 'could be very awkward . . . disruptive', that she 'would shout and throw furniture about . . . and wouldn't eat', concluding, 'if she thought I wanted her to do something, she wouldn't do it', and made it clear that she wanted to 'be with her natural mother'. But the truth of the matter was that Frederick West himself had orchestrated their hatred of one another.

One person who remembered the animosity between the eight-year-old and her babyish minder was West's other daughter, Anna-Marie, who wrote later: 'For a start Charmaine hated Rose and told her so. She would go out of her way to antagonise and aggravate our volatile stepmother. She never missed a chance to remind Rose about our real mother.' And that did not in the least improve Rosemary Letts's temper. As the weeks passed she became steadily more and more aggressive towards both children. 'She made us do most of the household chores despite our ages,' Anna-Marie remembered, 'and if we didn't do them right she erupted. Doing them right, of course, meant doing them Rose's way: there was no other. If you did it wrong you got a hiding.'

Another person who witnessed Rosemary Letts's loathing for

Charmaine West was her upstairs neighbour at 25 Midland Road, Shirley Giles. She had moved into the house at about the same time as Frederick West, and Mrs Giles's elder child Tracy, who was only two months older than Charmaine, had started to play with the eldest of the three children in Rosemary Letts's care. One morning Tracy went downstairs to borrow a cup of milk from her friend's flat. Years later she would recall: 'Charmaine was standing on a chair with her hands behind her back. All I could see was this huge brown leather belt. It held her wrists. The prong of the belt was stuck into the leather above the buckle. There was a lady beside her with a spoon in her hand.' Mrs Giles was told later by Rosemary Letts that 'Charmaine had been very naughty and she had to teach her a lesson, to teach her wrong from right', but the words might almost have been spoken by Frederick West, and the brown leather belt could certainly have belonged to his late mother Daisy.

Shirley Giles and her family left 25 Midland Road shortly after the incident with the spoon and the leather belt, but the injuries to Charmaine had not come to an end. At six-fifty in the evening of 28 March 1971 she had been treated at the casualty department of Gloucester Royal Hospital for a 'puncture wound' to her left ankle, which was the result of a 'domestic accident'. In fact, it was in all probability a knife wound – a stab from a kitchen knife. Not long afterwards Anna-Marie was taken to the doctor with a deep gash in the side of her head, requiring stitches, which Rosemary Letts insisted was the result of a fall. Once again it was nothing of the kind. The truth of the matter, as Anna-Marie was to recall, was that the seventeen-year-old Rosemary Letts had snatched her cereal bowl from her hand one morning 'and lashed out, breaking it across my head in one movement'.

The only child safe from Rosemary Letts's temper was her own baby daughter Heather, still only a few months old. She 'absolutely adored children until they were about one year old', Anna-Marie remembered years afterwards. 'She loved the helplessness of them, and she loved to do things for them . . . But the moment children developed signs of independence, such as crawling, walking or talking, things changed. Then they became a nuisance and would feel the sharp end of her tongue and her temper.'

No matter the punishment inflicted, however, Charmaine West never allowed herself to lose control. She refused steadfastly to let Rosemary Letts intimidate her, and took whatever violence was meted out to her stoically, never once allowing herself even to shed a tear. The tiny smiling girl, who still wet the bed, and whom Frederick West himself called 'fiery and comical', even had her collar-bone broken by her new 'Mum', but she was not even taken to the hospital for an examination. In the cold dark nights she would simply lie in the narrow single bed under the window in the rear bedroom that she shared with her half-sister, listening to the wind rattling the panes above her, and whispering: 'Anna-Marie, Anna-Marie, the witches are trying to get in. They're going to get us.'

Frederick West was released from Leyhill Prison in the early hours of the morning of 24 June 1971, and he took the bus home to Midland Road, Gloucester. Rosemary Letts and he celebrated by going to bed together as soon as Charmaine and Anna-Marie had gone to school, but otherwise it was a miserable home-coming. The floorboards were still bare, there was hardly any furniture, and as soon as he returned both the electricity and the gas supply were cut off. 'When I came out of prison they didn't pay any of the bills, just told the gas, electric and all that. So we all, more or less, slept in the front room . . . with a candle and an oil fire,' West recalled. 'Actually, the oil fire blew up some months later and set fire' to the small kitchen/breakfast-room. But the lack of light and heat served only to exacerbate further Rosemary Letts's already short temper. She had been left to 'hold the fort', she told West fiercely; now he had to 'sort things out'.

Exactly what happened to the West family in the next few weeks remains shrouded in mystery. Both Frederick West and Rosemary Letts have given relentless, conflicting versions of the events surrounding these summer months in 1971. One thing is clear, however. After these weeks were over, the lives of two more young people, Charmaine and Rena West, had been snuffed out, and their bodies buried in narrow graves. Rosemary Letts was to see her rival, and her rival's first child, brutally murdered.

Throughout the last months of his life Frederick West insisted regularly that Charmaine West did not disappear until 'about two or three weeks' after he was released from Leyhill Prison, although at one moment, as he did on so many occasions, he changed his mind and said he could not 'quite remember' when she left. But West did not deny that 'Rose never liked Charmaine really. I turned a blind eye to it, because I couldn't do nothing about it. I wouldn't separate 'em. It was either getting rid of Rose or putting them in a home . . . What the hell! I didn't know what to fucking do about it.'

In the end, however, with Rosemary Letts's insistent barking voice in his ear, West decided to 'sort it out'. Whatever the truth of exactly when Charmaine disappeared, there is no doubt whatever that Frederick West eventually confessed to the murder of the half-caste daughter of his wife Rena and the Pakistani 'Billy Boy'. In his early interviews with the police after his arrest in 1994, West admitted that he killed Charmaine 'about a week' after his release from prison, while she was sleeping in the back of his wife's car, and immediately after he had killed her mother.

In this first version he explained: 'Rena came and seen Rose when I was in prison, and Rose said, "Look, you'll have to wait 'til Fred comes", 'cause it was only a couple of weeks.' West then maintained that Rena had come to collect her daughter from Midland Road to 'take her away', shortly after his release from prison, but that he had arranged to meet her later, at a local pub, because Rosemary Letts was 'so upset' at the prospect of losing the child.

'I took Rena in the pub and got her absolutely paralytic, and then took her out to Dymock in the country where I know, and I strangled her and buried her.' He then went back to his wife's car, where Charmaine was asleep 'because her mother had given her lager or something' in a bottle with a straw.'

> There was Charmaine in the back of it. I thought, What am I going to do now? . . . So, anyway, I strangled her while she was sleeping 'cause there's no way I could have touched her in any other way and wrapped her up in the back and drove back to Midland Road.
>
> I sat there for . . . must have been an hour, just thinking, and then . . . I suddenly thought to get Charmaine and take her in . . . so I went to pick her up and of course she was stiff . . . I picked her up . . . out of the back and I mean she just flopped over, like . . . and I thought she was dead. There was no doubt about it . . . She'd peed all over the back seat and . . . everything and I mean you know her eyes was just open. She was lying looking at me and I closed her eyes, and then I carried her round the back.

West admitted matter-of-factly that he had put the dead child's body in 'a coal cellar under the kitchen', where there was 'probably two foot of slack coal in the bottom of it. So I dug that out and laid her along the back of the wall, on the house wall, the main building wall, facing in towards the wall . . . Charmaine was wrapped up in a lot of blankets,' West maintained. 'She wasn't cut up or nothing . . . she was fully clothed and everything. There were no clothes taken off her or nothing . . . She wasn't dismembered at all.' As soon as he had finished, he had gone back upstairs and climbed into bed to cuddle Rosemary Letts, who was crying – because she was 'so upset to have lost this girl she loves'.

That version of events bore little resemblance to the truth, and not long afterwards West adapted his story to disguise what had actually happened to the child. He suggested that the child's body 'must have been removed to the municipal tip' in Gloucester when a demolition firm had worked on an extension to the back of 25 Midland Road. Yet again, this was an attempt to throw the police off the track, and to maintain his story that nothing whatever had happened to the child – beyond his strangling her. Before the police began excavating Midland Road, West went even further in his effort to persuade them not to search for her body, and retracted his confession altogether, telling the police: 'You won't find nothing at Midland Road, 'cause Charmaine's in India.'

It was yet another of Frederick West's lies. The ugly truth was quite different. When Charmaine West's remains were eventually recovered from a small, square, nine-feet deep hole under the kitchen area of 25 Midland Road at seven-ten in the evening of Wednesday 4 May 1994, there was every sign that she had been both naked and dismembered when she was buried. The four-feet, five-inch tall girl had been planted, just as Ann McFall had been planted, her tiny

106

naked body stuffed into a well-dug hole just two feet square. Her hands were missing, and so were a great many of her foot and toe bones, as well as both her kneecaps, and there was also evidence that she had been all but cut in half, her legs torn out from her pelvis at the hips.

After the discovery of her skeleton, Frederick West refused to confirm that he was responsible for her death, repeatedly saying 'No comment' when questioned by the police. Nevertheless, only a few weeks later West told his first solicitor, Howard Ogden, that Rosemary Letts had killed the girl. It was an accident, West said in July 1994: 'She grabbed her by the throat and killed her.' But even that version of events he was to retract, suggesting just two weeks later that Rosemary Letts had told him: 'I gave her an overdose of aspirin or something, because you were trying to find Rena.'

West then revised that version, suggesting that Rosemary Letts had killed the girl after he had come out of prison, but that 'I never knew nothing about Charmaine'. In this version Rosemary Letts had told him that Rena had taken the girl 'to India', and he had not discovered until much later that Rosemary Letts and the pimp Rolf had disposed of Charmaine's body, putting it in a suitcase. They had then told him later that 'They wanted to put it on the municipal tip'. Not one of Frederick West's many versions of these events, whether to the police or to his original solicitor, rings true.

No one can be entirely sure how eight-year-old Charmaine West met her death, but there are a number of clues to suggest that she may have died in an even more horrifying way than West had the courage to admit. Shortly after the discovery of her body in Midland Road, for example, West was asked if sex or bondage had anything to do with the child's death, and, although he refused to answer the question directly, he nodded his head.

There is no doubt that Frederick West regarded an eight-year-old girl as 'a sexual object' who had to be 'broken in' to the ways of sexuality by her father. 'It's a father's job' he would tell his daughter Anna-Marie only a year or so later. 'I'm just doing what all fathers have to do. It's a normal thing, so stop carrying on.' Indeed, in the years to come West was to tell some of his other female children exactly the same thing, just as he was to sexually abuse some of them, telling them that his own father had done exactly the same thing before him.

Although the thought is a terrifying one, there is every reason to suspect that Frederick West raped his eight-year-old stepdaughter Charmaine in the coal cellar of 25 Midland Road just weeks after his release from prison in the early summer of 1971. West was almost certainly assisted in the task by Rosemary Letts, who was to help him do exactly the same thing just eighteen months later to Rena West's other daughter, Anna-Marie. The giggling couple from the caravan at Lake House were thereby to be forced even closer, their intimacy, forged by her father's adverse reaction and West's subsequent imprisonment, now confirmed. It was West's last test for the young woman from Tobyfield Road, her participation the final proof that she was trustworthy, and the final tie to him that she would never be able to break. For ever afterwards they would be isolated together in their own bizarre, evil world.

Bound with tape so that she could not move, her naked body tied with sheeting, gagged and then penetrated by a man who should have been her protector, with the help of a young woman then still only seventeen who pretended to be her mother, Charmaine West's murder was an act of irredeemable evil.

Whether the spirited eight-year-old girl with a large gap in her front teeth was killed because she threatened to tell her mother, or the school authorities, what Frederick West and Rosemary Letts had done to her in the cellar of 25 Midland Road can only be a matter for speculation. It is equally possible that she suffocated on the gag around her mouth, or was strangled by West in the act of intercourse, or stabbed by Rosemary Letts to stop her from screaming when the gag was removed. All are equally horrifying possibilities. What is certain is that her naked body was cut in half and more than forty of her bones removed. Charmaine West's young life was snuffed out as if it were no more than a candle's flame.

There was not even the faintest flicker of contrition. Frederick West and Rosemary Letts merely saw to it that her attendance record at St James's School was brought to an end that summer with the note: 'Moved to London.' And when her half-sister Anna-Marie arrived home from school on that July day in 1971, she was told Charmaine had 'gone off with her mother'. Charmaine West's death made Frederick West and Rosemary Letts partners. No longer simply the apprentice, she had become his accomplice.

Chapter Nine

Bloody partnership

'Search then the Ruling Passion: There, alone,
The wild are constant and the cunning known.'

Alexander Pope, *Epistles to Several Persons*,
'To Lord Cobham'

When her daughter Charmaine died, Rena West was not in Scotland
but in Reading, and she was travelling regularly to Gloucester. 'She
would visit Charmaine at school, and take her out for the day,'
Frederick West would recount later, "cause she was running some
sort of prostitute ring in Gloucester from a pub in Barton Street.' His
wife was also visiting Rosemary Letts at Midland Road, possibly to
recruit her sexual services and provide her with clients, but also,
perhaps, for sexual reasons of her own. 'Whether Rose and Rena was
having an affair, I don't know,' West himself explained. 'Could have
been. I wasn't there.'

Certainly, Rosemary Letts knew Rena West a great deal more
intimately than she would admit almost a quarter of a century later.
The Scottish woman was a familiar part of both her own and
Frederick West's life. Far from being someone whom Rosemary Letts
had never met, as she would insist at her trial, Rena West had shared
with her the caravan at Lake House, the room at Clarence Road in
Cheltenham, and the flat at Midland Road from time to time. Rena
West was no stranger to Rosemary Letts, any more than she was to
the West family.

But Rena West was almost certainly not at Midland Road when
her daughter Charmaine was murdered. In all probability she was
busy elsewhere, working as a prostitute, hoping, no doubt, that her
daughter was being looked after. Though she may have suspected, or
known, the fate of Ann McFall, it is unlikely that she would have
suspected that Frederick West would harm her first-born child. He
had shown no inclination to do so before, even bringing her back
with him from Scotland in the winter of 1965. But Rena West had
not reckoned with Rosemary Letts.

109

For the determined young woman from Bishop's Cleeve, Frederick West was everything she wanted. What was past was past. Now they were going to make a new life together. And there was no room in their relationship for a third partner, certainly no room for Rena West. The woman intent on 'having their son', as West had put it in his letter from prison, would not allow anyone to interfere with her plan. And by the beginning of August 1971 there was the added danger that Rena West might come to realise exactly what had happened to her daughter Charmaine. There seems no doubt whatever that Rosemary Letts demanded Rena West be killed in case she went to the police about Charmaine.

Fear for the fate of the child may have been the reason for Rena West's going once again to consult Walter West in Much Marcle. Several members of the West family saw her drive out to Moorcourt Cottage one afternoon in August 1971 and walk down to the fields to where West was working. The two of them remained there in conversation for the rest of the afternoon. It could very well be that Rena West went to tell Walter West that she suspected that his son had killed a second time, and that this time she would not cover up for him. But whether Walter West then warned his son that his wife was about to report the disappearance of Charmaine to the police can only be a matter for speculation.

Whatever the truth, one thing is certain. Shortly after her visit to his father, Frederick West decided to kill his wife. She now posed too great a threat to his relationship with Rosemary Letts, and she knew enough to threaten his freedom. Rena West's visit to Much Marcle was the last time that anyone in the West family, including Walter West, saw the twenty-eight-year-old Scottish woman alive. Significantly, near the end of his life West admitted: 'My father and Rena were close. Whether the old man was having an affair with her I don't know.'

In late August 1971, shortly after her visit to Much Marcle, West arranged to meet his wife at the East End Tavern in Barton Street in Gloucester at nine-thirty one evening. 'She was with a gang of Irish blokes' and was drunk by the time he got there, he recalled a quarter of a century later. 'Now Rena was always very loving when she got drunk, and that was how we came to go out there – to our favourite spot near Much Marcle.' Frederick West offered her a lift in a car that he had borrowed from Rolf, the pimp who was now helping him to find clients for Rosemary Letts, and he helped her into the front passenger seat. Half-way to Much Marcle, however, West stopped to help her into the back, ''cause she was so drunk'.

It was dark when they arrived at the entrance to Letterbox Field, on the road between Dymock and Much Marcle, but there was enough moonlight for Frederick West's purpose. He helped his drunken wife out of the car, took a rug out of the boot, and walked up the side of the corn-field in the moonlight to an oak tree on its western edge. 'I woke her up and we got out and we made love against . . . by the tree there, just on the edge of the field,' West told

110

the police twenty-one years later. Shortly afterwards they walked half-way back towards the car, sat on the bank 'and made love again there'.

'Then we went back to the car, and then I lost my head with her a bit and we had a right set-to, and a right row . . . and that was when she ended up getting killed . . . I just smashed her against the gate.' And ended her life, he said, by kicking his wife to death on the ground.

The confession bears the hallmark of every one of Frederick West's many and varied confessions. It attempts to portray him as a man suddenly overtaken by events, a man who acts spontaneously, a man to whom murder simply happens as if by accident. As ever, it is a gross distortion, but one built on a flimsy fabric of truth. In fact, Frederick West had chosen the site at which to kill his wife with considerable care, just as he had enticed her to the spot by preying on her remaining affection for him. There would have been a winning smile on his face as he made love to her twice in that moonlit field in Gloucestershire, a field alongside the one in which he had already buried his former girlfriend, Ann McFall.

It is almost impossible to believe that Rena West would have agreed to go out to Letterbox Field with him on that August evening if she had known for certain that Ann McFall's body was buried within a few hundred yards of the point at which they made love, although it is just possible that she may have convinced herself that she was still his only true partner, the one woman whom he truly loved. It is far more probable that her affection for West was far greater than even he would admit, and that she expressed it in the only way she knew – in the act of intercourse. It is all the more possible, therefore, that Frederick West killed his wife, as he had killed Ann McFall, in the actual act of sexual intercourse.

After his arrest Frederick West maintained at one point that 'I didn't know what to do then. It was the first time I'd been ever mixed up in anything like that, so the only thing I could think of was to bury her in the field'. Though it hardly fits into this 'spontaneous' explanation of her death, West then added that he happened to have a pickaxe and a spade, both of them needed to bury the body, in the boot of the car, as well as a curved two-and-a-half-feet-long Jamaican sabre knife, which he could use to dismember the body: 'I had that give me some years back for chopping nettles,' he explained.

'It was in the middle of summer and the ground was rock-hard,' he explained, so the process of digging a hole took him half an hour. 'Then the problem was it wasn't half big enough . . . and then I realised that I couldn't get her in there, so I then decided to cut her up and put her in there.' Shortly after eleven o'clock that night, Frederick West 'took her legs off and her head off', and buried his wife's body in the hole in Letterbox Field.

One reason why he decapitated his wife may lie in West's experience in the slaughterhouses of Gloucestershire and Herefordshire, as well as his determination not to leave traces of blood either on the side of the road or even in the field itself. He chose a method which he had seen when he had worked as a driver for the slaughterhouse, because he knew how effective it could be in ensuring that as little blood as possible was spilled on the ground. Near the end of his life West would explain to his first solicitor, Howard Ogden: 'When you kill veal, you must cut the head straight off – alive. They don't stun them or nothing, because every bit of blood's got to be got out.' There is every possibility that he laid Rena West's body over the small narrow shaft he had dug for her, and let the blood flow from her neck into the hole.

After he had finished he went back to the cattle trough in the field and washed his hands and upper body, because he had been working dressed only in his trousers. 'It was hot digging, and I was used to not wearing a shirt.' Then, after 'a cigarette', he 'tied all her clothes in a big chunky sweater she wore' and 'chucked them over into a fire' that he insisted was blazing in a nearby field, which West knew as 'The Allotments'.

Letterbox Field, like Fingerpost Field, where Ann McFall's body was buried, was within sight of Moorcourt Cottage. It was a field that he had helped to plough and reap as a child. 'The reason I know all these fields there are because I worked on them when I was a young kiddy . . . I was the only one that would mow it,' West recalled. He also planned with some thought an exact location for her body, burying her remains at the side of the field under an oak tree, not least because the ripe metre-high corn would shield him from any passing car. Besides, West maintained, 'being a farmer all my life, the last thing I wanted to do was destroy the crop . . . so where you get a tree the grain wouldn't grow.'

Though West would insist that he 'hadn't gone out there to kill Rena', and had gone only because 'we always went up there to sit on this bridge and watch badgers. It was quite a romantic little place to sit, actually. You could see foxes and all that, various animals', there is no doubt that he had chosen Letterbox Field for exactly the same reason he had chosen the next field as the final burial site for Ann McFall.

Rena West, like Ann McFall, had served her purpose for Frederick West; each had given him her own version of love. In his mind their deaths were to be his tributes to them, his works of art. For they bore his signature as surely and unmistakably as if they had been canvases he had painted. Both graves were to be within his sight whenever he wanted to see them, both within his control, set beside each other like tombstones in his own personal country churchyard.

West buried his wife within a hundred yards or so of the young Scottish woman's body, and he buried them both in an identical manner. Both Rena West and Ann McFall were buried in thin narrow shafts of almost identical shape and size: twenty-eight inches by fifteen across, and a little over three and a half feet deep. And both women were naked and dismembered when they were shoved unceremoniously into the Gloucestershire soil. Like Ann McFall, Rena West's

112

body was also interred with a number of bones missing, a total of forty-one in all. Her left kneecap was missing, as were a large number of hand and foot bones. Those bones may well have found their way into the boot of the car West had borrowed for the evening, to be taken back to Gloucester, to the small shed he had recently hired alongside his new allotment at Podmore, the allotment where he may really have destroyed his wife's few remaining clothes.

Only one stray item found its way into Rena West's narrow grave: a child's small red plastic boomerang with 'Woomerang, Boomerang' written on it. It almost certainly belonged to her daughter Charmaine, and was West's way of burying the newly dead child with her mother, a grim memento of his power over them both. Frederick West gave his own version of how the four-inch-long red plastic boomerang had found its way into his wife's grave. 'She must have had it in her pocket or something when I took her clothes off. It must have fell in.' The explanation does not hold water, not least because only moments before he had insisted she hardly had any clothes on when they made love – 'only a grey skirt, I think; she never wore much anyway' – and because he took pains to remove everything else that could possibly have identified the body of his wife. It was to be almost twenty-three years before the body of the young Scottish woman was recovered by the police, just four days before what would have been her fiftieth birthday.

Frederick West did not go to visit his father in Moorcourt Cottage the night on which he killed his wife, although he admitted later: 'If there had been a light on, I would have went in.' Instead, he took the car back to Gloucester, and went home to Rosemary Letts, the woman whom he had called 'His Darling Wife' just three months before in a letter which ended 'Mr and Mrs R West forever'. Rena West had been the first woman to expand his sexual horizons, introduced him to the pleasures, and profits, to be had from prostitution, as well as to the excitement to be gathered from more and more deviant forms of sexuality, but now her role had been usurped by a woman whom Frederick West admitted 'was just as vicious as what Rena was', Rosemary Pauline Letts.

Frederick West and Rosemary Letts would maintain steadfastly for almost a quarter of a century that Rena and Charmaine West had gone off together to Scotland, to London or to Saudi Arabia to start a new life together. And no one suspected that it was not the truth. Why should they? Rena West had been coming and going to and from Gloucester for several years, disappearing to Scotland, Reading, London or Manchester whenever she pleased, and certainly not remaining with her children. The local Children's Department had been aware of that since West's return from Scotland almost five years earlier. Charmaine, too, had made no secret of her desire to return to her mother, and she had certainly said so repeatedly at school. Who would be surprised, therefore, if both were to disappear within a few weeks of each other? It was a simple matter for Rosemary Letts to tell St James's School that Charmaine had left for

London with her mother, and for Frederick West to back up her story by telling anyone who asked: 'All her aunties and uncles and that live there.'

That was the version of events that Frederick West stuck to until the last few months of his life. But then, just as he retracted his other confessions, so he retracted the confession that he had killed his wife Rena. Then, instead of accepting the blame himself, he put it all on Rosemary Letts, just as he put the blame for Ann McFall's death on Rena West.

In this revised version of the killing of his wife, which Frederick West gave originally to his first solicitor, Howard Ogden, West insisted that Rosemary Letts had been assisted in the killing of his first wife by the ubiquitous Rolf, whom he had also implicated in the death of Ann McFall. West claimed that Rena West had been killed in their small flat in Midland Road while he was in Leyhill Prison, and then 'dumped in this bloody tank . . . in plastic bags, in the garage and covered up. It was an old water-tank'. In the last few months of his life he told Howard Ogden: 'Rolf cut Rena up with that sabre knife he had – that's how Rose got the notion of cutting them up, because Rolf showed her how to do it.'

Frederick West insisted that Rosemary Letts had told him that she had killed Rena West herself, after Rena had demanded to take both Charmaine 'and Anna-Marie as well'. 'Rena was killed for two reasons, I reckon,' West claimed. 'One was that she caught Rose with them kids tied up', and the other was that 'Rena was getting drunk and getting a bit loose-mouthed, and Rolf was getting sick of her because she wasn't toeing the line.'

In this version Rena West had been dismembered in Midland Road and placed in an old water-tank in the garage at the side of the flat. 'She could've laid in that bloody garage for two years or more,' West insisted. 'The body was actually in plastic bags, and there was a piece of asbestos on top of the bin, and then mattresses and blankets and all that. When I lifted the piece of asbestos, the stink was unreal, even with the plastic bags.' The tank was filled with battery acid and copper piping. 'But I wasn't going to put Rose in prison, having just come out, and I didn't wanna go back,' West maintained. So when Rolf had come round, he, together with Rosemary Letts and West, had taken the body out to Kempley. 'Me and him dug the hole again, and Rose sat in the car. But Rose and Rolf buried her. They tipped her out of the plastic bags.'

This second version of the death of Rena West is only partly convincing, although it is certain that Rena West's remains were the most decayed of any of Frederick West's victims when they were eventually recovered. It is possible that a dismembered body was dumped in the old water-tank in the garage of 25 Midland Road, wrapped in plastic bags, but there is at least a chance that that body in fact belonged not to Rena West but to her daughter Charmaine.

It seems only too likely that West did not bury the child immediately after her death, and did so only after considering for some time

Rosemary Letts, left, then aged three, with her mother Daisy, and elder brother Andrew on the beach in 1956. She was one of William and Daisy Letts' seven children

Frederick West's parents, Walter and Daisy West, in Much Marcle, shortly before his mother's death in 1968 at the age of just forty-four

Frederick West, right, aged two, with his brother John, who was just a year and three days younger than he was. They were the eldest members of Walter and Daisy West's six children (*South West News Service*)

Rosemary's father, William Letts

Frederick West the family man. Here he is seen at home with one of his two dogs, as well as a proud father and happy holidaymaker. Camping was one of West's few hobbies, and one which he kept up until the last years of his life

The new Mrs West with her first son, Stephen, born in August 1973, just nineteen months after Rosemary Letts had married 'bachelor' Frederick West in Gloucester. The first Mrs West, Rena Costello, had disappeared in 1971

Rosemary West at a Halloween party in the cellar of 25 Cromwell Street, Gloucester, which was being used as her children's playroom at the time

Heather West was Frederick West's second eldest daughter, and his first with Rosemary West. Determined and independent minded, she rejected her father's persistent sexual advances throughout her childhood. Her disappearance in 1987, at the age of sixteen, was eventually to bring the police to 25 Cromwell Street with a warrant to search for her remains, which were discovered beneath the patio in the rear garden *(South West News Service, right)*

Family portrait of eight of Frederick and Rosemary West's children. From left to right, Stephen, Mae and Heather stand behind, Tara, Anna-Marie (who is holding Lucyanna), Rosemary and Barry. The picture was probably taken in 1984, shortly after Anna-Marie's marriage and her reconciliation with her parents

where exactly would be the best place to conceal her body. Indeed, it is also possible that he may not have finally buried the girl's body until some months after her death, and shortly before he was due to leave Midland Road. There is no doubt, for example, that his neighbours in Midland Road were banned from the rear garden months later, in 1972, so that he 'could build an extension to the kitchen area', and at the same time encase his young daughter in what amounted to a bunker of a grave, hidden beneath five feet of concrete.

In the space of barely two months, Frederick West had killed twice more. But he showed no outward sign of any difference whatever. Neither he nor Rosemary Letts gave the slightest hint to anyone that anything untoward had happened in their lives. West found himself a new job, at Simon Gloster SARO in the town, where he started work on 2 August 1971, and was to remain for more than a year, while Rosemary continued acting as a part-time prostitute. As far as anyone who knew them at the time was concerned, life returned to what West and his partner liked to think of as 'normal'.

What that meant can be judged from the experience of a young woman who moved in next door to Frederick West and Rosemary Letts in the early autumn of 1971. Elizabeth Agius was then nineteen and the mother of two young children, one a baby of only two months. Not long after she moved in, she was struggling down the front steps of 24 Midland Road with a large pram when she encountered West. He introduced himself, helped her down the steep steps with her pram, asked if she had just moved in, and where her husband was. The young woman said he was abroad. When she saw West a couple of days later, he invited her to 'come in and have a cup of tea' and 'meet his wife'.

In fact, when West introduced Liz Agius to Rosemary Letts that afternoon, he called Rose his 'girlfriend'. And Mrs Agius recalled later: 'She looked about fourteen, and I took it that she could have been his daughter.' Over the next weeks, Mrs Agius became friendly with them both, and offered to act as their babysitter, and West would regularly pop in to her flat in the evenings to ask her if she was 'coming across for tea'. She also noticed that when he did so, West would often 'flick my backside with his hand', even when Rosemary Letts was present.

The search for sexual prey was still the dominant theme in Frederick West's life. On one occasion when Liz Agius babysat for them at the weekend, she asked her next-door neighbours whether they had had a 'nice evening' when they got home in the early hours of the morning. West told her, 'No, we only went driving and looking for young girls', and went on to explain that it was better if he took Rosemary Letts with him, because having another woman in the car meant the girls would think it was safe. He preferred young runaways, 'because they had nowhere to go', and was particularly keen to pick up 'girls between fifteen and seventeen' because 'hopefully they would be a virgin and he could get more money for a virgin' and they could 'come and live with them and go on the game if they wanted to'. Mrs Agius was a little shocked, but took it as a joke, one of West's relentless sexual nudges and winks. When he went on to tell her that he went out on his own as well 'to see what I can find and bring home', she dismissed it. 'Fred always made a joke about sex.' He had even smiled and said to her: 'Oh, what I could do to you!'

In fact, it was not long before the seventeen-year-old Rosemary Letts told her nineteen-year-old next-door neighbour that Frederick West was actually telling the truth, and went on to tell her that she was a prostitute. She earned 'extra money that way' and 'Fred didn't mind a bit', she told her. In fact, he 'liked to watch and listen' to know exactly what she did with her clients. 'There was a hole through the wall' so that he could watch whenever he wanted to, but if he was at work 'she'd tell him exactly what happened'. Then Rosemary Letts told Liz Agius that her husband wanted to have sex with her, and said 'she did not mind a bit'. She even asked if she would consider going to bed with them both at the same time. In the weeks that followed she repeated the suggestion several more times, but each time Mrs Agius refused.

The sexual suggestions did nothing to affect the friendship. 'They were such a nice couple. The type of people who don't hide anything from one another,' Mrs Agius recalled years later. Indeed, the two young women, each with two children, continued to see each other regularly, just as Frederick West continued to try to persuade Mrs Agius to go to bed with him. 'He said he would tie me up, and do all sorts of things to me', and always added, 'I could tie him up if I wanted to', or whip him and burn him with cigarettes. West's endless banter would rarely cease. 'He was a real sweet talker; he could charm most women,' she would remember. But she could only watch in fascination as Rosemary Letts fed his unashamed and ever-increasing interest in sex.

One afternoon Rosemary Letts showed Liz Agius two small shoe-boxes that she kept under the double bed in the front room at Midland Road. One contained an assortment of different-coloured capsules, while the other was filled with sugar cubes wrapped in silver paper. Rosemary Letts told her that they were both 'for protection against disease', although it is much more likely that the capsules were some form of sleeping-tablet, and the sugar cubes were a form of hallucinogenic drug. Frederick West's experiences among the hippies of Cheltenham, and the details of the drug culture that he had discovered then, were now being put to use, as Liz Agius was to discover herself. When she visited Rosemary Letts on the ground floor of Midland Road soon afterwards, she began to feel drowsy shortly after having a cup of tea they had given her. The next thing she remembered, she was to confess to the police two decades afterwards, was 'coming to' naked in bed with Rosemary and Frederick West.

By the time that Rosemary Letts celebrated her eighteenth birthday, on 29 November 1971, she was pregnant again. Anna-Marie was now seven, and her daughter Heather just one. She and Frederick West were hoping for 'their son', and now they were free to marry without her parents' consent. Rosemary Letts would tell her daughter many years later that she had thought they had 'better get married to make things legal', although it seems far more likely that West himself would have proposed they marry, aware that a wife cannot give evidence against her husband.

As West remembered in the last months of his life: 'Rose went to see her parents, because I had nothing to do with her parents through that time, and her father and mother said to her, "Look, he'll just give you a family of kids, then leave you, and not marry you", and Rose came back and said that to me. I said, "Right, let's get married", and that was it.' West booked the register office for the following Saturday morning. The marriage certificate was certainly more important to him than the ceremony, however.

As he did so often, Frederick West aped his father. He chose to marry Rosemary Letts on 29 January 1972, just two days after what would have been his parents' thirty-second wedding anniversary. The wedding was scheduled for eleven o'clock in the morning. 'But I was working until five to, and I was absolutely covered in oil, 'cause I was changing an engine up in White City for a bloke.' Rosemary Letts had to 'beg him to take off his overalls'.

Just as there had been for his first marriage to Rena, there were only two witnesses, and his wife would recall later that one was a friend of her husband's who 'had so many aliases that he had to scribble out the first name he wrote on the certificate'. For his part West would recall simply: 'I was there with my brother and Mick Thorneybrook. They were the witnesses. We came back home. My brother bought a bottle of Bristol Cream sherry. We had a quick drink and went straight back to work.' Frederick West signed the marriage certificate without a qualm, describing himself on it as a 'bachelor'.

The new Mrs Rosemary West watched Frederick West describe himself as a bachelor on his second marriage certificate, and signed the certificate alongside him as a true record of his status. There could hardly be a clearer indication that she knew only too well that Rena West had not gone back to Scotland, or to Saudi Arabia, or to London.

For if Rosemary Letts had seen Rena West take Charmaine away, as she was later to suggest at her trial, why would she not have enquired about her whereabouts when she saw her husband enter the word bachelor on their marriage certificate? The only conclusion is that she knew she was dead. Equally, if Rena West had come to 'collect' Charmaine from Midland Road, as the new Mrs West insisted at her trial, how could she possibly have agreed to take part in the marriage that she clearly craved – unless she knew that her rival could not possibly object? The only answer is that Rosemary West knew very well that both Rena West and her daughter Charmaine had met a violent death, and knew, too, that it was a secret that bound Frederick West to her for ever.

Marriage gave Rosemary West what she wanted: formal recognition that she alone was her husband's legal partner. It acknowledged that she had replaced Rena and become a woman in her own right – something of considerable importance to a child brought up to think of herself as her father's 'baby'. The marriage certificate anointed her adulthood and provided her with a mature confidence that she had lacked before the ceremony. And it demonstrated to the world, and in particular to her father, Frederick's and her love for one another. But their love, a love that they never ceased to proclaim for the next twenty years, was not born of joy, affection or respect, or of romance. It was born of blood, pain, suffering and death, and it craved those dark passions to sustain it.

On the way back from the ceremony, 'Fred found some money in the park which covered the cost of the marriage licence', Rosemary West was to tell her daughter many years afterwards. 'I remember he was over the moon. We had no honeymoon. We just went to the Wellington pub and bought one drink. He asked me what I wanted, and I said a lager and lime. He said: "You have a bloody Coke and like it." '

At the time of his marriage West was still working during the day for Simon Gloster and, after work, for his landlord Frank Zygmunt. It was a routine of two jobs that he would maintain, with only one or two interruptions, throughout the rest of his life. Two jobs satisfied his desire to 'keep busy', and to increase his family's income. Working as an odd-job man, labourer and part-time builder for Zygmunt also meant that he could always be on the move, 'shooting down' to look at something at any time of the day or night, for ever able to conceal his movements. If there was nothing to do, Frederick West would quickly become restive, dissatisfied at being idle, desperate to keep himself busy as if he were trying to keep a demon at bay.

One afternoon not long after his wedding, West burst into the kitchen at Midland Road, after being told that there was no work that evening. The new Mrs Rosemary West, now more than six months' pregnant, was having tea with Liz Agius. Seeing the two women, Frederick West disappeared into the front bedroom, only to reappear minutes later with a pair of handcuffs. Without warning, West grabbed Mrs Agius's left hand, yanked it towards him and clapped the handcuff around her wrist. 'Now I've fucking got you,' he shouted, with a smile. But his new wife was not amused. 'Get them off her,' Rosemary West shouted back across the kitchen. West removed the handcuff, the smile still on his face.

But West was not always so easy-going. When Liz Agius introduced him to her husband in her next-door flat one evening, he stormed off into the kitchen in a rage. When she followed and asked him what the matter was, West told her bitterly: 'He's able to have you whenever he wants and I can't.' A few days later, back in his own flat, he told his astonished neighbour: 'I'll kill him and put him right down there . . .Your husband should be six feet under there. If I can't have you, why should he?' But once again, Liz Agius took it as a joke, another of Frederick West's suggestions not to be taken seriously.

All the visitors to 25 Midland Road were equally forgiving. They had every reason to be. Even though she was now several months' pregnant, Rosemary West was still entertaining her male 'clients' in the afternoons, just as she had done in the past. They were still usually from the local bus garage, although she would also make love with one or two of her husband's friends, including a well-known local burglar, who had stayed with them in the flat from time to time, and their landlord. Sometimes she would suggest someone new, like a man she worked alongside as a barmaid in a local pub, and her husband would make no objection.

Whoever it was, Frederick West would usually stay while the man undressed – 'to see that Rose was all right' – and then disappear, often to watch covertly his wife making love – only to reappear later to join her and her 'client' in the small double bed in the ground-floor front room. Whether he took part or not, West insisted that his wife make as much noise as possible, and talk suggestively, throughout the act of intercourse. 'And I always made love to her again, after they'd gone, like. That was part of the deal.'

One or two of the Wests' neighbours at Midland Road were less enthusiastic about events in the ground-floor flat. But they were less concerned about the stream of visitors than the noisy arguments that would break out suddenly between Frederick West and his new young wife. One source of friction was West's continuing friendship with Liz Agius; another was his habit of disappearing in the evening for hours at a time, leaving Rosemary alone to look after Anna-Marie and Heather. But when one set of neighbours complained to the Wests, they were told to mind their own business. The Wests simply ignored anyone who disagreed with them. And Frederick West did exactly as he pleased. Indeed, he had also started to build a bathroom extension out from the back of his flat over the old coal cellar, just as a few months before he had bricked up the entrance to the basement from the garden. It was as if Frederick West were the owner of the house rather than simply one of the tenants.

In fact, West's relationship with his landlord Frank Zygmunt had grown steadily closer in the two years since he had first moved into Midland Road, and in the early summer of 1972, shortly after Rosemary West gave birth to her second child on 1 June, a daughter they named May June, Zygmunt suggested they should move. There was a house for sale on the other side of the park, nearer the town centre, which had been split up into bed-sitting-rooms, but which was now derelict and to be sold as a single dwelling. The price was £6500, and Zygmunt agreed to lend Frederick West £500 as the deposit, just as he agreed to help him apply to Gloucester City Council for a mortgage for the remainder.

Not that the prospect of becoming a houseowner at the age of thirty did anything to alter West's habits. About four days after the birth of their new daughter May June, Rosemary West wanted to be taken home from the hospital, her husband 'more or less wasn't allowing me to'. She discharged herself, and returned to the ground-floor flat at 25 Midland Road, but there was no sign of Frederick West. She recalled later: 'Anna-Marie was dirty and Heather was a mess.' Sensing the inevitable, Rosemary West went round and hammered on the door of a neighbour. There was a lengthy silence until, eventually, her husband emerged 'flushed and hassled'. Frederick West was unrepentant. He just smiled his naughty boy's smile.

In late July 1972, with Frank Zygmunt's help, Frederick West became the owner of the house that was to remain his home for the rest of his life, as well as his proudest possession, number 25 Cromwell Street. It was all but uninhabitable when the purchase was completed, but one of the first people a delighted Frederick and Rosemary West took to see it was their neighbour from Midland Road, Liz Agius. The couple 'who didn't hide anything from each other', in Liz Agius's words, told her they were going to rent rooms to 'single mothers or single girls as long as they were on Social Security because then the rent got paid'.

It was not the only plan they revealed to their young neighbour, as they showed her around the three-floored semi-detached house. 'There was a cellar with a little catch-door in the floor inside the house,' Liz Agius remembered years later. 'I went down just a couple of steps. Fred said it would make a good playroom for the children when they had parties', if he were to soundproof it. But then West turned to his neighbour and added: 'Or I could make this my torture-chamber.' Mrs Agius did not go down the rest of the steps into this cold, damp cave. Instead, she turned and told him: 'You're dreaming.'

They were macabre dreams, but very soon they were to come true.

Chapter Ten

The cellar

'Your worst enemy,
becomes your best friend,
once he's under ground.'

Euripides, *Herakleidai*

It bore all the hallmarks of a lair. The cellar was dark, dank and windowless, 'like a cold, wet, damp cave', in Rosemary West's own words, when she and Frederick West moved into 25 Cromwell Street in August 1972. The floor was wet underfoot, and the only light came from a single bulb at the top of the narrow wooden stairs that led down from the hallway above. The cellar stretched the length of the house, but without a torch it was almost impossible to see even that, though there was a small grating at the rear. A tall man would have had to bend down to stand, but neither West nor his wife needed to, the wooden beams across the ceiling just inches above their heads. A prison cell would have been more welcoming.

The cellar of Cromwell Street suited Frederick West's purposes admirably. It was remote, but still within sight; he could control who went into it, and who left it, and when. No one could visit it unless he asked them to, and no one could leave it without his permission. There was no window to tempt the inquisitive eye of a passer-by, and the brick was thick enough to be rendered soundproof with the addition of a membrane and some plasterboard. The square vent in the rear wall could be covered up easily enough. It was the perfect place in which to experiment. The first thing he did was to renew the lock on the door in the hallway opposite the front door. West kept one key for himself and gave another to his wife. She wore it around her neck, as she would wear a number of other keys to other rooms in the years to come.

The house above was neglected and run down. The one room back and front on each of the three floors was separated by a simple wooden staircase, and the bare floorboards echoed to the tread. They had been used as bed-sitting-rooms, and were to be so again before

121

long, but they alone were not the attraction to Frederick West. Nor was the small rear garden, bordered by the tin wall of the prefabricated Seventh Day Adventist Church to the right and three trees to the left, which backed down towards St Michael's Square beyond, with an elderly wooden garage just outside the kitchen window. All this was useful for his growing family, but it did not make West's eyes gleam. Only the cellar did that.

In the autumn of 1972 Frederick West started work on the house with the unusual degree of enthusiasm that he was to retain for his house throughout the rest of his life. Number 25 Cromwell Street was to become his proudest possession. In the years to come he would sit outside it and offer to show passers-by around the property, so intense was the pride he took in it. He would spend money on its renovation and improvement rather than spend anything on his family. When he stole, or received stolen property, it was usually for the benefit of his house. It marked him as a man of property, a man to be taken seriously. Much more than a mere accumulation of bricks and mortar, it represented everything that West wanted to demonstrate to the world. It was his kingdom.

But as far as Rosemary West was concerned, 25 Cromwell Street was every bit as much her house as her husband's, and she intended to make sure that West clearly understood that. She wanted a bedroom of her own, apart from him, in which she could entertain her clients, and she did not intend to be taken for granted. She was almost nineteen, the mother of two of his children and stepmother to a third, and she was not about to be ignored. He might think he controlled her, but she was still not 'a big soft chair' to be sat on. And a few weeks after they moved in, she set out to prove it. Rosemary West left her husband and went back to her parents.

Frederick West described what happened, and why, in his last months, and in doing so he explained a great deal about his relationship with the extraordinary young woman he had married. In particular, West acknowledged that while they lived together in Midland Road, 'Rose was actually treated like a schoolgirl by me, and this came to a head in Cromwell Street. Rose was sort of Anna-Marie's schoolgirl mate, and still more or less acted like a schoolgirl sort of thing. That went right on up until she'd had May, and suddenly one morning Rose had obviously realised that she was a schoolgirl part of this marriage.'

'What she did was, she didn't get any shopping in on Friday, and on the Sunday morning she got up early and said, "I'm going out for the day",' which came as a great surprise to her husband, who knew 'Sunday dinner was always something really special'. Anna-Marie elected to stay with her father, but Rose took her other two children with her and disappeared, not telling her husband where she was going. When she had not returned by five o'clock that evening, Frederick West decided to take his daughter and go to find her.

'I mean, I knew exactly where she'd be. I gets there, and I jumps out of the van, because you had to go across the green to her place in

Tobyfield Road, and I crossed the green. By the time I'd got to the door, her father's standing there, protecting his daughter, and he says, "Rose has left you".' Even twenty-two years later the idea made Frederick West laugh. 'So I said, "What's the crack then, what's wrong?" and he says, "You treat her like a child". I said, "Right, tell Rose that I'm going to sit in the van out the front there for ten minutes, and if she ain't there, there'll be somebody else in her bed tonight. There'll be another girl in her bed tonight".' With that he walked back across the small green verge outside the Letts's house and climbed into his van.

Within four minutes Rose was in the van with me and her father's following her, and he's saying: 'Oh, he's only kidding, he's only kidding.' Rose turned round and said: 'I know him, you don't, so shut up, Dad.' And so we went back home and we sorted it out. And from then on, that was where Rose had always had the say in the house, and I've had the say outside, work, my work, and everything.

As Rosemary West left the house with her two children to join her husband in his van, she told her mother Daisy Letts: 'You don't know him. You don't know him. There's nothing he wouldn't do.' More than two decades later, Mrs Letts remembered that her daughter had paused at the doorway, then added as she walked away from her parents: 'Even murder.'

But neither Bill Letts nor his wife took their daughter's remark seriously. 'We just thought it was the words of a highly strung girl.'

It was the first public sign that Rose West was no longer her husband's apprentice, that she had become his junior partner, and an indication that the force of their joint personalities was to prove even greater than his alone. But it would always be Frederick West who would dictate the pace and direction of their activities. No matter how strong her personality, or vicious her temper, it was he who told his wife what to do, and when. She became the creature he had always wanted her to be, and accepted the role willingly, recognising the influence it gave her.

Nevertheless, it was Frederick West who dictated the terms of their relationship. He was still capable of the violence that he had demonstrated to his first wife, still capable of holding her around the throat until the air all but left her lungs, still capable of smashing her head against the door if she annoyed him. He did not break any of her bones, and tried to choke her only when 'he's been angry'. But she was not afraid of the man she was now locked together with in a partnership that would not be broken for two decades. Rosemary West did not believe that he would kill her, confident that in the end her wits would save her from the excesses that she knew he was capable of. Besides, she, too, was capable of violence. Frederick West had been a good teacher.

Rosemary West had grown into an attractive young woman. With shoulder-length dark hair and wide-set brown eyes, she was slender but full-bosomed, with the look of a startled fawn. But the look was deceptive. As her stepdaughter Anna-Marie would remember, she 'made no attempt to hide her cruel streak'. The young mother would push the child's fingers into boiling water, or beat her stepdaughter repeatedly 'for not stirring the gravy in the right way and not mashing the potatoes properly', as well as for failing to hand her a tea-towel promptly enough. 'I was hit across the head with a broom on more than one occasion and I still have a small scar where she knifed my hand.

'It was as if she had mental blackouts,' Anna-Marie suggested, 'almost as if she didn't know she was doing it. When she had finished, she might look at you and say: "Your fucking fault. You should have done it properly." On other occasions she wouldn't speak; she'd just carry on with what she was doing as if nothing had happened.' When the eight-year-old girl complained to her father, Frederick West simply laughed and went back to work on his house. He would work there all day, then set off for the night shift of his new job as a fibreglass presser at Permali's factory on Bristol Road.

In the last months of 1972 West managed to make the cellar habitable. It was not an easy task. In the first week he lived in the house water and sewage had seeped up through the floor, submerging the cellar under two feet of water, a result of both a break in the sewer pipe that ran under the house and a rise in the water table. 'Cromwell Street used to be part of the moat round Gloucester,' West would explain later, 'that's why it was always flooding.' Nevertheless, West managed to divide the cellar into three interconnecting rooms. In the back room, nearest the garden, he kept his tools; the middle room, where the stairs came down from the hallway, he left empty; and the front room he began to convert to a playroom for his three children. He would work down there all day, after getting just a little sleep after his job at Permali's, sometimes bolting the door from the hallway behind him. When he emerged, his eldest daughter remembered the whispered conversation with his young wife, and their giggling.

On the top two floors upstairs, West installed two small kitchenettes, between the front and back rooms, and quickly started to look for lodgers to fill the four rooms. Frank Zygmunt's loan of £500 had to be paid back quickly, and he did not want to waste any time. The rent he intended to charge was £3 a week, and if he could get two lodgers into each one of the rooms, so much the better. His loan would be repaid more promptly. Frederick West offered Liz Agius, his neighbour from Midland Road, one of the two second-floor rooms, but told her 'she'd have to leave' her husband if she wanted to take up his offer. The implication was clear enough: she would have to consider working as a prostitute from the house. But when she refused West did not press the idea; he simply repeated his plan to look for young girls, and single mothers, who were receiving 'benefit – 'cause that way they can pay the rent.'

Rosemary West had different ideas. She wanted young men as well as young women in the house. If he was still pursuing young girls in his van, she saw no reason why he should not supply her with young men in the house. And it was she who won the argument. In the early autumn of 1972, when the first lodgers moved in to 25 Cromwell Street, they were all young men. One was Ben Stanniland, an eighteen-year-old, who shared the top-floor back room with another young man, Alan Davis, always known as 'Dapper'.

On the night they moved in, Frederick West invited them both out for a drink with his eighteen-year-old wife. The conversation was laced with sexual innuendo, and West's nudging questions about their 'girlfriends', full of suggestions that he had no objections whatever to their bringing them back to Cromwell Street. Not long after they returned to Cromwell Street that evening, Rosemary West appeared upstairs in the top back room the two young men shared and climbed into bed with Stanniland. After they had made love, she climbed out of his single bed into bed with his room-mate, Dapper Davis, and made love to him. 'In the morning', Stanniland recounted later, 'we were a bit dubious about going downstairs', but Frederick West 'made it clear it was OK'. What they did not know was that he had been watching them through a hole in the door.

Meanwhile, West told two of his other lodgers that 'if they couldn't pay the rent they would have to have sex with Rose'. He was drawing his young wife further and further into his bizarre sexual world, a world that probably also saw him supply young girls for prostitution in Bristol in return for a fee. Nevertheless, it was a world that Rosemary West found increasingly captivating. She wanted to explore it as much as he did. And if that was also what he wanted her to do to prove her love for him, she was more than happy to oblige. It provided her with a role in her husband's life, and she had no intention of neglecting him as she thought Rena West had done.

But Frederick West had also been encouraging his new wife to experiment sexually. Now eighteen, Rosemary West had discovered that she was attracted to both men and women, and the idea fascinated her husband. What had started as the acting out of his fantasy in making love to two women at the same time in his own bed had been adapted and extended by Rosemary West to West's becoming the voyeur watching her make love to another woman. The more she indulged her own new-found passion, the more excited he became at the prospect. Together, they had then added the element of bondage to their experiments, she anxious to capture a female partner, he to subjugate her so that she would never leave him. A young woman was now not simply to satisfy her husband's desires, but to satisfy hers as well. Now they were both a male and female rapist working in partnership, her bisexuality adding fuel to the flames of his all-consuming secret passion. It was to become a lethal combination.

And as soon as Frederick West had made 25 Cromwell Street habitable, he set out to re-establish the system that he had first used

125

in Glasgow and then taken with him to the caravan sites of Gloucester. He went looking for a new 'nanny' for his children, another young woman to groom as a potential partner, but this time also a playmate for his wife. And, as ever, West went looking for her in his car. Relying on the lodgers to babysit for them, Frederick and Rosemary West resumed the tours they had told Liz Agius about in Midland Road. They drove around the area looking for young women who might need a lift, and who might offer the possibility of sexual excitement. But now there was the added *frisson* of Rosemary West's sexual interest in young women as well as young men.

Shortly after ten-thirty one evening in early October 1972, one of their expeditions bore fruit. Frederick and Rosemary West drew up beside a young woman standing outside a pub in Tewkesbury, less than ten miles north of Gloucester. Just a few weeks away from her seventeenth birthday, Carol Raine was five-feet, two-inches tall, slim, with straight dyed chestnut hair and a wide-eyed smile. She was hitchhiking back to her home in Cinderford in the Forest of Dean from her boyfriend's home in Tewkesbury. Rosemary West spoke first. 'She asked me where I wanted to go,' Carol Raine would remember at Rosemary West's trial almost a quarter of a century later. 'They said they'd give me a lift, and I got into the front of the car.' At the time West owned a two-door beige Ford Popular, an unassuming little box of a car, in which the rear seat passengers had to climb over the front seat to get into the back. His wife climbed into the rear, as Carol Raine settled herself in the passenger seat, and they set off south towards Gloucester. Carol Raine said later, 'A woman in the car was a bonus; you felt safer.'

On the journey West and his wife asked the sixteen-year-old girl why she was hitchhiking and whether she had a job. She told the Wests that she used to hitchhike 'three or four times a week' and that she was unemployed. 'They were quite nice,' the girl recalled later, and by the time the car had reached Gloucester the couple had offered Carol Raine a job as a 'nanny' for their children. 'I was a bit surprised, but I'd always wanted to be a nanny. I told them that my parents would have to meet them first.' When West and his wife had dropped the girl outside her home in Cinderford, not long after eleven that evening, they arranged to come back and meet her mother and stepfather the following Sunday.

The Wests duly arrived at Carol's parents home in Cinderford the following Sunday, bringing with them Anna-Marie, Heather and their four-month-old daughter May June. 'They told Mum and Dad that they'd look after me,' Carol Raine recalled two decades later. 'And the children were cute, actually. I was pleased to get the job.' A few days afterwards the Wests returned to Cinderford to collect Carol and her belongings, and moved her into Cromwell Street. She was to share the first-floor back room with Anna-Marie.

Pretty, impressionable and a little vulnerable, Carol Raine had had sexual problems in the past. West sensed this; his extraordinary antennae had not let him down. An elderly family friend had abused her when she was six, and she had been indecently assaulted in a Gloucester park at the age of thirteen. Each of the experiences made her a perfect target for his sexual attentions, but for the moment West bided his time. Neither he nor his wife objected when her boyfriend came to stay for the night each week, nor did they object when – on the night before her seventeenth birthday in late October – an old boyfriend turned up to stay. The Wests even lent them their double bed in the ground-floor front room for the night, no doubt with a view to his watching through a spyhole in the door. To both Frederick and Rosemary West, Carol Raine must have seemed the ideal 'nanny', a dependent, sexually active young woman who could be groomed to do their wishes.

Paid £3 a week 'spending money', Carol Raine settled into life at 25 Cromwell Street, happy enough in the liberal atmosphere and relaxed sexual code. This was not the stiff world of a parental home where no one was allowed to do anything: quite the opposite. Cannabis and other drugs were available freely among the young people who came and went through the upper floors, visiting the lodgers, staying for a while in their rooms before disappearing again. And sexual intercourse was just as freely available. She herself had sex with both Ben Stanniland and Dapper Davis, just as Rose West had done. As Carol herself put it many years later: 'It was the hippie era and people were generally very friendly.' There is no doubt that sex, and everything to do with it, was the one persistent topic of conversation in Cromwell Street, and the Wests did everything they could to foster the atmosphere. It allowed them to participate in it too. And, as if to prove how liberal an environment they wanted it to be, the Wests made sure that there was no lock on the bathroom door.

Just as he had done at Lake House caravan park, Frederick West started to brag to his new nanny that he 'could do operations' and that he had carried out abortions – 'in case you ever get yourself into trouble'. Meanwhile, his wife got into the habit of walking into the bathroom while Carol Raine was in the bath. Rosemary West would stroke her hair, and tell the seventeen-year-old, 'you've got lovely hair' and 'lovely eyes'. Carol Raine remembered: 'I was a bit embarrassed really, uncomfortable.' The girl was also only too aware that West would pick on his wife from time to time. 'I didn't like Fred. I'd try to stick up for her and he would tell me to mind my own business.'

After six weeks or so with the Wests, their continued bickering, his bragging and the relentless sexual innuendoes began to take their toll on Carol Raine, and she announced that she wanted to leave. Rosemary West did not want her to go, but her husband 'didn't mind one way or the other'. In fact, he did mind. Frederick West was almost certainly incensed that she had refused his repeated invitation to take part in the 'gang bangs' that he and Rose had been proposing, and which other visitors to the house had witnessed with girls other than Carol Raine. Nevertheless, West was careful to disguise his fury behind his perpetual grin, and they parted amicably enough. Carol Raine went back to her parents' home in Cinderford, and back to hitchhiking to Tewkesbury on three or four nights of the week.

Only a few nights later, on Wednesday 6 December 1972, Carol Raine was standing outside a pub in Tewkesbury, trying to hitchhike back to Cinderford, when, once again, Frederick and Rosemary West pulled up beside her in their Ford Popular. Almost twenty two-years later, at the trial of Rosemary West, Carol Raine was to describe the events that followed that evening, events that Mrs West insisted she could 'hardly remember at all'. In contrast, Carol Raine's recollection was particularly detailed, and utterly horrifying.

'I felt a little bit wary,' she recalled. 'But Rose asked me if I wanted a lift back to Cinderford. I said, "Yes". Rose got out and pulled the seat forward for me to get in the back.' Carol Raine climbed in, but rather to her surprise Rosemary West climbed in beside her 'for a chat'. They drove to Gloucester, and then turned south towards the Forest of Dean. After telling the seventeen-year-old that they had missed her and their children had missed her, 'Then they started to talk more in a smutty manner'. Frederick West asked if she had had sex with her boyfriend that evening. 'I was embarrassed and said, "No". He said, "Have a look, Rose", and she grabbed me in the crotch. I had never spoken to them about my personal life before. Rose had her arm around the back of me, and she started touching my breasts over my clothes. I think that's when Fred said, "What's her tits like?" '

Rosemary West was trying to grab hold of the girl in the back of the Ford Popular with her and was laughing – 'not a nice laugh', in the words of Carol Raine. 'Then she tried to grab me between my legs. I was wearing trousers. I was struggling with her. I started panicking. They were saying things to each other. It was smutty talk about me, about my body.' With the street-lamps of Gloucester now behind him, Frederick West pulled the car up on to the grass verge beside a gate to a farm field near Highnam. He stopped the car, turned around, and started to punch the girl. 'He was calling me a bitch and that', and his wife was still struggling with her. After three blows to the mouth and side of her head, Carol Raine passed out.

When she woke up Carol Raine found that her arms 'had been tied behind my back with my scarf', and that both Frederick and Rosemary West were 'putting tape all the way round my head, over my mouth, and round the back of my hair. It was brownish, textured gummy tape. Rose was holding me and Fred was putting the tape round.' The seventeen-year-old was terrified. She could not open her mouth, and could breathe only through her nose. 'I had no idea what was going to happen to me. I didn't think I was going to go home again.' The defenceless girl was pushed down on the back seat, and Rosemary West sat on top of her, while Frederick West turned the car around and headed back towards Gloucester.

When they arrived at 25 Cromwell Street, West got out first to make sure that there was no one about, and then led the bound and gagged girl into the house and up to the first-floor room at the front, which contained a sofa and a double mattress on the floor. 'They told me to keep quiet. Fred said if I was good they would cut the tape off', which after a little time he did, using a sharp double-sided knife, a knife so sharp that it cut the frightened girl on the cheek. 'He apologised. He said he didn't realise the knife had two blades.' Apologetic or not, West then urged Carol Raine to sit on the sofa. 'Rose sat next to me and started trying to kiss me. She was touching my breasts and legs over my clothes. Fred was still there. I said something like, "Get off, leave me alone". She just continued. But I think it was then that Rose went and made us cups of tea.'

For a moment it seemed that the ordeal was over. Frederick West untied the girl's arms and gave her a mug of tea. But there was a naughty boy's smirk etched on his face. Neither West nor his wife had the slightest intention of allowing their former nanny to leave Cromwell Street without her taking part in the sexual plan they had for her. As soon as she had finished her tea, they both started to undress her. Then 'they tied my hands back up and gagged me with cotton wool'. While his wife undressed herself, West led the panic-stricken girl across to the double mattress on the floor. 'I had no clothes on at all. I was put on the mattress on my back.' West then blindfolded Carol Raine, and he started to do exactly what he had bragged he did to so many of his friends over the past few years. He started to examine her as if he were a back-street abortionist.

'It was like being examined in the genital area,' the seventeen-year-old would recall two decades later. 'It was both of them. I could feel fingers inside me. They were discussing my genitals, about the size. They said I had "chubby lips", and Fred said he could improve my sex life. He could flatten the vaginal lips, and the clitoris would be showing more. I'd get more pleasure.' The blindfolded, bound girl recalled: 'I was scared they might put something in me, or even operate in some way.' Frederick West's operation did not involve surgical instruments, however. It depended only on a two-inch-wide leather belt that his father and mother would have recognised at once.

Rosemary West held the girl's legs apart, and West hit her vagina with the belt's buckle about ten times. 'I remember seeing the belt when he was hitting me. I can't remember if the blindfold was taken off, or just rolled up.' No consideration whatever was shown for the helpless girl lying in front of the Wests. Indeed, no sooner had her husband finished hitting Carol Raine viciously with the belt buckle than Rosemary West knelt between her legs and performed oral sex on her. 'Fred was watching and then took his clothes off and went behind Rose and started having sex with Rose at the same time. I could see all this. It lasted only ten minutes or a quarter of an hour.' Throughout, Carol Raine recalled later, 'Rose was grinning and laughing. Wickedly, I suppose. She looked evil to me.' By contrast, Frederick West 'seemed quite calm'.

129

When Rosemary West left to go to the bathroom outside the door, West raped the naked, bound girl, though 'It was only a few seconds', she recalled. But moments after he climaxed, he started crying and apologising for what he had done, and when his wife returned to the first-floor room he did not mention the rape. Instead, West settled down to sleep on the sofa beside her, leaving Carol Raine bound and gagged on the mattress. Not surprisingly, the seventeen-year-old did not sleep. She even tried to escape by getting up and going to the window, but she could not lift it. Demoralised, she went back and lay on the mattress on the floor.

At about seven o'clock the next morning there was a knock on the front door downstairs. 'Fred got dressed and went to answer the door. There was a man's voice outside the door. I tried to make a noise to get this person's attention', but the attempt failed. Rosemary West put a pillow over her head to stifle the screams. 'When Fred came back into the room they were both really angry.' Frederick West told the terrified girl that he would 'keep her in the cellar and let his black friends use her, and when they had finished they would bury her under the paving-stones of Gloucester'. West also told her: 'There's hundreds of girls buried under there.'

But Frederick West did not carry out his threat. Though Carol Raine was utterly helpless on the mattress in front of him, and even though he had already buried the bodies of at least two young women and a child, West decided to keep his former nanny alive, at least for the time being. He was intent on abusing her still further. When his wife went downstairs to see the children, West raped Carol Raine for the second time. 'When he had done it, I was crying.' After he had pulled up his trousers, West again 'started crying', his victim remembered years later, and 'apologised for hurting me'. He told her she was 'there for Rose's pleasure', adding that his wife 'gets hard to handle when she's pregnant' and 'needed a woman to play with'.

As soon as his wife returned to the room, and as if nothing untoward had taken place, Frederick West suddenly announced to Carol Raine that they 'would really like me to come back and live with them'. The astonished girl recalled, 'Fred asked me first, when he was on his own', but she quickly realised that 'this would be my chance to get away from them. I said, "Yes." ' But she also said that she would have to go back to Cinderford to collect her things. Clearly pleased at the prospect, West untied the girl and encouraged her to take three baths and wash her hair, to get rid of the sticky gum that was still stuck to it from the adhesive tape she had been gagged with the evening before.

'I helped clean the room, and saw the children when Rose brought them upstairs.' While she was doing so, one of the lodgers, Ben Stanniland, knocked on the door to borrow the hoover, but she did not say anything to him. She had already decided to stick to her own plan of escape. The Wests wanted to go to the local launderette; not long after eleven o'clock that morning, she went with them. 'Fred went off to park the car or go somewhere and dropped us off.'

Luckily for Carol Raine, Ben Stanniland came into the launderette shortly afterwards, and, while Rosemary West was talking to him, the seventeen-year-old girl seized her chance. Had Stanniland not been there, it is entirely possible that Rosemary West would have set off in pursuit. As it was, Carol Raine left the launderette. 'I just kept walking. I walked straight through Gloucester.'

But Carol Raine did not go home to Cinderford. Too embarrassed to tell her mother what had happened, she went instead to see a friend. 'I didn't tell anyone else straight away.' She just sneaked into her home later in the evening and 'got into bed'. It was to be the following evening before she plucked up the courage to talk to her mother. Then, although her stepfather was reluctant, the police were called. For a moment it looked as though the truth about Frederick and Rosemary West's sadistic sexuality might emerge into the bright light of day. In fact, it was to remain in the shadows for the following twenty years.

Though her face was puffy and bruised, and there were rope burns on her legs and back, as well as grazes where the tape had been cut off, Carol Raine was not exactly treated as an innocent victim. 'The police found out that I had slept with two of the lodgers,' she remembered many years later, 'and made me feel so bad about it that I didn't want everybody finding out. If I had been a little innocent convent virgin it would have been different, but because I'd had partners it was as though it was nothing important.'

Nevertheless, on Saturday 9 December 1972 the police arrested Frederick West at Permali's, where he was working weekends as well as night shifts, and then went on to question his nineteen-year-old wife at Cromwell Street. When one detective asked if Carol Raine's allegations were true, Rosemary West replied: 'Don't be fucking daft. What do you think I am?' And when he then went on to ask if he could search their Ford Popular, she merely added: 'Please your bloody self.' In the car the detective found a button from Carol Raine's coat, and a subsequent search of the house itself revealed both a 'partly used roll of masking tape' and a collection of pornographic photographs. After her arrest, Rosemary West told the police she would not say anything 'because I promised my husband I would say nothing'.

But Frederick West's uncanny sixth sense of what made a victim was vindicated once again. Although Rosemary West admitted a lesbian approach to Carol Raine, just as her husband admitted assault, their victim's reluctance to embarrass either herself or her family saw to it that both he and his wife would be let off. Though there was talk of a charge of rape, the police did not press it. Perhaps West seemed too innocuous, too placid and humble a man to fit the stereotype of a sexual offender at the time, and the police accepted without much hesitation that he and Rosemary West would each plead guilty to one charge of indecent assault, and another of actual bodily harm, if rape was dropped. After being warned about what cross-examination in the witness-box might reveal about her sexual

131

encounters, and with her stepfather still reluctant to see her involved, Carol Raine agreed to drop the more serious charge.

When Frederick and Rosemary West stood beside each other in the dock at Gloucester magistrates' court in the morning of Friday 12 January 1973, West could not have felt more confident. He had done all this before and got away with it. He knew Carol Raine had decided not to give evidence 'to save embarrassment', and he was quite prepared to appear contrite, if it would speed their release. West also knew enough about the legal system to apply for legal aid, even though he was pleading guilty, and not to make the mistake of defending himself. The thirty-one-year-old West and his nineteen-year-old wife listened intently as their counsel made the pleas of mitigation on their behalf. Conrad Sheward painted a portrait of them as a happily married couple, telling the three magistrates that, although his clients were newly married, they had been living together as 'man and wife for two years', and had two children of their own, as well as one from 'Mr West's previous marriage'. Sheward then revealed that Rosemary West was pregnant with her third child.

As he was to do so many times in the years to come, Frederick West had sensed instinctively how to operate the legal and administrative system to his advantage. He may well have consulted his friend and patron, Frank Zygmunt, over some of the details, but his innate ability to confuse those in authority with his special mixture of humility and obsequiousness was being honed all the time. The chairman of the magistrates, John Smith, told both him and his wife that although the court was bound to take a very serious view of 'offences of this description', 'We do not think that sending you to prison will do you any good'. Frederick West bowed to the bench and clasped his wife's hand. For her part, Rosemary West just stared straight ahead. Once again Frederick West had proved to himself that he could get away with anything. More important still, he had proved it to his wife.

Though Rosemary West would strenuously deny that she was responsible for the assaults on Carol Raine, just before the end of his life West was to give another version of the rape, this time one that placed all the blame on his wife. 'Rose had tape in the car, ready to tape her mouth up, and she tied her hands with the whatsername,' West told his solicitor in 1994. 'So when Rose attacked the girl that night, I didn't know what to bloody do.' West confirmed, however, that his wife had suggested that they give her a lift. 'I was busting for a pee, that's what it was, and when I turned towards Cinderford there's a big lay-by, which I knew, and I pulled in there, got out, walked to the gate, dropped me zip, and next minute she screams. I run back to the car, and Rose said, "I got me hand up her cunt". I said, "What?" She got her over on the side, wrapping tape round her and God knows what 'er ain't doing. What can I do? Take the blinking girl home like that?'

Impossible though it is to believe, West insisted that he took Carol

132

Raine back to Cromwell Street to cut off the tape. But when he went to get a knife, 'the next minute when I come back through the door Rose has got her legs open beating her between the legs. I said: "For fuck's sake, keep away from her, leave her." I got her together, and sorted it out, and apologised and everything. That's why we only got fined twenty-odd pound.'

In the last months of his life Frederick West maintained steadfastly that he had never once mentioned anything about putting her under the paving-stones of Gloucester, even though Carol Raine was the second person to remember his threat about burying someone 'down there'. Liz Agius, too, had heard West say her husband should be 'down there', pointing to the cellar, and Rosemary West herself suggested during her trial that her husband had always maintained that the cellar 'was not a place to have pregnant women or small children'.

Nevertheless, Rosemary West also explained that her husband could be both 'very persuasive' and 'very intimidating'. Frederick West, she insisted, 'could charm the birds out of the trees, literally. He had the gift of the gab'.

Frederick West intended to put that to good use. There would be no more mistakes like Carol Raine. In future no one would be given the opportunity to report to the police what he did to them. He did not intend to return to court again, to risk a more serious charge being levelled against him. Carol Raine had been a trial run, an experiment. In future there would be no more mistakes. He would see to that. And the cellar was the perfect place. No one would interfere there. No one was likely to come in.

Chapter Eleven

Suffer the little children

'Great crimes come never singly; they are linked to sins that went before.'

Racine, *Phaedre*

Frederick West was his father's son, and so it was probably inevitable that one of the first people he would choose to abuse in the cellar of his house in Cromwell Street would be his eldest daughter. He had created her. She was his of right, his to do with as he chose. That was how it had always been in his family. He would hear no argument on the matter. In his mind, Anna-Marie West had to be prepared for her sexual role, the bearer of the next generation of Wests, and at the same time she could satisfy his own lust for her. The fact that she was only eight and a half years of age, a plain, innocent, rather reserved little girl, made no difference whatever. If she objected, the new blue polythene membrane he had used to line the cellar's walls and ceiling, to protect against the damp, would muffle any sound.

As West confided to one of his new lodgers in the first weeks of 1973, he had decided to convert the 'cellar into a dungeon' for sex parties. The Carol Raine court case had brought him 'loads of kinky letters', he told him, which had convinced him there was an appetite for 'parties'. In his spare time on the night shift at Permali's factory, he constructed a four-feet long metal bar shaped in a U, with two small wings at either end of the U. To an outsider it might have looked harmless enough, a decoration for a gate perhaps, or the first part of an elaborate signpost, but in fact it had a far more sinister purpose.

It was a purposeful Frederick West who led his daughter and his wife down the wooden steps into the cellar of Cromwell Street early in 1973. Rosemary West shut and bolted the door behind them. As Anna-Marie was to write almost a quarter of a century later: 'As the three of us stood at the bottom of the stairs I suddenly began to get nervous. All of a sudden there was an atmosphere I couldn't fathom.' The girl had been in the cellar before, but 'had never actually played there – I was kept too busy doing the housework for that'. When she asked her father what was going on, he said nothing and looked across at his wife. 'Rose had a strange smile on her face as if she was really going to enjoy herself but wasn't going to say why.'

As another of his daughters, May, would recall after his death: 'Dad used to say the *first-born* child to a daughter should be the father's', adding: 'Dad didn't like us pushing him away. If you did, he used to get quite violent. He had a look which was really scary.' Like many other incestuous fathers before him, West harboured the desire to create another generation of incestuous children. For her part, Rosemary West made no secret of her dislike for her stepchild Anna-Marie. Her own two daughters, Heather and May June (who was to change her name to Mae) were now both walking. To Rosemary, the plain little girl who slept in the ground-floor back room at Cromwell Street was more of a nuisance than a child to be protected and nurtured. Anna-Marie was not hers, and Rosemary West saw no reason why she should not suffer. If she did, she might learn a little more respect for her stepmother.

West told his daughter: 'Just do as you are told. Take your clothes off and put them on the floor.' But the child was not quick enough for his wife. In one movement, Rosemary West ripped her step-daughter's dress off. Then she and her husband pinned the child down on a mattress on the floor and tied her hands and ankles to the U-shaped metal frame West had constructed. He then tore up old sheets into strips to tie her to it. When the child asked what they were doing, she was told to 'shut up and be quiet'. It did nothing to reassure the eight-year-old, who started to scream. Her stepmother sat on her head to stop her, but when the child panicked at being unable to breathe, she took some of the sheeting strips and gagged her.

It is almost impossible to imagine the terrifying impact that this ugly, perverted assault must have had on the eight-year-old child. But the Wests justified it by telling the sobbing girl that she 'should be very grateful, and feel very lucky that I had such caring parents that thought of me'. She was even led to believe that 'all loving parents were acting the same'. In particular, Frederick West told her it would make sure she could satisfy her husband when she married: 'It's going to help you in later life. I'm just doing what all fathers have to do. It's a normal thing, so stop carrying on. This will make sure you get a husband when you're older. You'll be ready for him, and you'll be able to have children.' West then proceeded to take a smooth white plastic vibrator out of a clear Pyrex bowl of water on the floor beside the mattress and insert it into his daughter's vagina.

'I remember the pain as they inserted something inside me,' Anna-Marie was to write in 1995. 'It hurt so much I just wanted to die.' She could neither move nor speak, and she had no idea what was happening, or why. There was also a buzzing noise that she did not understand. While it was happening, her stepmother started 'rubbing and scratching' her breasts. The ordeal 'seemed to take for

135

ever and the pain was so bad I almost lost consciousness.' As it went on, she remembered 'looking at the glass bowl on the floor' and seeing that had filled with what looked like frog-spawn. 'It was all red. It frightened me.' Eventually, Frederick West and his wife removed the vibrator and left their daughter in the cellar. But they did not release her. They merely removed the rudimentary gag, so that she could breathe more easily. 'They just upped and went, leaving me bound hand and foot.' She lay there motionless, save from shivering occasionally with fear and cold.

Unspeakable though it is, the child's ordeal was not over. After a time the Wests returned and assaulted the helpless little girl, tied to a frame on a mattress in the cellar, for a second time, repeating the previous process. Only this time, after they had finished, they released her. But not before they had threatened her with 'a good hiding' if she told anyone about what had happened. Frederick West left his wife to untie the girl. In Anna-Marie West's own words: 'It was the beginning of the agony I was to endure for many years to come. They didn't help me as I struggled towards the daylight, barely able to walk. In fact, Rose laughed at my predicament. She seemed to find the whole thing incredibly funny.' Rosemary West told her stepdaughter: 'Everybody does it to every girl. It's a father's job. It's something everybody does but nobody talks about.'

Over the next few years Frederick West would steadily refine the abuse he subjected his eldest child to, reminding her repeatedly how lucky she was to have this 'preparation' for adulthood. Anna-Marie West accepted the abuse unquestioningly, which almost certainly saved her life. Her acceptance meant that she did not suffer the fate of her fiery, rebellious half-sister Charmaine. West calmly and relentlessly, abused his daughter until she was unable to refuse. He trained her as expertly, and as tirelessly, as a circus trainer might tame a wild beast, making her his creature every bit as completely as he had the young woman who was only eleven years her senior, her stepmother. West systematically abused his daughter, as determined to subjugate her as he had been to subjugate Rosemary Letts. West carefully shaped both their sexual appetites, malevolently encouraging them both to lose any sense of right or wrong, and then he cast them as rivals for his affection.

In the years to come Frederick West reworked the horrifying metal contraption he tied his eldest child to that afternoon in early 1973. His later device was a cylindrical cup, once again with small brackets at each side, designed to attach to a belt around her waist, so that she could wear it all the time, rather than being tied to it immobile. He would place a vibrator inside the metal cup, which was then inserted into her vagina, and force the girl to walk around the house wearing it, dressed only in a little miniskirt. The device 'used to hurt and pinch because it was metal', she would remember later, but 'Rose would get a real kick out of it, and if Dad came home from work and found me in it he would just laugh with her'.

Frederick West had sexual intercourse with his eldest daughter

136

repeatedly throughout her childhood, on one occasion coming down to the cellar after his wife had again tied the young girl naked to the U-shaped metal bar. 'Rose started hitting me with her fists,' Anna-Marie recalled, 'and swearing at me and calling me names.' Her stepmother then hit her with a leather belt, before once again abusing her with a vibrator, 'pushing it deep inside'. Then: 'I remember my father being there. He had work overalls on. I remember looking at my dad, pleading with him with my eyes.' The appeal did no good. 'My dad had sexual intercourse with me, and then he went. I presume it was his lunch hour.' On 6 July 1973, her ninth birthday, Anna-Marie fainted at the swimming-baths at school and was taken to Gloucester Royal Hospital, where she was detained overnight for observation. The staff noticed small cuts and bruises on the child's tiny unformed breasts, but accepted her explanation that they were the result of an accident.

West would also take his eldest daughter out with him in the evenings to steal 'sand and gravel that was on the side of the road', or he took her out at the weekends to the small building jobs he had agreed to do, including the flats he would 'do up' in his spare time after work. 'On other occasions he would do it in the back of the van he used to transport his tools. He would park somewhere remote.' West kept a mattress in the back of the van for the purpose. Afterwards, 'He would ask me not to tell Rose and he would give me a few pounds to buy sweets.' Anna-Marie West wrote many years later:

When my father did these things to me there was almost a sense of affection about it. He would kiss me on the mouth, which I hated. It was almost as if I were his girlfriend, not his daughter. But it was the only kind of love I knew from him, and I never complained. I didn't mind keeping it a secret from Rose. In a way it was something I had over her, something I knew and she didn't.

That was precisely Frederick West's strategy, and his wife responded to it as he predicted she would, by abusing her rival for his affections still further. On one occasion Rosemary West forced her step-daughter into a boiling bath, then spent 'an age' smothering the scalded girl in baby oil, and on another she made Anna-Marie stand naked against a blank wall so that she could take a photograph of her young but developing body. The child was encouraged to believe that she deserved this relentless mixture of punishment and abuse. 'I believed them and so I tried harder to please everyone,' Anna-Marie wrote later. The child, no matter how abused, still wanted to love and admire her parents, and particularly her father.

Frederick West's obsession with sexual experiment knew no bounds. The abuse of his daughter merely fuelled the flames. In the floors above the cellar at Cromwell Street, West watched in fascination as a string of young girls came and went from the upstairs rooms, visitors and girlfriends of his four male lodgers. Ever the voyeur, and yet also consumed by a ludicrous jealousy that convinced him every girl should want to make love to him before any other man, he took to creeping around the house at night to see who was sleeping where, and with whom. He would sit on the wall outside the house to engage the girls in conversation as they came and went, inviting them into his own rooms on the ground floor 'for a cup of tea' and to 'meet Rose'. Each and every young girl West saw he wanted to possess.

Rosemary West was keen to encourage him. Her own sexual awareness, too, had been groomed to obsession. She was as anxious as he was to discover new experiences. The men he invited to their house to share her bed, either with him or without him in it, were a part of her daily life: now not only prostitution but also fascination. But now there were female as well as male partners. She knew how much the idea of watching her make love to a woman excited her husband, but making love to a woman for her husband's benefit – even with his participation – was not enough. She had learned of his passion to possess and subjugate every woman, and realised, too, that the most explicit form of subjugation, the one form of sexuality that was guaranteed to please him, involved placing the woman in some kind of bondage.

At first Rosemary West may have been cajoled or bullied by her violent husband to experiment with bondage, but as her own sexual awareness developed so her pleasure in sado-masochism flowered, until she became as hypnotised by it as he had become. 'I knew Rose was vicious,' Frederick West admitted just before his death. He had seen her viciousness in action. 'Rose was fucking cruel,' he would insist. She had harnessed her own desire, and used it in turn to manipulate her husband with his own obsession. The combination of their two passions was to be far more powerful even than his alone.

At first the extent of his wife's enthusiasm for bondage may have taken Frederick West by surprise. Certainly, towards the end of his life he would tell his solicitor: 'Rose wanted to be tied up, hung up, left in the fields, everything.' At that time he denied that he had ever done so, even though he had told the police two years previously that he had tied her to a five-barred gate near the Gloucestershire village of Minchinhampton late at night and made love to her. 'She wanted me to,' he confessed, 'but there was other blokes doing it to her. Sometimes she came home and she'd been well fucking beaten, mind. She had some deep fucking cuts in her arse and back and that, where she'd been whipped.'

This violent sexuality was to pervade their life together in the years to come. Once Rosemary West had learned of that violence, she had wanted to experience it for herself. West had complied willingly. First the act of bondage between them was probably enough. But as her experience had grown, and her confidence increased, so her desire had grown to violently subdue young women, willing or not, thereby only further fuelling her husband's desire. Carol Raine was lucky enough to survive the experience. But it was a turning-point. Although Frederick West continued to believe that he could always escape punishment for his sexual crimes, Rosemary West was not prepared to take the risk of appearing in court again. If there was the slightest doubt in either of their minds about the safety of letting their victim go, they would urge each other not to take it.

Not that West allowed an atmosphere of violence to permeate life at Cromwell Street. He was too careful to make such an elementary mistake. Bondage and sado-masochism were to be kept under ground, buried deep within his secret world, never to be allowed too near the surface. They were the dark side of his sexual life, to be concealed behind a healthier mask. To his lodgers he presented himself only as an approachable, hard-working labourer and land-lord, proud of his house and his family, but nevertheless with a perfectly healthy interest in anything to do with sex. 'There were so many girls and so many blokes going in and out of the house that I hadn't got a bloody clue who they were,' he explained at the end of his life. 'All the girls, all the blokes, in Cromwell Street, if they wanted to run somewhere, I would take them. All the girls I got on great with. I used to talk fucking dirty to them, and they'd talk dirty back.' The role of the smutty but affable landlord was one of Frederick West's favourites.

Lodgers of all kinds would find their way to the modest square house in the centre of Gloucester. Young men or women might stay for one night only, sleeping on one of three mattresses on the floor of the front room on the first-floor. Or they might share temporarily with a friend or friends in another of the rooms. 'People used to come and go at all hours of the day and night,' one lodger recalled many years later. 'And Fred never seemed in the least concerned. There were girls on the run from local homes, boys who had nowhere to go for the night: endless parties.' At one point that winter about twenty members of the Scorpions motor cycle gang stayed at Cromwell Street for a time. 'And there were always drugs if you wanted them.'

With Frederick West's active encouragement, sex in all its forms permeated the house, and Rosemary West was its principal partici-pant. 'It would be easier if people asked me who Rose didn't have sex with, not who she did,' West said in the last year of his life. 'I mean, there were so many. When I was in Permali's, the blokes were taking an hour off and going up and fucking Rose. I never thought nothing of it.' What West did not say was that he was also charging them for his wife's sexual services. But West's fellow workers were not his wife's only lovers. There were also his lodgers and their friends. Frederick West did not object if they smoked marijuana in their rooms, or took hallucinogenic drugs, just as he did not object if they made love to his wife. He even informed one of them that if she looked 'moody' when he paid the rent to her, he 'should take her to bed'. The young man thought he was joking, but found out that he was not.

Another lodger was not so fortunate. Propositioned by his land-lady, he 'regularly had sex with Rose' while Frederick West was at work. 'Fred knew all about it, just like he knew all about everyone else.' But that did not prevent West trying to strangle the young man one evening, after he had found him asleep in his lounge after clearly having made love to his wife. Waking to find West's hands tight around his throat, a fight had broken out, which resulted in the lodger being charged, and fined, for an assault on his landlord.

On the surface at least, Frederick West would not react so violently towards the stream of young women who increasingly found their way to Cromwell Street. He would make them welcome, grinning as they confided their problems to him, and he suggested they should 'talk it all over with Rose', gently drawing them into the sexual net that he was carefully constructing. Rosemary West played her part to the full, participating in group sex with three of the male lodgers on more than one occasion, sexually propositioning the more amenable girls who came to the house looking for a room for a night or a week.

Lynda Gough was one of the young women who found her way to 25 Cromwell Street in the first weeks of 1973. Five feet, three inches in height, with long straight light brown hair, which she often tied back in a bun, and large framed glasses, she was nineteen at the time, exactly six months older than Rosemary West. An impetuous, friendly girl, who had suffered some learning difficulties as a child, she had lost the tip of one finger in a childhood accident, as well as one of her front teeth, which meant that she wore a dental plate, but that did nothing to curtail her outgoing open smile. The eldest daughter of a city fireman, she had worked as a seamstress at the Co-op in Gloucester since leaving school two years before, where one of her contemporaries had been the missing Gloucester girl Mary Bastholm. Indeed, it is possible that Lynda Gough and Rosemary West may have even worked together as seamstresses at one point, although that was not the reason she arrived at Cromwell Street. The reason was much more straightforward. Lynda Gough had become Ben Stanniland's girlfriend, and she came to the house to visit him.

Lynda Gough and Rosemary West could almost have been sisters. Born within a few months of each other, both had left school without academic qualifications, both shared the same long hair, largish breasts, the same large-framed glasses and slightly surprised smile, and the same interest in sex. Rosemary West would have watched with interest as Lynda Gough's relationship with Ben Stanniland foundered, and Gough transferred her affections to his fellow lodger, Alan Davis. Before long she had sampled the sexual appetites of some of the other lodgers as well, and Rosemary West knew that it would only be a matter of time before she would come to depend on her for help and advice. Young, rebellious and with a streak of mischief, eager to explore the world around her, Lynda Gough rapidly became Rosemary's friend, and a confidante. Frederick West was working long shifts for Permali's, and then going on to help Frank Zygmunt in an effort to pay off the loan, and, on the surface at

140

least, the open-minded, high-spirited fireman's daughter was exactly the sort of friend Rosemary West craved. She could help with the children, babysit for her from time to time, and share her life. As the weeks passed, she saw less and less of the lodgers and more and more of Rosemary West. But Lynda Gough was to become more than a friend. In the early spring of 1973 Rosemary West seduced her.

'Rose was knocking off Lynda before I was,' Frederick West recalled in the last months of his life. 'She used to come there a lot.' In mid-March his wife told him that Lynda Gough wanted a room, and West was only too happy to agree to her moving in, even though he already had four male lodgers sharing the top two rooms at Cromwell Street. The prospect of a pretty young girl, whom his wife suggested privately that she might be able to pass on to him, was too good an opportunity to miss. 'She had a massive bust on her, but the rest of her body was skinny,' West would comment appreciatively years later. Once again he offered a job as their nanny. She could share the room with Anna-Marie, just as Carol Raine had done a few months before.

In early April, just as he had done for Carol Raine, West drove his wife out to their new nanny's home, although this time it was to take the girl out for a drink rather than to satisfy her parents that they were a suitable couple for their daughter to live with, and he took care to stay in the car out of sight when his wife went to knock at the girl's front door to collect her. A fortnight later, during the morning of 19 April 1973, Frederick West went back again to her home near the Oval in Gloucester, this time to help her to move her belongings. Once again he was careful not to be seen. Neither of Lynda Gough's parents were at home. Their daughter left them a simple note: 'Dear Mum and Dad, Please don't worry about me. I have got a flat and I will come and see you some time. Love Lin.' It was to be the last contact that Mr and Mrs Gough would ever have with their eldest daughter.

'Lynda was a bit kinked in different ways,' Frederick West recalled years later, 'because she had black magic magazines. She was into virgin's blood and God knows what. She was a bit fucking weird.' In fact, it was no more than the natural curiosity of many young people, but West and his wife ruthlessly exploited it. Lynda Gough became their willing slave in a series of bizarre sexual experiments. Seduced first into sex with Rosemary, and then with both of them, the Wests then relentlessly proceeded to extend their sexual experiments with Lynda Gough into bondage and sado-masochism. Though the nineteen-year-old could not possibly have foreseen the outcome, it was to lead to her torture, mutilation, dismemberment and decapitation.

It is impossible to say with absolute certainty how Lynda Carol Gough met her death, but Frederick West went into considerable detail in his first confessions to the police. He started by suggesting: 'It was their fantasies I set up for them', and went on to say 'It was new to me, I hadn't had anything to do with that sort of thing much before.' West said the young fireman's daughter wanted to 'bathe in a

141

virgin's blood. That was her fantasy and she was hell-bent on that'. This, he insisted, 'was building up for about three weeks and she was getting obsessed about it by the day'.

Lynda Gough had 'just moved in as a tenant', when West decided to fulfil what he was later to describe as her fantasies. 'She was heavy into this kinky sex and all that, so we worked out . . . or she worked out a bizarre thing to do with tying up, hanging up . . . She wanted to use her hair to bond herself with. She had such long hair.' West recalled that they had 'tried to several times, different ways and that', but 'the problem was the basement wasn't high enough'. West had already cut a slot in one of the beams in the cellar – 'for her hands and that to tie up to', but when he did so 'she was standing on the floor'. So he 'dug a big piece out' of the bricks and stones that lay on the cellar floor at the time, so that he could suspend the girl from the cellar beam. But Frederick West did not hang Lynda Gough up by her hands. He suspended the nineteen-year-old by her ankles, with her head hanging into the hole he had dug in the cellar floor.

'The bondage sex thing was planned up with Lynda. She had no jewellery or glasses or nothing, they were all left in her room, 'cause she came down practically naked,' West explained twenty years later. 'She stripped off and oiled herself, and put funny markings on her face and body . . . off these books she had', using different coloured lipsticks. 'Anyway, she said, "I'm all ready and all this", but then she wanted her bust tied up, massive bust she had on her.' West duly did so. 'Anyway, she was all roped up, and she kept laughing her head off, making weird noises and God knows what.'

By this time, according to West, Lynda Gough was tied up across this hole. West had attached a rope to her ankles, and she was hanging on to it, supporting herself with her arms. 'She had a rope round her neck and her arms were just up in the air for some reason, she was holding herself up like that . . . 'cause then her legs went up and . . . she dropped down on her arms to hold her.' Frederick West pulled the rope tied around Lynda Gough's ankles and lifted the young woman up until she was suspended over the hole in the brick and ash floor in the cellar. 'So anyway, she was just hanging there . . . and she was enjoying every minute of it. Then she wanted me to pour oil over her, and water, and God knows what over her, jelly and something she got, supposed to be love potions.'

Until this point, West's version of the events surrounding Lynda Gough's death may bear some resemblance to reality. But from this moment onwards Frederick West concealed from the police, and from everyone else, the precise details of ordeal that the adventurous nineteen-year-old suffered in that damp, dark cave beneath the paving-stones of Gloucester. The horrifying truth is that she was almost certainly kept captive in the cellar for several days, and regularly tortured and abused, until she was finally killed. Lynda Gough may have started out fulfilling her own 'fantasy', and she ended up part of Frederick and Rosemary West's 'fantasy', and she could never have suspected the sexual abuse, degradation, torture

142

and mutilation that she would be subjected to in the gloom of that sinister basement. The Wests may even have told her that they loved her, but it was not a love that any human being would recognise.

Gagged, tied and hanging naked by her ankles, Lynda Gough was abused sexually by both Frederick and Rosemary West. Indeed, she may well have been expecting some kind of sexual experience. But what she could not have been expecting was the relentless sadistic extension of that experience. Their sexual intercourse with her would probably have been followed by abuse with a vibrator and a dildo, a rubber phallus, in both her vagina and her anus. But the sexual abuse would not have stopped there. Other people may well have been invited to have sexual intercourse with the helpless girl as she hung there in the cellar like a carcass in a slaughterhouse. And the more she twisted and turned to avoid the humiliation and the pain, the greater pleasure Frederick West would have taken from her plight. The greater her agony, the harsher would Rosemary West's actions have become. Then her sexual torment would have been followed by physical torture.

In the hours, even days, before her eventual death, Lynda Gough was reduced to nothing more than a slab of meat. Her fingers and toes were almost certainly cut off while she was conscious, as were her hands and wrists shortly afterwards. Both her kneecaps were removed, as were seven ribs and her breastbone. But she could not speak, she could not protest; she was utterly helpless. She was condemned only to suffer. And the longer she remained alive, the more tempted Frederick West would probably have been to try to keep her so, to extend the experience. The sexual excitement he felt would have grown as the time passed, as would his wife's. Lynda Gough's stricken body was part of the ritual of their unspeakably evil love.

The Wests did not stop. They would never stop, no matter how much their victim pleaded with her eyes. Neither Rosemary nor Frederick West showed any mercy whatever to the helpless young women who had fallen into their clutches, just as they showed not a moment's remorse or contrition. Theirs was a satanic devotion to the pursuit of pain in others, a devotion so fierce that it almost defies description. There was an element of ritual involved in her killing, as West was eventually to hint to the police. Indeed, it may well have been Frederick and Rosemary West, rather than their victim, who wanted to drink blood, as West made love to the mutilated young girl's body as she hung dead in front of him.

Frederick West would never admit exactly what happened to Lynda Gough. At one stage he explained that she was 'getting unbearable' and that he just 'lost his head . . . put a rope round her neck and strangled her', but at another he suggested rather that she had strangled herself by accident. Neither explanation rings true, but in his second version of events West insisted that he was interrupted shortly after he had pulled the helpless girl over the hole in the cellar floor.

'Somebody rang the bell, and somebody answered the door and somebody shouted "Fred". So I thought, Bloody hell, I shall have to go up and see, 'cause they knew I was there . . . they could probably hear us. So anyway I went up, and it was somebody come to see me . . . and I stood there talking to them for about twenty minutes, almost half an hour, I suppose.' Significantly, Frederick West did not recall who the person was he had spent half an hour talking to at the front door; all he could remember was: 'I'm trying to get from them to get back to her because I had no shirt on. I only had just me jeans on, and anyway I finally got away . . . When I got back down, the flipping rope that was holding her legs . . . had snapped and she was hanging there. She was strangled. Hanging by the neck into this hole.'

The story is as much of a lie as West's insistence while he was telling it that 'There is nobody else involved. I did it all on my own.' Indeed, it was a lie which he was to retract in the final months of his life, suggesting instead that his wife 'and another person or persons' had been responsible – that he had had nothing to do with the nineteen-year-old's death. In fact, there is little doubt that Frederick and Rosemary West systematically sexually abused Lynda Gough's helpless body, just as they removed more than 120 of her bones after they had done so. As for her 'laughing', that would have been impossible, as the Wests had placed a surgical plaster over her mouth, and then covered that with a length of two-inch-wide brown parcel tape, which they had wrapped around her head completely, to gag her. Nor was she tied only with rope: strips of fabric were also knotted and tied around her, as was a long length of string.

When Lynda Gough's lifeless body was eventually cut down from the beam, Frederick West set about disposing of it with the same calm, methodical care that he had brought to the bodies of his first wife, his 'angel' Ann McFall, and his stepchild, Charmaine. He cut her head off, disarticulated both her legs at the hips, leaving knife-marks in the upper thighs, and removed the bones he wanted as trophies. But he did not dig a small, narrow hole for her remains, as he had done for Rena West and Ann McFall. Instead, he painstakingly removed her dismembered body from the cellar piece by piece, presumably by pushing it through the small vent at the rear ('There was no back entrance to the cellar at that time'), and threw it into an inspection pit beneath the elderly garage attached to the back of the house. ('It just had a board on top of it'.) West discarded Lynda Gough as if she were no more than another piece of junk that had once littered the cellar floor. He even threw the dental plate she wore into the hole with its one tooth attached, though not her glasses. Frederick West then filled in the pit with the loose earth and rubble from his excavations in the cellar to cover his tracks. And it is hard to believe that there would not have been a smile on his face as he did so.

West would also have made sure he could help himself to whatever money Lynda Gough had in the house. He never neglected an opportunity to steal, no matter the circumstances, and he would not have done so now. Like a modern-day Fagin, he studiously went through her belongings, taking what he fancied for himself, as he did wherever he went, and collecting almost three plastic bags full of other clothing and possessions as he did so. West remembered later that he discarded about twenty 'witchcraft' books at the time, but 'Lynda's bra and pants and all that got flushed down the toilet'.

For her part, Rosemary West took some of Lynda Gough's clothes for herself, just as she helped herself to some of the girl's collection of cheap rings and necklaces. Those clothes that were too blood-stained to wash were pushed into the plastic bags her husband had filled and left out with the household rubbish for collection. Those that were not, she put into the washing-machine, to clean and wear herself. The action appalled even Frederick West. 'I thought, Fuck me, she'd killed her and had her fucking clothes on. She's wearing the girl's shoes and she'd killed her, and her dressing-gown,' West explained in the last months of his life. 'I said, "You wore her fucking clothes after you killed her." She said, "I washed 'em." '

Unlike Ann McFall and Rena West, Lynda Gough was missed after her disappearance into the hands of the Wests. Her parents, John and June Gough, were more than a little concerned about their daughter and her whereabouts, although, as Mrs Gough would explain years afterwards: 'Both her father and I felt, "Let her have her head for a bit, she'll be back." ' The Goughs simply wanted to know if their eldest child was happy, and all right. For a time the Goughs did nothing, but about a fortnight after finding her daugh-ter's note Mrs Gough went in search of her. She visited her daughter's workroom at the Co-op in Barton Street, only to discover that Lynda was not there. Eventually, she discovered that Lynda had been visiting 25 Cromwell Street.

On the first Saturday morning in May 1973, June Gough walked down the side of the Wests' drab narrow three-storey house in the heart of Gloucester in pursuit of her daughter Lynda. The door was opened by Rosemary West, whom Mrs Gough immediately recog-nised as 'the lady who called for Lynda when she went out for a drink' only a matter of weeks before. But she was rapidly joined on the front doorstep by her husband, Frederick West, who told Mrs Gough in no uncertain terms that her daughter was not there.

'I told her mother she'd left,' West admitted at the end of his life. 'I told her, "She's gone to Weston".' But Mrs Gough noticed that Rosemary West looked as though she was wearing her daughter's cardigan, and she was definite that Rosemary was wearing her daughter's shoes. 'But those are Lynda's slippers you're wearing,' she told the nineteen-year-old Mrs West. 'And there's some of Lynda's things' on the washing-line in the garden. Frederick West did not flinch. 'I told her she'd left 'em behind.'

'There wasn't a great deal of conversation forthcoming' after that, Mrs Gough would recall in 1995. She and her husband would go to visit Weston-super-Mare in search of their daughter, just as they would consult a policeman neighbour, telling him of Mrs Gough's experience at Cromwell Street, but they would never officially report their daughter Lynda as missing. Like thousands of other parents with missing daughters, they would simply hope that one day she would walk up the path to their front door. It was a hope that was to be destroyed when Lynda Gough's remains were recovered from beneath the bathroom extension of the Wests' ugly, square little house at 2.25 p.m. on Monday 7 March 1994. As Frederick West himself admitted in the last months of his life: 'That was the first one at Cromwell Street. There ain't no doubt about that, because the basement was stones then, bricks, just bricks laid on that ash stuff.' But it would not be the last.

Lynda Gough's disappearance was explained to the lodgers by Rosemary West. She went upstairs shortly after eight o'clock one morning and told one of them that she had 'hit our daughter while she was babysitting' and that 'she wouldn't be coming round to the house again'. Not one of the lodgers questioned her explanation for a moment. Why should they? By this time there were eight young men living in the four rooms on the top two floors of Cromwell Street, each paying £3 a week, and to every one of them Frederick West seemed every bit as harmless as he must have done to the police. Always grinning, always cheerful, he was nothing more than an unexceptional, ordinary bloke. As one lodger put it more than twenty years later: 'He was a very placid man', although 'totally obsessed with sex. He never tired of talking about it, and he was unable to hold a conversation on any other subject'. Young women might be coming and going constantly in the house, but all the while Frederick West was simply 'hammering', 'doing do-it-yourself' and working 'down the cellar'. The lodgers did not pay all that much attention to him.

For a moment, just for a moment, the Wests must have held their breath in the summer of 1973. Lynda Gough had been missed, and her mother knew that she had been at Cromwell Street. The chances had to be that a policeman would arrive before too long to ask questions. In fact, not one but two policemen did arrive that summer, but it was not to investigate the disappearance of the Gloucester fireman's daughter. Instead, Detective Constables Castle and Price raided the house, and the lodgers, for drugs: 'Two or three times a month for years', Frederick West would recall years later. 'That's where I come to know him [DC Castle] very well.' West maintained that they had come round after Lynda Gough's disappearance to search one of her lovers' rooms, 'and they found heroin needles'.

The drugs raids were the beginning of West's long relationship with the police, a relationship that would lead to his convincing almost every officer he ever dealt with that he was no more than a small-scale thief and fence, who ran a 'relaxed' lodging-house in the city centre, a place where the lodgers sometimes smoked cannabis and experimented with other drugs. Frederick West's deliberately

146

humble, self-effacing approach to all forms of authority drew the police into his net just as effectively as it drew in impressionable young women. What neither group suspected was how great the degree of arrogance that humility concealed.

Astonishing though it may seem in retrospect, the fact that West was almost certainly supplying young girls for prostitution in Gloucester and Bristol; the fact that he was encouraging his wife to act as a prostitute in his own house, and charging his workmates for her services; the fact that he was prepared to keep young women prisoners in his cellar until they agreed to provide him and his friends and clients with sexual services; and the fact that a number of young women went missing from his house – all went unnoticed.

Detectives came and went regularly in the upper part of Cromwell Street, looking for drugs, and on one occasion actually arresting one of the lodgers for possession of cannabis, but they did not sense that the landlord may have had entirely different, and much more frightening, criminal ambitions. As the psychiatrist and child-abuse expert Dr Eileen Vizard put it after his death: 'Frederick West must have learned quickly how to ingratiate himself with the authorities who became such a familiar part of his daily life, grooming them just as he had groomed Rosemary West to trust him, and – in their case – to underestimate him.'

Frederick West's docile servility served only to underline how insignificant he was, how little notice needed to be taken of him, how little regard he seemed to deserve. As the years passed, and no policemen arrived at his door to enquire about the whereabouts of missing young girls, so his approach to the police became more and more confident and more sophisticated. Still humble, West may have considered offering titbits of information about the Gloucester underworld to officers he felt comfortable with, and whom he wanted to trust him. He may even have considered offering police-officers his wife's sexual favours, but it would not have been an obvious bribe, more the offer of friendship. It would have been exactly the same technique that he used to entice young women into his house: Frederick West took exceptional care never to appear dangerous.

Chapter Twelve

The master builder

'The sleeping and the dead
Are but as pictures; 'tis the eye of childhood
That fears a painted devil.'

Shakespeare, *Macbeth*

For a few weeks in the summer of 1973, Frederick West curtailed the late-night expeditions in his recently acquired second green Austin A35 van, and concentrated instead on building an extension to his house. Rosemary West was only a few weeks away from giving birth for the third time, and the Seventh Day Adventist Church next door in Cromwell Street was being rebuilt. It seemed an appropriate moment. West recruited several of his lodgers to help him move the elderly wooden garage from the back of Cromwell Street to the bottom of the garden, and then he started to erect a ramshackle lean-to in its place. The idea, he told the lodgers, was to create a small bathroom on the ground floor. Now there would be four children in the lower floors of the house, and the family needed more space. But West did not do the work alone.

Rosemary West helped him. 'She could mix plaster all right. She dug holes, everything,' West would recall many years later. Indeed, one visitor to the house not long afterwards recalled seeing her putting tar on the extension's roof by lamplight in the darkness, wearing a heavy coat and wellington boots, while heavily pregnant. When she complained of feeling tired, West suggested that she have a daily glass of Sanatogen. But the purpose of the twelve-feet-long by six-feet wide extension was not only to provide a bathroom and shower for his growing family at 25 Cromwell Street. The new building would also conveniently cover the garage's former inspection pit, which now contained the remains of Lynda Gough.

On 19 August 1973, not long before her twentieth birthday, Rosemary West gave birth to her third child – the son that she and her husband had longed for since they had lived at Midland Road. It was the first birth that West himself attended. Frederick West had already decided to christen the boy Stephen Andrew West – Stephen after his own father's middle name – and made plans for him to be baptised in a local church, as they had done for both their other children. 'We were very pleased we had Stephen – our first boy,' Rosemary West would recall years later. Almost from the moment he was brought back to Cromwell Street, his father called him 'Boy' rather than Stephen, as his own father had called him.

Then, quite suddenly, Frederick West found he had not one but two sons. A few weeks after Stephen West's birth, West's past caught up with him. Not in the shape of Lynda Gough's parents, or indeed any other relative of one of the women he had killed, but in the shape of his former lover from Scotland, Margaret McAvoy, who had given birth to his son in July 1966, whom she too had christened Steven. Unsettled, and increasingly unhappy, Margaret McAvoy had traced the man who had driven her around Glasgow in his ice-cream van, and become her lover, with the help of the Department of Health and Social Security, and an official of the DHSS had arrived at Cromwell Street to suggest that he might offer financial support to the child and his mother. Frederick West had refused point-blank, but Margaret McAvoy had then written to him herself, asking if he would look after Steven for a time. Only too aware that the last thing he wanted was a full-scale investigation by the DHSS, or any other official body, West agreed reluctantly to look after his illegitimate son.

'Margaret couldn't drive,' West would recall, 'except me up the wall. So we got a lift off Rose's Dad, who'd just been made redundant, to collect the boy. He took us to Preston in his new Mazda . . . She was on the verge of a nervous breakdown, that was the whole problem.' Frederick and Rosemary West met Margaret McAvoy in a car-park, where the seven-year-old was handed over to the father he had never met and a young woman who was most certainly not his mother. He was to remain in their care at Cromwell Street for the next six months or so, another burden for Rosemary West to bear on her husband's behalf, and another child who would feel the rough edge of her tongue, and her temper.

When Rosemary West unpacked his suitcase back at Cromwell Street she discovered that he still wore nappies in bed at night, which brought back memories of another of her former charges, Charmaine, and which did nothing to endear the boy to her. Over the next few days she introduced Steven McAvoy into the bizarre, sealed world of Cromwell Street, a world in which he would not be expected to talk to other children, to bring friends home, or indeed to do anything at all Rosemary West disapproved of. He would also not be expected to contact his mother.

Steven McAvoy was sent to St Paul's School in New Street with Anna-Marie West for a time in the autumn and winter of 1973. 'At home in the evenings I would try to teach him to read and write properly,' Anna-Marie remembered two decades later, 'but it was very difficult for him.' Rosemary West did not make matters any easier. She complained that he had never been trained to look after his belongings, or to help in the house. She hit him when he called her 'Stepmum' not 'Mum', and snapped at him continually, growling that she had to bully him to get him to go to school, and that he was 'disruptive' when he got there. Years later Steven McAvoy would explain that Rosemary West had punched and kicked both him and Anna-Marie repeatedly, dragging them by their hair around the sitting-room at Cromwell Street.

Anna-Marie herself remembered one incident in which her stepmother 'launched herself at us' after she had found a letter from Steven's mother which Rosemary West neglected to hand on to her son. She had been reading the letter to the boy when her stepmother had returned unexpectedly. 'Neither of us were quick enough to get away. We were still on the floor and easy targets as her fists and feet flailed. Steven probably came off the worst. She ground her stiletto heel into his face and just missed his eye. To this day he still has a scar there.'

But the seven-year-old boy was not subjected to physical abuse alone. The Wests also drew him into their sexual world. Both Frederick and Rosemary West treated him as they did their other children. West called the first-floor bathroom, which had no lock on it, his 'conference room'. His younger daughter Mae would explain later: 'Dad would call us in while he was on the toilet and we'd have to sit on the edge of the bath and talk to him.' Rosemary West expected Steven McAvoy to do exactly the same thing when she was in there, either in the bath or on the lavatory. But it did not stop there. Just as she did her other children, she also encouraged him to watch her making love to her husband.

Steven McAvoy learned quickly that Cromwell Street was no ordinary semi-detached house in an English county town, just as Frederick West was no commonplace householder. If West came home from work early, he might eat an onion like an apple, or make himself a snack by putting a thick lump of lard straight from the chip-pan on to a piece of bread. He would never wear new clothes, preferring instead to wear anything he found or stole from his building jobs. When his wife bought him a new pair of jeans, he used them as a draught-excluder for several months before putting them on, insisting 'they were too clean'. West would scour the pavements of every street he walked down looking for loose change, and would take special care to search the ground around telephone boxes, ''cause you always find money there', and 'he moaned if he had to spend fifty pence'. As his daughter Mae recalled: 'At least ninety-nine per cent of the contents of the house were stolen, including the lino on the floor.'

Inevitably, Steven McAvoy visited the cellar in Cromwell Street, and discovered that by this time West had put in two half-glazed doors with frosted glass in the plasterboard walls he had constructed to make it into three separate rooms. Frederick West himself remembered that the boy had found 'two old gas-masks in the front basement room – the one nearest Cromwell Street', but he did not elaborate on the uses he might have put them to. In all the period that Steven McAvoy was staying with the Wests, Frederick West was just a little more careful about whom he invited into the cellar of Cromwell Street, and what went on there. Steven McAvoy might be his illegitimate son, but he did not want to take unnecessary risks while the boy was still in contact with his mother.

But the stream of visitors to Cromwell Street did not abate during Steven McAvoy's time there. The eight male lodgers continued to come and go relentlessly, and Rosemary West's father Bill Letts became an increasingly frequent visitor now that he had taken retirement from Smith's Industries. Indeed, it was probably Letts and his daughter who persuaded Frederick West to take a holiday that summer, and to leave Cromwell Street for a week's break on a caravan site at Westward Ho! in Devon, close to the Letts' family home in Northam.

As Mae West remembered: 'Dad would never have bothered to take us all away, but Mum nagged him and nagged him.' But the prospect of sex in a caravan again almost certainly proved too great a temptation to refuse. It had been one of Frederick West's passions since his days at Sandhurst Lane in Gloucester, where he had enjoyed unsettling the neighbours by making love to Rena West so noisily that some of them had complained. Something about it satisfied the exhibitionist within him, the man proud of his priapic prowess, so proud that he delighted in astonishing his fellow residents on a caravan site. 'My first sex with Rose was in a caravan,' he recalled cheerfully towards the end of his life.

But now there was an added attraction: the prospect of sharing the experience with Bill Letts. In 1973 Frederick West set out to manipulate his father-in-law just as he had manipulated so many of the other men and women whom he came into contact with. Though West was capable of describing Letts as 'an evil bastard', with 'that little round face and little beady eyes', and a man who had that 'evil look', that was only a subterfuge to conceal how close the two men were in their approach to sex and to young women. Letts was to become another willing victim of West's rapacious sexual drive, the older man relentlessly ushered in to the perverted sexual world that he had created with his wife.

In the beginning Frederick West was more than prepared to tolerate Bill Letts's sexual relationship with Rosemary. 'He was never sexually abusing her,' West maintained at the end of his life. 'She was more willing than he was. I caught them at least half a dozen times, and she was enjoying it.' But it did not stop there. Letts, almost certainly, became one of the men whom West would invite to participate in the sadistic sexual practices that he carried out in the cellar of Cromwell Street. Indeed, at one stage West even considered converting the cellar into 'a granny flat' for Letts to live in, so close had they become and so keen was he to sustain their relationship. The two men, both abusers, and both in turn hypnotised by

Rosemary West's sexuality, forged a link in 1973 that was to last until Letts's death in 1979.

For her part, there is no doubt that Rosemary West exploited their fascination with her throughout their holiday in Devon together, satisfying both her husband and her father at various times during their stay, and relishing the sexual charge that she drew from the experience. It was the first real opportunity for her to rebuild the relationship she had always enjoyed with her father, and explore the new power it gave her over him, while at the same time it allowed her to exploit Frederick West's appetite for voyeurism. Beyond even that, it also allowed her to satisfy his appetite to spend time in bed with her and another man, even if that man was her father. Rosemary West may even have sensed that in the very act of sleeping with a girl and her father, West was reliving something of his own childhood in Much Marcle, but whatever the exact truth there can be no denying that Frederick West maintained in the last months of his life: 'Rose's father was heavy into her, and she was heavy into him, because what Rose tried to do, I think, was to get me the same as him.'

With Rosemary West's willing assistance, West and his father-in-law were to come to share a common bond that was to bind them together for the rest of their lives, a bond so close that only Rosemary West would ever fully understand it. In the years ahead Bill Letts would become as important a part of life at Cromwell Street as the children. But he was not the only relative to assume a central role in the lives of Frederick and Rosemary West at Cromwell Street. There was another: Frederick West's younger brother John.

John West, only a year younger than his brother, was to become as regular a visitor to Cromwell Street as Bill Letts, and for not dissimilar reasons. He, too, came to fall under his elder brother's manipulative spell. 'They always had a strange relationship,' West's son Stephen would maintain years afterwards. 'Very strange.' John West had become a Gloucester council dustman, whose round included Cromwell Street, and he had taken to visiting his brother's house every afternoon after his round was over. Sometimes he would bring a toy he had found on the round as a present for the children, and sometimes he would come just for a cup of tea.

As Frederick West gradually renovated and extended Cromwell Street, so he carefully invited those people he trusted to share some of its secrets and perversions. And once his visitors had been invited in, he was reluctant for them to leave, just as he was reluctant for the young girls who were to become his victims to leave. 'Dad never wanted anyone to leave him if he could avoid it,' his son Stephen would explain after his father's death. 'He could never stand the idea.' So, though Rosemary West may have physically abused him, neither she nor her husband were anxious to relinquish Steven McAvoy once he was in her hands. Both saw it as a threat to their power.

By the late autumn of 1973, however, Margaret McAvoy had recovered sufficiently to want her son returned to her. Neither

Frederick West nor his wife made any attempt to do so. In fact, they did exactly the opposite, refusing her persistent requests to return her son. West liked the idea of having fathered another son, just as he liked to boast that he had at least one other illegitimate son in Scotland, whose parents ran 'a coach company'; and he might even have 'twenty or thirty children up there'. Now that he had Steven McAvoy with him, and his wife seemed to want to keep him, West saw no reason to let him go. Indeed, he ignored the whole matter for months.

'So then she put the Social Services on to me – like for holding her son and all this,' West would recall. 'And I said: "Look, Margaret, if you want him, come and fetch him, he's here." . . . Anyway, Margaret did.' According to Frederick West's version of events, Margaret McAvoy had wanted him to drive the boy back to Scotland, but West had refused, and thought nothing more about it until the Social Services had arrived to support her claim. Only then had he relented. His daughter, Anna-Marie West, remembered many years later that Margaret McAvoy had been forced to break into the house to take her son away, but West himself remembered only: 'Eventually she and her sister came and took him back on the train.'

Frederick West's appetite for sex was as persistent as ever. Even though there were now four children, aged nine, three, one and three months, living with him and his wife in the ground floors of Cromwell Street, sex was still his obsession, his only hobby. He still spent whatever spare time he had combing the streets of Gloucester and the surrounding area for likely girls. Not that he would always have to go out to find them. A steady stream of young women still crossed the threshold of Cromwell Street to see the lodgers, just as Lynda Gough had done. Some of them came alone, some brought their friends. Then their friends in turn would arrive at Cromwell Street to see the men upstairs, or to see if there were any drugs for sale. But most of all, perhaps, to discover precisely what the attractions were of this modest square house that had developed such a reputation among the young floating population of Gloucester.

Frederick West regarded any girl who found her way to Cromwell Street, by whatever means and for whatever reason, as 'fair game' and 'begging for it'. "Cause what we used to have in Cromwell Street . . . from about eight o'clock in the morning you'd have girls from seventeen, eighteen, nineteen leaving to go to work and they had their drug parties at night up there . . . then you'd get all the teeny-boppers coming in then for the day . . . And then they'd disappear about half-four or five and then all the girls come back in. It was just a continuous flow going in and out all the time.'

If they did not find their way to his door, West went searching for them, exactly as he had done for more than a decade. At heart, Frederick West was still a poacher, for ever on the lookout for prey, and happy to seize it whenever it presented itself, no matter where that might be. And, as ever, he was quick to sense the likeliest targets, the vulnerable girls who needed someone to confide in,

153

someone to listen quietly as they poured out their stories of broken homes and unhappy childhoods. West had quickly realised that one of the most fruitful sources of girls were the local children's homes.

When he picked them up, West would often ask them cheerfully: 'Oh, don't your boyfriend take you home?' In the last months of his life he recalled: 'It was just conversation I made. It's a typical thing to say to a girl when you pick her up late at night, you know. Why ain't your boyfriend took you home, 'cause normally a boyfriend takes them home. You don't leave them to thumb a lift on their own.' If they proceeded to explain about how they had fallen out with their boyfriend or their parents, West would take care to appear sympathetic, anxious to 'help 'em out in any way I could'.

These were the girls whom he lured into his house, gently beckoning them with promises of help and friendship, calming their worst fears with the prospect of a bed for the night and the support of his wife. They were the young women who were to make up the majority of his victims, the innocent and the vulnerable, young women who all too often did not fit into the pattern of a conventional family life, and who were therefore only too willing to respond to his apparently unconditional offer of kindness.

Once they had taken the bait, however, Frederick West would seldom let them out of his grasp. If they were sexually promiscuous, he might first seduce them himself, or offer them to his wife for her to seduce them, but if they were not, it would not deter him. If they turned down his propositions, that would make him only more determined than ever to have them. They might be drugged or beaten until they were prepared to allow him to satisfy himself and anyone else West invited to take part in their sexual torment, before being pressed into prostitution for his financial benefit, either operating on an *ad hoc* basis out of Cromwell Street or passing into the hands of a local pimp. 'He simply couldn't bear any girl leaving him,' his daughter Mae explained after his death. 'He would do anything to keep them, just as he would do anything to hang on to his own children.' Frederick West would rather kill them than let them leave voluntarily.

No one can say for certain where or when Frederick West first met one such girl, Carol Ann Cooper, who was always known as Caz. But she fitted precisely the pattern he so often searched for. Caz Cooper may never have visited Cromwell Street, but she would have known girls who had. She may have met West in one of the cafés in Gloucester, where he would still play the one-armed bandits and watch the young girls come and go with their boyfriends. Caz Cooper was certainly friendly with one or two bikers, members of the Scorpions who had camped at Cromwell Street from time to time, the same sort of young men that West had spent so much time with as a younger man in Newent, roaming the countryside on his 1000-cc motor bike. She may have spoken to him without remembering him, or been introduced to him without knowing. Or he may simply have spotted her across the café and waited for his

154

opportunity to engage her in conversation.

Frederick West would have smiled and offered to buy the young girl a cup of tea, just as he had offered Rena West a cup of tea twelve years earlier in another café in Ledbury. Or he may have watched her leave the café and stand at a bus stop, just as he may have watched Mary Bastholm leave work and stand at a bus stop almost six years earlier – indeed, just as he had watched the young Rosemary Letts do at about the same time. West may even have stood waiting beside her at the stop, engaging her in conversation as they waited together, and then sat beside her on the bus journey, just as he had done with his wife.

One thing is absolutely certain. Frederick West would have watched the fifteen-year-old girl carefully before he approached her. In spite of his outward appearances, he had become a methodical, watchful man, conscious that he had a great deal to hide, and not prepared to risk acting too spontaneously. He would have listened as she told him the story of her life, gently drawing out the details of her parents and whether she was alone.

Carol Cooper could hardly have been a more perfect candidate for Frederick West's attention. As her friends maintained years afterwards: 'All she wanted was to be loved.' West would have offered that above everything. The bait that he proffered to young women like Carol Ann Cooper was the love that she and many other girls like her craved, the love of an ordinary family. Born in Luton in April 1958, the child of parents who had separated when she was four, she had lived first with her mother, who had died four years later, and then with her father, who by then had remarried and moved to Worcester. That relationship, too, was destined to fail, and in 1971, Carol had been taken into care by the local authority and placed in the Pines Children's Home in Worcester. She was then thirteen.

As Carol's time at the Pines wore on, so she became steadily more rebellious. A tall, strong, outgoing and determined girl, she took to running away for a day or more at a time, and to occasional bursts of shoplifting. She herself tattooed the word CAZ on her left forearm, as well as a series of dots on the knuckles of her left hand; she dressed in denim and the regalia of the bikers she met on her forays into Worcester and the surrounding countryside. By the age of fifteen, she was sometimes spending the night with them in stationary railway carriages. By the late autumn of 1973, when she crossed the path of Frederick West, Carol Ann Cooper was five feet, six inches tall, with shoulder-length brown hair, blue eyes, a small scar on her upper lip, and a broad devil-may-care smile. As one friend put it, she 'would do anything anyone asked her, right or wrong, because she was seeking attention all the time.'

On Bonfire Night in 1973, a firework had gone off in Carol's left hand, burning her as it did so, and when she was allowed to leave the Pines on Friday night that weekend, to stay with her grandmother, her left hand was still bandaged. At lunchtime the following afternoon, on Saturday 10 November 1973, she met her boyfriend of the time, Andrew Jones, in Worcester, and together with a large group of friends they went to the Odeon cinema. After watching the film they went on to a local fish-and-chip shop and sat on the steps of the Scala cinema to eat them. The plan was for Carol to return to her grandmother's home that evening rather than the Pines, because she had been given her first weekend pass, which allowed her to sleep elsewhere.

But she did not set off at once. 'Carol and me had been getting a bit niggly with each other,' her boyfriend remembered many years later. 'She put her arms around me and asked me to kiss her, but I wouldn't. She was standing opposite me. I think she was crying and I went over to her and made it up.' They arranged to meet again the following evening at six o'clock, and Andrew Jones then gave the fifteen-year-old girl her bus fare for the trip to her grandmother's. At 9.15 that evening, Carol Ann Cooper climbed on board a number 15 bus at The Trinity, in the centre of Worcester, to make the short journey to Warndon. She never arrived.

The bus journey was not long enough for Frederick West to have engaged Carol Ann Cooper in conversation for the first time, and there is no evidence that he ever violently abducted anyone from a public place. But at some point during the brief journey she certainly encountered him. And it is highly unlikely that it was for the first time.

Many years later Frederick West would insist that he had known Carol Ann Cooper 'for probably twelve months', and that he had 'met her in a café in Tewkesbury', although he 'didn't see her a lot . . . it was just a couple of times a week or something'. At another point he maintained he had picked her up 'when she was hitchhiking' from Worcester to the Pines Children's Home some time earlier that week in November. Indeed, it seems highly likely that Carol Cooper had visited Cromwell Street, possibly as a babysitter, before her disappearance on that Saturday evening. She would simply be one of the scores of young girls who found their way to the house, attracted there by its reputation for drugs and its relaxed sexual atmosphere.

The truth of the matter is that West almost certainly arranged beforehand to meet Carol Cooper on that Saturday evening in November 1973, drawing her into a secret with him which he pledged her not to 'tell anyone'. Indeed, it is even possible that he may already have been her lover. As a number of other impressionable young girls had been before her, she may well have been flattered by the attentions of this older, more worldly man, and been fascinated by his extravagant stories. He, in turn, may have suggested that she get an early bus from Worcester that evening to allow him time to take her to Cromwell Street, with the promise that he 'would run her home' afterwards. Whatever the precise ruse, Carol Ann Cooper never reached her grandmother's home at Warndon. Instead, she found herself in the cellar of 25 Cromwell Street.

As he was to do on so many other occasions, Frederick West gave several conflicting versions of what happened to Carol Ann Cooper after she had reached Cromwell Street, but in each one of them he insisted that he knew her before the night she disappeared. He even had a nickname for her – 'Skinny' – 'for the simple reason that I didn't shout out her real name when I was making love to her and nobody else'. West described her as a 'fairly big girl' with a 'd-i-y perm', and called her 'a prostitute in Tewkesbury', adding: 'She was quite professional in her job . . . making love.' In his first version of her death, given to the police shortly after his arrest, West suggested that he killed her after picking her up in his lorry and making love in a 'lay-by on the Worcester road' near the Bunch of Grapes pub.

> She's sat in the lorry. She didn't put her clothes back on. She just sat on her clothes in the lorry naked . . . and I said, 'What do you want to sit like that?' or something . . . and I said, 'You're going to have to get dressed . . . because we're going out into the lights now' . . . and she said, 'Oh, let's make love once more' and then we made love again . . . and then she said, 'Of course, this will cost you double', and I said, 'What do you mean, cost me?' . . . and she said, 'Well, it will, or I'll scream rape on you' . . . I hit her straight over without even thinking.

West maintained that then he took her body back to Cromwell Street, where his wife was asleep in the ground-floor front room. 'Anyway, I checked that Rose was asleep and there was nobody about, and I went down in there and dug a hole and put her in.' He then suggested that he 'cut her up' with his nine-inch-long sheath knife, which he kept 'on the right-hand side of me belt'. The reason he brought her back to his house, he suggested, was that he had no means of digging a hole; otherwise he 'would probably have buried her on the way back somewhere . . . out round Tewkesbury some-where . . . I wouldn't have taken the risk of bringing her back if I'd have had . . . something to bury her with'. West also maintained that he did not know she was only fifteen years of age. 'She certainly looked a lot older than that to me, and she acted a lot older, I mean sexual-wise.'

The significance of Frederick West's first version of the events surrounding the death of Carol Cooper is that he insisted throughout that his wife knew nothing about it. 'Rose had nothing to do with it,' he told the police after his arrest. 'Rose didn't even know anything.'

Towards the end of his life, however, West totally altered this version of Carol Ann Cooper's death, and put the blame firmly on his wife's shoulders instead. 'The first I seen of her was at home, at my place. I didn't pick her up nowhere. I took her back on a motor bike. I don't know how she got back to Cromwell Street . . . She was only at the house, as far as I know, one day . . . I came home from work and she was there.' In this second version West maintained: 'These girls were always in the bloody bedroom with Rose, that's what I couldn't understand. It seemed a peculiar place to keep girls. I said to Rose, "That's a schoolgirl, she can't stay here." I took her to

Worcester, and dropped her. That was the first time and the last that I'd ever seen her.'

But then he added: 'Rose told me it was kinky love sessions that went wrong. That's how the girls came to get killed.'

In the last months of his life Frederick West insisted that Carol Cooper's death was just one example of his wife's attitude to sex and to women. 'I think the cruelty bit in her was for women, she wanted to hurt women. She'd have to do what she's done to them.' In his words, Rosemary West was 'fucking strong. I had a fucking job to handle her at times, mind, when she got rough with me', and she had become addicted to sado-masochistic sex. 'I'd be making love to Rose and all of a sudden she'd smack me in the bloody face, nearly take your bloody head off. Then she'd say, "Do the same to me! Do the same to me!" '

In the last months of his life Frederick West insisted that he would never agree, but every indication is that it was only under his tutelage that his wife had grown increasingly violent in sexual relations. Indeed, it is more than likely that the first person to be suspended from the beams in the cellar of 25 Cromwell Street and sexually abused was Rosemary West herself, and that she and her husband then decided to subject other people to the experience.

The inescapable fact is that Frederick and Rosemary West both knew perfectly well how Carol Ann Cooper came to die, and why. Although West threw up repeated smokescreens to conceal the ugly reality of what they both planned, and executed, in the cellar of Cromwell Street, when the remains of the poor fifteen-year-old's body were eventually recovered from the floor in the centre of the rear section of the cellar, it was only too clear that she, too, had been sexually humiliated, tortured, mutilated and dismembered, just as Lynda Gough had been only seven months earlier.

There can be little doubt that Carol Ann Cooper, too, found herself suspended above the same hole in the brick and ash floor. The discoloration of the soil which contained her remains, when they were found, indicates that her dismembered body decomposed where it lay – three feet beneath the cellar floor at Cromwell Street. Almost certainly, Carol Ann Cooper met her death exactly as Lynda Gough had done, hanging from the beams in the cellar of Cromwell Street above the hole that he had dug specifically for the purpose. This time, and on each occasion in the future, it is more than probable that Frederick and Rosemary West added extra dimensions to the sexual humiliation and torture that they subjected their victim to.

The Wests clearly made sure Carol Ann Cooper could neither move nor cry out when they abused her. There was an elasticated band of cloth three inches wide and six to eight inches in diameter wound around her jaw and lower face like a headband when her remains were recovered from beneath the cellar floor. It was a more elaborate form of gag than the one Lynda Gough was forced to wear, as this time it was not only made up entirely of surgical tape, but was also wound several times round and round the head. Along with it were two pieces of braided cord, like dressing-gown cord, as well as loops of fabric, which must have made up part of her bindings.

Frederick West never admitted that Carol Ann Cooper died in bondage in the cellar of Cromwell Street, although he did confirm that 'kinky sex' was the reason for her death. Once again he was at pains to conceal behind other explanations the ugly truth about his crimes, explanations that to any other man – and to almost any police-officer – would seem horrifying enough. To admit to a senseless, brutal killing was his way of keeping his and his wife's secret: that they had, in fact, killed in infinitely more terrifying and repellent ways, after sexually humiliating and abusing their victims for several hours or days.

It is certain that Carol Ann Cooper was abused sexually by both Frederick and Rosemary West. Once again, rape would have been followed by abuse with a vibrator. Both Wests may have flayed her with a cat-o'-nine-tails and burned her flesh with cigarettes, as West himself had suggested that Liz Agius did to him. And Frederick West would have taken infinite pleasure in watching the horror and fear in the gagged girl's eyes as she hung in front of him. Once again, other people may have been invited to abuse her while she was kept alive in the cellar, and once again the sexual torment was followed by physical torture.

When Carol Cooper was eventually recovered from the narrow hole three feet beneath the cellar floor, fifty of her bones were missing, including most of her wrist bones, and thirty-five finger and toe bones. The conclusion is inescapable. They were cut off by the Wests, almost certainly while she was still alive. Her pain would only have increased the pleasure of her captors, her terror only increased their sense of power over her. Like Lynda Gough before her, Carol Ann Cooper was reduced to a carcass above the hole in the floor in that grim, dank room, and then, like her predecessor, this fifteen-year-old girl was disposed of, as if she were no more than a lamb to the slaughter.

Carol Ann Cooper may even have been still alive when her head was severed from her body between the fourth and fifth cervical vertebrae. But even death did not bring an end to her humiliation. Her head was not simply dropped into the hole beneath her. It was kept and placed in the hole the right way up. Her legs were disarticulated from her pelvis at the hips, with the help of a sharp knife, leaving fine cuts on her thigh bones. There were cuts on other bones as well, and the lower third of her breastbone was entirely removed. Indeed, it was never recovered from her grave. Like so many other bones, it was to disappear as mysteriously as the Wests' victims. And all this took place while Frederick and Rosemary West's children were asleep directly above them on the ground floor of 25 Cromwell Street.

When Rosemary West was shown a photograph of Carol Ann Cooper in April 1994, twenty-one years later, shortly after her arrest for her murder, it was one of the few occasions on which she showed any emotion. She began to cry. It is the clearest evidence there could be that she remembered only too clearly what happened to this vulnerable, open-faced young girl who only 'wanted to be loved'.

It is all but impossible to imagine what must have been in Frederick West's mind as he climbed back up the wooden stairs from the cellar after dismembering Carol Cooper's body and dumping it in pieces in a small hole in the ground. But he no doubt told his wife 'not to worry' as 'he'd sorted it out', just as he no doubt went into the garden to wash the blood off his chest and arms with a hose. He would probably have demanded a cup of tea, as he did on so many other occasions, and then made himself a sandwich by cutting the end off a large loaf of bread and putting irregular-shaped chunks of cheese on top of it, as if he had just returned from a day in the fields.

Murder had become a matter of routine to Frederick West. Carol Ann Cooper was merely another victim. As the forensic psychologist Professor David Canter puts it: 'His victims had become arbitrary objects. His objective was violent control over others, and control over his own anger towards women.' West's desire for the love he had always sought as a child had been translated into a search for 'true love', a love that he could trust, but which itself concealed the darker desire for sexual conquest. Once a young woman had complied with that, she could not truly love him, and could therefore not be allowed to survive. Once West had possessed her body, it had to be kept as a trophy of his success, and a grim reminder that this was one certain way that a woman could be trusted never to leave him.

West did not believe for one moment that he was going to be caught. He had chosen Carol Cooper with care. He knew it was unlikely anyone in her family would connect her with him, his wife or his house. Mrs Cooper was not going to arrive on his doorstep as Mrs Gough had done, for the simple reason that no one in her family would know that she had even been there. As far as the world at large was concerned, Carol Ann Cooper had simply disappeared into thin air, and that was precisely what he had planned. He had even taken the trouble to bury the bandage on her left hand along with her.

An obsession with aberrant sexuality had become the focus of Frederick and Rosemary West's life. Every spare moment was now devoted to it, every thought directed towards its further exploration, every opportunity to extend its experience to be seized without hesitation. What had begun as a fascination only a few years before had become a fully fledged addiction. The Wests would go to extraordinary lengths to attract young women, resorting to subterfuge in unexpected ways. Shortly after Carol Ann Cooper's disappearance, for example, Rosemary West took to visiting the local nightclubs in Gloucester, calling herself Rose Letts and describing herself as a 'nanny' to this family in Cromwell Street. More than one young woman found themselves friendly with the now twenty-year-old woman without realising that she was married to the man she introduced as her brother 'Fred'. Rosemary West may have been doing so – in part – to establish her own independence from her husband. For his part, Frederick West was happy enough – if it brought another young woman to his door. His son Stephen was one day to explain:

> Dad saw sex in everything. You could never get away from sex. If he went for a walk in the park with the dogs he would see people at it on park benches, even though none of us could ever see anything. He would say that girls had run out at him, waving their knickers in the air, or that they'd begged him to make love to them on the side of the road. He was obsessed with sex . . . Dad was never discreet. Mum never wore underwear, and the first thing he did when he came home was to stick his dirty hand up her skirt and smell it . . . Our parents didn't care. They didn't give a damn . . . It was like making a cup of tea for them.

Certainly, Frederick West made no secret of his obsession at Permali's, where he was still working, though he, like most other factory workers in Britain at the time, was just about to go on to a three-day working week in response to the international oil crisis in the wake of the Yom Kippur war in Israel in October 1973. West would invite some of his fellow workers to 'pornographic films shows' in his cellar every Sunday from noon to six o'clock and brag to them that he could 'persuade' girls to go into prostitution by 'keeping them locked up in a room without food and water', although he and his wife 'would always have sex with them first'. But West's workmates simply thought he was making up the stories.

For all his openness about his sexuality, Frederick West nevertheless took meticulous pains to conceal much else in his life. He would pretend to have only one elderly A35 van, but also keep a motor cycle elsewhere, just as he would rent an elderly caravan without telling anyone. He would insist that 'all he had in the world' was 25 Cromwell Street, yet also secretly hire an allotment and a shed in another part of Gloucester. He would appear to have no money, yet somehow always find 'pounds at a time – lying in the street', 'which he'd probably really stolen', according to his son Stephen. West liked nothing more than to appear no more than a simple labourer, a jobbing part-time builder, but he would always be on the lookout to steal or receive stolen property.

No matter how straightforward and predictable West may have appeared, he took elaborate pains never to reveal anything about himself or what he was doing if he could possibly avoid it. Frederick West took pride in his growing nickname of Freddy the Fox, "cause no one can ever work me out'. On the surface he seemed only too understandable, yet beneath he was a secretive, elusive man, a man never prepared to answer a direct question unless he had to. As his younger brother Douglas once said of him: 'Fred was not the sort who volunteered information without being asked a question, and you couldn't be sure you got the truth from him if you asked him.'

Ever active, West filled his days during the three-day week at Permali's by doing more work for his old landlord Frank Zygmunt. The Pole wanted six flats constructed in two houses that he owned in Midland Road, and West was only too happy to help. The extra money meant that he could pay off the loan on Cromwell Street more quickly. He was always ready to fill his time by making money, as Rosemary West filled hers by looking for more clients as a prostitute.

On the surface West was as keen as he had always been on his wife's activities as a prostitute. He liked to watch, just as he sometimes liked to participate, and the extra income was welcome. But West was still, on occasions, ambivalent about it. As his daughter Mae would record years afterwards: 'Dad was quite happy for her to do it, as long as she got no enjoyment from it. She couldn't do anything right. He was jealous, even though he wanted her to do it. She had to pretend to the customer that she was having a good time. But if Dad thought she was really enjoying it, then he'd go straight upstairs and punch her.'

In her turn, Rosemary West learned a great deal from her husband, practising her own form of intimidation on her children, and particularly on her stepdaughter Anna-Marie. 'To watch her go into one of her major rages,' the girl would remember many years later, 'was like watching a horror movie. Her expression would change: you would see coolness transforming her face. Then her eyes would disconnect. When she got really angry and began to hit you, she would froth at the mouth and spit.' Rosemary West would hit the child with a thick black leather belt that she had taken to wearing under her clothes, often dampening it before hitting her, 'to inflict as much pain as possible', as her husband had taught her.

They used Anna-Marie as a guinea-pig for their other sexual experiments, just as they had used Charmaine West before her. 'They frequently practised forms of restraint on me. It was usually Rose who did the tying up. Sometimes I would be tied with my hands behind my back, sometimes tightly in front of me . . . I might be secured to the bed with my legs spread-eagled or bound together . . . She seemed to be trying to establish which way caused the most pain.' The materials used varied. Old sheets would be ripped into strips as bindings or a gag, builders' rope or nylon clothes-line used as restraints, and carpet tape as another form of gag. 'She had canes and whips, including a cat-o'-nine-tails . . . She might use just one of them or a selection. When she had completed her experiments she would encourage Dad to rape me or they would both insert objects into me.'

Beyond even the abuse of their children, Frederick and Rosemary West's evil partnership had been cemented with the deaths of Lynda Gough and Carol Ann Cooper; as well as the secrets of Mary Bastholm, Charmaine and Rena West. Tutored by her husband, Rosemary West had learned to manipulate his appetites by showing

162

him forms of sexual violence that he might not have imagined without her help, while for his part he delighted in forcing her into ever more extreme forms of perversion. The combined force of his perversion and her violence had become a lethal concoction, one so deadly that it almost defied belief.

Chapter Thirteen

Slaughter of the innocents

'Alas, that spring should vanish with the rose!
That youth's sweet-scented Manuscript should close.'

Omar Khayyám, *Rubáiyát*

Dirty and dishevelled, his hair caked with sweat, his fingernails filled with the fibreglass of Permali's factory, his overalls dark with grease and stains, Frederick West was never clean and tidy. 'It was impossible to persuade him to take a bath,' his daughter Mae remembered after his death, 'absolutely impossible.' With his gypsy looks and his smutty conversation, he was a filthy, leering little gnome of a man, a man whom some women might find repulsive rather than attractive.

And yet, and yet, he was so much more than that. West's appearance was but his first camouflage, for like a chameleon he would change coat and colour whenever it suited him. He would not have looked out of place in the costume of Mr Punch or the court jester, because his eyes would have glinted with the same devilment, and he would have waved his truncheon or his staff with exactly the same abandon. In spite of the grimy overalls, he was the likeable rogue, and one who could charm a woman.

For no matter how unattractive Frederick West may have appeared, there can be no doubt that he had a powerful impact on many young women. Nor did he have to rely for his success on violence or abduction. There was something in him that attracted women anxious to mother him, and to participate in what they might have seen as his 'naughtiness', unaware that his perpetual grin concealed a far, far darker truth than they can possibly have imagined. No matter what we now know of West's murderous record, there were many young women who found him, in his own daughter's words after his death, 'great fun to be with'.

Frederick West was no haunted loner, brooding in his room for days at a time, prepared to venture out only at night, like some modern-day Mr Hyde. He was no Jack the Ripper, Dennis Nilsen, or even Hannibal Lecter. West was a gregarious man who took pleasure in sitting outside his house in the evening engaging passers-by in conversation, a man who was for ever taking complete strangers into his living-room for 'a cup of tea' and to meet his wife. West thought nothing of talking to people in the street, or in the park, nothing of engaging in lengthy conversation the waitress in the café he had just 'slipped into' for a moment, nothing of smiling broadly and complimenting a girl on the colour of her dress or the sheen in her hair. And it was not only vulnerable, unhappy young women, the refugees of care, who fell for his particular, devilish charm.

Lucy Partington was not a runaway, nor was she a waif and stray who had once been in care: quite the opposite. Born in March 1952 and educated at Pates Grammar School for Girls in Cheltenham, she was a twenty-one-year-old third-year undergraduate at the University of Exeter, studying medieval history and English, when she encountered Frederick West. Her parents were divorced; her father Roger, a PhD from Oxford, was a research scientist with ICI in the north of England, and her mother Margaret worked in an architect's office in Cheltenham. Lucy was the third of their four children, and the novelist Sir Kingsley Amis was her uncle. Bright, serious and dedicated, she was a member of the university's medieval music group, the Musica Ficta, and was hoping to do a further degree at the Courtauld Institute in London. In November 1973 Lucy Partington had converted to Roman Catholicism after undergoing instruction from a priest in Exeter. She could hardly have been a less likely victim for Frederick West.

But unfortunately for her she looked astonishingly like Rosemary Pauline West. They shared the same dark shoulder-length hair, parted in the middle, the same shy and slightly surprised smile. More than that, she had exactly the same long hair and glasses as Lynda Gough. It was a look that particularly appealed to West.

On 20 December 1973 Lucy Partington returned to her mother's home in Gretton, a few miles north-east of Cheltenham, for the holidays. She spent Christmas with her mother and brothers, and had planned to set off to visit her father on Teeside on the morning of Friday 28 December. But the evening before she went to visit her friend Helen Render at her home near Pittville Park in Cheltenham. Disabled and all but confined to a wheelchair, Helen Render was one of Lucy Partington's oldest friends, who called her 'Luce the Moose', and the two young women spent the evening discussing the future. While they were together, Lucy Partington even composed a letter to the Courtauld Institute applying to study for an MA in medieval art. She took the letter with her when she left Helen shortly before ten-fifteen that evening. Lucy Partington was never seen again.

It was sleeting on the evening of 27 December 1973, and Lucy would no doubt have pulled up her collar against the wind as she walked down Culrose Close and Albemarle Gate towards the bus stop on the Evesham road to catch the last bus to her mother's house in Gretton. But, like Mary Bastholm before her, Lucy Partington

165

disappeared from somewhere near a bus stop, although this time one on the Evesham road in Cheltenham rather than one on Bristol Road in Gloucester. What exactly happened to her remains one of the most unhappy mysteries in Frederick West's murderous career. For the twenty-one-year-old student was not to be found for more than twenty years, when, at last, her remains were unearthed from beneath the cellar floor at 25 Cromwell Street.

What is not clear is how, precisely, they came to be there. For Lucy Partington had no known connection with Cromwell Street or Frederick West. She was certainly sensible enough not to accept a lift from a man, or a man and woman, at night without a considerable amount of thought. She had not visited the Wests. She had not visited their lodgers. She was not a resident of a local children's home. She was not a vulnerable teenage girl who might fall for the blandishments of a man who seemed to want to help her. And yet Lucy Partington must have accepted a lift from Frederick West at some point on that December evening in 1973.

Frederick West himself insisted that he had known Lucy Partington for some months before she disappeared. He also insisted that they used to make love regularly in Cheltenham's nearby Pittville Park, and that he had even given her a nickname, 'Juicy Lucy'. According to West's first version of events, on this particular December evening in 1973 he had been waiting for her when she left her friend, and Lucy Partington had been sitting in his van waiting for the bus to arrive when they had started to argue. 'She said she wanted me to run her out near her home or summat, and what she was actually saying was "Come and meet my parents".'

In his first confessions to the police, West maintained:

So I met her this night, and picked her up, and what she'd done, she'd found my phone number . . . 'cause she come the loving racket . . . and wanted to come and live with me and all this rubbish . . . anyway, we had a row over it . . . I mean, it was always made clear to these girls that there was no affair, it was purely sex, end of story, and if they ever tried to threaten to tell my wife . . . they could be in serious trouble.

Anyway, I reminded her that I said . . . like, any messing with my home and you're in deep trouble . . . and, oh, she got quite nasty about it. She said I wanna come and live with you and all this crap, and I just grabbed her by the throat.

West then suggested that he had killed Lucy Partington in his van that evening, driven her body back to Cromwell Street, and pushed it down into his cellar through the vent in the back wall.

Though it is difficult to believe, Frederick West insisted repeatedly, throughout his police interviews that he and Lucy Partington had been 'having an affair' for several months, and that he had first met her 'in the early summer' when he had taken his children to the boating-lake in Pittville Park on a Sunday afternoon. 'I got going with her after,' West said firmly. 'It was all secret, hush, hush.'

I met Lucy as I said in the first place, in the park, right, in Pittville Park . . . when I was walking the children. I was sat on the seat talking to her, and they were playing, throwing stuff in the lake, you know, and feeding the ducks and all that. And then I took the children home and I arranged to meet her back at night, and I came and met her on that hill, and, um, we had a bit of sex romp and that, and that was it. Then I didn't see her again for a long time, for a while, quite some time, then I met her again, that was on the other side of the park . . . I was there with the children then again, and Rose was there somewhere. But I think Rose was down on the swings . . . and I took them up to see the peacocks up the top and . . . I seen her and I went across and had a chat to her . . . and then I met her the following night again. Then I didn't see her for a while after that.

West remembered the twenty-one-year-old well. 'Fairly slim, shoulder-length black hair, a student,' he explained in the last year of his life. 'I had the children with me when I met her, and that's what fascinated her towards me. I think it was the children; she came talking to them and that.' Certainly West knew that she 'used to catch a bus from Pittville Park', because 'she had a mate up there', and he maintained steadfastly that she would meet him either before or after she 'had been to see her mate'. West said that he used to 'park in Pittville Park and wait for her . . . I met her quite a few times', keeping the van out of sight.

'I mean when we met, like . . . it was sex and virtually straight away, and then had a chat, used to lie on the grass and have a chat, and then probably sex again . . . because we only met more or less in the dark, like, in late evening . . . She was a very talkative girl, actually; she used to try and cram I suppose a week's news into a couple of hours, like . . . 'cause we get on well together, I mean, too well, that was the problem.' West agreed to meet Lucy Partington in the park, he claimed, because he was afraid that his wife's parents, or her brothers, might see him. 'Her brother used to walk that road regular, all hours of the day and night, to his girlfriends in Cheltenham . . . and he did catch me and Rose once in the park, or seen us, and went back and reported it to his parents . . . And the last thing I wanted them to do was to go and tell Rose I was meeting another girl in Cheltenham.'

As a result, West claimed, he would never risk taking Lucy Partington to a pub or a café, or indeed to anywhere else in Cheltenham, for fear of encountering his brother-in-law. It was this fear of discovery that had caused the difficulties that night. He said that the twenty-one-year-old undergraduate had 'got my phone number and address from somewhere, and if I didn't go with her properly or something, her wanted me to see her parents, her wanted me to do bloody everything. Then she was going to ring up Rose, go and see my wife, tell her we were having an affair . . . because she reckoned I was taking advantage of her.' It was this threat, West maintained fiercely, that led to his strangling her in the park, putting her body in the van, and taking her back to Cromwell Street.

Yet again this was not to be Frederick West's only explanation for the death of one of his victims. Ever anxious to portray himself as a fertile man who fathered children whenever he had even a brief sexual relationship, West went on to suggest that Lucy Partington was pregnant when she confronted him on that December evening in Pittville Park. In this expanded version West said they made love, and then she told him: 'I'm pregnant and I want a thousand pound off you . . . or eight hundred pound . . . for an abortion.' West went on to explain: 'That's where the row took up there, because I don't reckon she was pregnant. I think she was having me on. So then we had a violent row, and that's how it all happened . . . All I can remember,' he added, 'we had one almighty row . . . argument and practically a fight in the back of that park, 'cause she was threatening me.'

Both versions of Lucy Partington's death are difficult to believe. After Frederick West's death, for example, her mother, Margaret Partington, explained that her daughter had 'barely spent any time' in Gloucestershire or Cheltenham during 1973, and certainly not long enough either to have met West or to have embarked on an affair with him. Her mother insisted that she had simply been too involved in her work, and in travelling throughout the year, to have had even the opportunity to consider it.

Shortly before his death, however, West remained adamant that he knew Lucy Partington well. 'I mean, I ought to know when I met somebody . . . We used to meet in the park . . . and then whatever we'd be doing we done, and that was it, and then she would go off up across the bank.' West accepted, however, that he probably had not used his real name. 'She knew me as Steve . . . I used the name Steve quite often . . . Never used no surname.'

Lucy Partington's friends and family are also convinced that she was a virgin when she encountered West on that snowy night in December 1973. Indeed, they believe that she had a firm set of moral principles that would have prevented her from embarking on any kind of sexual affair, let alone with someone as unlikely as Frederick West.

Nevertheless, West never once chose a victim by accident. He was a painstaking and careful man, and preferred to target his victims after observing them carefully. Also, although he was to change his version of the events surrounding the deaths of his victims, he never once retracted his explanation that he had met Lucy Partington before the night she disappeared in December 1973. It is possible, therefore, that West did meet her in Pittville Park, and that she did indeed talk to him when he was with his children. West might, for example, have engaged her in conversation, and discovered that she had recently become a Catholic. Religion was a subject that he liked to discuss, and he would no doubt have told her about the baptism of his own children. The topic could hardly have been less threatening; indeed, his interest in it may well have intrigued the undergraduate.

It is also possible that Lucy Partington met Frederick West more than once, but that she did not embark on any kind of sexual relationship with him – and that in turn led him to want to possess her sexually. It is only too likely that she made it very clear that she had no interest in him as a sexual partner, and that it was her very rejection of his sexual advances at their meeting or meetings that led to his targeting her as a potential victim. But Lucy Partington could hardly have sensed any danger from West. If she had done, she would certainly not have accepted a lift as she knew that one of her friends, Ruth Owen, had been propositioned by a white-skinned, dark-haired man about ten or fifteen years older than she was, at a bus stop in the area only a few years earlier

In the circumstances, it seems reasonable to assume that Frederick West had, in fact, met Lucy Partington before that wintry night in December 1973, and, therefore, that she would get into his A35 van. He may have been waiting opposite the stop, knowing that she went to see her friend in the evenings and often caught the last bus home. She would not have known what was in his mind, and seen him only as a man she had met with his children. The friendly smile from a man she knew, someone who had always seemed harmless enough, only ever anxious 'to help out', would have eased any suspicions that she might have had. That may well have been the technique that he had used five years earlier with Mary Bastholm, whom he had first met in the Pop-In café, probably with Ann McFall.

So it is difficult to believe that Frederick West did not know Lucy Partington, but it is still just possible. In that case he may have used the system he had pioneered with Carol Raine fifteen months earlier, and taken Rosemary West with him in the van that night, knowing that any young woman would feel safer if she saw another woman of the same age in the car too. That was the technique that West had explained to Liz Agius in Midland Road, and which the Wests had then applied to Carol Raine.

It is also possible that West may have slightly amended his system in the light of his experience, and that instead of pulling up at a bus stop with his wife beside him in the front seat, he had deliberately dropped his wife off beforehand to stand at the stop and pretend to wait for the bus. When Lucy Partington, or whomever the intended victim might be, arrived at the stop, she would find Rosemary West already standing there.

If Rosemary West were then to engage the girl in conversation while they were both standing at the bus stop – for example, by suggesting that they must have just missed the bus – and then 'by chance' her husband happened to drive past, what could be more natural than for the young woman to offer her companion a lift in her husband's car? Lucy Partington might even have recognised her companion at the bus stop as a young woman who had caught the bus from Bishop's Cleeve to Cheltenham and back over the past few years. Certainly, Rosemary West would have been careful to talk about her children, and how anxious she was to get back to them. What could possibly be the danger in accepting a lift with a young woman like that? What could be more persuasive than a young companion of the same age? What could be more reassuring to a girl alone?

Frederick West had dedicated himself to appearing unfrightening. It was his finest disguise, the one subterfuge guaranteed to succeed. It was only when he returned to the safety of his own house, and, in particular, to the security of his cellar, that he would reveal himself in his true colours. To any young woman unfortunate enough to fall into his clutches, the effect must have been truly terrifying. The man who had pretended so effectively to be nothing more than someone 'anxious to help out' was suddenly revealed as someone who could only be called a monster. But by that time the young woman was almost certainly bound and gagged, and could do nothing more than watch in terror as her captor used her to live out his fantasies.

In the final months of his life, West would try to deny all knowledge of the killing of Lucy Partington, and place the blame for her death firmly on his wife. 'I never seen her in me life,' he would tell his original solicitor, Howard Ogden. 'Rose's old man picked her up on the way through.' He then went on to suggest that Lucy had been 'supplied' by his father-in-law and his wife 'to a fucking party or something. I don't know if Rose was supplying these girls to the same lot that Rena was in Bristol'. But West maintained: 'Half the time I didn't know who was in the bloody place. Rose was putting them in and taking them out, letting them stay, enticing them. They were bloody young girls . . . Rose was having casual sex with some of them but she never mentioned that to me.'

As he did so often, Frederick West may have used a small sliver of the truth to conceal the ugly reality of what actually happened to the unfortunate undergraduate when she found herself his prisoner in the cellar of 25 Cromwell Street. His father-in-law, Bill Letts, for example, may have been involved in some way, ''cause Rose's father spent most Christmases over at our place then'. And there is no doubt that West preferred to hold his own 'parties' in the basement of his house rather than 'supply' girls to anyone else's; just as his wife's violent sexual appetite would have been heightened by her newly discovered pregnancy. Equally, West would also have taken a particular delight in the humiliation of a girl who was his social and intellectual superior.

The possibility must be that on this occasion, for the first time, Frederick West indulged his passion for photography. He had recently acquired an eight-millimetre movie camera, and had made no secret among his friends that he 'wanted to make movies'. But the movies he wanted to make were not cheerful representations of his growing family. West wanted to make pornographic films, using his wife and friends as the actors, and almost certainly featuring the plight of the young women who fell into his hands as victims. Though West was to deny it firmly in the last months of his life, there must be a suspicion that he filmed the torture of some of the young women who died at Cromwell Street, hiding the film under the floorboards, and taking it out to watch with his wife after his children had gone to bed. Whether he actually filmed the death of his victims can now be no more than a matter for speculation, but there must at least be every possibility that he created what later were to become known as 'snuff movies' – films of the deaths of his victims. The one person who would never feature in his home-made pornographic films was West himself; he was too cautious a man for that, too determined never to lose control of events.

Certainly Frederick and Rosemary West's sexual horizons had expanded still further, now that they were confident that they had succeeded in getting away with the murders of both Lynda Gough and Carol Ann Cooper. The Wests by now used their victims to demonstrate their love for one another. 'If you really love me, you will kill her,' Rosemary West would have said to her husband. 'If you don't want me to leave you for her, then you'll have to kill her,' Frederick West would have replied, both demanding that their partner kill to secure the strength of their mutual love. Each encouraged the other to greater and greater excess, exciting the other to demonstrate and prove their love for one another.

After her arrest the police suggested to Rosemary West that she had become fascinated by Lynda Gough's interest in black magic and satanism, which led them to want to torture and humiliate their victims as part of a ritual in which other people who shared their views participated. There is no clear proof that this took place, but Rosemary West's declared interest in 'bathing in virgin's blood' to 'make herself more beautiful', and in washing in 'virgin's urine' for the same purpose, suggests that a ritual element may have played some part in their killing. The fact that Lucy Partington was a virgin when she fell into the hands of the Wests may have substantially increased her attraction to them both, adding an extra tragic dimension to the abuse that she was subjected to at their hands.

Whatever the precise truth, there can be little doubt that Lucy Partington, too, found herself in the cellar of Cromwell Street, just as Carol Ann Cooper and Lynda Gough had done before her. But this time the Wests almost certainly kept Lucy Partington alive for considerably longer than they had their previous victims. Part of the evidence for this is that Frederick West remembered it was snowing on the night that he and the twenty-one–year-old undergraduate had their row in Pittville Park, whereas in fact snow did not fall in Cheltenham until three days later. But more significantly still, though he had nursed a hatred of hospitals since his motor cycle accident at the age of seventeen, Frederick West suddenly presented himself at the casualty department of Gloucester Royal Hospital at twenty-five minutes after midnight on the morning of 3 January 1974 – seven

171

nights after Lucy Partington's disappearance – for treatment to lacerations of his right hand. It seems only too probable that West had not started to dismember the body of the poor young woman until that evening.

What exactly happened to Lucy Partington during those seven days can only be guessed at. But there can be no doubt that the Wests made sure she could neither move nor cry out when they abused her. An oval band of sticky tape some sixteen inches in circumference was found wrapped around her skull when her remains were unearthed from the familiar two-feet-by-two-feet narrow shaft that West had dug for her three feet below the cellar floor at Cromwell Street. Two hairgrips and many fragments of hair were found stuck to the tape, and once again some additional surgical tape seemed to have been used to form a gag.

Just as with their other victims, a gag alone was not the only restraint the Wests resorted to. Two pieces of cord, knotted beneath the jaw, were also found with Lucy Partington's remains, acting as what may have been some kind of rudimentary noose around her neck, and there were also other pieces of rope found with her skeleton. The only possible conclusion is that this peaceful, serious girl found herself hanging helpless in the Wests' cellar in the days after Christmas 1973. It seems likely that she, too, was mercilessly abused just as her predecessors had been abused, with the addition of new and even more horrifying variations.

It seems only too possible that she was kept alive for several days in the cellar of Cromwell Street, the door locked from the hallway above and the only keys in the hands of Frederick and Rosemary West. They must have taken a grim delight in her imprisonment, for they probably chose quite deliberately to suspend the naked undergraduate by her arms in a corner of the cellar wallpapered with nursery characters. Certainly, no mercy can have been shown, for once again after the sexual abuse had ended, torture would have begun. The police suggested to Rosemary West after her arrest that parts of her skin had been removed while she was alive, and she had been subjected to other forms of horrifying sadistic abuse involving the use of fire.

No fewer than seventy-two of Lucy Partington's bones were removed. Her right shoulder-blade and left kneecap were missing when her remains were recovered from the semi-liquid clay beneath the floor of Cromwell Street; so were three of her ribs. Not one of these bones was ever discovered. The only possible conclusion is that Frederick West removed them, as he had removed the bones of each and every one of his other victims. West also removed fifty-two foot and toe bones from the seventy-six in her body, as well as eleven of her fourteen ankle bones and three of her sixteen wrist bones. It seems only too possible that he did all this while she was alive.

Once again Frederick West chose to decapitate his naked victim before burying her. When it was eventually recovered, Lucy Partington's skull was found upside-down in the narrow shaft that he always dug, with the knotted 'loop of tape' noose beneath it. Her legs had been disarticulated at the hips and shoved into the hole on either side of her torso. Indeed, her body had had to be manoeuvred into the hole, as there was a sewage pipe running across it which would have made the task even more difficult. No clothes or belongings of any kind were discovered with her skeleton; not her rust-coloured knee-length raincoat, nor her pink, flared brushed-denim jeans, not even the brown canvas satchel with the name L. K. Partington stencilled on it that she had been carrying on the night she disappeared. Nothing whatever was found with her remains when they were discovered twenty years later.

There was, however, one extra element in her narrow grave: an eight-inch-long, black-handled kitchen knife with a specially sharpened blade and a rounded tip. The only possible conclusion is that it had been used to dismember her body, thereby making the fine cut-marks that appeared on some of her bones, and that it had then been thrown into the hole in disgust when it had slipped and inflicted the lacerations to Frederick West's right hand that led him to hospital in Gloucester.

In the first days of January 1974 Lucy Partington became the second body to be buried beneath the cellar of Cromwell Street by Frederick West, his third victim within a year. Killing had become an addiction for him, one that he would never be able to break, and one that he had, in turn, seduced his wife Rosemary into joining. Their love for one another had been sealed in the blood of three innocent young women in Cromwell Street. They were now for ever bound to one another by this evil love.

Margaret Partington quickly reported her daughter Lucy's disappearance to the police, and an extensive search was mounted for her throughout the New Year holiday in 1974. Just as they had been in the case of Mary Bastholm almost exactly six years before, teams of officers were recruited to search the area and to question motorists and pedestrians to see if they may have seen the missing undergraduate. Officers combed Pittville Park, a television appeal was launched, and a reconstruction staged of her trip to the bus stop, all in the hope of jogging the memory of any passer-by, but to no avail. As a distraught Margaret Partington said at the time: 'How anybody could disappear and just vanish completely in three minutes baffles me.' It would continue to baffle the police for twenty years.

Frederick and Rosemary West could not fail to have been aware of the police hunt for Lucy Partington. The details were reported extensively in their local paper, the *Gloucester Citizen*, and recounted on the local television news. West himself admitted later that he had seen 'photographs of her on lampposts' and heard the details on television. He may well also have turned up to watch, with a sly smile on his face. There is even some evidence that within a few years West would actually volunteer to take part in the search for a missing girl, so intrigued was he by the procedure – and so anxious to see that his concealment of her body had been successful.

An interest in the search for every missing young woman was

almost certainly the reason that the only television programmes Frederick West watched with any regularity were news bulletins. 'Dad always came home in time to see *News at Ten*,' his son Stephen would recall after his father's death, 'and we all had to keep quiet while it was on.' That was not the only news programme he watched. 'If he was at home he would look at the six o'clock, the seven o'clock, the nine o'clock, the ten o'clock and the one at midnight,' his daughter Mae would remember. 'They were the only programmes he was ever interested in.' In contrast, West did everything he could to prevent his children watching television soap operas as they grew up. 'He told us they were too depressing,' Stephen West remembered, 'especially *EastEnders*.'

Frederick West himself had no need of soap operas. His life was dramatic enough. He had now killed two young women, Carol Ann Cooper and Lucy Partington, within six weeks of each other. But once again he reacted cautiously, anxious not to draw any unnecessary attention to himself. After the Christmas and New Year break, West quietly returned to Permali's and to his part-time building work, for all the world the personification of innocent endeavour. The fact that, by then, his previous two murders had gone undetected served only to increase his confidence. That did not mean, however, that he was not careful. He decided to leave the next killing until the next public holiday from work, Easter 1974.

But now, for the first time since Carol Raine, Frederick West picked up a girl he had not specifically targeted, a girl he did not know. Nevertheless, Thérèse Siegenthaler fitted the pattern that he had come to look for. She was another student, another twenty-one-year-old, another slim girl with shoulder-length straight dark brown hair, another girl who wore glasses and was a little shorter than he was, at about five feet, four inches, and another hitchhiker. Born in Switzerland, one of five children whose parents had divorced when she was eleven, Thérèse Siegenthaler spoke fluent English, although with a Swiss-German accent, and was studying sociology at the Woolwich Polytechnic in south-east London. Though she looked a little younger than her years, and wore no make-up, she was none the less physically self-assured and more than capable of looking after herself. A student of judo, she worked at weekends in the Bally shoe shop at the Swiss Centre in Leicester Square, London, to supplement her income, and was well used to hitchhiking. She was also sexually aware.

Thérèse Siegenthaler had planned to visit Ireland during her Easter vacation in 1974 to meet a Catholic priest. She had gone to a party at a friend's house in London on the night of 15 April, and the following morning had gone back to her lodgings in Deptford, London, to collect her belongings. She had then set off to catch a ferry to Ireland, although whether she was intending to travel from Fishguard or Holyhead is not entirely clear. When she was last seen, Thérèse Siegenthaler was wearing a black PVC three-quarter-length jacket and carrying only a small bag, her Swiss passport, as well as enough money for the week she intended to be away. She already had tickets for the theatre in London in the final week of April, and did not intend to miss it. But Thérèse Siegenthaler never fulfilled her plan. Like Lucy Partington four months before her, she disappeared. The whereabouts of the twenty-one-year-old Swiss girl remained a mystery for two decades, until her remains, too, were discovered buried beneath the cellar floor of 25 Cromwell Street.

Yet again, Frederick West provided an elaborate series of conflicting versions of the events surrounding the death of Thérèse Siegenthaler. But, as usual, certain elements in his description of the killing never changed. He admitted throughout, for example, that he had given Thérèse a lift in his van, that he had taken her back to Cromwell Street alive, that she had been involved in a sexual experiment with him, and that he had buried her beneath the cellar floor once the experiment had gone wrong. As ever, he was also at pains to suggest that he had never intended to murder her; it was all an unfortunate accident. West was as anxious as he had been in the case of Lucy Partington to insist that he and Thérèse Siegenthaler had been lovers. It was part of a carefully conceived smokescreen to conceal the true depths of his inhumanity.

'I had an affair with her. She was on holiday over here, and she threatened to tell Rose,' West told the police shortly after he had first admitted killing the Swiss girl, and once again he offered his tried and tested motive for her death. 'It was made quite clear that I was married to Rose . . . and every one of 'em did exactly the same thing . . . "I love you, I'm pregnant, I'm gonna tell Rose, I want you to come and live with me" . . . and that was the problem.'

Frederick West maintained that the sociology student had a 'nice figure, petite' with 'blondish/mousy hair' and that he had picked her up 'just outside Worcester'. Indeed, in this first version of events West went on to suggest that they had then twice made love in a lay-by, and that shortly afterwards she had asked him for money. 'I just lost me head with her,' he said, explaining that he had hit her, and then taken her home to Cromwell Street 'after Rose had gone out to the Bamboo Club.' West suggested that he had driven his green A35 van round to the back of his house in Cromwell Street, and had put the Swiss girl's unconscious body through the vent into the cellar at the back of the house. Soon after he had joined her there, West explained that he strangled her 'to make sure she was dead'.

Within a matter of hours, West was to alter that version of events, and explain instead that he had picked up the girl 'outside Evesham' and that she was heading for Cheltenham. In this second version the Swiss girl had told him about Amsterdam, and tulips, and had then told him that 'she fancied sex'. As a result they had 'pulled off down a lane. It was dark'. Afterwards, he had asked her: 'Where do you want me to take you? The other side of Gloucester? Because it would be easier to get a lift.' But the student had replied: 'Oh no, I'll just come home and stay with you . . . because I've got nowhere to go.'

West maintained that he had protested, but the young Swiss girl had threatened him, saying: 'I'm the one with the wet knickers . . . I've only to say you've raped me . . . you're in big trouble.' As a result he had agreed to take her home to Cromwell Street. After they arrived he decided to strangle her – but only after he had 'made her a cup of tea and they'd made love again'.

Under interrogation, however, Frederick West admitted that even this second version of events did not represent the truth. When it was suggested to him, for example, that Thérèse Siegenthaler may have been gagged with tape, West suddenly volunteered the fact that 'it was . . . I think it was grey tape . . . what you seal boxes with', and went on to admit, unprompted, that some of his victims were tied up. A matter of hours later he even expanded on that explanation and said 'the Dutch girl [as he called Thérèse Siegenthaler] was the one I had the kinky bondage with . . . because that was what she wanted to do . . . She wanted a mask made on her face . . . and her nose trussed up and all this.'

A few hours later West refined his version of events still further, this time to explain that he had picked up the twenty-one-year-old in his van in Evesham, and had given her a lift to the Trustee Savings Bank in Barton Street, Gloucester, so that she could change some money. He had then arranged to meet her again a week later: 'She said: "I'll go on to Monmouth and that and then I'll meet you back at the end of the week." . . . She was going touring, like.' It was only when she had come back that he had taken her to Cromwell Street, 'where it all went wrong'. In this version Thérèse Siegenthaler 'walked in' to Cromwell Street because she 'wanted bondage, and I mean that was arranged and we did it'.

Frederick West maintained firmly that the Swiss girl 'was too excited to get this flipping bondage thing going. I mean, she was all sort of geared up when she come back. I mean, when we finally got into the basement . . . I mean I looked round and she was absolutely starkers except for her ear-rings . . . I mean, that's how geared up she was.' West now claimed that every single one of the victims that he buried in the cellar had 'wanted to have bondage sex, or kinky sex, and that's all it was . . . It was their thing. They wanted to try or do it . . . Each one was their own fantasy.'

In this version the fantasy had once again got out of hand, and as a result West had taken Thérèse Siegenthaler into the front room of the cellar in Cromwell Street and laid her on the floor. 'I tried to get the taping off. I couldn't even get it off her. I don't have nothing to rip it with . . . When you get two or three pieces together you can't rip it, and by this time she's in, you know, looking as though she's in some pain and that – so I just strangled her.' Frederick West even gave his reason. 'I don't believe in suffering, anybody suffering, like myself. If anything happened to me I would rather somebody just end me there and then, than let me lie there and suffer, 'cause suffering is a thing I can't take, like with animals . . . Anything that's suffering should be put to sleep, not allowed to suffer.'

Once more Frederick West was at pains to portray himself as no more than somebody who had only wanted 'to help out these girls'. He even told the police: 'After anything happened, when the girls died, I mean my stomach used to knot up and I felt sick and giddy and felt really ill, and I just wanted to get out from home like, get out altogether, give myself a chance to try and get control of myself again.' Indeed, West explained: 'When I buried the girl and got rid of her clothes and that . . . I had to dive for it, the door, go out for a long ride somewhere.'

This was, yet again, a carefully sanitised version of the truth of what had actually happened to the young women who had fallen into his hands. Frederick West would never accept the pain and suffering he had clearly subjected any of his victims to, baldly claiming instead: 'I couldn't let anybody suffer for a few seconds if I could help it . . . I don't believe in suffering anyway . . . I mean, I couldn't torture anybody or anything.'

The truth was very different. No matter precisely how Thérèse Siegenthaler found her way to 25 Cromwell Street, and it seems possible that, for once, West had picked up a hitchhiker at random (though he may have arranged to meet her on a second occasion), she, like Lucy Partington, Carol Ann Cooper and Lynda Gough before her, found herself a helpless prisoner in the Wests' locked cellar. The confident Swiss girl may have been tempted to visit the house on some entirely harmless pretext, just as some form of drug to make her drowsy may have been slipped into the tea that Frederick West so kindly made for her when she arrived.

None of the Wests' four children, even Anna-Marie who was almost ten, would have taken the slightest notice of another young woman in a house that was regularly populated by a stream of unknown young women at all hours of the day and night. After his children had disappeared to bed, Frederick West and his wife would no doubt have led the by now pliant and drugged young girl through the locked door that opened on to the stairs into the cellar. Thérèse Siegenthaler was never to climb back up those stairs, or be seen again by anyone, until, almost exactly twenty years later, her remains would be unearthed from beneath a false fireplace in the front corner of the cellar's front room, the one nearest Cromwell Street.

No one can be sure how Thérèse Siegenthaler came to die, but Frederick West's own admission that some form of sexual bondage played its part in her death hardly seems open to dispute. A knotted loop of cloth was found very near her skull, which, when it was cleaned, was found to be a cloth scarf that had been folded or rolled and then tied to form a loop of almost fourteen inches in circumference. There were brown hair fragments in the knot, and there seems no doubt that it formed a gag around her mouth. Even though the knot could have been pulled free, the Swiss girl would have needed a free hand to be able to do so. No ropes were found with her remains, although West himself suggested that some of the girls had been 'anxious to try out a harness' that he had made out of plastic. West

177

would not have thrown away something that he had gone to some trouble to make. Indeed, a large number of sexual harnesses of varying sizes and strengths were finally recovered from Cromwell Street.

The pattern of the previous deaths makes it almost inevitable that Thérèse Siegenthaler suffered a fate similar to that of her predecessors in that damp, dark cave beneath the paving-stones of Gloucester. Once again a number of bones were missing when her jumbled skeleton was recovered from its tiny two-feet-by-two-feet hole dug three feet or more beneath the cellar floor. Her left collar-bone was missing, as were five ankle and nine wrist bones, as well as twenty-four of her seventy-six finger and toe bones, a total of thirty-nine missing bones in all. Like Lucy Partington before her, the Swiss girl had fine knife-cuts on the upper end of her thigh bones, which may have been made when her legs were disarticulated from her pelvis at the hips; and, like Lucy Partington, she had been decapitated.

Frederick West confirmed that that had been her fate, and even went on to describe in grim detail what he did. 'I used to put their head over the hole and cut their head off,' he told the police, adding, 'And of course that was most, the bulk, of the blood gone . . . it would just rush out . . . Once you've cut the jugular vein, blood just rushes out.' West told the police that he made sure 'always' to cut his victims' heads off first, because that way he kept the bloodstains to a minimum.

But then West tried to convince the police that he did not enjoy this horrifying task, trying to confuse them, as he had confused so many in the past, into believing that he was an ordinary man. 'There are no words to describe it, actually. You feel terrible. There is just no words to explain what you go through . . . Both mentally and physically, like, you are absolutely shattered,' West said a month after his arrest. He went on: 'Once you go to try and cut somebody's head off, you then freeze mentally, and you just carry on and . . . from then on you don't know what you're doing . . . your mind is gone . . . and you're in so much pain in your stomach and you're shaking so much . . . I mean, like people say once you've done a thing it becomes easier. It does not – believe me, I can tell you that it does not get easier.' In retrospect such claims are revealed as being pathetic lies, lies that not even the guards at Belsen would have attempted to sustain. There was no conceivable justification for the mutilation of the bodies of these innocent young women, no claim of medical experiment, or the demands of national pride or sovereignty. West disarticulated and decapitated his victims for no other reason than convenience, once he had achieved his own gratification at their expense.

When it was pointed out to Frederick West that he might have disposed of the bodies of his victims in a different way, for example by burying them in larger holes that did not demand that he decapitate them, he dismissed the idea at once. 'It don't work like that . . . When it happens you panic there and then. You got to do summat quick.' He insisted that his idea was always the same, that he 'always wanted to make the body fit the hole'. It was another of West's distinctive elaborations of the truth.

Frederick West chose to decapitate his victims to confirm his supreme control over them, to render them nothing but ciphers, and therefore no longer women as human beings, to be craved at one moment and feared the next. They were, to use Professor David Canter's terminology in his 1995 study *Criminal Shadows*, 'victims as vehicles' of West's own emotions. 'These are offenders whose native intelligence and life opportunities have enabled them to present a sociable face to the world,' Professor Canter explains. 'These are the criminals who come nearest to exhibiting pure evil. They know what the story of human relationships ought to be, but this always appears a part they play, not a role with which they are at one. They can recognise what empathy may mean, but they never feel it.' To have left his victims' bodies intact would have been to belittle his victory over them. Frederick West could not have tolerated that.

When Rosemary West was finally questioned about the death of the twenty-one-year-old Swiss student two decades after her disappearance in April 1974, she steadfastly refused to make any comment whatsoever; just as she denied any recollection of her at her trial. During her police interviews, Rosemary West simply sat and stared at the ground when she was asked at length about the events that may have led to Thérèse Siegenthaler's death. She refused even to comment on the suggestions that the girl might have been drugged, then bound and gagged by the Wests, then held prisoner in the cellar of Cromwell Street. She refused to comment on whether the young student's fingers and toes had been removed while she was still alive. She also refused to acknowledge that she would have known that Thérèse was almost exactly a year older than she was.

But Rosemary West did pause for some time when she was asked if the Swiss girl had been scalped before she was buried. It was almost one of the very few moments of emotion that Rosemary West ever allowed herself to display during her interrogation, perhaps because the memory of this particular atrocity was too vivid to be forgotten.

Rosemary West rapidly recovered her composure, however, and went on to refuse to comment on whether the girl had been made to kneel over a hole that Frederick West had dug in the floor before she had been beheaded. She also refused to discuss what might have become of a contraceptive coil that Thérèse Siegenthaler may have had fitted, and which would have required a medical operation to remove. The device was never recovered from the young Swiss woman's grave, suggesting that Frederick West, the man who had boasted so persistently of his skill at abortions, may have removed it – either before or after her death.

Lucy Partington and Thérèse Siegenthaler had a great deal in common. They were both students, and almost exactly the same age. They both wore their shoulder-length brown hair parted in the middle, just as they both wore glasses. They were both about the same height and shared the same slim build. More significant still, they both had no link whatever with number 25 Cromwell Street – except for their striking resemblance to the woman who was mistress of that house, the twenty-year-old Rosemary Pauline West.

Was Frederick West deliberately seeking young women who were exactly like his wife? Was he doing so in order to subject them to a sexual humiliation that he would have liked to subject her to, but did not dare? Did she sense that, and help to do so to protect herself from him? Or was she aiding and abetting him to target young women exactly like herself as a way of making her seem even more attractive to her husband – knowing that the victims would never agree to participate in his evil love-affair as she had done? Did West kill these poor girls because his wife demanded it, or because they did not measure up to her?

Though Frederick West offered explanations for many other things in his life, these were questions that he never answered.

Chapter Fourteen

Immaculate conceit

'Any fool can tell the truth, but it requires a man of some sense
to know how to tell a lie well.'

Samuel Butler, *Notebooks*

Frederick West was a compulsive and felicitous liar. Lying came to
him as easily as breathing, and required no more thought. It was as
much a part of his personality as his relentless sexual appetite. But,
like much else in his life, West brought a meticulous care to his lying.
Throughout his life he had steadily refined a technique that made
everything he said seem straightforward, but which also effectively
concealed far more than it revealed. West would layer half-truth on
half-truth – to disguise the lies beneath – apparently open and yet in
fact obscuring almost everything of the truth. It was a technique that
he must have used on the young women who became his victims, the
apparently open-faced, talkative little man, who took pains to lace
every sentence with an exaggeration or an irrelevant detail.

Ask Frederick West if he knew someone, and he would never
answer directly, always asking instead where they lived, before
digressing into an endless description of the best route to take to
their house. Ask him if he had committed a crime, and he would
embark immediately on a description of the events that might have
led up to it, only then to digress again until it was almost impossible
to recall the detail of the original question. West went to considerable
trouble to seldom answer any but the most direct questions, and even
then to do everything in his power to confuse and fog the questioner.

In the last months of his life West explained his technique to
Detective Constable Hazel Savage in an interview room at Gloucester police station. It was the first and only time that he ever did this,
and it revealed the subtlety of his approach. 'What happens is,' West
confessed, 'I'm talking away to them . . . and suddenly it comes into
my mind, shit, I'm telling them the truth, you know what's been
going on . . . So then I shove something in there . . . to get away from
it.' This use of irrelevant detail, West admitted, was 'because I want

to get away from it, to give me a chance to think'. It was the only occasion on which West admitted that he knew when he was lying and when he was not, and how he managed to cope with the situation. The only difficulty he encountered was 'that you get to a stage where you . . . just don't know what you are actually saying . . . You've got everything mixed up. So you've got to try and get out of it, to give your mind a chance.'

West maintained throughout the 145 police interviews conducted at the end of his life that he would never explain anything to anyone unless somebody asked him the correct, direct question, and even then he would still lie rather than tell the truth. 'When you've got so much on your mind, it, well, suddenly runs into each other in your mind and . . . the only thing you can think of is to dive out of it, to give you a chance . . . because the last thing I want is for you to be able to come back and say, "you lied to me about that".' It was not the reaction of a simple or blunt man.

West took enormous pleasure in practising this technique. Anyone he met was to be deceived, to be lulled into the sense that they understood him, while he kept the reality studiously hidden for himself alone. Though he could barely read, and certainly could hardly write, his native wit and self-confidence carried him through triumphantly for years. He particularly enjoyed practising his technique for deception on the police. West revelled in the police drugs raids that regularly swept through Cromwell Street. He would seize the opportunity they brought him to lie with a persuasive fluency that no one would detect – except perhaps his wife Rosemary. As she was to put it: 'The police coming round was just a joke to him. He thought it was funny.' It gave him an opportunity to deceive, and there was nothing that West relished more.

Frederick West nevertheless recognised that he could have been an even more persuasive liar if only he had been able to write notes of what he had said, to give himself an *aide-mémoire*. As he confessed to his first solicitor, Howard Ogden, in the last months of his life: 'Where I'm buggered up, see, is I think of things, but I can't write it down. I can't write. I've got to fucking remember it, and it's not that easy.' Easy or not, West managed it with a fluency that confused police-officers, social-workers, doctors, psychologists, probation officers, prison officers and his victims for almost half a century. And very few people whom he came across guessed that they were being duped.

'Dad always told me he would just let out the bits of information that suited him,' West's son Stephen explained after his father's death. 'It meant that he could always make people like the police run about after him, for example. If they thought he was going to tell them something new, they would take an interest.' When he talked about it, Frederick West giggling gleefully, hugging himself with pride, then quickly returned to his pretence of humility and subservience.

And if the police could be taken in, what chance would a

vulnerable young girl stand against him? West used exactly the same techniques on them as he did on those in authority. He lied and lied again, exaggerated and boasted, twisted and turned their emotions, all in an effort to confuse, an effort to entice them to forget their fears – and trust him. In the twelve months between the middle of April 1973 and the middle of April 1974, West had used the technique to such effect that the bodies of four young women were now buried beneath his house in Cromwell Street. Lynda Gough, Carol Ann Cooper, Lucy Partington and Thérèse Siegenthaler stood silent witnesses to his appetite for lies, deception, sexual excess and murder.

But to the young men and women coming and going in his rooms at Cromwell Street, Frederick West was still simply an affable landlord, albeit one with an 'open marriage', as he liked to describe it to everyone he met. West told one of his female lodgers at the time that 'Rose liked women and he liked to watch', while at the same time he encouraged a young Jamaican to have sex with his wife, calling the young man 'the best friend I ever had'.

In the early summer of 1974 Frederick West left Permali's factory in Bristol Road, Gloucester, for a new job nearby, in the light fabrication shop at Muir Hill Wagon Works, which was then owned by Wingets of Rochester, Kent, which made the shells of railway wagons. He was to remain an employee there for ten years, with only one brief break. Endlessly talkative, and yet relentlessly hard-working, West was for ever chattering to anyone who would listen. One fellow worker remembered him as 'a bragger and a liar', but also 'a friendly sort who got on with most people'. And, just as he had at Permali's, West made no secret at his new job that his wife was a prostitute 'who liked women and blacks in particular', telling anyone who might be interested that he had made eight-millimetre pornographic films of her making love, which he 'showed to friends' in his cellar on Sunday afternoons. West even boasted that he kept the master copy 'hidden under the floorboards'.

When West invited his fellow workers to Cromwell Street, some were astonished to find that he had decorated the first-floor bathroom of the house with Polaroid pictures of his wife's 'private parts'; one called him a 'pervert' as a result. Undeterred, West recruited some of them to help him work on his house in Cromwell Street. In the summer of 1974 they assisted him as he laid the first concrete floor in the cellar. West told them that he was still considering 'lowering the floor', but that before he made up his mind to do so he wanted to keep to a minimum the 'smell of sewage' which he said had begun to permeate the room from a 'broken pipe' beneath. It was more likely that the smell came from the decomposing bodies of four young women, but no one who worked in the basement with West noticed anything particularly unusual.

Upstairs, the Muir Hill men were often introduced to some of the young female lodgers. West would brag that he would sometimes turn his lodgers 'into prostitutes'. One was a Swedish or Dutch girl who seemed to be pregnant, but there was also a girl called Marilyn from the Forest of Dean, together with a Gloucester girl, also called Marilyn, as well as the daughter of an American serviceman from the US Air Force base at Lakenheath in Suffolk, called Donna. They were just some of the many young women who seemed to flood in and out of the house at all hours of the day and night. Twenty years later the police would make strenuous efforts to locate them all, to satisfy themselves that they had not suffered the same fate as the four women buried beneath the house, but they would not succeed in every case. The women were a part of the mystery that would surround Frederick West for ever.

Nothing about the West family was commonplace. Many years later one visitor remembered that when one of the female lodgers, who was pregnant, had told her landlord and landlady in broken English, 'I am with child; it is Fred's', Rosemary West had replied immediately, 'No it isn't; it's yours', and started laughing along with her husband. Another recalled West telling off his eldest child, Anna-Marie, then nearly ten, for 'screwing in the park'.

In the summer of 1974 the Wests' other children were still tiny. Heather was three and a half, Mae two and Stephen only just one, and, hardly surprisingly, Rosemary West's temper was short. The violence that had been part of her life since her childhood was ever present. On the night of 13 August 1974, for example, West remembered: 'I came in from work late, and she said, "The children have broken the telly. I want a new one".' Frederick West did not take his wife's complaint too seriously. But Rosemary West quickly grew angry when he refused to respond. Giggling, West picked up the broken television and ran towards the living-room door, only to see his wife run after him brandishing a kitchen knife.

'I slammed the fucking door straight in her face, and the knife come "bang" straight into the door,' West remembered. 'Next minute there's one almighty scream. So I put the television down and opened the door. One of Rose's fingers is hanging down and the other one is hanging off.' Even though two of her fingers had been all but severed, his wife was not crying. 'So I grabbed a towel, covered her hand, took her out the front. This is twelve o'clock at night.' Frederick West remembered that his brother John had been 'standing by the front gate' when they got outside. 'We took her down the hospital.' At Gloucester Royal Hospital that night Rosemary West insisted that it was simply 'an accident'. She had been 'playing with knives' while 'cutting wood'. The stony look on her face would not have changed as the hospital admitted her for the night with 'a deep laceration across the ring and little finger on her right hand'.

Rosemary West was detained in hospital for two days, but the accident did nothing to dissuade her from using knives. Time after time when she lost her temper she would turn on her children with a knife in her hand, jabbing the point at them. Her second daughter

Mae remembers one occasion on which her mother was cutting meat in the kitchen:

> She was shouting, as usual. For some reason she picked on me and came at me with a knife. I was sitting there on the top step in the lounge and she came towards me. She flashed at me with the knife. I was crying and said, 'No, Mum, no Mum, no Mum'. She kept slashing the knife at me and there were little nicks all over my rib-cage . . . You never knew what Mum was going to do next.

At this time it was always Rosemary West who disciplined the West children. Her son Stephen recalls: 'The slightest thing would set Mum off . . . Mum had no self-control. She would just flip and have no idea what she was doing . . . Mum would hit out with anything she could lay her hands on. If she'd had a sledge-hammer she would have belted you with it. A rolling-pin was one of her favourites. She would just lash out and you would be sent flying.' Frederick West, on the other hand, 'was the same as my mum, but he didn't flip as often. Mum was like that every other day.' By comparison with his mother, Stephen West insists, his father was 'more abusive than violent – but he snapped very quickly. Dad would flip four times a year. But when he did go he was like a madman.'

The lack of self-control that brought abuse to the Wests' children was reflected precisely in the abuse of the young women who became the Wests' victims at Cromwell Street. Within the confines of their own home, the Wests sustained their unquenchable, secret desire for sexual abuse and violence, as four young women had already discovered to their cost, each one suffering more and more extreme humiliation at the hands of the Wests. The gags used to prevent their screaming had become more subtle and precise, the ties that secured them to the beams more elaborate and sure, their imprisonment longer, their deaths ever more horrifying. And the Wests' appetite for all of this showed no sign of diminishing.

In November 1974, almost exactly one year to the day after the disappearance of Carol Ann Cooper, and almost exactly a further year after the abduction of Carol Raine, another young girl was to fall into the hands of Frederick and Rosemary West. Her treatment was to prove beyond any doubt the extent of the depravity that they were now eager to explore.

Shirley Hubbard was a pretty, spirited, vulnerable girl of fifteen and a half when she found herself at Cromwell Street. And, like so many of the other girls who did so, she was a child of a broken, unhappy home. Born in Birmingham on 26 June 1959, the daughter of Glenys Lloyd and John Owen, her parents had separated when she was two, and, as a result, their daughter Shirley had been taken into care. She had spent the next four years shuttling back and forth between one parent or the other and local authority care, until in 1965, at the age of six, she was finally placed with foster-parents,

James and Linda Hubbard, who lived in Droitwich, Worcestershire. Shirley spent the rest of her childhood with the Hubbards, and in 1972, at the age of twelve, adopted their name.

By the age of fifteen Shirley Hubbard was five feet, six inches tall, slim but well proportioned, with shoulder-length fair brown hair, hazel eyes, and 'a nice smile' which meant that 'she could usually get her own way', in the words of a friend. If she failed to do so, 'she would usually show off'. She had also tattooed herself on the left forearm with SHIRL in one-inch-high block capitals. Shirley Hubbard was also something of a flirt. 'She always reacted positively to the presence of a man,' according to one acquaintance, and from the age of fourteen would regularly slip out of her downstairs bedroom window at night to meet one boyfriend or another. Shirley also liked to hang around the fair when it appeared in Worcester, and 'liked older men, who were strangers in the area', according to her friends. In the autumn of 1974 there were rumours, for example, that she was seeing an older, married man working on some houses being built at Briar Hill in Droitwich, who 'would take her out in his car'.

In October 1974 Shirley Hubbard ran away from her foster-home during the night, taking most of her possessions and clothing with her. She left Linda and Jim Hubbard a note: 'I've run away. Don't try and find me. I'll be in touch.' She was missing for five days, only to be discovered camping with a soldier in a field about five miles from Worcester, and brought back to her foster-home by the police.

But a month later, on 14 November 1974, she disappeared again. Once more, she cleared her room of most of her possessions and clothing, probably stuffing them into a duffel bag, but on this second occasion she was never to return. On that Thursday, Shirley Hubbard set out from her home in Droitwich for her temporary job on the make-up counter at the Debenhams store in Worcester, where she was doing a week's work experience. It was half-day closing, and at one o'clock that afternoon she met up with her new boyfriend, Dan Davies, who worked at the John Collier tailor's shop in the town. His brother Alan, who worked on the travelling fair, had been one of Carol Ann Cooper's boyfriends for a while the year before, but Caz Cooper and Shirley Hubbard had never met, at least to the best of Dan's knowledge. That afternoon Dan Davies and Shirley Hubbard sat on the banks of the River Severn eating a bag of chips and watching the world go by. They then went to his house, where they talked to his brother and sisters.

Shortly before 8.30 in the evening, just as Carol Ann Cooper's boyfriend had done exactly a year before, Shirley's boyfriend set off to put her on a bus home, this time from Worcester towards Droitwich in the north, rather than from Worcester towards Warndon in the east. And, just as Caz Cooper's boyfriend had done a year earlier, Dan Davies arranged to meet his girlfriend at seven o'clock the following evening before he put her on to a waiting bus not long after nine o'clock. And, exactly like Caz Cooper one year before her, Shirley

Hubbard was never seen again after she boarded the bus in Worcester on a November evening.

The similarities between the cases of the two girls are striking. It is possible that Frederick West had continued to haunt the centre of Worcester in the wake of his success with Carol Ann Cooper, and had spotted the happy-go-lucky Shirley Hubbard in the town. But it is far more likely that he had been introduced to her by one of Caz Cooper's friends, and that she had fallen under the spell of his extravagant stories, the mature father-figure she had spent much of her life searching for. West may very well have been the 'older, married man' she had been having a relationship with in Droitwich, for there is no doubt that West had done odd part-time building jobs in the town. Indeed, just as he may have done with Caz Cooper, West may even have suggested that she get an early bus from Worcester that evening to allow him time to take her to Cromwell Street, with the promise that he 'would run her home' afterwards. It is only too likely that Shirley Hubbard may even have decided to accept the offer of a room at Cromwell Street from Frederick West, and packed her belongings in Droitwich as a result.

Frederick West would no doubt have been offering Shirley Hubbard a place where she could 'be herself', away from 'the pressures' of her foster-home, and he would probably have offered to 'run up' and collect 'the rest of her things' with her whenever she wanted. It would have been his way to welcome her into a secret that only they shared, a secret that would cost the fifteen-year-old her life. The older man whom Shirley Hubbard found herself with this time, the man in whom she placed her trust, and who seemed only too prepared to look after her, was not the father she so clearly longed for. Frederick West did not like a young woman to leave him, not once she had found her way into his care, and certainly not once she had discovered his secret appetite for abuse. Though Shirley Hubbard's disappearance was reported to the police on 15 November 1974, her whereabouts were to remain a mystery until her skeleton was recovered from beneath the cellar floor of 25 Cromwell Street almost two decades later.

When Frederick West first confessed to killing the five young women whose bodies were discovered beneath the cellar floor – a confession he later retracted – he bracketed Carol Ann Cooper and Shirley Hubbard together, calling them 'Worcester Girl One' and 'Worcester Girl Two', and insisted that he did not remember even their names. He also told the police that their bodies were fully clothed, that they had not been mutilated, and that, once again, the only reason that he had killed them was that they threatened to tell his wife of their relationship with him. 'It was made quite clear,' West maintained, 'that I was married to Rose . . . and every one of them did the same thing . . . "I love you, I'm pregnant, I'm gonna tell Rose. I want you to come and live with me." And that was the problem.' It was also a bare-faced lie.

It was not the only lie that West was to tell in the case of the two

Worcester girls. Time after time he would amend and modify his version of their deaths. Indeed, throughout the first stages of his police interviews he would even suggest that he picked them both up together 'in Tewkesbury one day', but that he had then picked up the 'one without the firework burn' – that is Shirley Hubbard – 'a few weeks later'.

> I picked her up just outside Worcester, and I was just generally talking to her as I was going along, and the next minute . . . she's got me fly undone and messing about . . . I just pulled in and . . . we made love. I think we made love twice . . . one after the other and then she, that's right, then she said 'That'll be ten quid' or something, and I said, 'Well, I don't carry money . . . and anyway I wouldn't pay a prostitute . . . If you'd said that in the first place,' I said, 'I'd have told you to get lost.' . . . Then she started shouting and she said, 'You're the sort of person who goes with slags' or something to that effect . . . And I just lost my head with her. Because as soon as she said that I thought of Rose, and Rose is no slag as far as I am concerned. So I went for her.

At this stage Frederick West was also insisting that 'there is nobody else involved. I did it all on my own . . . Let's get that straight now.'

West was never to give any direct details of how Shirley Hubbard came to meet her death. Nevertheless, at about this time Frederick West did confess to one of his workmates at the Muir Hill Wagon Works that he had worked as a pimp or 'stick man' in Scotland, and that while he was there he had learned how to make girls do what he wanted them to. He told his fellow worker that he would 'lock them in a room for a couple of days without food and water, to make them behave'. West had gone on to explain that he had recently picked up a fifteen-year-old girl outside the city and taken her back to Cromwell Street, where he had had sex with her. Rosemary West had then joined in, and afterwards West had suggested that she should consider a career as a prostitute – presumably working for him and his wife.

The girl had refused, and so they had tied her to the bed and 'sexually tortured her'. Rosemary West had used 'instruments to penetrate the girl', West confided, but he had nevertheless left the girl tied up in his wife's hands and had gone to work. But when he had come home again 'she was in a bad way'. Not for the first time, his fellow worker did not take him seriously, clearly thinking that it was simply another of West's wild sexual exaggerations. But it seems only too probable that the fifteen-year-old girl Frederick West was describing was Shirley Hubbard.

The degradation that the previous four young women were subjected to in the cellar of Cromwell Street was repeated on Shirley Hubbard. But, again, the Wests further refined their technique, this time gagging their victim in a quite horrific way. The Birmingham-born girl was taped up in such a way that she would have been completely unable to see either what her tormentors were doing or even who they were. Shirley Hubbard's head was covered from chin to scalp in two-inch-wide parcel tape, wound overlapping around her skull eleven or twelve times, with a final loop under the chin. Only the very top of her head was left uncovered. The mask – for there can be no other word for it – would have made it impossible for the fifteen-year-old to either see or speak, or indeed to hear at all clearly. It would also have made it impossible for her to breathe.

But Frederick West did not want their victim to die of suffocation: at least not until she had been kept alive long enough to gratify their own sexual desires, and the desires of anyone else whom they chose to invite into the cellar of Cromwell Street. To ensure that Shirley Hubbard could breathe, therefore, West inserted into the mask two U-shaped pieces of thin clear plastic tubing each approximately eighteen inches long and an eighth of an inch in diameter. The idea was straightforward: the tubes were designed to fit into the girl's nostrils so that she could still breathe, even though her head was completely encased in a shiny mask.

During his police interviews, Frederick West became confused over which girl had actually been forced to wear this dreadful mask, suggesting at one moment that it might have been 'the Dutch girl', his name for Thérèse Siegenthaler, only to change his mind and realise that he had made a mistake. West finally accepted that Shirley Hubbard, whom he described only as 'Worcester Girl Two', had, in fact, been the young woman subjected to this hideous mask of parcel tape. Indeed, West did not deny that he had 'trussed the girl up' and 'attempted to hang her upside-down on a hook in the cellar ceiling' for 'kinky sex'. Yet again, he claimed, 'enjoyment turned to disaster', as the girl managed 'to slip off', 'fall on to the cellar floor' and 'die as a result of her injuries'.

Part of West's confession to the police, a confession that, like all his others, he was to retract, is almost certainly true. In his later conversations with his first solicitor, West confirmed that 'Worcester Girl Two', Shirley Hubbard, had been at 'Cromwell Street for two or three days, possibly a week' before her death, although he tried to shift the blame for her murder entirely on to his wife. 'Rose kept her out of the way,' West insisted. 'These girls were always in the bloody bedroom with Rose, that's what I couldn't understand. It seemed a peculiar place to keep girls.'

West maintained that he had told his wife, 'That's a schoolgirl, she can't stay here', and told his solicitor that he then 'took her to Worcester, and dropped her. That was the first time, and the last, that I'd ever seen her.' But West went on to admit that he and Shirley Hubbard had had a drink together in a pub called the Swan With Two Necks, claiming that 'From there, she left on her own'. West specifically denied that he had been working on the houses at Briar Hill in Droitwich, although he then became confused about where he was actually working at the time, suggesting that he was still 'at Permali's'. Even more significantly, Frederick West did not explain

189

how Shirley Hubbard came to find her way back to Cromwell Street and into the cellar of his house.

Regardless of Frederick West's facile denial that he 'never tried it on with nobody', Shirley Hubbard, like the four young women who found their way into the cellar before her, was brought to Cromwell Street and ruthlessly and brutally used by Frederick and Rosemary West as an object for their sexual gratification. The novelty of their horrifying new mask would have temporarily increased the intensity of their sexual excitement, just as it would have allowed them the opportunity to invite other people to abuse the girl without fear of their victim's recognising them. But it also brought a disadvantage. The mask would have prevented West from seeing the terror in his victim's eyes. To use Professor Canter's terminology again, Shirley Hubbard was not solely an 'object' for Frederick West's use; she was also a 'vehicle for his emotions'. The experience of not seeing the impact on her of his depraved actions would have diluted the pleasure he received by applying the mask in the first place.

Frederick West could have indulged his appetite for medical examination on the naked and helpless girl, as he did with Thérèse Siegenthaler. He may have experimented again with fire or flames, which may account for the top of his victim's head being left free from the tape that covered the rest of her skull, just as he may have mutilated other parts of her body with cigarettes or oxy-acetylene. He may have whipped her with the cat-o'-nine-tails, or West may have given vent to another of his sexual obsessions, the possibility of mating a girl with a large dog. In the years to come West would return repeatedly to his interest in this perversion. He accumulated an extensive collection of pornographic videotapes featuring women being abused by animals, including both an Alsatian dog and a boar pig, and suggested repeatedly that he wanted his wife Rosemary to make love 'to a bull'.

Faced with this onslaught of depravity, one can only pray that Shirley Hubbard would have subsided into unconsciousness. For once again Frederick West removed a number of bones from his victim's body before disposing of it: forty of Shirley Hubbard's bones were missing when her remains were unearthed from their narrow shaft of a grave beneath his cellar floor two decades later, including seven of her sixteen wrist bones, which may indicate that she had been suspended by her ankles.

Even two decades later West showed not the slightest remorse or contrition. He simply told the police in his first interviews that he had used his sheath knife to dismember the girl. 'It was sheer force of habit,' he explained. 'I mean, it's handy to have a knife with you anyway, for numerous reasons . . . When you're building, cutting plastic, cutting anything. It wasn't carried as a weapon. It was carried as a tool.' It was also a tool that West used to decapitate Shirley Hubbard between the fifth and sixth cervical vertebrae. This time his victim's remains suggested that her neck had been cut from front to back, rather than from back to front, which indicates that it was carried out while she was suspended above the narrow hole that he had dug for her remains. But Shirley Hubbard's head was not allowed simply to drop into the hole beneath her. When it was recovered, it was erect, as if it had been placed specifically in that manner. And the mask of sticky tape was still around her skull.

Shirley Hubbard's dismembered body was eventually buried in the front of the three cellar rooms at Cromwell Street, the one nearest the street. And Frederick West later told the police that he had dug the hole at an earlier point "cause I was preparing the drains for a bathroom'. West then created a false chimney-breast nearby, and some time afterwards, in an act that can be seen only as the expression of his dark, bizarre sense of humour, he decorated the walls with wallpaper bearing the image of Marilyn Monroe.

Beyond the cellar, life at Cromwell Street continued on its familiar, routine path. West was now working relentlessly, at the Wagon Works in Bristol Road during the day, and as a jobbing builder – both on his own house and other houses – after his shift was over at Muir Hill. His appetite for work was undiminished, not least because it allowed him to conceal his actions. If anyone ever enquired where he was, West would say cheerfully 'working twelve hours a day'. It was the perfect cover. The ploy failed on just one occasion revealing his appetite for petty theft. On 25 March 1975 Frederick West appeared at Gloucester magistrates' court on a theft charge, for which he was fined £50 and ordered to pay £10 in compensation. He took particular care to thank everyone obsequiously for their 'kindness'. But in spite of his abject apologies to the magistrates, his contempt for the law had not diminished in the least. West took an intense and secret delight in allowing the cellar to become a storage site for stolen goods.

No one can be sure whether Frederick and Rosemary West sustained their passion for anniversaries by finding themselves another victim shortly after Christmas in 1974, as they had done with Lucy Partington the year before, for if they did so their victim's body was not interred beneath their cellar floor. But Frederick West certainly marked another macabre anniversary in April 1975. Almost exactly a year to the day after Thérèse Siegenthaler had disappeared while hitchhiking to Ireland by way of Gloucester, another young girl, Juanita Mott, went missing while hitchhiking on another road nearby. This time the girl had a clear connection to the Wests. Like Carol Raine before her, she had not only visited Cromwell Street, but she also knew the Wests well. Unlike Carol Raine, she would not survive to tell the tale.

Like Shirley Hubbard and several of Frederick West's other victims, Juanita Mott was the product of a broken home. She was born on 1 March 1957, the daughter of Ernest Mott, a United States serviceman who had returned to the United States, and Mary, who remained in England and lived in the Coney Hill area of Gloucester. As Juanita grew older she had become more and more difficult to handle, and as a result had spent periods in care. Juanita Mott had left school at fifteen, but in May 1973, shortly after her sixteenth birthday, had suffered an ectopic pregnancy, an experience that probably unsettled her still more. By that time, Juanita Mott had become a 'very strong-willed, independent girl', in the words of a friend; 'always on the go – nobody would know where she was', in the words of another. Attractive and outgoing, she was five feet, four inches tall, with dark shoulder-length hair, with a fringe she would sometimes dye blonde. 'Leggy and gangly', as another friend put it, her skin somehow always 'looked tanned'.

Juanita Mott had also had her share of trouble with the police. After staying with her mother and grandmother in Gloucester, she had started living in bed-sitting-rooms in the city, and early in 1974 found herself at number 4 Cromwell Street, where one friend remembered her as 'not very bright, naive and a bit dopey'. While she was there, Juanita Mott was charged with stealing a pension book and remanded to Pucklechurch Remand Centre in Gloucester. She received two years' probation, and moved into a flat in Stroud Road, and then into another in Albany Street, both only a few minutes' walk from Cromwell Street, where some of the lodgers from 25 Cromwell Street, and their friends, were regular visitors. It was probably there that she first encountered Frederick West, although she was also a regular at the Pop-In café in Southgate Street, where Mary Bastholm had worked.

In the middle of 1974 Juanita Mott confided to a friend that she had met a man called Freddie, who looked like a gypsy and wore an ear-ring in his ear. Indeed, West may well have offered the young woman a room at 25 Cromwell Street, for when she again found herself in trouble with the police in 1974 for a deception involving Giro cheques, and back in Pucklechurch Remand Centre, she wrote to West at Cromwell Street.

There seems little doubt that Juanita Mott accepted Frederick West's offer of a room at Cromwell Street. Not only was she probably infatuated with him, but she would also have felt at home. She, like so many of the other lodgers, shared difficulties with the police and the Social Services department, and used the address as a place at which to hide for a time, a place where no one would ask too many questions. As West himself admitted: 'That's why half of them was there. I mean, a lot of the girls that was there didn't use their own names.' Juanita Mott did not stay at 25 Cromwell Street for very long. There is no clear explanation for her decision to move out, although it is possible that West may have told her, as he told other young women who came to lodge at Cromwell Street: 'If they couldn't pay the rent they would have to have sex with me – or Rose.'

By March 1975 she had gone to stay with a family friend, Jennifer Frazer-Holland, in Newent – one of Frederick West's old stamping-grounds on the road from Much Marcle to Gloucester. Juanita Mott had stayed with her in the past, and Jennifer Frazer-Holland knew her well. She recalled years later that Juanita did not have a 'particular boyfriend' at the time, but that she would sometimes 'stay out all night'. Nevertheless, Juanita had promised that she would be at her friend's Newent bungalow on Saturday 12 April 1975 to babysit Jennifer's young children, while she got married. The evening before Juanita set out to hitchhike from Newent into Gloucester. She did not return to babysit the following day, which was 'totally out of character'. Though she was reported missing to the police, Juanita Mott was never seen again.

Whether by accident or design, Juanita Mott encountered Frederick West on the road from Newent to Gloucester on that Friday in April 1975. It may have been a chance encounter, but it is far more likely that he had arranged to meet her, or that he knew that she usually travelled into town on that day of the week. West may even have asked someone else to find out whether she was likely to be hitchhiking on that day. And, as he had with Carol Raine before her, West may have taken his wife with him that day, to make it more likely that she would accept a lift. If Juanita Mott had refused the offer of a lift, if Thérèse Siegenthaler had done so, or Lucy Partington, they might have escaped the terrible fate that awaited them at Cromwell Street. If there were ever an argument against any young woman, no matter how strong or sensible, hitchhiking in any circumstances whatever, it is the life of Frederick West. Evil can come in the least frightening packages.

In fact, West was pursuing Juanita Mott as a 'present' for his wife, a morsel to tempt her. For there is no doubt that, like Carol Raine, Rosemary West had set her heart on sexually possessing the attractive girl, who had celebrated her eighteenth birthday only a month or so before. Like Carol Raine, Juanita Mott may have rejected Rosemary West's advances, or refused to participate in the bizarre sexual experiments that had become her passion, or declined the Wests' offer for her to become a prostitute. Whatever the precise reason, her refusal ensured that Frederick West would make her his target on his wife's behalf, his morbid sweetmeat to succour her depraved sexual desire.

Twenty years later Frederick West maintained only that Juanita Mott 'used to come to visit' Cromwell Street, but that 'she never lived there'. He described her to the police as a 'black-haired girl, fairly big built', who had an 'American father', although he also suggested that she 'might have had a baby, 'cause she had stretch marks'. West insisted that she used to 'come and visit friends at Cromwell Street', and that she had then become friendly with him over a period of 'probably a couple of months'. Juanita Mott, he said, used to come 'down the basement helping me and that . . . when there was nobody there, like'.

As with his other victims, West also boasted about the fact that he and Juanita Mott had become lovers. Indeed, he claimed that shortly after their affair started they were 'making love two or three times a day' in the basement. In his first explanation of her death to the police, he even suggested that he had killed her after they had finished making love on a mattress on the cellar floor. They had been

193

in the basement laying carpet tiles, West suggested, and she 'could have tied something round her head to keep her hair away from the glue' they were using. 'We were both undressed. I never made love with clothes on . . . and she was undressed.'

As the erection went, so I slid out of her, and then I still lay on top of her talking . . . I said something to the effect, 'Oh, this is getting serious', or something – and she said, 'Oh, yer, I think it's about time that I told Rose and we sorted it out'. I mean, I never had no inclination of that whatever. I got quite a shock when she said she was going to tell Rose and . . . start going together, making it serious . . . I thought, No way can I allow that to happen. I just lost me head. I just strangled her with me hand.

In a later version of these same events, West amplified the story slightly, and suggested that Juanita Mott had told him she was pregnant, and, like Lucy Partington before her, 'was going to tell Rose if I didn't go away with her'.

In an even later version, one in which he blamed his wife entirely for the eighteen-year-old girl's death, Frederick West again painted himself as little more than the innocent helper, a man anxious to 'help out' these girls. He told his original solicitor that he had taken 'the Mott girl back to Stroud Road several times, and to Newent . . . Juanita used to come and talk to me quite regular'. He insisted that he had not picked her up thumbing a lift to Gloucester from Newent on Friday 11 April: quite the reverse. 'I took the Mott girl out to Newent. She had been staying on and off for a considerable time, I think . . . She wanted to go to America to see her father, and I was helping her to make some money to go . . . giving her money when I could get a few bob on the side, without Rose knowing.' It was yet another attempt to cast himself in a good light, the one good Samaritan whom the vulnerable young girls who found their way to Cromwell Street could rely upon.

He did not deny that some of the young women who found their way there suffered a terrible fate. 'We used to get loads of girls – but what I didn't realise was that Rose was enticing them there,' West maintained. 'I believe the girls ended up at these parties in Bristol. They were drugged. They were sexually abused. But I don't believe they were killed there. They were taken back to wherever Rose had 'em – and then they were tortured and killed by somebody else.'

The person who was actually supplying young women for prostitution and 'parties' in Bristol, or anywhere else for that matter, was Frederick Walter Stephen West. Indeed, significantly, West told the police when he first admitted the killing of Juanita Mott, that: 'she enjoyed getting hurt when she was making love'. That single remark, more than any other, holds the key to her fate. For Juanita Mott became the sixth young woman in the space of just two years to be sexually abused, tortured, decapitated and finally dismembered in

194

the cellar beneath the pavement of number 25 Cromwell Street.

The Wests' appetite for sexual sadism had grown into a consuming passion. The mask that had covered Shirley Hubbard's face entirely had clearly not satisfied them, no doubt because it denied the opportunity for them to see the horror in the eyes of their helpless victim, and so this time they gagged their victim with her own clothes. When Juanita Mott's remains were recovered from their narrow grave beneath the cellar floor, two pairs of tights, one within the other, a brassière and two long white nylon socks were found wrapped around her skull, 'under the chin and over the top of the head' in the words of the forensic pathologist who discovered them. Significantly, Rosemary West often wore long white nylon socks.

Frederick West had also perfected a sexual harness to keep his victim utterly immobile while he and his wife abused her. A length of plastic-covered rope, like a clothes-line, more than ten feet in length, was found knotted around Juanita Mott's body, with two small loops of ankle and wrist size specifically tied within it. Another seven-feet length of rope may have been used to tether the girl to a place in the cellar. For it seems almost certain that on this occasion, the Wests did not suspend their victim from the beams in the cellar, but instead incapacitated her on the floor – on the mattress that West himself said that they had used to make love on. For when Juanita Mott's remains were recovered, nineteen years after her disappearance, both her kneecaps were missing. And, as Rosemary West's children would bear witness in the years to come, their mother would often hit them on the knees when she wanted to incapacitate them. Juanita Mott's kneecaps were probably removed while she was alive to ensure that she remained the Wests' prisoner.

Like every one of Frederick and Rosemary West's victims, Juanita Mott would have been subjected to relentless and horrifying sexual abuse. In the years to come they would specifically keep for their own amusement a videotape of a young woman, drugged and bound, whose captors inserted a clear plastic tube into her vagina, through which they encouraged two live mice to enter her one after the other. Every videotape they kept reflected in some way their own depraved behaviour. In the circumstances it is literally impossible to imagine the shock or the terror that this would have induced in any young woman, nor the excruciating pain that could have been caused by the animal itself, if it were allowed to remain there for any time. Such inhumanity is the final sign that Frederick West's violent criminality was, as Professor Canter put it, 'nearest to exhibiting pure evil'.

During his last police interviews, Frederick West was reminded that the eighteen-year-old's body had also been viciously mutilated before it was buried. When the officer began to describe the bones that were missing from the body, West suddenly started to panic. 'I feel terrible,' he said suddenly, one of only a handful of times on which he actually displayed emotion during his long series of police interrogations. It was one of the rare occasions on which his voice trembled.

In fact, no fewer than eighty-eight of Juanita Mott's bones were missing when her remains were recovered from her tiny grave beneath the stairs that led down into the cellar of Cromwell Street. The upper part of her breastbone and her right first rib were missing, along with both her kneecaps, all but one of her 16 wrist bones, six of her 14 ankle bones, and 58 of her 76 finger and toe bones. Each and every one of them must have been removed. It would seem as though her hands were cut off entirely, for there can be no other reasonable explanation for their absence, not least because her fingernails were recovered from the familiar small narrow shaft two feet square into which Frederick West had stuffed what elements there remained of her body.

Juanita Mott also suffered a depressed fracture to the base of her skull 'as if a ball-ended hammer had been hit against the skin', in the words of the forensic pathologist who unearthed her remains. No one can be certain whether the blow was inflicted before or after her death, but there must be at least a possibility that she was struck with a hammer while she was still alive, yet another brutal humiliation for this helpless victim whose only mistake had been to accept a lift from Frederick West.

Once she was dead, West disposed of her body in his usual way. It was decapitated between the fourth and fifth cervical vertebrae, both her legs were ripped from their sockets and disarticulated at the hips, and she was shoved into a hole in the floor of the cellar and covered with clay soil. Her bindings, the bundle of material that formed a gag, a seven-feet length of rope and a pair of knickers, which presumably belonged to her, were stuffed into the small hole along with her. All passion spent, it was as if she had never existed.

Chapter Fifteen

Rosemary's babies

'Life's aspirations come in the guise of children.'

Rabindranath Tagore, *Fireflies*

Juanita Mott was the last young woman to be buried in the cellar of Cromwell Street. By the spring of 1975 there was hardly any room there, and the smell, which Frederick West could not blame on a broken sewer for ever, had begun to permeate the rest of the house. If there were to be more killings, he knew the bodies would have to be planted elsewhere. And there were to be more killings. Now he could not stop.

On 1 April 1975 Frederick West rented an allotment at Cheyney Close in Saintsbridge, Gloucester, and gone on to construct a small shed, six feet by three feet, six inches, on the site. It was another place to take his friends where they could smoke dope and watch pornographic films, and it may also have been another place at which to dispose of a body. The fact that he planted runner beans, potatoes, rhubarb and tomatoes, but seemed rarely to bother to cultivate them – even though he had a growing family – may give some indication that its purpose was not solely horticulture. Besides, West was no stranger to allotments; there had been others in the past, not least in Glasgow. They were a natural hide. What could be more innocent?

Another reason for abandoning the cellar as a repository was the simple fact that West now needed the room for his family. West had realised that his children were rapidly reaching an age when they would begin to ask more and more questions about what was happening down there. His eldest daughter, Anna-Marie, was almost eleven now, sullen at one moment, aggressive the next, and due to change to senior school in September 1975. His second child, Heather, was already four and a half, while Mae was almost three and Stephen almost two. West knew that the cellar could provide bedrooms, especially if he wanted to keep a 'special' room for his wife to entertain her 'clients'. The cellar had to be habitable.

197

West also needed the cellar for storage. His appetite for petty theft was still insatiable, and he had invited a local burglar, whom he had first met when they worked together in 1971, to come to Cromwell Street and live with them. The two men would use the cellar to hide whatever they needed to, secure in the knowledge that the police raiding the upstairs of the house never bothered to look down there. Rosemary West was the only other person to have a key to the door.

Rosemary West was twenty-one now, a woman who had had three children, mature enough to start to question what she wanted from life, a woman anxious to make her own stand, even if she was also still hypnotised by the small, swarthy man who used to come home stinking of the factory and the building site night after night. She started to develop longer-lasting lesbian relationships, and, as the year progressed after Juanita Mott's death, she began to stake her claim for at least some independence. In the summer Rosemary West took a holiday in Devon with another girl, leaving her husband to look after the children with Anna-Marie's help. 'They went for a week in a red Mini,' West recalled rather plaintively in the last months of his life.

Shortly afterwards, Frederick West threw the lodgers out of Cromwell Street, not because he did not want to keep them but because the local authority had inspected the house and told him that he would have to install a fire-escape and a fire-alarm. West had no intention of doing either. He simply decided to wait until the council had re-inspected the house, seen that there were no lodgers, and gone away. No sooner had the inspectors done so than West started to advertise in the *Gloucester Citizen* his 'bed-sitting-rooms' for £7 a week.

West also advertised for partners for his wife in contact magazines like *Experience*, and would arrange for the candidates to come to Cromwell Street to be vetted. If they proved acceptable and agreeable he would then film them with his wife. 'He was always looking for people to be in one of his films,' one fellow worker from the time remembered many years later. But Rosemary West's viciousness, a sadistic streak that she revealed only gradually during a sexual relationship, sometimes made it difficult to find willing partners. Frederick West also told one of his workmates at the time that he had 'invited three lesbians down from Birmingham for Rose', but one of them had been so terrified when 'her pubic hair had been bitten out' that she had 'run out into the street half-naked'. West said that he had been forced to 'run down the street after her, catch her, calm her down and take her back inside'.

West would also drive his wife to meet lesbians in other parts of the country. In the autumn of 1975, for example, Rosemary West embarked on an affair with a woman in Swindon who had replied to one of his advertisements in a contact magazine. His wife had never learned to drive – indeed, she never would – but her husband was only too happy to take her there, wait for her and then drive her home. On the way back to Gloucester he would insist she tell him 'every single detail'. For her part, Rosemary West was quite content to satisfy his curiosity. It gave her a sense of power over him. It was proof she was now capable of standing on her own two feet, a sexual being in her own right rather than simply her husband's creation. Frederick West, meanwhile, liked to brag about her sexual conquests.

One seventeen-year-old girl who found her way to Cromwell Street in the second half of 1975 bears witness to this. First taken there by a friend, she thought the Wests were a 'very pleasant couple', especially when Frederick West offered 'to run her home' in his A35 van. She went back a few weeks later, and Rosemary West invited her to her bedroom to see a jacket she had been making, and then persuaded the girl to take off her clothes and lie down on the bed. As Frederick West himself explained years afterwards: 'Rose had terrific powers of persuasion over these girls. If you could persuade a girl to undress in a bedroom, and that you're measuring her up for a dress, you've got some power.' When the girl was naked, Rosemary West had proceeded to kiss her neck, and then work down her body until she was sucking and licking her vagina.

'I was bewildered by it all,' the girl remembered later. But, a few weeks afterwards she returned to Cromwell Street, and on this occasion Rosemary West took her down into the cellar and laid her on a 'single mattress on the floor'. The rest of the room, she remembered, 'was full of toys'. Once again Rosemary West persuaded the girl to take off her clothes, and licked her vagina, but this time she went on to insert a vibrator into her. 'She did it so quick, it hurt me a lot,' the girl told the court at Rosemary West's trial two decades later, 'and she held it up there inside me. I had to ask her to take it out because it was hurting so much.'

The seventeen-year-old was a virgin. She ended up bleeding so badly that Rosemary West handed her a baby's nappy to use as a sanitary towel. But the girl did not complain. She simply put on her clothes and left. The events were never reported to the police. The girl never visited her family doctor. She was too embarrassed. There was never any official investigation, no official visit to Cromwell Street, no enquiry to ask how on earth the girl came to be harmed. There was no investigation whatever. Instead, Rosemary West joined her husband in the firm belief that she could always get away with whatever she wanted. Like him, she was untouchable.

Another person who suffered at the evermore confident hands of Rosemary West was her stepdaughter Anna-Marie. Now eleven years of age, the girl had 'never really been happy at school', and years later she would confess: 'I felt I didn't fit in . . . I was never allowed to invite other girls and boys home or to go to their houses to play.' In fact, this was part of Frederick West's plan. He and his wife were intent on maintaining their private world, away from the gaze of anyone who might not approve of it, and that depended on their absolute control over their children. Anna-Marie had become the guinea-pig for that control, just as she believes she was a guinea-pig for some of their attacks.

'They frequently practised forms of restraint of me,' Anna-Marie was to remember two decades later. Rosemary West experimented with sheets ripped into strips, builders' rope, nylon clothes-line, carpet tape and 'fabric to put across my mouth'. Once her step-daughter was bound, she would assault her with belts, canes and whips, as well as the cat-o'-nine-tails. It is hard to escape the conclusion that the attack reflected a little of what must have happened to the Wests' victims, not least because 'when she completed her experiments she would encourage Dad to rape me, or they would both insert objects into me'.

Between them, Frederick and Rosemary West carefully created their own bizarre and distorted reality. As the distinguished clinical psychologist George Kelly described it, the Wests formed their 'own distinctive alternative universe', and used this as a guide for their own actions and their responses to the world. It was a world that neither of them wished to see invaded. Their house might be filled with lodgers, but they did not finally impinge on the reality of the Wests beneath them. Nor did they impinge on the horrifying reality of what went on in the cellar. It was only when one of the young women lodging or visiting there stepped across that invisible threshold, and thereby joined the Wests' alternative universe, that they were in danger for their lives.

Frederick West would impress on his children, for example, that they should remain within the confines of the house whenever possible. 'We don't want to have anything to do with people outside. We don't need them. There are people out there who will hurt you . . . You're with people who will protect you,' he told his eldest daughter time after time. It was the reason that West would come to construct the extraordinary wrought-iron gates that barred the way to the front door of 25 Cromwell Street throughout the last twenty years of the family's time there. The gates were his protection against a world that he did not want to intrude upon him, a barrier to be crossed only on invitation.

Within the walls of Cromwell Street, West was the master of his universe. Still a thief and a part-time fence – he was fined £75 for receiving stolen goods in November 1975 – he relished his wife's prostitution, and her appetite for lesbian relationships, just as he relished the medical details of her pregnancies and menstrual cycle. He took an equally fascinated interest in the development of his daughter Anna-Marie's breasts, and her journey into puberty. It was a fascination that he would retain throughout the rest of his life. His crudeness expressed itself in phrases like 'I see Harry Rags is riding in the two-thirty', as a way of indicating that his wife's, and later his daughter's, period may have started. 'We always wondered how he knew, but he did,' his eldest daughter was to remark.

It was not the only indignity that Anna-Marie West was subjected to. Rosemary West also took pornographic photographs of her stepdaughter with a Polaroid camera, and hit her repeatedly, although always taking care to make sure that the bruises did not show. On another occasion, when Anna-Marie West displeased her, Rosemary West stripped the girl, and instructed her younger children to paint the words 'Black Hole' on her stepdaughter's naked buttocks with an arrow pointing towards her anus. Rosemary West took a photograph of the girl, who was then told to remain naked until her father came home. When he did so, Frederick West simply laughed.

West exercised a delicate and subtle control over the house and its inmates. He took particular pleasure, for example, in goading his wife to lose her temper, and standing back to see what damage she might inflict on her children once he had ignited the fuse to her formidable and vicious temper. Rosemary West, in turn, would try to amuse him by humiliating Anna-Marie, or beating one of the younger children, knowing that he would never object. On one summer evening, for example, she took her stepdaughter out to a pub for the evening, persuaded her to drink rather too much barley wine, and then helped her husband to rape her in the back of his van on the way home. It was Rosemary West's means of keeping her husband entertained and calm.

Frederick West would demand sexual intercourse at any time, just as he had always done, referring to it as 'going off to bunny land', and Rosemary West had become only too willing to oblige. West's sexual grooming of the young Rosemary Letts had borne fruit; she was now as sexually obsessed as he was, and equally determined that she should be guaranteed her own gratification. Under Frederick West's instruction, sex, and everything to do with it, had become an addiction, to dominate his wife's life just as intensely as it dominated his. As Anna-Marie West would put it: 'That was Rose for you. Sex on demand – at any time, any place and with anybody she could get her hands on. If she wanted it at that moment, she got it. It didn't matter if it was Dad, one of her so-called friends, a woman or a child.' Frederick West had created a woman in his own sexual image, and seen her appetites grow until her perverse desire matched his. Their evil love had blossomed.

In the years to come, Frederick and Rosemary West would do everything within their power to usher all their female children into their alternative universe, their world of sexual experiment. Before the end of 1975, for example, Anna-Marie was being offered as a sexual favour to some of the men who came to the house as regular clients of her stepmother. Sometimes her father would watch through the spyhole he had made in the door of 'Rose's Special Room'. West himself would have sex with her 'quite frequently' in the back of his van and 'sometimes in the woods'. And in time her two younger stepsisters, Heather and Mae West, would find themselves used as sexual bait for men. Anna-Marie West reacted to this abuse she suffered by becoming aggressive and delinquent at school, her rage and unhappiness expressing itself in a determination not to be ignored, a desire for revenge on a world that had not allowed her a childhood. As one friend in the first year at Linden Secondary School in Gloucester remembered: 'Anna seemed to know more

201

about sexual things than the rest of us. Her knowledge of sex seemed beyond her years.'

One man who had been ushered into the sexual world of Cromwell Street by Frederick West was his father-in-law William Letts. Letts's relationship with his wife Daisy had hardly improved in the years since their separation at Bishop's Cleeve, and he had become an increasingly regular visitor to his daughter's and son-in-law's house. One reason was simple enough. Letts had retained a sexual relationship with his daughter throughout the years she had been married to West, and with her husband's blessing. Only two decades older than Frederick West, Letts was also attracted to the house by the possibility of other sexual conquests. Indeed, he may well have been one of the men invited into the cellar from time to time.

In the last months of his life Frederick West talked at length about his father-in-law and his relationship with his wife. 'He was fucking her regular. That's why she was going over there. He was bringing her back, and fucking her on the way. But I actually caught them in bed. He was well in.' The idea appealed to the voyeur in West. 'I never knew that Rose was ever abused. Rose never told me that her father had ever abused her. Whenever I seen her with him she was more than willing to get them off, and having a good time at it.'

Rosemary West's sexual relationship with her father did not put her husband off for a moment, even though he would describe Letts as 'an evil bastard' with an 'evil look', who had a 'little round face, and little beady eyes'. Early in 1976 West started work on the cellar with 'the idea of making it into a self-contained granny flat' for Bill Letts. He had already concreted over the ash and gravel that had been its flooring originally, in the wake of Juanita Mott's death. The project was shelved, however, probably not least because of the dangers of disturbing the bodies of five young women, but West nevertheless invited Bill Letts to stay in one of the lodgers' rooms at Cromwell Street.

Frederick West's and Bill Letts's friendship went even further than a sexual ménage à trois. When Letts decided to take early retirement from Smith's Industries in Bishop's Cleeve in 1976, at the age of fifty-five, the two men decided to go into business together and launch another café in Southgate Street in the centre of Gloucester. The few thousand pounds that Letts had received on retirement was used to buy the lease and acquire the necessary catering equipment, and as his share West did all the conversion and building work that was required. In doing so he was almost certainly realising one of the dreams that had filled his life since his days above the Rendezvous Café in Newent, the dream of owning a place at which to meet young girls. The two men called the café the Green Lantern. It even had the benefit of a cellar.

During the hot summer of 1976 Letts took his daughter and the West children to a holiday camp in Westward Ho! in Devon, not far from his family home at Northam. Frederick West remained in

Gloucester, working night shifts at Muir Hill and spending what time he could during the day preparing the café for its opening. But the holiday did not turn out exactly as Bill Letts may have planned. He rapidly became incensed at his daughter's promiscuity. Rosemary West started to work her way through the camp orchestra, 'like a dose of salts', as Anna-Marie West remembered. 'There was an almighty row between Rose and her father and the result was that we packed our bags.'

In the last months of his life Frederick West would recall some of his experiences with his father-in-law in a section of his prison memoir *I Was Loved by an Angel*. He did so in fourteen pages of his ninety-eight-page memoir which describe his relationship with Shirley Robinson, another young woman who was about to enter his life. The memoir starts with his memories of Bill Letts and their café, and it reveals precisely the byzantine sexual relationships of Cromwell Street at the time.

'Rose's father . . . was living in my family home in Cromwell Street,' West wrote. 'Rose's mother and father were separated. I was working nights and helping to get the café ready for opening day.' One night West injured his thumb on the heavy press he used at Muir Hill, and went to hospital for treatment.

> I stopped home to see Rose. It was about 11 p.m. Rose was in bed, so I went into the bedroom . . . I didn't put the light on in the room. I sat at the bottom of the bed. I was telling Rose what had happened to my hand at work. Then Anna came running downstairs and said to Rose: 'Grampy's going to sleep with me.' Anna had not seen me. Anna thought I was at work. Rose said: 'Go back to bed. He's not going to eat you, he's only going to fuck you . . . I am sure you will love that.'

Frederick West insisted in his memoir, which he hoped would eventually be published, that the thought appalled him. 'I went upstairs to him and said, "What's going on?" Anna was with me. Bill said, "Rose said Anna could sleep with me but Anna is playing up" . . . I said to Bill, "You're out of this house in the morning".' West maintained that he then took his eldest daughter to her room, where 'Anna told me Rose had been sleeping with her dad and now Mum got men coming from the pub at night, when you're at work, and Mum told me to sleep with her dad so he did not go downstairs to Mum's room'. According to his memoir, Frederick West's only response was to tell his daughter to 'lock her door' and to go back to work himself.

'When I got home in the morning Rose and her dad was in the kitchen having breakfast . . . He said to me: "Do I have to go?" I said, "Yes." "Where can I go?" I said: "To the café." There was a flat on top of the café. "You can go there." ' At that point, according to Frederick West's version of events, his father-in-law left Cromwell Street and went to live above the Green Lantern. But their partnership did not dissolve. As West would explain eighteen years later: 'It was a joint venture. I wanted to keep an eye on him, what he was up to . . . He was a devious bastard, and he was a bastard with young kids too.' In that respect, as in many others, the two men had a great deal in common.

'I was going home from work one morning,' West wrote in his memoir. 'I stopped to see Bill. I went to the back door. I looked up to the roof at the back of the café. There was Bill by the bathroom window. He had sacking over him. I said: "What you doing up there?" He said: "Shhhh." He came down to me. He said, "I picked up two young girls in Bristol. They were coming to Gloucester. And they stayed the night. And they're having a bath together. If you get up on the roof you can see them." ' Frederick West maintained in his memoir that he refused the offer. 'I said: "No way. I am not into that." '

In spite of what Frederick West may or may not have told his father-in-law about his dislike for the abuse of his daughter Anna-Marie, there is no doubt that both he and his wife independently sexually abused the twelve-year-old. In the same year that Letts moved to live above the Green Lantern, for example, the girl was forced to perform oral sex on her stepmother. 'She kept urging me, "Come on, do it properly",' the girl would recall. 'And then, "Use your fingers". It was absolutely horrendous. And all the time it was happening she was squeezing and scratching my breasts. She had long fingers and quite long nails, and she scratched me until I bled. She grabbed the skin at the base of my throat and twisted it until I could barely breathe.'

Meanwhile, West himself would take his eldest child with him on his part-time building jobs, many of which were in other houses in the neighbourhood, and often for members of the West Indian community. 'What they didn't know,' she was to recall, 'was that when they left us alone in the house, or in a different part of it, my father would have sex with me. On other occasions he would do it in the back of the van he used to transport his tools. He would park somewhere remote on our way to or from a job. Often he would give me money afterwards, and said: "Sorry, love. Here, have some pocket-money, but don't tell your mother".'

The delicate but immensely strong thread of love that binds an abused child to her abuser is only too clear. 'It was the only kind of love I knew from him, and I never complained. I didn't mind keeping it a secret from Rose.' Frederick West was subtly choreographing a jealousy between his wife and eldest daughter which would persist throughout the rest of his life, redoubling his influence over them both. At one level they were rivals for his sole attention; at another they were merely members of a harem of women prepared to do his bidding. But both were to play up to the roles he cast for them.

In the late summer of 1976, for example, Rosemary West started to dress up her stepdaughter and take her out with her in the evenings to pubs and clubs, where she would introduce the girl as her 'sister'. One seventeen-year-old who met them together one evening at a local sports and social club was absolutely convinced they were sisters. 'They looked very alike,' he remembered. When Rosemary West suggested that he leave with them and go back to Cromwell Street, the young man thought he was being offered sex with her younger 'sister', but, in fact, he made love to Rosemary West herself against a wall in the street after Anna-Marie had gone inside the house.

In the autumn of 1976 Frederick West resigned from the Muir Hill Wagon Works and devoted all his energies to the Green Lantern. His sister-in-law Glenys Tyler was also working at the café with her father Bill Letts, while West was helping every day. Now, as well as the old green A35 van with the windows down the side, which were covered by curtains, West acquired a blue Transit van with scaffolding poles welded to it, which supported a large roof-rack. West would use it for transporting jobs, some of them for Glenys Tyler's husband Jim, but in the evenings he had developed a new pastime. The size of the van allowed West to indulge this hobby. He would take his wife with him to look for clients, and allow them to have sex in the back of the van while he stood and watched.

West was still using what other spare time he had for building work for a variety of people in Gloucester. 'He was a meticulous plumber and painter,' one resident recalled many years later, 'even though he looked terrible. And he was extremely reliable.' West's ability as an odd-job man and builder was particularly popular among the West Indian community, and he took every opportunity to encourage the black men he met to consider having sex with his wife, not least because he was convinced they had 'larger ones' than white men. Frederick West approved: 'Rose only had big fucking blokes. She didn't want little worms playing about with her.'

Certainly, by the end of 1976 Rosemary West having overcome her initial suspicion of black people, had had a number of Jamaican and black West Indian lovers and clients at 25 Cromwell Street. She had another objective beyond prostitution, however. Still only twenty-three, Rosemary West wanted another child, and her husband was fascinated by the possibility that she might become pregnant by one of her black lovers. In the first weeks of March 1977 both interests were satisfied. Rosemary West discovered that she was pregnant – by one of her black lovers. The news delighted her husband, for they kept no secrets from one another. They were, in the words of one of their lodgers at the time, 'always together', and 'they always knew what each other was doing'.

Rosemary West's appetite for sexual intercourse did not diminish during pregnancy: quite the opposite. 'When Rose was pregnant she was always extra sexy for some reason,' as Frederick West put it. She might be slightly less mobile, but that did not mean that either she or her husband wished to abstain from their diet of violent and perverse sex. It simply meant that she needed to stay at home rather more. That did not present the Wests with a problem, as Cromwell Street was still providing shelter to large numbers of itinerant young people.

Its reputation as a safe haven among the vulnerable and unhappy girls in Gloucester had grown steadily, carefully nurtured by Frederick West. In Jordan's Brook Community Home in Gloucester, for example, a former approved school, several of the resident girls knew that Cromwell Street was a place where they could find temporary accommodation if they absconded – even if only overnight. Over the preceding year Jordan's Brook girls had been finding their way to the Wests' house with increasing regularity.

One Jordan's Brook girl, who first visited Cromwell Street in 1976, remembers Rosemary West as a 'big sister' or 'young mum', who was 'always a shoulder to cry on' and said she could 'go there any time'. Many years later the girl, who was then only fourteen and had been placed in care the previous year, would recall: 'It was nice because I felt as if someone really cared.' She met Frederick West, but 'only casually, and very briefly'. During the first part of 1977 she visited Cromwell Street regularly, usually on Friday mornings between ten o'clock and midday. She would sit and talk to Rosemary West before returning to Jordan's Brook. 'I was a bit upset about the people in care,' she would recall, 'and about the system. We would talk about it and she was fine. A couple of occasions we would talk about girls' things, periods and sex and things, which seemed pretty normal for that age.'

On one occasion early in 1977 she and another young girl absconded from Jordan's Brook and slept rough on the streets of Gloucester for a night. The next evening they went to Cromwell Street together, where the door was opened by Rosemary West wearing only a bra and pants. 'I got the impression she was going to bed,' the girl remembered many years later. Frederick West appeared, and there was a suggestive conversation, but 'Yvonne and myself stayed the night – on the sofa'. Not long afterwards, however, on one of her Friday morning visits to the Wests' house, things went a little further. While Rosemary West was comforting the girl: 'She was quite close and started kissing my neck and touching my breasts on the outside of my clothes,' the girl recalled eighteen years later. 'It was a bit odd and a bit strange. I didn't like it at all. I pulled to one side and she stopped and didn't apologise or anything.'

Nevertheless, throughout the early summer of 1977, the first months of Rosemary West's new pregnancy, the girl, who was now fifteen, continued to go to Cromwell Street on most Friday mornings, continued to visit the place she had come to think of as a home, and continued to talk to the 'big sister' cum 'young mum' who lived there. Until, on one Friday morning, on the way to visit her mother, she called to use the lavatory. As usual, Rosemary West answered the door; but that was the last familiar thing that would happen to the girl that morning. 'She was wearing a chiffon blouse type of thing, loose, and a skirt. She was wearing nothing under the blouse as far as I could see.'

Rosemary West ushered the girl inside her house, and suggested she use the first-floor bathroom. But afterwards she did not simply allow the fifteen-year-old to leave; instead, the pregnant twenty-three-year-old mother led the girl into a first-floor front bedroom. Nothing could possibly have prepared her for what was about to happen. 'There were three other people in the bedroom,' the Jordan's Brook girl would recall. 'Fred and two young girls. They were both naked. He had some shorts on.' One girl was thirteen or fourteen and blonde, the other a little older with a tattoo on her forearm had dark spiky hair. 'I was dumbstruck with what I was seeing.'

Without uttering a word, Rosemary West started to undress the fifteen-year-old that she had just led into the room. 'I didn't know what to do. She started. I ended up finishing,' the girl remembered afterwards. 'It felt like a fair-ground ride where you are stuck against the wall.' Not to her hostess, however. 'She said it was OK, things like that. We are all girls. It just seemed as though everything was supposed to be normal.' Rosemary West then removed her own clothes, while her husband stood on one side of the bed. The room now housed four naked women and Frederick West.

The young blonde girl was led towards the bed by Rosemary West, who started to caress her, all the time reassuring her that there was nothing unusual in what was happening. 'She looked very distressed and frightened,' the girl from Jordan's Brook recalled. 'She was face downwards. I looked away.' When she looked back, she saw Frederick West wrapping one-and-a-half-inch-wide brown parcel tape around the young blonde girl's wrists, fingers and thumbs – 'and across her chest', so that they seemed 'like bandages'. The parcel tape was then tied around her ankles, and she was turned over on the bed so that she was now lying on her back. Her legs were then tied 'quite far apart'. The girl looked away again, and then heard a noise, the noise of a vibrator.

Remembering these events almost two decades later, at the trial of Rosemary West, the girl broke down in tears time after time as she relived the events on that Friday morning in Cromwell Street. It had taken her many years even to pluck up the courage to tell the story in the first place, and she agreed to give evidence only on the understanding that she would remain anonymous, so ashamed and upset had she been by what took place on that summer's morning in 1977.

'Rose had a vibrator, and a candle, and a tube of what I presume was lubricant,' she explained. The vibrator was used on the bound young woman. 'I could see tears on her face.' Then Rosemary West said suddenly: 'Are you enjoying this, Fred? Is it turning you on?' West by this time was also naked. As soon as his wife removed the vibrator, he had sexual intercourse with the helpless fourteen-year-old lying on the bed in front of him. His wife put her hands on his buttocks as he did so. 'She had tears on the side of her face. She looked very pale.' Frederick West left the first-floor front bedroom shortly afterwards, and his wife removed the tape from the prone girl's wrists. 'Rose was stroking her cheek and saying, "It's OK". It was like Jekyll and Hyde. All aggressive one minute, then all motherly again.' The remains of the tape were ripped off her body, leaving the young blonde 'in a trance-like state'.

The fifteen-year-old from Jordan's Brook, who was known at Rosemary West's trial as Miss A, was then herself led towards the bed. She told the court that she thought, God, I'm next. The woman who had acted like a big sister towards her for almost a year 'held my wrist and led me to the bed and sat me down. I wanted to scream. I wanted to kick. I wanted to cry. But I just felt numb. She used words like, "Relax, it's fun". She laid me down and just caressed and touched me a little . . . then she got the tape. I kept thinking "Why?" '

Frederick West came back into the room as his wife started taping the girl's wrists and arms behind her back. Her ankles were then taped apart, and she 'felt something hard and cold go inside me – in my anus'. Rosemary West was murmuring to her gently, 'Enjoy, relax'. Then she felt fingers 'searching around' her vagina, and she could see West himself masturbating beside her. She felt 'something cold and hard again', but waxy this time, which 'could have been the candle' pushed inside her after the fingers had been removed. 'Then Rose said, "Fred, you're enjoying this" ', as she continued to abuse the girl relentlessly.

'It seemed like for ever,' Miss A would recall, until West himself 'came up from behind' and started to have intercourse with her. His wife meanwhile started twisting the girl's nipples viciously, and then turned to caressing her husband's bare buttocks again. 'He was talking about coming over my back, and I remember stuff being rubbed into my back. It must have been by Rose, because the hands were quite soft.' Frederick West then left the room again, and his wife took a tiny pair of scissors and snipped through the tape around her wrists. Then: 'It was pulled off hard, like the hairs being pulled out of your arms.'

Eventually, the Jordan's Brook girl was allowed to pick up her dress and return to the bathroom. 'I felt horrible. Dirty. I just wanted to scrub it away,' she remembered. 'Blood had gone down my leg. From my anus, I believe. I just wanted to cover myself up. I came out of the bathroom and stopped for a second and then I just ran down the stairs and went.' She fled barefoot across the park at the bottom of Cromwell Street and started to hitchhike. 'I felt so ashamed. I felt thick and stupid. I couldn't go to the police because then there was a stigma about children in care, that if you were in care you were bad. I couldn't go to my mum. I couldn't go to my dad. There was nobody.'

Miss A finally went home to her mother's house, but she did not tell her, or anyone else, about her experiences at the hands of the Wests on that Friday morning in 1977. When she returned to Jordan's Brook on the following Monday she still did not confide in anyone. But six weeks later she went back to the Wests' house in Cromwell Street. It was another Friday morning, but this time she 'took a can of petrol and some matches', which she intended 'to put through the letterbox of their house and set it on fire'. The girl stood by the iron gates that Frederick West had just erected to bar the entrance to his front door, but she did not push the bell. 'I wanted to do it so much,' she recalled, but her nerve failed her. 'I walked back – and just went home to Tewkesbury.' It was to be seventeen years before the girl from Jordan's Brook would tell anyone what had happened to her in Cromwell Street in the summer of 1977.

Once again the Wests had chosen their victim with meticulous care. Miss A was no stranger to Frederick or Rosemary West (although at her trial Mrs West denied she knew her at all). In fact, the Wests probably knew far more about her than even she suspected, for her visits to Cromwell Street on Fridays were not her only contact with the West family. Miss A certainly knew Graham Letts, Rosemary West's brother, because they had run away together, and lived for a time in a flat above a tea-shop in Cheltenham. Miss A had almost certainly told Graham Letts that she had been abused by her father and her brother at the age of twelve, and she may well have told Rosemary West exactly the same thing during their conversations in Cromwell Street. Miss A may also have told her that her brother had not been her only boyfriend.

Although the opportunity to abuse Miss A may have presented itself unexpectedly, there is little doubt that the Wests would have targeted her as a potential victim shortly after the start of her visits to Cromwell Street. Because of her history of sexual abuse, proven sexual track record, and suggestion of mental instability, the Wests would have been certain that there was every chance that she would never be believed – even if she did report the events of that morning to the police or the Social Services. Frederick West, in particular, would no doubt have prepared his own subtle version of events should he ever be questioned about the girl and what may have occurred in his first-floor bedroom, which would have maintained that she had been both a willing and active participant in a 'gang bang', as he liked to call them.

Miss A was not to be the last girl from Jordan's Brook Community Home to find her way to Cromwell Street, nor was she the last to be brutally abused there by Frederick and Rosemary West. During her visits, however, West began an affair with a seventeen-year-old girl called Shirley Robinson, a young woman who looked for a time as though she might become the third Mrs West. Not surprisingly, their relationship did nothing to endear her to the increasingly pregnant Rosemary West.

Chapter Sixteen

The next Mrs West

'Love that is fed by jealousy dies hard.'

Ovid, *Love's Cure*

On a visit to the Green Lantern café in the spring of 1977, Frederick West met the girl who was to make almost as great an impact on his life as Ann McFall had done ten years before. Though he was not to realise it at first, Shirley Robinson forced West to question his love for his second wife, and threatened his marriage to Rosemary West. In the process she became the only woman ever truly to test the strength of the Wests' love for one another, and she was to pay a terrible price for doing so.

Shirley Robinson was also the only other woman, apart from Ann McFall, that Frederick West was to force himself to write about during the last days of his life. He described their meeting, and their love-affair, in the memoir that he called *I Was Loved by an Angel*. Laboriously writing in biro on sheets of lined A4 prison paper, West remembered that he met her a short time after he had 'asked the police to have a look' at a hand-gun that his father-in-law Bill Letts had at the café.

'A week or two later I stopped at the café,' Frederick West wrote, 'and there was a girl sat in there. I said "good morning" to her and went out to the kitchen. Bill said to me: "I got a girl to work with me." I said: "Is that the girl in the café?" He said: "Yes." I said: "Where's she from?" He said: "I picked her up in Bristol . . . She is looking for a job." ' West went back into the café, introduced himself, and asked the girl her name. 'She said: "Shirley Robinson." That was the first time I seen Shirley. I got to know her well.'

That was undoubtedly the case. West's relationship with Shirley Robinson was to last longer and remain closer than his relationship with any other of his English-born victims. She was to live with him and with his wife for more than fifteen months, and, like Ann McFall before her, she was to come within a matter of weeks of bearing his child. And, once again like Ann McFall before her, she was the child of a broken and unhappy home.

210

When Shirley Robinson first encountered Frederick West she was seventeen years of age, a brash, precocious girl with a broad Wolverhampton accent, about five feet, two inches tall, with light brown shoulder-length hair and a wide-eyed, mischievous smile. Born in October 1959 in Rutland, where her father was working at an RAF base, she had spent an unhappy childhood being pushed from pillar to post. The year after her birth, the family were posted to Singapore, only to return to Darlington in England after a year, where her younger brother Kevin was born in December 1961. Less than a year after that, Shirley's parents separated. The three-year-old Shirley Robinson stayed first with her mother, and then, for a rather longer period, with her father, before returning once again to her mother, who by this time had married again. Things did not work out, and in 1974, at the age of fourteen, she was taken into care in Wolverhampton.

By this time Shirley Robinson had become withdrawn and rather sullen, a girl who did not easily make friends with other girls. As a result she was sent to the secure extra-care unit at the Crescent School in Downend, Bristol, where eventually she was to settle down. One reason for the change may have been that she had become a lesbian. In 1975 she embarked on a lesbian relationship in Bristol, and took a job in the evenings in a gay pub in the city. She went on from there to work at a local boot factory, but that did not last long, and early in 1977 she worked briefly as a housemaid in a hotel in Chipping Sodbury. By the beginning of April she was at the Green Lantern café in Gloucester and, almost certainly, starting to visit 25 Cromwell Street.

'She told me she was a lesbian,' West was to explain in his memoir. Indeed, in this version of events it was almost the first thing that Shirley Robinson said to him when they met at the Green Lantern. 'Shirley was a happy-go-lucky girl,' West wrote. 'I called in the café every morning and night', but one morning 'Shirley was looking ill. So I asked her what was up with her. She said Rose's dad was giving her a hard time, and could I get her a bed. I asked Shirley what he was up to. She said he had taken the lock off the bathroom door and her bedroom door and he just kept walking in and . . . "touching me up . . . I only go with girls".' West did not hesitate. He offered her a room in his house. 'So Shirley moved to Cromwell Street.'

The attraction for Frederick West was only too clear. Here was another young woman whom he could watch make love to his wife, and who might then be prepared to take part in one of his 'films'. The fact that she was a self-confessed and active lesbian certainly increased his fascination for her. In the last week of June 1977 he helped her move out of the flat above the Green Lantern and into the small room beside the bathroom on the first-floor of Cromwell Street. As he did so, Shirley Robinson would no doubt have told him every detail of her unhappy childhood, and the abuse that she had suffered at the hands of adults. Her confidences can only have broadened the grin on Frederick West's face.

West was well aware that the seventeen-year-old's attractions for his pregnant wife would be even stronger. The girl was a potential lover for his wife, someone to be seduced without having to venture out into the local pubs or clubs, a morsel that he could bring home for her delectation. His plan worked. Shirley Robinson definitely 'got on well with Rose'. Frederick West noted as much in his memoir, adding, 'They were going out at night'. There is no doubt that at some point in the summer of 1977, and at about the same time as Miss A was suffering so dreadfully at her hands, Rosemary West and Shirley Robinson began an affair. West was not only aware of it; he encouraged it. Lesbianism fascinated him, though he could not abide its male counterpart. Frederick West believed all homosexual men were 'dirty bastards', while lesbians were 'clean and straight'.

The Green Lantern café was not proving a success. Its debts were mounting rapidly. Bill Letts had recruited the help of his wife and family to help him to run it, but the café could not support them all financially. And Frederick West knew it. The one thing he never lost sight of was money, particularly his own, and he had no intention of supporting the Letts family. 'So I went and said to Rose's dad, "We will have to close it down",' West wrote in his memoir. 'Bill went back to live with his wife, Rose's mum.'

West recruited Shirley Robinson to work for him instead of the café. The collapse of the Green Lantern had forced him to go back to the Muir Hill Wagon Works, but he was also still working as a part-time builder, and he needed help. West was converting and refurbishing flats for Frank Zygmunt's widow and son. Zygmunt himself had died shortly after West had moved into Cromwell Street, leaving his property to his family. And, by chance, some of the first flats that West had worked on were at 24 and 25 Midland Road, where he and Rosemary had lived at the start of their relationship. One of his first jobs had been to refill the cellars of both 24 and 25 Midland Road with aggregate – thereby burying his stepdaughter Charmaine still further.

This building job at Midland Road was one reason why Frederick West had originally told the police that they 'wouldn't find nothing at Midland Road', because the demolition men 'must have taken Charmaine's body to the tip'. Indeed, West maintained strenuously in his police interviews in 1994, before Midland Road was excavated, that: 'You pull it down, there'll be nothing there.' West clearly hoped that he had covered his tracks effectively during his building work there, and was particularly keen that the police should not try to recover the child's body. If they did, it would give the lie to his persistent claim to them that 'she was in one piece, no doubt of that'. To recover her remains would reveal that the child's body was most certainly not in one piece.

Frederick West took Shirley Robinson with him to work at Midland Road. 'She worked like a man,' he wrote. 'Shirley spent all her time on the job, seventeen hours a day. I worked on my job by day,' and then 'went to work with Shirley till we went home at eleven

212

or twelve at night'. And it was while they were at Midland Road that Frederick West, too, embarked on an affair with the tiny seventeen-year-old girl, whom he had nicknamed 'Bones' because of her thinness. Three or four months after they started working there together, West would record in his memoir, 'Shirley was undressing to change out of her working clothes. She said: "You want to have sex with me?" I said: "You're a lesbian." She said: "Lesbians have sex with men." I had never made love to a lesbian. I wondered what it would be like. So I said, "Yes." So we had sex.'

Their relationship did not end there. According to Frederick West: 'Shirley said: "I want a baby." I said: "What for? You're a lesbian." She said: "I have a girlfriend in Bristol and we would like a baby." I said: "No baby. A baby has to have a mother and a father, not two girls. What about when the child goes to school?" So Shirley said: "You can have sex with me when you want to." I said: "We will see." So Shirley got dressed and we went home.' But not until, West maintained, he had instructed her: 'You are not to tell Rose.'

Even if his account of the beginning of their affair is to be believed, the reason for Shirley Robinson's sexual approach to Frederick West almost certainly had nothing to do with a desire for a child, at least at the outset. She was to confide to a friend some months later that it had simply been her way of paying the rent for her small room in Cromwell Street, as she had discovered that it was a system that West had used in the past. It is also certain that Shirley Robinson's individual sexual relationships with Rosemary West and Frederick West then expanded into a ménage à trois, with the Wests sharing the girl as a lover, often at the same time and always in the same bed.

Shirley Robinson continued to work with Frederick West, just as she continued to have sex with him. One of the jobs they did together was at 7 Cromwell Street, where they worked throughout one weekend towards the end of the summer of 1977. 'We started on Saturday to strip the walls . . . The householder and his mates were helping,' West would recall. Then: 'It was opening time at the pub, so my helpers went to the pub. Shirley and I did not go. Shirley was on the stepladder working on the ceiling. She said to me: "How long will they be at the pub?" ' West told her: 'They won't be back till the pub closes.'

Shirley said: 'I will take my overalls off . . . catch them.' So I look up. She kicked them off at me to catch them, so I did. I looked up and said: 'You got no pants on.' She said: 'No, it's too hot to wear them.' So Shirley said: 'Catch me.' So she jumped down to me to catch her. I did. We fell on the floor. Shirley held me tight and said: 'Please make love to me. I am in love with you.' . . . So I made love to Shirley. Then we got on with the work.'

Shortly afterwards the seventeen-year-old girl with the strong Black Country accent discovered that she was pregnant.

By this time Rosemary West was eight months' pregnant with the child she had conceived with a Jamaican. The fact that she was bearing another man's child, the first time she had ever done so, may have made West feel an unexpected jealousy – even though he may have been enthusiastic about the idea at the outset. In the circumstances Frederick West may just have seized the opportunity to make his wife jealous in return, and himself urged Shirley Robinson to have his child, rather than succumbing to her suggestion. The prospect of having two women fight over him was certainly still one of Frederick West's passions, just as his appetite for making his wife angry had not deserted him.

Ten days after Shirley Robinson's eighteenth birthday in October 1977, she was confirmed as six weeks' pregnant at the Health Centre at the Park in Gloucester, where she had registered as a patient in June, after moving into Cromwell Street. Less than two months later, and just after her own twenty-fourth birthday, Rosemary West gave birth to her third daughter and fourth child, whom the Wests christened Tara. Frederick West told one friend afterwards that they had decided to christen his latest daughter Tara because it was the name of the 'hotel that Rose often used'; Tara was later to be referred to in the family as Mo.

The night of the birth of Rosemary West's new child certainly remained imprinted on her husband's mind, and may give a clue to his attitude towards her pregnancy. In his memoir West recalled that he had been working on their house with Shirley Robinson that evening:

> When Rose came in with a black man and said to me, 'Get my case. I am going to hospital. I am in labour,' I said, 'I am going with you. That's my baby'. Rose said to the black man, 'My husband will take me' . . . so he went. I said to Rose, 'Why did you want him to go with you?' Rose said, 'I was in bed with him when I went into labour. I said he could come and see me have the baby.' Rose said, 'I thought you were at work.' I said, 'If you stayed at home a night or two you would see me.' Rose said, 'I need a man to keep me happy.' I said, 'Thank you, Rose.' I could not believe how hard Rose could be to me.

Nevertheless, Frederick West accompanied his wife to the hospital that night and remained with her throughout the child's birth. 'I stayed with Rose all day because Rose was upset,' he wrote, 'because the baby was not black, she was brown. Rose asked the midwife if the baby would go black. She said, "Yes." So Rose got happier about it.' She even took the trouble to keep a menu card from her stay in hospital that day, noting on the back: 'Best meal I've had for a long time. Little more salt needed, otherwise excellent. Mrs R.P. West.' Her husband registered the baby's birth himself, declaring that he was indeed the natural father. There was no suggestion whatever that the little girl should not be brought up as a member of the West family. Shirley Robinson, meanwhile, signed a greetings card of congratulations, alongside two of the Wests' other children, Stephen and Mae.

At her trial Rosemary West maintained that she did not know that Shirley Robinson was pregnant by her husband. But before his death Frederick West insisted equally forcefully that she knew very well. 'One night Rose said, "Shirley is pregnant by you",' he wrote. 'I said, "Shirley did not tell me. I only made love to Shirley twice." Rose said, "Shirley told me that." ' Although West would go on to insist that Shirley Robinson had 'set him up' to get her pregnant, it seems certain that West hoped for this extraordinary confrontation between these two women in his life, perhaps not least to teach his wife something of a lesson.

Certainly, West knew the enmity that the two pregnancies would arouse. 'I went to see Shirley,' he wrote, 'and said to her, "Why did you tell Rose and not me?" Shirley said, "I know Rose is having a black baby and I am having yours. Ha. Ha." I said, "How did you know that Rose was having a black baby?" She said, "Rose told me. Rose said you did not want no more children. So she had to go and get one." ' West replied by warning Shirley Robinson: 'Don't trust Rose. She can be violent.' Shirley said, 'I know that Anna told me.'

There can be no doubt that Rosemary West planned revenge. Clearly aware of Shirley Robinson's pregnancy by her husband, she entered into direct competition with her rival. And barely three months after giving birth to her mixed race child Tara, she herself became pregnant by Frederick West.

Now there were two pregnant women living within the crowded confines of Cromwell Street, which also boasted two female lodgers on its top floor and Shirley Robinson one floor beneath them, whose small room was opposite another occupied by the Wests' eldest daughter Anna-Marie. The two young women would often go to collect Shirley Robinson's unemployment benefit together on Thursday mornings. Anna-Marie West is also in no doubt that her stepmother knew that Shirley Robinson was pregnant by her father. It may well be that Shirley told her so herself.

Heather, Mae and Stephen, the Wests' three younger children, had been sleeping in the cellar, but once their father had completed the twenty-five-feet-long extension to the back of the house they moved to bunk beds behind some curtains on the ground floor. Frederick West, meanwhile, had seized the opportunity to make entry to the cellar a little more difficult. He locked the entrance in the hall, and made the main access down some steps in the new rear living-room, which he covered with a trapdoor. The ground-floor front room remained 'Rose's Special Room', where she entertained her clients, and which the Wests took care to keep locked; they slept together in the rear bedroom on the ground floor.

In the first stages of her pregnancy Shirley Robinson had maintained her sexual relationship with both West and his wife. 'Shirley said, "I am still a lesbian and love girls",' West wrote, and went on:

215

'Shirley said. "You will love me now I am having your baby, and you know it's yours, and it will look just like you." Shirley and Rose got to be good friends and were going out at night together. Shirley would leave me at work about eight o'clock and go home and out.' The eighteen-year-old girl helped West work on an extension to Cromwell Street, which his wife had demanded he create in the last stages of her pregnancy with Tara.

In the spring of 1978, however, when Rosemary West's second pregnancy within a year had been confirmed, her attitude to Shirley Robinson changed dramatically. From being her sexual partner, she became her enemy. The woman whom she had been happy enough to welcome into her house, and into her bed, was now a threat, and one that she wanted her husband to deal with. But for a moment at least, Frederick West did nothing. He did not 'sort it out for her', as he had done on so many occasions in the past. He simply ignored the situation. Even more significantly, West refused signally to subject Shirley Robinson to the treatment that he had meted out to some of the other young women like her who had made their way to Cromwell Street.

West may well have felt angrier than he had been prepared to admit over the birth of Tara. He may also have been intent on teaching his wife a lesson that no matter how dominant she may have felt in the house, he was still firmly its master. Perhaps, too, he was more attracted to the young woman in the small first-floor bedroom than he had admitted to his wife. Certainly, Anna-Marie West would remember her father 'taunting' his wife that Shirley was going to be his 'next wife'. And there is no doubt that in the spring of 1978 Rosemary West sensed her husband might be grooming the young woman to take her place. There is also no doubt that that was exactly what Shirley Robinson had in mind. The eighteen-year-old had even told one of her fellow lodgers that Frederick West was going to leave his wife for her, and that Rosemary West was 'jealous'.

'The next thing was Rose was telling everyone she hated Shirley,' Frederick West was to recall at the end of his life. 'So I said to Rose, "What's going on?" She said, "It's got nothing to do with you" . . . Rose said "Work the cow's fingers to the bone and do not pay her, give all the money to me and I will pay her." ' As Shirley Robinson's pregnancy progressed, so her relationship with Rosemary West deteriorated still further. 'It became very tense in the house,' Anna-Marie would recall – until, in March 1978, when she was six months' pregnant, Shirley Robinson moved out of her tiny cramped room in Cromwell Street to live with a woman.

Rosemary West may well have given the girl an ultimatum that she had to leave their house, for Shirley Robinson admitted to one of the lodgers that she was 'more frightened of Rose than Fred'. But Shirley Robinson had retaliated by telling her landlady that she was certain she was going to give birth to her husband's son, and that she and West had even chosen a name together – Barry, after the Welsh rugby union player Barry John. Frederick West was now in a quandary, trapped between two women, both pregnant by him, one apparently determined to remain, the other to become, Mrs West. For once, West dithered.

After Shirley Robinson moved out, he 'went to see her two or three times', he wrote. 'I missed her. We got on so well together, and Shirley was having my baby. Shirley knew I was missing her. So as long as I went to see her, the longer she would stay away. So I stopped going to see her. Within a week Shirley was waiting for me outside of my work . . . She said, "Your baby is missing you and I am." I said, "Come home with me." We went to see Rose. Rose said, "Shirley can have her old room back." '

In the wake of Shirley Robinson's return, Frederick West admitted that: 'Rose and Shirley did not have much to do with each other. Shirley made friends with the girls in the top room.' At the outset West seemed pleased that the girl had returned. Early in May 1978, barely a month before she was due to give birth, he even went to have a full-scale studio portrait of himself, dressed in his best suit, standing beside the small girl in her best dress. It could almost have been a wedding photograph. West later explained it by saying that she had wanted it 'so she could send them to her father and friends', but West himself kept two of them, no doubt to Rosemary West's intense annoyance.

As the birth of Shirley Robinson's child in June 1978 drew closer, Frederick West's attitude steadily began to change. Though the eighteen-year-old would make every effort to tell him how much she loved him, and would follow him around whenever she could, she was now more than eight months' pregnant, tired and irritable, and no longer able to work with him every evening. No doubt under intense pressure from his wife, West began to change his mind. Shirley Robinson had become a liability. West told one of his lodgers, Liz Parry, who was paying £7 a week to live in the top-floor front bedroom that Shirley was getting 'too possessive', while Rosemary West confided to her that 'no matter what Fred did' she would never leave him.

Over the months she had lived at Cromwell Street, Liz Parry had become friendly with Shirley Robinson, and now the pregnant girl, too, confided in her. 'Shirley was frightened of the Wests,' she would recall seventeen years afterwards. 'She wanted to stay in my room to keep away from them.' For about a week Shirley Robinson slept in her bed, while she slept on the couch. As Liz Parry would remember: 'Shirley was becoming quite emotional about Fred.'

At some point in the second half of May 1978 Frederick West finally reached a decision about Shirley Robinson. Shortly before his own death seventeen years later, he ended his brief memoir of her with the words: 'Shirley said to me, "Is Rose going to leave you?" I said, "I have no idea what Rose is doing. I wish I did." Shirley said, "I will always be yours. I love you, Fred." ' They were the last words West would write about the young woman who was eight and a half months' pregnant when her life was brought brutally to a close one May morning at 25 Cromwell Street.

When West confessed to the murder of Shirley Robinson, he deliberately avoided going into any detail of precisely what happened. In his first interviews he was intent on maintaining that he alone had been involved, and no one else. West told the police simply that he had 'strangled her in the hall, in the living-room', when 'Rose was in hospital having a baby'. He also maintained that 'I don't think Rose even knew Shirley . . . As far as I know Rose never ever met Shirley.' As time passed, however, Frederick West gradually expanded on this first account. He explained that the eighteen-year-old was 'six months' pregnant', but insisted that she 'was going to have the baby for another girl in Bristol', telling the police she was 'pure lesbian' and adding that 'I don't know if she actually raped Anna, but she had sex with Anna-Marie'.

West also maintained that the reason he had killed Shirley Robinson was because she had threatened to 'tell Rose' she was pregnant with his child. He said the girl had been waiting for him on his allotment at Saintsbridge, and had wanted to have sex with him. 'I said, "I ain't got time to mess with you. I got to get home." . . . So we got in the van . . . We went home . . . and she was nagging on about me having sex with her . . . I remember I kept saying to her all the time, "keep to the agreement, the baby is yours" and that was the end of it.' When they got back to Cromwell Street, West explained, she had gone upstairs, but when he had joined her she had continued to nag him. 'I turned round and hit her actually, smacked her across the floor, knocked her across the room. She went flying down on the floor.'

Shirley Robinson had not been killed by the blow.

> She wasn't dead . . . So I got her outside and locked the back doors and stayed outside with her. And I sat on a block there used to be . . . Then I just sat there looking at her, and . . . it was going through me mind at the time, she's going to absolutely ruin me marriage . . . She's going to destroy the lot . . . There was loads of spare cable chucked on the floor there, all cut up. So I just went over and picked a piece of that up, and come back and just put it round her neck. I mean, I just didn't think to kill her, I wasn't thinking nothing.

All this took place 'in the late evening', West maintained, and that after he had killed the girl he had hidden her body under 'this big heap of cut-off cables . . . And left her there . . . Locked the patio doors . . . and I picked up a bag and I went to the hospital'. When he got back, Shirley Robinson was 'stiff, cold', so West had lifted a slab outside his back door and beside the wall of the neighbouring church. 'But then I couldn't get the hole anywhere near big enough, because it was going to take too long. So I went in the back door and got the knife . . . and just cut Shirley up there, took her arms and legs off, and then I packed her up . . . just pushed her in with a spade.' He admitted that he had ripped 'a summer dress thing' from her body 'to stop the blood getting on the patio, because I had nothing else'.

'It had been carefully planned with Shirley not to say anything,' West claimed to the police. 'I mean, I didn't want to get involved with Shirley or involved with any woman apart from Rose.' He had even 'chucked her out once' but 'she would not bloody stop calling me, and coming and looking for me all the time'. Finally, West insisted she had given him no alternative other than to kill her. 'I was aware that Shirley was carrying a child of mine . . . and I mean the last thing I wanted to do was hurt a child of mine.' But Rosemary West, he insisted fiercely, 'is the only thing that matters in my life, nothing else, not even my children'. Like almost every other word of Frederick West's first confessions, this was a bare-faced lie.

In a second version West came just a little closer to the truth. For a start, he accepted that his wife had not been in hospital at the time of Shirley Robinson's death, and that the girl had wanted him to pose for a photograph with her as 'the father of the baby'. This time he maintained that Shirley Robinson had met him at his allotment after he had left the Wagon Works for the day at four-thirty. 'Shirley wanted me to go and live with her . . . so we went up on to Painswick Hill . . . to talk it over right . . . She came up with "you love me" and all that . . . but I mean I wasn't interested, no way, and she knew that . . . or it was made clear to her.' In this second version West said that he then took the girl back to Cromwell Street, only to find that his wife had gone out for a walk in the park with Tara, Heather, Mae and Stephen. West insisted that it was then that he had killed her, because 'What Shirley had done is gone upstairs and told Liz.'

West then claimed that he had put the girl's unconscious body in the wash-room he had recently created at the back of the house, strangled her with cable 'to make sure she was dead', cut her up with a bread knife, dug the small hole 'and carried the pieces out and dropped them in the hole . . . I took the big piece out first, and then the head, and then the legs. I didn't have much room to put it in, so it had to be packed.' He had dismembered the girl's body on her own summer dress, and washed her blood from his chest and arms in the sink. 'If Rose had come out, she had no suspicion that I was doing anything, apart from building that wash-room . . . Rose didn't know nothing.'

The reality, of course, was quite different. Although Frederick West would maintain steadfastly throughout the majority of his police interviews that his wife knew nothing about the death of Shirley Robinson, or indeed about her pregnancy, there is no doubt that Rosemary West knew her intimately. She had made the critical decisions about her future – until her pregnancy. It seems certain, for example, that Shirley Robinson was allowed to remain at Cromwell Street in the spring of 1977 only because Rosemary West wanted to seduce her and then pass her on to her husband, just as she had done with Miss A at exactly the same time. Indeed, at one stage in their bisexual relationship Rosemary West may even have told the girl that she would help her 'look after' Frederick West's baby for her. But when Shirley Robinson made it clear that she intended to become the next Mrs West, Rosemary West's attitude towards her changed completely. Her lust for her turned to loathing. In the circumstances there can be no doubt that she knew of the girl's death. She helped her husband kill her.

Girls were brought back to Cromwell Street by Frederick West for his wife's sexual delectation. He brought them to her in the lair he had created in his cellar, like the poacher he was by nature, and he delighted in the sexual enjoyment that his wife so obviously derived from their abuse, just as he relished the opportunity to despoil and sexually humiliate them himself. At the outset West had allowed Shirley Robinson to escape that fate, perhaps because his wife found her particularly attractive, or because he too was fascinated by her. Whatever the reason, West had dithered, and Shirley Robinson had seized what she saw as an opportunity – marriage to an older man, the father that she had always longed for.

As a result Shirley Robinson became the greatest threat Rosemary West had faced in the eight years she had known her husband. Rena West, by comparison, had been absent for long periods of time, returning only rarely to see West, and to help him to introduce the young Rosemary Letts into their sexual world. Nevertheless, Rena West had been killed at her successor's insistence, and Shirley Robinson now suffered exactly the same fate. Rosemary West wanted the bright young girl killed. After all, she did not want to give her husband an opportunity to change his allegiance, and see him kill her, as he had his first wife.

At the end of his life Frederick West gave a very different version of the death of Shirley Robinson from the one that initially he gave to the police. In it he explained clearly that he had only been trying to make his wife jealous. In fact, West confessed that if Rosemary West had not been pregnant with a black child, 'Shirley probably wouldn't even have got the one she got. It was a way of getting even with Rose, I suppose, not intentionally, but that was the way it went.'

West told his first solicitor, Howard Ogden: 'Shirley and me had a good relationship. She loved the idea of having a baby . . . but Shirley conned me, and I realised that after, but I never quarrelled with her over it.' He even confessed that she was 'much like Ann McFall – happy-go-lucky, carefree – I belong to Fred and I don't care who knows it', and confirmed that he had indeed made love to her one day while they were stripping wallpaper at 7 Cromwell Street. But he added:

What I didn't realise was that Shirley had grown fond of me . . .
The next thing I finds out, she's only gone and told Rose . . .
From that time on Rose fucking hated her, and you could see it.
    Let's be fucking honest. Shirley was madly in love with me, and I knew that. But I was trying to cool it down with her. Because it could never be nothing. From the time she said about

220

pregnancy I said if it ever happens it is your child . . . I'm not leaving Rose. I wouldn't leave my kids for another woman. That's the thing I've fought all my life – to give my kids a mother.

But Frederick West also knew that 'Rose fucking hated Shirley. She was always going to belt her face in if her ever got hold of her. Made that quite clear to everybody.'

Shirley Robinson wanted West 'to go to Germany with her – to meet her father, who was going to send the money for the trip', but West thought: 'I ain't fucking getting mixed up with that, and that was what we had the few words about.' Shortly afterwards, he recalled, the girl had turned up outside the Wagon Works factory, saying: ' "There's me carrying your baby and you're not bothered about me at all." . . . Straight in front of everybody.' Clearly desperate by this time, she also told West outside the Muir Hill works: 'Once I have the baby, you don't want me with you.' In the last months of his life, however, West maintained firmly that that had been 'the last time I ever saw Shirley'.

In this final version of Shirley Robinson's death, West blamed his wife for killing her. 'Rose was after Shirley . . . give her a good hiding. I didn't think she'd kill her. I thought she'd just give her a fucking pasting, and get rid of that baby or summat.' But West insisted that Rosemary West never gave him the details of exactly how the eighteen-year-old finally met her death. 'Rose never had the time to kill Shirley at home . . . I am a hundred per cent sure that Shirley was not attacked at home. So where she was I don't know. Where she was killed. And how she got back there . . . Rose wouldn't tell me . . . All she said was, "I sorted that bitch out. She had the full length of my arm up her cunt, and that sorted her out . . . I had the fucking head off that bitch. I hated the look on her fucking face. It gave me great pleasure cutting her head off." '

Whatever the brutal revenge Rosemary West wreaked on Shirley Robinson her remains were found buried in an identical manner to every other victim in Cromwell Street, as well as to both Rena West and Ann McFall in their adjoining fields near Much Marcle. Like every other young woman who suffered at the hands of Frederick West, Shirley Robinson was to be abused, tortured and mutilated before she died. Even more horrifically, the eight-and-a-half-month-old baby in her womb was to be abused with her.

Like Juanita Mott before her, both the girls' kneecaps were missing from their skeletons when they were recovered from the back garden alongside the church wall. And, just as in Juanita Mott's case, there must be a strong possibility that they may have been removed while she was still alive – to incapacitate her completely. It also seems certain that she, too, would have suffered extensive sexual abuse and humiliation at the hands of the Wests.

Shirley Robinson may even have suffered some form of vile and macabre abortion at the hands of the Wests. For Frederick West suggested in a private conversation towards the end of his life that

Shirley Robinson may have gone into labour during the last moments of her life. If that is the case, Rosemary West may indeed have 'sorted out' both Shirley Robinson and her unborn child, as her husband claimed. Certainly, when her remains were recovered the baby was not in the position the Home Office forensic pathologist, Professor Bernard Knight, felt it should have been in. The unborn child's head was not in Shirley Robinson's pelvis, and it had not been left intact in the abdomen. Frederick West himself insisted: 'I never touched the baby at all', but accepted that his wife had told him that she 'had her fucking arm up her. That's why that baby was up where it shouldn't be. Rose . . . rammed it up her.'

The reality of her ordeal may have been worse even than this. When her remains were recovered, her right thigh bone had been severed with what the pathologist described as a 'heavy but very sharp weapon'. Shirley Robinson's right leg may have been broken while she was still alive. Indeed, a good many of her fingers and toes, as well as both her hands and feet, may have been removed at the same time. Yet again, a victim's bones were removed as souvenirs: twenty-eight of Shirley Robinson's thirty wrist and ankle bones, and forty-two of her seventy-six finger and toe bones were missing when her body was unearthed from the familiar small, square shaft that Frederick West had dug for it.

Significantly, three of Shirley Robinson's vertebrae also were missing. She may even have been decapitated – while she was alive – for her skull was certainly removed between the fourth and fifth cervical vertebrae, and found face down in her tiny grave, just as her legs had been disarticulated from her body at the hips. There were also no fewer than twenty-one fine cut-marks on her bones. There seems no doubt that Rosemary West had indeed lost her temper with Shirley Robinson, and taken considerable pleasure in both her humiliation and her murder.

The only familiar items missing from Shirley Robinson's grave were any form of mask or binding. But there would have been little need to tie or bind a woman in the last month of her pregnancy, especially if her kneecaps had already been removed. Or it may simply indicate that the Wests used a different form of gag, which they took pains to remove, or that they drugged the girl senseless before keeping her in the cellar that Frederick West had taken such pains to make more difficult to enter while building his new extension.

When Liz Parry returned to her room at Cromwell Street on the day of Shirley Robinson's disappearance, she did not go downstairs and knock on the door to the Wests' section of the house. She merely thought the girl had probably made it up with her landlords, and went to bed. The following morning Frederick West made a point of coming upstairs to see her to tell her that 'Shirley had left to visit relatives in Germany'. Liz Parry later recalled that 'the Wests seemed very happy'. With Rosemary West nodding her agreement beside him, West went on to tell her gleefully: 'Another reason Shirley had to leave. She was planning to rip my knickers off me.'

Shirley Robinson was never seen alive again, though the Wests would tell Liz Parry that they were 'keeping in touch' with the girl, who had given birth to a little boy, whom she had named Barry. The Wests also implied that Shirley was 'going to return to Cromwell Street', and that when she did so Rosemary West was going to look after the baby for her. Anna-Marie West, too, was told by her father and stepmother that Shirley Robinson had gone to Germany. But a few days later another lodger, Claire Jones, saw Rosemary West bundling Shirley Robinson's few belongings into plastic bags. Her landlady pushed the door closed when she saw her. When Rosemary West came to give evidence at her trial in her own defence, she maintained that she remembered Shirley Robinson 'but not well', that they had never had any lesbian relationship, that she would never remove 'anybody else's things', and that she 'never had a clue' that Shirley Robinson was pregnant with Fred's baby.

Like Lynda Gough before her, Shirley Robinson was to return to haunt the Wests. Though they may have thought that they had put any inquisitive officials off the scent – by withdrawing her claim for supplementary benefit, and claiming her unemployment benefit fraudulently for a time – they were visited eventually by Peter Gregson, an official from the Department of Health and Social Security, on 8 August 1978. Gregson remembered seventeen years later that the lady who answered the door informed him that the young woman he was enquiring for had 'gone to Germany'. The lady, of course, was Rosemary West.

It was the last time anyone came in search of Shirley Robinson. For the seventh time in his six years at Cromwell Street, Frederick West, with his wife's help, had managed to make a young woman disappear into thin air without anyone really noticing.

Chapter Seventeen

The house of dreams

'Just as dumb creatures are snared by food, human beings would not be caught unless they had a little nibble of hope.'

Petronius, *Satyricon*

Frederick West's morbid fascination with gynaecology was not restricted to an interest in abortions. He was also intrigued by the possibilities of genetic engineering, so much so that in the wake of the birth of Tara, his wife's first half-caste child, he became increasingly fascinated with the possibility of repeating it, artificially. No sooner had Rosemary West given birth to his own fifth child and fourth daughter Louise, in November 1978 than West embarked on a series of bizarre medical experiments designed to ensure that his wife would give birth to another half-caste child – whether the father in question knew about it or not.

West's plan was straightforward enough. If Rosemary West had sex with a Jamaican client using a condom, West would take the used condom away as soon as her client had left, and meticulously protect its contents. He would then mix them with the contents of another coloured client's condom, which he had stored earlier. And a short time afterwards West would insert this newly mixed semen into his wife by means of a small syringe, in the hope that she might conceive. To store the semen from the first condom, West would sometimes 'persuade' a young woman to keep the first condom inside her vagina for a time to maintain the semen at body temperature. But if his wife's client did not use a condom, West was not to be deterred. He would insist that she allow the man's semen to dribble out into a small pot that he kept especially for the purpose, and again mix it with an earlier client's, and, as before, insert the mixture with his small syringe.

The objective of West's experiments was to ensure that his wife became pregnant with a half-caste child but was prevented from knowing, for certain, the identity of the father. It was a means of control over the woman who obsessed him. It allowed him to manipulate her sexuality, indulge his own fascination with what he saw as the greater potency of her black lovers, while at the same time alleviating his natural jealousy, for he was always the one in control of the experiment. He was the 'mad scientist' setting the parameters for his own bizarre world. Most important of all, it meant that Rosemary West would never be able to form any kind of permanent relationship with one of her coloured lovers, and thereby threaten their own love for one another.

West never sought to cloak his murders in the respectability of medical 'experiment'. Not for him the alibis of Joseph Mengele, or the creation of a master race. His attempts at artificial insemination were simply another part of his fascination with sex. When he was eventually caught, West made no attempt to explain his killings of young women as merely an investigation of their genitalia or reproductive organs: far from it. For him, their deaths were simply 'kinky sex that went wrong', to use his own macabre phrase, not part of some greater scheme to redefine the human species. West offered no justification for so many of the deaths beyond his own sadistic lust and sexual gratification.

When Frederick West was first asked about his medical experiments, when he was arrested by the Gloucestershire police in 1992 on charges associated with child abuse, he admitted freely that he carried them out, but denied that he had ever stored the semen in another young woman. But there is evidence that West did, in fact, do so, using at least one young woman to store the contents of the condoms. Instead, West gleefully admitted to the police that all he and his wife used to do was: 'Just shove it in the bag and take it with us.' He went on to explain that 'We go up the hills . . . and use it the same night . . . within an hour and a half', because, he concluded, 'What you must remember is whenever a coloured bloke makes love to her, then I make love to her within half an hour of that . . . because that is our thing, like.' West saw nothing strange or unnatural in this behaviour.

His fascination with the female reproductive organs knew no bounds. West also explained to the police in 1992 that he had been experimenting with ways to make a film inside a woman's vagina, and had even found and kept a medical device for the purpose. 'It was left at home by a midwife one time,' he maintained, and he and his wife had adapted it to their own purpose. 'We put it in her, look in with a torch and things like that, and try to film inside as well,' he told the police proudly. 'It shows the womb, like, inside.' At the time, West admitted only that he performed this on his wife, but there must be the suspicion that it may have been yet another of the humiliations that he meted out to his victims.

One young woman who may have been forced to undergo these and other medical experiments was Frederick West's eldest child, Anna-Marie. Now fourteen, she had been abused by West and his wife for six years, regularly supplying him with sexual favours, and suffering physical abuse from his wife with equal regularity. She, in turn, became, by her own admission, 'aggressive, if not delinquent'. Indeed, it is difficult to see how she could have responded to the abuse in any other way, so distorted was the world she inhabited. One of Anna-Marie West's first boyfriends was told by West himself that he was 'not shagging her enough', even though he knew his daughter was legally under age. The boy also suspected that West spied on them while they were in Cromwell Street. On another occasion the fourteen-year-old girl was told by West: 'You don't want no fucking schoolboy. You want someone who'll sort you out. He won't know what to fucking do with it.'

The girl was also still being introduced to her mother's clients, with whom she was expected to have sexual intercourse. 'Sometimes I had to go first, sometimes second,' she would recall many years later. If she refused, the punishment could be brutal. Shortly after her fourteenth birthday in July 1978, she was treated in the casualty department of Gloucester Royal Hospital for 'puncture wounds' to both feet, wounds uncannily similar to those suffered by her sister Charmaine seven years earlier. The summer before, Anna-Marie West had been detained overnight at the same hospital for what was described as 'an accident at an ice-rink', but which also might well have been inflicted with a kitchen knife. In the school year that ended in the summer of 1979, she was absent sixty-eight times.

Not long afterwards, at the age of fifteen, Anna-Marie West became pregnant by her father. But she did not give birth to the incestuous child that Frederick West may have longed for. The pregnancy was diagnosed as ectopic, and she was again admitted to the Gloucester Royal Hospital, although no one explained what was wrong with her. West himself accompanied her, explaining only: 'The doctors think there might be something wrong inside. They are going to put you to sleep and have a little look.' She remembered afterwards that West did not stay long, but that when he came back briefly – 'He hated hospitals' – it was simply to tell her that she was now all right. He visited her just once more in the week she was there.

Within a matter of months Frederick West's eldest child was to run away from Cromwell Street. Disturbed and distraught, she would tell her friends that she thought her mother was 'a slag' because she worked as a prostitute, and how often her father grabbed at her breasts when she passed him. Finally, Anna-Marie West, who was to change her name to Anne Marie shortly afterwards, could stand no more. For the first time she realised that 'other people didn't live in the way we did at Cromwell Street'. As she would explain fifteen years later, until then: 'I associated everything with sex . . . To get love you had to provide sex; if someone gave you something or offered to help you in any way, you repaid them with sex. If you wanted something from someone, you offered them sex. To avoid beatings and provoking Rose, and to please her, you had sex with her or with the men she had chosen . . . The only love and affection I ever knew from my father came after he had had sex with me.'

226

Within the walls of Frederick West's house that was perfectly normal behaviour, entirely acceptable within the 'alternative universe' that he had so deliberately set out to create for himself and his family. Life there went on much as before, although now there were five of Rosemary West's children, Heather, aged nearly nine, Mae, six, Stephen, five, Tara, a little under a year, and the new baby, Louise, as well as Anna-Marie. The upstairs rooms were still filled with lodgers, and the house still had its criminal associations. One local burglar used it as his permanent address for a period of 'home leave' from prison, and there were persistent rumours that West still allowed other criminals to hide in the cellar, or to leave their stolen goods there. Certainly, the neighbours would often see Frederick West and his wife leave the house in the late evening in his green Bedford van, with a sliding door at the side, not to return until the early hours of the morning. More often than not they would then carry planks of wood and other building materials into their house, which they had presumably 'found' on their expedition.

But it was not only stolen sand and cement that Frederick West would go looking for in his van. There were still the attractions of young women, and he had carefully nurtured his latest local source. Jordan's Brook Community Home in Hucclecote, Gloucester, which had housed Miss A, the girl he and his wife had attacked in the summer of 1977, still catered for some particularly disturbed young people among its twenty-four residents, and West made sure that many of them got to know the reputation of 25 Cromwell Street for providing accommodation for the night 'with no questions asked'. In 1979 Frederick West was working on a house near Jordan's Brook, and he would regularly offer the inmates cigarettes or a lift in his van if they needed it. Inevitably, he would also joke relentlessly about sex, inviting any girl who might 'need a bed' to come to visit him. By then, some of the Jordan's Brook girls had even given Frederick and Rosemary West a nickname. They called them Mr and Mrs Shackles.

One of the girls at Jordan's Brook at the time was a sixteen-year-old named Alison Chambers, who had arrived there in December 1978 from a children's home near Pontypridd after running away and threatening to 'go on the game' as a prostitute in London. Born in Hanover in Germany, where her father had been serving in the RAF, she had become a rebellious teenager after the breakup of her parents' marriage. Her mother Joan had married again when her daughter was thirteen, and moved to Swansea, but Alison Chambers had not been altogether happy with her and, as a result, in 1977, at the age of fourteen, she had been taken into care in Wales. Soon after Christmas 1978 she had moved to Jordan's Brook in Gloucester.

A little over five feet, two inches in height, Alison Chambers was a neat, cheerful girl, with blonde hair and bright blue eyes. She had quickly settled into life in Gloucester, although one member of the staff was to remember later that she was 'obviously insecure' and prone to exaggeration, particularly when it came to stories about her boyfriends. 'It was as if she wanted constant attention,' she would recall. Like so many of the other young women who were to find their way to Cromwell Street, Alison Chambers was in pursuit of her own version of love.

Not long after her arrival at Jordan's Brook, Alison Chambers was sent out on a Youth Training Scheme to prepare her for the end of her period in care on her seventeenth birthday that September, and to introduce her to working life. In the early part of 1979 she had worked as a waitress in the Road Chef café, but by April she was 'very, very happy' to be employed at a firm of solicitors in Westgate Street, Gloucester, where she acted as a junior receptionist and general assistant. By that summer Alison Chambers had also started to make her way to 25 Cromwell Street. One of the lodgers at the time remembered her coming regularly in the early evening, always smartly dressed and carrying a handbag, a girl who looked 'as though she'd come from work', made to feel welcome in a house where she was always known as Al or Ali.

The world of Cromwell Street must have seemed enormously attractive to the impressionable young woman. It was not only a place to stay for an hour, or the night if necessary; it was also a haven from Jordan's Brook, the institution that Alison Chambers had grown to 'loathe', as she told a friend. Rosemary West's five children no doubt made Cromwell Street feel more hospitable than the children's homes she had been used to, and Frederick West's elaborate and exaggerated stories would certainly have impressed her. Once again he was the older man who seemed to take an interest, a man with a family who could be relied on, the father she wished she had. And yet again West delighted in playing up to her fantasies. He even bought her a necklace with her name engraved on it.

But it was not just the Wests themselves who made Cromwell Street attractive to Alison Chambers and to some of the other girls from Jordan's Brook. There was also the fact that the household made no secret of its interest in sex in all its forms. That brought the house a glamour, and a fascination, which no ordinary house could match. It was this that led the girls to congregate outside it on the pavement on some evenings, talking among themselves. The stories of the red light that went on in the ground-floor lounge when Rosemary West was 'entertaining one of her clients', or the stories of the 'wailing' that would emanate from her ground-floor front bedroom, must have made the place seem even more exciting. Several of the girls who found their way there were almost certainly encouraged to earn extra money by acting as part-time prostitutes for the Wests, who offered them to their friends and visitors. Others, including Alison Chambers, participated in both the Wests' sexual life.

Cromwell Street was a house of dreams, a place where Alison Chambers could forget that she was, in fact, a resident of a children's home, a place where she could confess her deepest secrets. Her best friend at the time remembered years later that they had both discussed with Rosemary West running away from the home; Rosemary had produced a black and white photograph of a farm which she said she and her husband owned. Rosemary West told Alison Chambers that she could have her own room there, where she could write the poetry Alison had told her she wanted to, and where Alison could ride the horses in their stables. 'Alison was captivated,' her best friend would recall sixteen years later. She photocopied the picture of the 'farm' and drew ivy on it: she even told the other inmates of Jordan's Brook, though some of them thought it was only her 'story-telling'.

The 'farm' that Alison Chambers fell in love with could have been another of Frederick and Rosemary West's elaborate deceptions, another means of drawing a naive and vulnerable young woman into their net, but there is no doubt that the farm existed, even if the Wests did not own it. Many years later one young woman from Jordan's Brook even remembered being taken there and 'tied to a slab' by the Wests as part of a satanic ritual in which eight men stood and watched as she was raped by Frederick West. One of the girls who visited Cromwell Street at the time remembered later that Alison Chambers was given its location as 'Stoke' or 'Stoke Valley' up the Tewkesbury road out of Gloucester, near a fish farm. Stoke Orchard, barely a mile or two from the Wests' original meeting-place in Bishop's Cleeve, is certainly near the Tewkesbury road out of the city. And, by a strange coincidence, just over a year after Alison Chambers was told about it, the Wests confessed to a Gloucester magistrate that they had 'recorded themselves making love . . . in a van parked on a disused airfield at Stoke Orchard' at almost exactly the same time that they were telling the sixteen-year-old Jordan's Brook girl about their 'farm'.

The attraction of the new life that Cromwell Street seemed to offer proved too great for Alison Chambers to resist, as did the sexual possibilities that the Wests offered. By the end of July in 1979 she had almost certainly become the lover of both Frederick and Rosemary West. And on 4 August, after discovering that she would have to stay at Jordan's Brook beyond her seventeenth birthday in September, she packed most of her belongings and absconded from the home. She confided to her best friend that she was going to live at Cromwell Street, but asked her not to tell the staff at Jordan's Brook. Instead, Alison told her to tell them that she had 'run away to Wales'. The two girls then arranged to meet the following afternoon so that Alison could collect the few clothes she had left behind. But when her friend kept their appointment the next day, the sixteen-year-old girl with a faint Welsh accent did not turn up. The following day the police were notified.

Alison Chambers was to be heard from again, however. In September 1979 she wrote to her mother and stepfather 'to let you know exactly what I am at present doing with myself and my life'. She went on: 'I can understand that this is little consolation to you, after my taking off from Jordan's Brook House, but I feel I owe you at least that.' The German-born girl, who was just about to celebrate her seventeenth birthday, then told her parents: 'I am at present living with a very homely family and I look after their five children and do some of their housework.' This letter was sufficient to satisfy the West Glamorgan County Council that she was not a missing person, and that she should be released from care. It was also enough to persuade the police that she was no longer a missing person.

'All I'm doing,' Alison Chambers explained, 'is trying and I might say succeeding in living a normal everyday life with worries that are shared and with happiness that is true. Also I'm living in a happy and relaxed atmosphere and not a strained and cold atmosphere. I cannot say I feel sorry for running away because that would be untrue, but I am sincerely sorry for any anxiety I've caused the family.' And she ended her letter. 'I just wanted to let you know I'm safe, and shall continue to write to let you know how I'm coping. One thing I don't want anyone to do is to worry about me because I don't deserve it, so please don't. I love and miss you all. Please believe that. Until I write again, take care of yourselves. All my fondest, Alison.'

This heartfelt, honest plea for freedom was the last anyone heard of Alison Chambers until her left thigh bone was unearthed from beneath the patio in the garden of 25 Cromwell Street fifteen years later. Alison Chambers did not sense the danger that lurked there, did not sense that the Wests' nickname of the Shackles might have had an ugly rather than simply an erotic, clandestine, sexual connotation, and did not sense that her trust might cost her her life. Tragically, she may well not have been the only victim the Wests took from the impressionable young women boarded just across Gloucester in Jordan's Brook Community Home.

No fewer than twenty-two young women were to go missing, their 'whereabouts unknown', after they left the children's home between 1970 and 1994. The whereabouts of another forty-two young people who left its care, including Alison Chambers, were 'not recorded'. Some of them may well have made their way across Gloucester, using alleyways and side-roads, just as Alison Chambers and her best friend had done in the summer of 1979, to ring the doorbell beside the iron gates at the front of 25 Cromwell Street. Some, too, were probably offered a lift there by the dirty, dishevelled little man the girls also knew as 'flirty Fred'.

A number of those missing young women must have fallen into the hands of Frederick West, whether in Cromwell Street or at the farm that his wife told Alison Chambers about. West's prodigious sexual appetite and his addiction to violence and murder, now fuelled by the killing of at least eleven young women, could not have stopped. The only realistic conclusion is that West did lure many more young women to Cromwell Street, or elsewhere, for his sexual gratification, and their humiliating death. The possibility that he then disposed of their bodies in the style that he had perfected in another site, or sites, is too great to be ignored. Though he would insist throughout his final police interviews that 'there are no more. I can't make up

230

people I killed', the statement was another lie, as he hinted in the last remaining months of his life.

Frederick West probably persuaded Alison Chambers to write the letter to her mother and stepfather. It bears all the hallmarks of his natural skill at covering his tracks and confusing the outside world. He would have known that it would have deflected even the most inquisitive official from his door. The letter was too perfect a cover to have been an accident. And it worked triumphantly. The letter was sufficient to persuade West Glamorgan County Council, which was responsible for Alison Chambers, to release her from its care, as she seemed to be making her own way in the world. The tragic result was that Alison Chambers met her end in Cromwell Street. Indeed, her thigh was the first human bone discovered there, though at the time no one knew to whom it belonged.

When Frederick West first confessed to her murder, he gave a most unexpected explanation for it. Anxious to divert attention from his connections with the girls from Jordan's Brook, West insisted that Alison Chambers had turned up at Cromwell Street to blackmail him with a copy of the portrait photograph he had had taken sixteen months earlier with Shirley Robinson. In his first version of the reasons for her death, West maintained that the sixteen-year-old from Swansea, who had not even arrived in Gloucester when Shirley Robinson disappeared, was, in fact, 'Shirley's mate'. Clearly confusing her at first with another young woman, whom West said was 'big-boned' and twenty-two years of age, West went on to insist that the girl he only ever knew as 'Shirley's mate' had turned up at Cromwell Street 'several years' after Shirley Robinson's death and said to him: 'As far as I can gather you killed Shirley.'

But West rapidly changed his story, suggesting instead that she had arrived 'between twelve months and two years' after Shirley Robinson. 'She came to the door and asked if Shirley was there, and I said, "Shirley don't live here now", and she said, "Yes, yes, she does . . . I've got a photograph here of you with Shirley".' West said he then told her to 'go to a café or something and have a cup of tea and come back later', because 'Rose was cooking the dinner'.

Then West began to heap lie upon lie, confusing the dates and events, in his customary elaborate attempt to conceal the truth. He suggested that 'Shirley's mate' was the girl Shirley Robinson had told him she was 'having the baby for', and that he had sent her down to his own café in Southgate Street (though it had closed two years earlier). 'I said: "I'll come down and pick you up." . . . So anyway I . . . sent Rose out to sleep for the night . . . went down with the van, drove past the café, she came out and . . . went back home with her to try and sort it out.' Back in Cromwell Street, West explained:

She said that Shirley said in her letter that if she didn't turn up in so long or something then to come and get me and I'd know where she was. I said, 'What do you mean by that?' and she said . . . 'That you could have knocked her off, killed her.' She was telling me about Shirley, and if she didn't find her she'd go round and get the police, and all this lot, so we had an argument, a row, and I punched her on the jaw first, and knocked her on the floor and strangled her.

He went on to tell the police that he had buried the girl's body under a 'big paddling-pool' in his garden, which was made out of blue engineering bricks. 'All I done was lifted him up and packed her underneath him, and dropped him back on top of her.' Finally, Frederick West confessed that he had cut the girl's body up into four pieces, a head, torso and two legs, with his sheath knife.

Barely a day after this confession West changed his story again. This time he told the police: 'I don't actually believe this girl was old enough to actually be associated with Shirley. She didn't seem to me to be. The only thing I can't understand is where she got the photograph from and the so-called letter. I never actually seen the letter but I've got the photograph off her.' This time, he explained that the girl had turned up looking for 'Cromwell Road and not Cromwell Street' and that he had been driving her around looking for 'Cromwell Road' when 'she produced this photograph, because I think what she was doing was building up courage' to ask him. In this second version West suggested the girl was 'too young-looking' to be Shirley Robinson's 'lesbian friend', and that he had simply 'dropped her off'. But: 'Then she turns up again, later, and she starts the same crack again, and she starts putting threats. She wanted money to go off somewhere.' And West still maintained that he never knew her name.

It was another tissue of lies. But one with a deliberate and well-thought-out purpose. Like every other confession Frederick West gave during his interviews with the police, it was designed to divert any possible suspicion away from Rosemary West. 'Rose would definitely not have seen her,' West insisted as he described the girl as 'about five feet two', with 'blonde crinkly hair . . . just to her ears', and 'blue eyes', estimating her age as 'fourteen, fifteen, sixteen, if that'. In this second version the girl had turned up 'a month or two' later, but West had prevented her from even entering Cromwell Street, and had instead set off to drive her back to Bristol when she had started demanding money. 'Then she starts giving me all that, evil of the day, all she could think of. What she was going to do to me and what she was going to tell the police that I'd done.' He pulled into a lay-by, 'had a right shouting match' with her, then decided to drive her back towards Cromwell Street. When they were nearby, in a garage off Saint Michael's Square, behind his house, 'she set going again, so I grabbed her by the neck with me hands and choked her'.

It was now after midnight, West maintained. 'So I . . . put her along under the window by the back door', took a piece of 'thirty amp cable' and twisted it around her neck because 'I wasn't sure she was actually dead'. West then realised, or so he claimed to the police, that he could not make the hole under the paddling-pool in the garden any bigger 'without using a sledge-hammer' – 'plus the fact that Rose is in bed' – and so had been forced to cut her up into the four pieces he had originally described.

When the police finally identified Alison Chambers as 'the girl under the pond' Frederick West changed his story for a third time. This time he claimed that she had been living at number 11 Cromwell Street, and that he had 'done her room up for her and she stayed there for a while . . . 'cause she had nowhere to stay'. When the house had first been converted to multiple occupancy, West went on to explain: 'There was a load of girls ran away from Jordan's Brook and was there . . . I mean, it used to be a regular place for them to go.' Once again West took scrupulous care not to suggest that she, or any other Jordan's Brook girl, had been anywhere near his own house in Cromwell Street.

'She was looking scruffy,' he told the police. 'She wasn't scruffy in the first place. No, she was quite well dressed, but she'd worn the same clothes over and over . . . and she had an iron mark on her jumper.' West insisted that the girl 'was turning up too often, watching me', and 'I think what she was really after was a handful of money off me 'cause she thought we got money, or I got money'.

West admitted that some of the girls who arrived at Cromwell Street 'were obviously trying to make money other ways', and added, 'a lot of them were on the game'. As a result, he said, there were 'girls that accepted what we did and, you know, and forgot about it, went home and on their way . . . See, I had affairs with so many different girls, I mean, you're not talking one or two, and . . . everyone didn't end up in disaster, by no means.' When the police suggested that the girl he was calling 'Shirley's mate' was, in fact, Alison Chambers, West simply replied: 'Don't mean a thing. I never asked her her name.' But he went on to insist: 'This girl never stayed with us.' Throughout each of his three different confessions, West also neglected to reveal to the police that the sixteen-year-old Alison Chambers was naked when she was buried, and that she had clearly been subjected to some form of sexual abuse.

Like its two predecessors, this third confession, too, was a pack of lies. But that is not altogether a surprise. Frederick West was by this time desperately trying to conceal the extent of his killings, and was confused about which young woman he had buried and where. Without the ability to write any sort of list, he would have been struggling to keep track of the lives of a number of young women, not all of whom he would confess to killing. West certainly confused Alison Chambers with another young woman, whose identity we do not know but who became one of his victims – the big-boned, twenty-two-year-old whom he first described as the body in his garden. She would not be the first young woman whose life would become a mystery once she entered Cromwell Street.

The Wests attracted young people, many of whom concealed their identities and their reasons for being there. Many of them were to fall under the Wests' spell, and went on to disappear without trace not long afterwards. Several of the lodgers remember a pregnant young woman with khaki shorts, hiking-boots and a German accent as having been there at this time, but Frederick West would never confirm it. Once within the doors of Cromwell Street a number of young women seemed simply to have vanished without trace, although no one can say with absolute certainty how many.

When the body of Alison Chambers was recovered from beneath the rear bathroom window of 25 Cromwell Street, her skull was found to be bound tightly with a one-and-three-quarter-inch-wide plastic belt, passing from under the chin to the top of her head. The buckle was still on the top of her head, with fragments of her hair trapped in it. The only possible explanation for a belt that would have clamped the girl's jaw tightly shut was that it had been used to stop her screaming. When West was confronted with its existence, he insisted: 'She wasn't actually bondaged . . . it was just whatever was on her was put on her . . . so I could keep her together and lift her.' He went on: 'I can't even remember putting a belt on her head.' But that, too, was clearly a lie.

There can be only one conclusion. Once again Frederick West's victim had been subjected to relentless and horrifying abuse. Just as the other victims had been in the past, she would have been systematically violated both by West and his wife Rosemary. This time the Wests may have pushed the boundaries of their humiliation still further: Frederick West may have filmed her death. West was well aware of the commercial potential of 'snuff movies', which depict the sexual torture and death of a young woman. Only a few years after Alison Chambers's disappearance, West even bragged to a young woman whom he met in Cromwell Street that he was 'interested in them'. There must be at least the possibility that one of his victims provided him with the chance to exploit what he would have seen as an opportunity for a profit from this form of pornography.

A part of Frederick West's version of the events surrounding the death of Alison Chambers may contain some elements of the truth. It is possible that the girl may have found the picture of Shirley Robinson with West and begun to ask embarrassing questions about it, and about the girl. These questions may in turn have provoked Frederick West to kill her. She may even have made a naive attempt to blackmail him when she discovered that the girl had disappeared, or when she was taken to see the 'farm'. Her discovery of the photograph may have infuriated Rosemary West, who may not have known that her husband still had it. Or Alison Chambers may have refused to accept West's invitation to become a prostitute, and found herself imprisoned in the cellar of Cromwell Street for 'a day or two to see sense'.

No matter what West told the police it was a lie to say that neither Frederick nor Rosemary West knew Alison Chambers. She had worked for them for a time as a 'nanny', just as some of her predecessors had done. And like them she had suffered a terrible fate. When her body was recovered, her remains were dreadfully jumbled, but, once again a significant number of her bones were missing. In particular, both Alison Chambers's kneecaps were absent from the familiar two-feet cube shaft she was found in; just as both kneecaps were absent from the graves of Shirley Robinson and Juanita Mott. They must have been removed to incapacitate her.

Like her predecessors, Alison Chambers had been mercilessly mutilated. Her upper breastbone had been specifically removed, as had sixty-three of her seventy-six finger and toe bones, and no fewer than twenty-seven of her thirty wrist and ankle bones. Though the police meticulously recovered even the girl's fingernails and toenails from her tiny grave, a total of ninety-six of her bones were missing. The only conclusion is that at least some of them were removed while she was alive, but, gagged with a purple belt, she would have been unable even to protest.

No one can say with certainty what became of Alison Chambers's hands and feet, or her kneecaps. They may have been kept by the Wests as morbid souvenirs for a time, only to be thrown away when they had forgotten which of their victims they belonged to, or burned and kept in a tiny jar or pot on their mantelpiece so that they could relive the memory of what they had done to her. But it is also possible that they were disposed of promptly. It is conceivable that they were flushed, as so many of the bones of the other victims may have been flushed, into the sewer system of Gloucester through a hole that Frederick West had specifically constructed for the purpose in his cellar. It is also possible that some of them may have been burned on his allotment in Saintsbridge, or disposed of in a septic tank at the farm the Wests had taken such pride in describing to Alison Chambers. One thing is certain; they were removed to humiliate and depersonalise a vulnerable and innocent girl who had been looking for nothing more than a happy and secure home, and thought she had found one with Frederick and Rosemary West.

Finally, in the last months of his life, in conversation with Howard Ogden, his first solicitor, West admitted that Alison Chambers, whom he still described as 'Shirley's mate', had, in fact, lived with him and his wife for 'a month or more after she'd left Barnwood in Gloucester', and that she had befriended one of the lodgers. By this time he was placing the blame for all the killings at his wife's door, explaining only that: 'When I caught them young girls there, they'd have to fucking go.' Unbelievable though it may sound, West also suggested: 'If the girl did stay at all at our place, I mean, I'm not saying she didn't because if anybody was in trouble . . . I helped them out the best I could with . . . no bad intentions whatsoever. I mean, I like people to look upon me as somebody they can trust.'

One other unlikely event may have contributed to the death of Alison Chambers. At some point in the summer of 1979 West paid for his wife to abort her third pregnancy in three years. Though the reason is not entirely clear, West told Howard Ogden many years later that: 'She reckoned it was mine. So I went and paid for her to

235

have an abortion.' That explanation could well be true, for West was apparently determined that his wife should conceive another half-caste child as a result of his experiments with the semen of her black male clients. Nevertheless, it was also to be the only abortion that Rosemary West would ever allow to be performed on her. It could well have infuriated her so intensely that she took part of her revenge on Alison Chambers.

What is not in question is that within a few weeks of Alison Chambers's disappearance Rosemary West was pregnant again – with her sixth child – though she was still not quite twenty-six years of age. Frederick West would later question whether this latest child was his, suggesting to Howard Ogden that his wife had conceived after making love to her father, Bill Letts. But that was a gross, and mischievous, lie. Letts himself had died the previous May, at the age of fifty-eight. Indeed, this too may have unsettled Rosemary West, who had sustained her sexual relationship with her father throughout her life, and that, too, may have contributed to her anger towards Alison Chambers.

'Rose used to go on holiday a lot with her dad,' West would explain subsequently, 'long weekends and all that.' His death came as a shock to both the Wests. 'He had this sinus trouble, where he had to have his nose drilled out every so often,' Frederick West explained, 'because the bones used to grow over in his nose. He had it all his life. And he went into hospital and had it done. They put him under anaesthetic and he went straight out.' Rosemary West attended her father's funeral in the council cemetery in Cheltenham alone, and perhaps in memory of the man who had first introduced her to deviant sexuality, she paid him a distinctive tribute by wearing deliberately provocative clothes, including a pair of black stiletto heels.

Only a matter of weeks later Rosemary West was to tell Alison Chambers about the farm that she and her husband shared, and only a matter of weeks after that the sixteen-year-old absconded from Jordan's Brook. After her disappearance, Rosemary West would lead some of the other girls from the children's home to think that Alison had actually gone to live on their farm. But in the months and years that followed, no one ever went to find the farm, or to look for the girl with the soft Welsh accent. At the trial for her murder, Rosemary West even denied that she knew her.

The police did visit 25 Cromwell Street some months after Alison Chambers's disappearance, but it was in pursuit of missing goods rather than missing girls. The worst of the drugs raids of the mid-1970s had come to an end, but Frederick West's appetite for petty theft and receiving had not dimmed, and that had attracted the attention of the police. Only a year earlier an old friend from Leyhill had been arrested again for storing stolen property in the cellar of Cromwell Street. And in the summer of 1980, only a few weeks after the birth of his second son and seventh child (whom West chose to christen Barry – in a grim memorial to Shirley Robinson), he was arrested for receiving some of the proceeds of a burglary at a local health centre in December 1979, including five tape recorders and a number of tape cassettes. They were found in the top cupboard of one of the first-floor bedroom wardrobes.

One of the tapes so shocked the police that when West eventually came to trial on 2 October 1980, the contents were not read out in open court. Instead, the jury were simply handed a transcript. When questioned about it, West confessed it was a recording of his making love to his wife in the back of his van the previous December on 'a disused airfield near Stoke Orchard'. But he went on to explain that he had been going to phone a detective constable he knew, Malcolm Mustoe, about the goods 'and return them'. West also told the court that he had given information 'about a well-known Gloucester criminal who had been his lodger to DC Mustoe before'. West was sentenced to nine months' imprisonment for the offence, but the sentence was suspended for two years, and he left the court after having to pay just a fine of £50. The evidence leaves little doubt that Frederick West was operating as a low-grade police informer at the time. It would have suited his purposes admirably. There could hardly have been a shrewder ruse to distract their attention from any connection that he might seem to have with a missing girl or girls. Once again it was Frederick West's means of 'grooming' authority, of ensuring that he would always remain underestimated, the small-time thief and informer who was no danger to anyone.

West walked a tightrope on the very edge of the law, but he walked it so skilfully, and with such a measured tread, that he never seemed in danger of falling. Both the police and the underworld seemed to trust him. One of the criminals to whom he gave room at the time remembered many years later, for example, that West would regularly go out at night in his green Bedford van, taking a fork, spade and pickaxe. He even recalled that on one occasion both the Wests went out one evening taking with them a petrol-driven garden cultivator, called a 'Merry Tiller'. West could hardly have needed it for his small allotment, especially as he would later insist that the 'council took it off me 'cause I never looked after it'. But no questions were ever asked, no reports made. Frederick West made everything seem perfectly normal.

On another occasion, in the years immediately after the disappearance of Shirley Robinson and Alison Chambers, a resident in another house in Cromwell Street, then still only a small boy, remembered seeing West emerge from his house one evening covered in blood from his shoulders to his knees 'in patches'. He ran to tell his mother, but she was watching *Minder* on television and did not pay much attention. The boy also remembered many years afterwards Heather West, then aged nine, telling him that there was blood all over the kitchen at Cromwell Street. But again no one seemed to take the slightest notice.

In the summer of 1980, however, shortly after her sixteenth

birthday, Anna-Marie West disappeared from Cromwell Street altogether, severing every tie with her mother and father for almost three years. In her account of her life, written fifteen years later, she maintained that she wanted to start a new life, and that on the morning of her disappearance her father had thrown away all her belongings and stripped her room. She reported him as asking his wife: 'I don't think she'll be a problem, do you?' Rosemary West did not answer.

In the last months of his life Frederick West gave a rather different version of his eldest daughter's departure. In conversation with Howard Ogden, West maintained that he had always told Anna-Marie 'to accept Rose', but that her 'love turned to hate'. He then suggested that 'Anna-Marie was frightened to tell me what was going on', and went on: 'At sixteen, Anna-Marie said, "Get that fucking bitch out of here, and I'll look after the children." Straight to her face. Rose was sat there.' West insisted that he 'couldn't do it', and that as a result his daughter had left, but not before she had hit him 'straight in the face'.

The strain of sustaining the carefully insulated world of Cromwell Street was beginning to take its toll on the Wests. And their children were growing up.

Chapter Eighteen

Rose's chocolates

'They must need go whom the Devil drives.'

Cervantes, *Don Quixote*

By the time of their tenth wedding anniversary in January 1982, Frederick and Rosemary West were consumed by an evil, all-pervading lust. It had darkened and corroded the love that they had first shared in Bishop's Cleeve until they could no longer distinguish one from the other. He had nurtured the viciousness that she had inherited from her father into an appetite for sadistic sexuality and domination, and she, in turn, had become his full and fearsome partner. Her wickedness had seduced him to explore the extremes of his own vile sexuality, driving him beyond gratification towards a motiveless violence. Together they had urged each other on to plumb ever greater depths of depravity.

Ultimately Frederick West remained unquestionably the master of their ugly symbiosis. West remained the hunter, the provider of their sexual prey. And West dictated the terms his wife had to live by. He had to approve her violence, sanctioning its use when he returned to Cromwell Street, for ever the final arbiter of their relationship. If his wife would not abide by his decisions, his anger could be fearful, as his children knew only too well. 'Dad was really quiet,' West's eldest son would remember, 'but he snapped very quickly. He used to threaten us by saying, "I'll fucking kill you, you bastard".' West might only lose his temper a handful of times a year, 'but when he did go he was like a madman'. He would punch his eight-year-old son relentlessly for twenty minutes at a time, and he would think nothing of kicking him with his steel-capped boots.

To Rosemary West, equally, violence was an everyday occurrence, a habit as ingrained in her as her prostitution. She would hit her children with anything to hand, be it a knife or a hammer – sometimes simply because she could not find a dishcloth or a teatowel. She would put her hands around her son's throat so tightly that he blacked out, and carried the imprint of her fingers for two

239

weeks, and never offer a word of explanation or apology. 'We were so scared of her when she was younger,' her second daughter, Mae, would recall, 'because she was really nasty. She'd hit one of us, and then she'd want to hit us all because she was in the mood.' But she never hit her husband. Rosemary West had seen at first hand the terrible damage he was capable of inflicting on a young woman.

Frederick West's physical strength underpinned his strength of character. What he wanted he would get, by whatever means, and no matter how long it took him. He could be patient, placid and persuasive when it suited him, just as he could be violent, vicious and venal. He controlled his own inner rage with an iron hand of self-discipline and concealment, and he expected nothing less from his wife. If she failed to deliver that, his revenge could be swift and brutal.

On one occasion, probably around the time of their tenth wedding anniversary, West even confirmed this power over his wife in writing. He made her sign an astonishing declaration. It read simply: 'I Rose will do exactly what I am told, when I am told, without questions, without losing my temper, for a period of three months, from the end of my next period as I think I owe this to Fred.' It was a clear indication of how far the giggling couple from Lake House caravan site in Bishop's Cleeve were driven by Frederick West's strength of character. But the declaration also revealed how strong his wife's own role had become, in that he needed her to signify in writing that she would not lose her temper. Their interdependence had matured in the dozen years they had been together, as each demanded more and more extreme demonstrations of their love.

In Cromwell Street they would disappear into the first-floor bathroom together, which West always called 'his office', for lengthy whispered discussions, more often than not about sex. It was their one consuming interest, their obsession. And it was this fascination with sex in all its forms, and the violence that both Frederick and Rosemary West always needed to accompany it, that lay behind their murderous partnership. In the last few months of his life West confirmed this in a series of conversations with his first solicitor, Howard Ogden. At the time he was intent on placing the blame for the killings of all but one of the young female victims entirely on his wife. Their conversations revealed a great deal of the interwoven, sinuous nature of the Wests' sordid partnership, though they certainly did not reveal everything. The transcriptions do not make pleasant reading, for they demonstrate the extraordinary depths to which human beings can sink.

'I know how they were killed,' Frederick West explained baldly. 'Vibrator. Pushed in with Rose's foot. That big bastard. That's why Shirley's baby was fucking up the wrong place.' West said that he had watched his wife do it. 'Obviously she bound their mouths up with that fucking tape round their gobs. And then what she'd do, she'd push the vibrator in as far as she could into them, then get hold of their legs and just push it in with her foot.' The vibrator in question

240

was more than a foot in length and four inches in diameter. 'She did so much damage to them with that, that she had to fucking kill them.'

West insisted that it was this that had led to the death of Alison Chambers. West said his wife had told him: 'I put her on a bloody vibrator and let her wriggle on that', and had then confessed, 'And she was a beautiful young juicy thing . . . She hadn't been fucked much.' Why did you kill her? he asked her. 'Oh, I fancied her,' she said.

'She wanted to hurt women,' West went on. 'She'd have to, to do what she's done to them.' He then maintained that, unlike his wife, he did not enjoy group sex.

I only ever tried it once, and I didn't like it, because Rose acted too bloody vicious. What she did to that little girl was unreal. I was making love to the girl, and Rose got a vibrator and shoved it straight up her arse. Fuck me, the girl nearly went right through the fucking wall.

I would never allow Rose to tie me up. She fucking tried for years . . . No way was I going to let her tie me up. I didn't believe in it, and I didn't have anything to do with it . . . But there was blokes doing it to her, and sometimes she'd come home and she's been well beaten, mind. She'd have no knickers on, like. She'd been fucked all day, and I'd come home from work and she'd sit deliberately on the edge of the settee with her legs wide open and . . . say: 'Look at that . . . I bet you wish you had something that could fill that.' . . . It never stopped. It didn't stop at all. There was no let-up. She used to run around naked in front of Stephen and that. She used to run around . . . flaunting it . . . She did it everywhere. 'It's my cunt and I'll show it to who I want to.' . . . She'd go and pick up any old tramp . . . She thought every bloke would want to fuck her, and if they didn't, she got nasty about it.

Rose didn't want the gentle part of it. She wanted some big nigger to throw her down and fucking bang on top of her, and treat her like a dog . . . that was sex to Rose. 'I don't want any of that soppy shit,' she said. 'I want fucking. Not fucking about with. Or chatting up.' And she'd get aggressive. Rose didn't have many women friends, because she made it too blatantly obvious she was after other things . . . She used to have spates in which she just couldn't get enough.

Frederick West also admitted to Howard Ogden that he 'tried bondage once', when he 'made that harness out of plastic, so it didn't break. The red one. I put it on her once, and even then I didn't like it.'

The truth of the matter is that Frederick West liked it, and everything else his wife did, a great deal. He had carefully groomed a sado-masochistic sexuality in his wife, and steadily drawn her into his own fantasies, until she was capable of creating fantasies for him: no longer the willing pupil but now the dominatrix in the rituals of their sexuality. For West was no baffled onlooker during any of the events he described so crudely to his solicitor. He was the grinning watcher, the voyeur peeping through the hole that he had specially constructed in the door, the man with the film or video camera, the ringmaster subtly pulling the strings of his wife's sexuality.

Indeed, West's fascination with vibrators and dildos may have been the result of his own sense of sexual inadequacy. For there is no doubt that he and his wife experimented with larger and larger replica phalluses, and West made repeated reference in his conversations with Howard Ogden to Rosemary West not liking some 'little thing wriggling about' in her. No medical record exists of the size of West's penis, whether erect or not, just as no record exists of his having truthfully revealed the details of his aberrant sexuality to any psychologist. But, significantly, West did admit that his favourite sexual position involved his entering his wife from the rear, while she was lying with her head far away from him, which may indicate that he may have become increasingly self-conscious about his penile size, his sexual ability, and his attractiveness to her, as their marriage progressed.

Whatever the truth about Frederick West's fears of inadequacy, he encouraged his wife to keep significant detailed records of her sexual conquests. These not only took the form of photographs of the erect penises of some of her clients, and of her own vagina in a variety of sexual states, but also consisted of a detailed diary in which she would record the size of her clients' penises, and in which she would also give them marks out of ten for their sexual performance. At her husband's insistence, she would keep the photographs and the diary in her 'Special Room' for him to consult at any time. Frederick West even installed a two-way mirror in the bathroom of his house in Cromwell Street so that he could see for himself the size of some of his wife's clients, creeping up the stairs after them to peer through the mirror while they were urinating.

But West did not stop there. As the 1980s progressed, he made a series of videotapes of his wife for their joint use. And once again there was an emphasis on the size of a man's penis, and Rosemary West's ability to 'take it'. The bigger the man, the more Frederick West liked to record it on video – and the more enthusiastic Rosemary West would become to demonstrate that she could sexually accommodate almost anyone or anything. As these experiments with videotape progressed, she took increasing pleasure in demonstrating to the camera, and her husband's watching eye, her capacity to derive sexual excitement from inserting into her vagina the largest vibrators and dildos, as well as cucumbers and pint beer glasses. She would then urinate over a towel, or into the glass, and pour the urine over her naked body. At one stage, a friend of the family estimated that West may have made masses of these amateur videos of his wife, but he took great care never to appear in any of these videotapes himself. West preferred the concealment and anonymity of being behind the

I Was Loved By an angel.
ana, I met ana in glasgow in
Scotland she Was the children
Nanny. she Work for My Wife +
Rean I had Nothing to do With
ana has she Was a young girl.
she allways made Me a cup
of Tea When I came in and My
Dinner, and allway gave Me
a Beautiful Little Smile as a
happy and Joyful young Lady,
she Wood chat to Me allways
a bout the children and Watt
thy had been Doing all day,
she Wood clean Up and go to
Bed, I Wood do My Books and go
to Bed, Rean Wood cum in 4-5-6
in the Morning Mostly Drink
and Just Dropped on the Bed
I got up at 6 to 6 30 ana Was up
and Mad the berakfast for me
and the Children I Went to Work

The first page of Frederick West's 'autobiography', *I Was Loved by an Angel*, written while he was in prison

Shirley Hubbard was only fifteen when she disappeared in November 1974 after running away from her foster parents' home in Droitwich, Worcestershire. She was never heard from again. A mask of adhesive tape was found around her skull when her remains were eventually recovered from beneath the cellar of Cromwell Street twenty years later *(Popperfoto)*

Juanita Mott, the daughter of a US Army serviceman, went missing in April 1975 at the age of eighteen, while hitchhiking from a friend's home in Newent into Gloucester for the evening. Juanita had been a lodger at Cromwell Street, although she was not living there when she disappeared. Her remains were recovered from beneath the cellar floor in 1994 *(Press Association)*

Shirley Robinson was eighteen when she disappeared from 25 Cromwell Street in the early summer of 1978. At the time, she was eight and a half months' pregnant with Frederick West's child. Her body, together with that of her unborn child, was recovered from the garden of Cromwell Street in 1994 *(Popperfoto)*

Alison Chambers absconded from a Gloucester children's home in August 1979, a few weeks before her seventeenth birthday. She failed to turn up for work the following morning at a local firm of solicitors, where she was an office junior, and was never seen again. A regular visitor to Cromwell Street, her remains were eventually recovered from the back garden in 1994 *(Popperfoto)* camera, perhaps only too conscious of his own penile size.

The majority of these video recordings were made in the top-floor bedroom at Cromwell Street, and kept there, where they could be discovered easily by the Wests' children. For Frederick West made no secret from his children that he wanted his wife to mate with a bull. 'That's why they had bulls on each corner of their four-poster bed,' Stephen West would recall later. 'He used to say, "The only thing that would satisfy you is a bull",' and claim that he was going to get one to 'sort her out'. Both Stephen and Mae West discovered rubber suits, masks, whips and vast piles of pornographic magazines in both their mother's own room and their parents' bedroom. Frederick West even made a sign for the end of the four-poster bed which he built himself. It was of exactly the same design as the wrought-iron sign denoting '25 Cromwell Street', and he screwed it to the four-poster bed. It read simply: 'Cunt.'

Frederick West did not disregard commercial pornography either. It was as much a passion as his own amateur efforts, for he depended on it, just as he did on his wife's exploits, to help him to sustain and satiate his own rapacious sexual appetite. As the 1980s progressed, West went to elaborate lengths to assemble his own collection of pornography. At one stage he had seven video-recorders, all of which he had stolen, and was duplicating pornographic videotapes for sale. At the outset he simply offered them to his friends and workmates, but he then gradually extended his range, possibly to the extent of supplying them to local video stores for sale 'under the counter'. West certainly suggested to a woman friend that he had made a profit from selling some that he had made himself, telling her that he had been paid £150 a time for recordings which involved the humiliation and beating of women, adding that he 'didn't understand how some women survived the beatings'.

Significantly, much of West's collection of commercial pornography featured the abuse of women by groups of men, including scenes of bondage, where the victim is bound and gagged by her attackers, and then subjected to repeated sexual abuse, often involving the use of artificial devices, including vibrators, and sometimes also involving urination. Several of the tapes showed a 'teacher' instructing his pupils on the elements of sexuality, a role that West clearly saw himself fulfilling to his family and to the young women who crossed his path. One tape, in particular, featured a young girl hung up by her arms from a beam in a cellar and abused by two men, one black, one white, while she is helpless. Another showed a young woman apparently drugged, and then gagged with masking tape, before being abused by two men.

Other tapes showed lesbian scenes, in one of which two women simultaneously insert the same cucumber into one another. But his collection also contained a considerable number of tapes that featured scenes of bestiality, where a woman mates with an animal or animals, including on one tape a pig, reflecting West's fascination with animal sexuality from his country childhood. There is no doubt that although West may have drawn some ideas for his own sexual experiments from his video collection, he would also have derived an even more intense satisfaction from the discovery that he had already experimented with perversions that he subsequently found on these commercial videotapes.

The voyeur in Frederick West came out in his collection of pornographic videotapes. They, probably more than anything else, captured his sexual insecurity, his sense that he alone was unworthy of a woman's love, and that he could never fully satisfy his partner. This in turn meant that if he did achieve some form of sexual conquest, the woman was immediately demeaned in his eyes, revealed as nothing more than 'a prostitute'. How could she have been anything else if she had allowed him sexual contact? This mixture of vanity and self-loathing drove his sexuality to greater and greater extremes. It was one reason why West wanted his wife to become a prostitute. It was a way of resolving the conflict within him, and making a profit at the same time.

Every kind of sexual perversity fascinated him. So, just as he had experimented with making audiotape recordings of himself and his wife making love in his van, so in due course would he create a videotape version – shot from the vantage-point of a tree – which showed his wife making love to a client in the van. And when he took her out to find clients in Gloucester or a neighbouring town, West would suggest that she wore a fur coat and stiletto heels but nothing else, and would take photographs of her in the outfit. He would then offer the photographs for sale to his friends, just as he would later offer pornographic videotapes for sale. The combination of a source of profit and the indulgence of his own sexual imagination ensured that pornography in all its forms was Frederick West's only other hobby.

West's eagerness for experiment, and his domination over his wife, an eagerness that gave rise to his desire for her to mate with a bull, led him to refer constantly to her as his cow. Frederick West even insisted that Rosemary West sign a document confirming it, just as he had made her sign the earlier declaration promising that she would not lose her temper for three months. Once again the document reveals a great deal about their relationship, and the extent to which West set the tone for much of his wife's sexual activity. It began: 'I, Rosemary West, known as Fred's cow, give my cunt to be fucked by any prick at any time he so desires without ever saying no.'

'My arse is to be smacked,' it went on, 'until I say I've had enough, my back hole is to be hurt until you say you've had enough. My tits I give to anyone that do not like them, to screw, bite or suck them when I'm being cocked, apart from my husband who can have them at his pleasure. My baby box is to be filled by anyone who says so when I'm told.' The document concluded: 'I give my mouth to be fucked by anyone I'm told and to be shut by Fred when I open it too wide. My tongue is to lick anything out when I'm told. My fingers is for wanking or fingering my cunt, or any other girl's cunt when I'm told. I must always dress and try to act like a cow for Fred, also to bathe and wash when I am told. Signed Mrs R.P. West.'

Exactly how West persuaded his wife to agree to sign this remarkable document, which he took pains to preserve in Cromwell Street, or whether indeed it was her own suggestion, is unclear. It is obvious, nevertheless, that his knowledge of her involvement in the killings of ten young women would have given him a powerful hold over her; just as her knowledge of his murderous nature would have given her an equal power over him. But the document brings into the clearest focus the intense relationship between the two. It was a relationship that had its foundation in a mutual depravity and lust, but which the Wests imagined to be love.

Rosemary West's sexual adventures with other men and women were a vital part of her attraction to her husband, one reason why Shirley Robinson's apparent single-minded devotion to Frederick West alone – to the exclusion of all others – may have worked against her, just as it may have worked against Ann McFall before her. Though it may have concealed his own sense of sexual inadequacy, West nevertheless made no secret of his cheerful and willing participation. One of his wife's partners, for example, a Jamaican who lived nearby, was a regular participant in the Wests' ménage. 'He would go out in the van with us,' West would recall in the last year of his life, 'and knock about, like. We got in the fields and Rose would run about naked, and we were naked as well, and . . . like carry on amongst ourselves and had a very good time. We'd made sure we were well out from anywhere and nobody seen us, like. And, I mean, we never ever got caught. We did it for years.'

West even urged his wife to save her semen-soaked knickers from her sexual encounters, particularly with coloured men, and provided her with glass storage jars to keep them in. One jar that West provided, and which remained, when filled, one of his prized possessions, had originally contained Rose's chocolates. The choice of that particular jar for these bizarre mementoes of Rosemary West's sexual promiscuity was no accident, but a reflection of his sense of humour. His wife 'didn't wear knickers at home', he told the police; she 'only wore them to go out for sex'. While a relationship with another man was still going on, West insisted that his wife put her knickers in the glass jar as soon as she got home, 'as souvenirs of her sex life', and then date them in ink.

Once the relationship with a particular man came to an end the Wests went a little further. 'At the end of an era, at the end of the passion, when it faded out,' West explained to the police, 'then they'd be burned and put in another jar.' The charred remains of his wife's underclothes were then kept in tiny pots on her mantelpiece. 'The idea was that in years to come we could say – well, that represents so-and-so, and that represents so-and-so . . . It was just something we thought up between us – to have these knickers in these jars – and then when you're sixty or seventy years old, like, you could say, "Well there's twenty in there" . . . They were nice pots, I mean, and the tops were sealed on, glued on.'

The knickers were collected systematically by the Wests throughout Rosemary West's years as a prostitute. 'Rose always had two bedrooms,' West explained. 'She would have one bedroom on her own. And her bedroom was always kept locked. She kept the set of keys on a chain round her neck, always.' Among the decorations were pictures of his wife in a variety of sexual positions, and 'Rose used to have the habit of putting nude figures of her niggers' along the bar that West eventually constructed for her use on the first floor of Cromwell Street. She was still advertising for clients in sexual contact magazines, using the name Mandy, just as Rena West had done before her, as well as bringing home men whom she met in local pubs like the Pint Pot and the Wellington. The clients would be offered a drink in the bar room that West had created on the first floor, before being ushered upstairs to the top floor. He had decorated one wall of the bar room with a large photograph of the Great Barrier Reef in Australia. There was a tiger-skin rug on the floor, and a chandelier in the ceiling, and West erected a sign above the bar which read 'Black Magic'.

Frederick West also collected his wife's knickers from the back of his Bedford van where a mattress made it their own mobile brothel. 'We would go out to different pubs on the road to Ledbury,' he remembered. 'It was a regular weekend thing, possibly one night in the week as well.' In 1985, however, he bought a second-hand white Ford Transit, once owned by Group Four Security, and fitted it out as a more sophisticated version of the same thing, once again designed to allow Rosemary West to operate as a prostitute – but under his protection. The reason for both vans, West maintained, was the 'fear of being seen by somebody from the church' for some of his wife's black clients, who would prefer to 'go by the river' or 'up on Painswick Hill'. West would still insist on making love to his wife immediately after she had finished with a client. 'That was part of the deal.'

Prostitution and pornography were two of Frederick West's definitions of love. Neither detracted in his mind from his love for his wife. Though to some they may have appeared depraved, to him they were proof of their love for one another, ways in which his wife and he could demonstrate their love. It was the basis of their relationship. 'There's a difference between evilly locking together and love,' he told the police. 'I mean, we're not evilly locked together at all. Rose might look a bit hard-faced and that, but Rose is soft as a kitten, and I know that because I've lived with her so long and controlled her life for so long.'

Even though Frederick West was finally to try to place all the blame for the killings on his wife, telling Howard Ogden that she was a 'callous' woman, 'with no feelings at all', he would nevertheless profess his undying love for her. Indeed, West even explained: 'I still think the world of Rose now, although these things have happened', and went on to suggest that his original love for 'his angel' Ann

McFall had been transformed into a love for his wife. 'Ann was passed into Rose, and I have been living with Ann in Rose all these years.'

On another occasion West told the police that he had always taken particular care when his wife was working as a prostitute. 'I mean, I make sure nobody harms Rose. I worship that girl, my wife. We've got a very special thing in our minds . . . and we didn't get married because we had kids. We got married 'cause we love each other . . . It's got stronger.'

Certainly, by the summer of 1982 their love for one another had been amply proven by the birth of seven children. Now that Anna-Marie had left, Cromwell Street was home to Heather, almost twelve, Mae, now ten, Stephen, nine, Tara, four and a half, Louise, three and a half, and Barry, just two; and in April 1982 they had been joined by the Wests' latest child, a girl whom they named Rosemary. In fact, the Wests' latest daughter was not Frederick West's own child. Her father was actually one of Rosemary West's long-standing black friends and clients. But West treated her exactly as he did Tara, his other mixed race daughter, whose father had since left Gloucester to return to Jamaica. 'It didn't bother me,' he explained to the police a decade later. 'I couldn't care less. They're my children and that's all there is to it.'

By that time Cromwell Street had become home to the Wests alone. The last lodgers, Liz Parry and Ped Brewer, had finally left a year earlier after Frederick West had refused to carry out an informal notice served on him by the local authority specifying that he repair parts of the upstairs of the house. From now on the Wests would take in lodgers only occasionally, and without informing anyone, thereby allowing West to avoid having to conform to any regulations.

Shortly after Rosemary's birth, Frederick West set about laying a concrete patio across the part of his back garden immediately outside his back door, the part that contained the bodies of Shirley Robinson and Alison Chambers. And, as he always did, he recruited his family to help. Then, gradually, West had begun to alter the two upper floors of his house. The top floor was turned into two bedrooms. In one West put the four-poster bed that he had made at work, complete with its indelicate wrought-iron sign. He also decorated each post at the corner with a wrought-iron bull, and placed a further bull and cow in the act of intercourse on its side. In the other top-floor room West put a king-sized bed with a lace canopy. Above the bed he suspended a concave mirror, and at its foot he erected a video camera. It was here that Rosemary West would make some of the amateur videos of her own sexual exploits, and here, too, that West would listen to her as she entertained her clients. He concealed microphones in the speakers of a hi-fi system in the room, so that he could listen to her on a baby alarm intercom on the ground floor.

'Every door in Mum's part of the house had a picture of a half-naked or naked woman on the back,' West's daughter Mae would recall. 'The house was pretty shabby before Mum started

247

working as a prostitute, but once she started earning money they started spending around the house. Dad didn't care about our part; it was all brown paint and cheap carpets.' The children were not allowed to go into the top two floors of Cromwell Street once West had started the conversion. But they were expected to answer the telephone to their mother's clients, take a telephone number and tell them that 'Mandy would ring them back'. They were not required to answer the door to the clients. Frederick West had taken care to install a second doorbell marked 'Mandy' for his wife. Significantly, in view of his pornographic videotape collection, her nickname was 'Mandy the Mouse'.

'We occasionally met some of the men who went with Mum,' Mae West would recall. 'They seemed OK and weren't perverts. They just sat with us playing, before Mum was ready to see them. While she was working I would look after the younger children. It would only be for an hour at a time, and usually two or three times during the day when she disappeared upstairs.' When Frederick West was at home he would sit in the ground-floor lounge with the speaker of the intercom pressed to his ear. 'He sometimes put his ear to the doorway to hear what was going on as well,' Mae West remembered. 'To us kids it was nothing, it happened all the time,' his eldest son Stephen would recall. 'We would hear all the loud noises up and down the stairs and just carry on with what we were doing.' To the West family in Cromwell Street, this was commonplace, their definition of love.

Rosemary West would sometimes summon a client herself rather than wait to be approached, referring to her ledger before she did so. Stephen recalled: 'If she fancied a coloured bloke who was well endowed she would look it up and ring them instead.' At other times West would continue to take his wife out in his van. 'Dad even put a little gas fire and a carpet in back of the van,' Mae would remember, 'because it got so cold. Then they would take a flask of tea and his usual bag of sex aids. I think Dad used to drive along when Mum was having sex in the back, and he'd film it on a tripod that he had bolted to the back. This would happen throughout the year.' To Frederick West, as to his family, this was entirely normal: his alternative universe.

That family was not neglected, however. Sometimes West would suddenly decide that they were going out for the day on a trip to the Forest of Dean, and put seats in the back of his van for them all to sit on. He would also take them for a week's break once a year to a holiday camp at Barry Island in Wales, and then in a caravan that he had acquired, which he would tow behind his van, for other family holidays at sites at Brean, near Weston-super-Mare, or Craven Arms in Shropshire. 'But Dad never cared for holidays all that much,' Stephen West remembered. 'He couldn't see the point in them. He'd always rather be at home in Cromwell Street.' West liked the familiarity, and the safety, that Gloucester and his house represented. He would always prefer to make forays from there, rather than risk completely unknown territory for very long.

Less than six months after the birth of the Wests' mixed race daughter Rosemary in April 1982, Rosemary West was pregnant again. The father was the same coloured man – who made a habit of coming to the house on Sunday morning, thereby earning himself a nickname – and in July 1983 she gave birth to her eighth child and sixth daughter. The Wests decided to christen her Lucyanna, though they would always refer to her by the nickname of Babs. Immediately after the birth, Rosemary West agreed to be sterilised. The operation did nothing to soften her vicious temper. Her children were still made to do most of the household chores. 'One of us would do the kitchen, the washing-up and wash the kitchen floor; another would scrub the bathroom floor and clean the whole bathroom. We had to clean the inside of the toilets, putting our whole arm in and really scrubbing,' Stephen West recalled of the year he reached the age of ten. 'If we did it wrong, she would give us a clout and we wouldn't do it wrong again.'

But it was not only the odd clout. Her violence towards her children was persistent and calculated. On one occasion in that year Rosemary West rang her eldest son's school to demand that he return home. When Stephen West arrived he found his thirty-year-old mother 'really calm, I couldn't understand it'. She told him to go into the bathroom, and ordered him to take his clothes off. His mother then tied his hands together with wire, and ordered him to lie face down on the floor so that she could tie his hands to the porcelain base of the lavatory. 'I couldn't understand what was going on. I was naked and I felt pathetic,' he remembered eleven years later. 'Mum looked so pleased with herself. She was completely calm as she tied my feet together.'

Rosemary West proceeded to beat her son with a leather belt for twenty minutes, standing on his legs so that he could not move. 'She kept whacking me with the belt, always the buckle end, and she aimed it at the base of my spine.' She also kicked him repeatedly in the stomach, shouting at him as she did so: 'What have you done wrong?' The boy had no idea, until finally Rosemary West accused him of removing some pornographic magazines from her room upstairs. Eventually, she simply sent him back to school. That afternoon her eldest child Heather returned home with a note from her own school explaining that they had confiscated some sex magazines from her. Rosemary merely laughed and said: 'Don't worry. Stephen got your beating.' When Frederick West got home, 'Dad just laughed. They were laughing together.'

'Mum and Dad wouldn't have changed if the Pope had knocked on the door and said, "Treat your kids better",' Stephen West would write after his father's death. 'They would have told him to fuck off as well. Funnily enough, none of all this made any real impression on us as children. It's what you got used to, it was normal life. We knew no different. All we thought was that these were Mum's and Dad's moods and tempers.'

Then, in the summer of 1983, three years after leaving their house without a word or an explanation, Anna-Marie West contacted her parents. She arrived at Cromwell Street with her boyfriend, Chris Davies. 'My father was very welcoming,' she would remember, 'but that was often his way when anybody new came into the house. He would be all friendly while he worked out whether they would be of any use to him.' Within a few months Anna-Marie (who had started to call herself Anne Marie) was pregnant, and on 14 January 1984, at the age of nineteen, she was married in the same Gloucester register office that her father and stepmother had married in twelve years before. One of the guests was West's own father, Walter West, then almost seventy, who came with West's younger brother Douglas and his wife, whom Walter lived with in Much Marcle. The entire West family then retired to Cromwell Street. At Frederick West's insistence, the reception was to be held in the basement.

Walter West's legacy still cloaked the shoulders of his eldest son. In June 1984, when Frederick West became a grandfather for the first time, at the age of forty-two, with the birth of Anne Marie's daughter Michelle, he started telling his two elder daughters, Heather and Mae, that it was 'the right of a father to take his daughter's virginity', and explaining to them that his father claimed that he had had done it to his sisters, and that he intended to do the same to them. There is evidence that he may already have attempted to abuse Heather, whom one friend of the family remembered hearing scream out 'No, no, please' in the middle of the night some time before this. Certainly, Frederick West told both his daughters repeatedly that he had 'created our bodies and that this gave him the right to look at our bodies', in Mae West's words.

From then on the two girls, now aged thirteen and twelve, who slept in twin beds in a room in the cellar of Cromwell Street, would go to bed fully clothed, and 'only undress under the bedclothes' to avoid their father's attentions. West would retaliate by trying to catch them in the shower, bursting into the bathroom and pushing his hands through the curtain to touch his daughters whenever he could. They responded by trying to stand guard for one another while they took a shower. In a rage West would call his daughters 'lesbians' and tell them that they both needed a 'good sorting out'.

Their father's sexual approaches were not entirely a surprise. There had been rumours in the family of what may have happened to Anna-Marie in the past, and neither Frederick nor Rosemary West had ever made the slightest secret of their own sex life. As Mae said: 'Sex had to be every night or he'd think Mum didn't love him', and her father would put his desire for his wife in the crudest terms. 'He'd say, "I had a good ride last night" . . . then he would say to Stephen, "You'll soon be ready to sleep with your Mum", and Mum and Dad would laugh.' For his part, Stephen West remembered: 'I just ignored him and let it wash over my head. I know he would have liked it if I had shown some interest, but I don't think he would have tried to force me.'

Frederick West reserved his principal attentions for his daughters, reminding both Heather and Mae West: 'Your first baby should be your dad's.' He told them that if they got pregnant, they could hand the baby over to their mother. 'He reckoned we would just be able to call it our brother or sister.' West made every effort to catch his daughters naked, and if they tried to cover themselves with a towel 'would try to rip it off'.

Recently made redundant from the Muir Hill works, which had closed in 1984, West was at home for a time, working for himself as a jobbing builder, still interested in finding 'lesbians for filming', as he told one next-door neighbour. With time on his hands there was more opportunity to pursue his hobbies. There was also ample time for him to abduct and kill more innocent young women. Psychologists consulted by the police after West's arrest were certain that he had continued killing throughout the early 1980s as relentlessly as he had through the previous decade, but he refused to confirm that this was the case, contenting himself with the remark: 'I'm not in a counting match. To try and get as many as I can.' They were clearly secrets that he intended to keep.

Frederick West saw no need to make any explanations or excuses for his actions. He saw them as a private matter, something that he need discuss only with his wife. He made it clear to the police that he thought that his business was his own, and he communicated that same thought to his children. They took it as commonplace, therefore, that he would cut holes in the doors so that he could see his daughters undress, and put his hands up their skirts whenever they were wearing school uniform. 'He didn't see himself as a paedophile; he just saw it as natural, natural to see what he had produced,' Mae would explain a decade later. 'But he'd get nasty if I tried to fight him off.' On one occasion West broke the door when she slammed it in his face; on another he 'threw the hoover at me for refusing him'. Yet there is every sign that most members of his family, no matter what they may have been subjected to, remained loyal to him and to their mother throughout their time at Cromwell Street. 'That was their reality as a family, the only love they knew,' as one social-worker put it many years later.

Heather West, however, found it increasingly hard to cope with her father's relentless sexual attentions towards her. She hated his insistence on keeping a record of her periods, for example, the suggestion that she should not remain a virgin after the age of fifteen, and his threats that if she refused to allow him to make love to her he would 'get someone to sort her out'. All took an increasing toll on the pretty dark-haired girl as she began the progress through puberty. In the mornings West would appear in her bedroom and pull the sheets off his eldest unmarried daughter. West would then 'sometimes get on top of us', then go out, only 'to come in again a minute later when we were getting dressed and fumble with us', as Mae West described a decade later. 'The whole atmosphere was really making Heather miserable.'

Heather West became steadily more withdrawn, rocking back and forth on her chair, biting her fingernails to the quick. At Hucclecote Secondary School she took to writing 'FODIWL' on the front of her exercise books, an acronym for 'Forest of Dean I Will Live', and a school friend recalled later that she was 'quite unhappy, particularly at home', and was planning to 'join the Army or go and work in a holiday camp'. Her school attendance record, at ninety-seven per cent, was excellent. In June 1985, at the first birthday party of her niece Michelle, Heather West stood alone, apart from the rest of her family. 'She seemed desperately afraid of her parents,' a friend of the time remembered nine years later.

One of Rosemary West's clients as a prostitute at the time, who had arrived at Cromwell Street after answering an advertisement in a contact magazine and became friendly with both the Wests over a period of about eighteen months, was eventually to report his fears about Heather to the local Social Services department in an anonymous telephone call. Arthur Dobbs would remember at Rosemary West's trial for murder nine years later that he had done so 'because I thought something funny was going on' after Rosemary West had told him that her husband was 'having sex with one of the girls'.

But when Frederick West was visited by a social-worker he responded as he always did to anyone in a position of authority over him, by being as humble and charming as possible. 'He always called you sir or madam,' recalled one social-worker who dealt with West at the end of his life. On this occasion he took considerable pride in showing the female social-worker all over his house, and ending his tour in the cellar. He even confided to her that he knew very well who had made the complaint, that it 'was all a matter of jealousy', and that he 'intended to go round and sort it out with him'. West's obsequious manner worked. There was absolutely no firm evidence against Frederick West, and the local authority let matters rest.

Heather and Mae West, meanwhile, made a pact between themselves. They vowed that they would never allow their father to have sex with them. It was a pact that was to cost one of them her life.

Chapter Nineteen

Heather

'A simple child
That lightly draws its breath,
And feels its life in every limb,
What should it know of death?'

Wordsworth, 'We Are Seven'

By the late spring of 1987 Heather West was sixteen and a half years old and on the brink of adulthood. With dark hair, dark eyes and a square, almost mannish jaw, she looked Spanish. There was certainly a sensuous, Mediterranean quality to her character, a fiery pride not easily dimmed. On top of that, 'she seemed more sexually aware than other girls of our age', in the words of a friend at Hucclecote Comprehensive School in Gloucester.

That was hardly a surprise. Heather West and her younger sister Mae had been fighting a running battle to repel their father's sexual advances for four years, a battle that had intensified as the months had passed, fanning still further Frederick West's determination to possess and subdue his wife's eldest child. By the spring of 1987 West not only wanted to penetrate his daughter Heather, but he wanted also to destroy her spirit and bend her to his own will. And the more she repelled his advances, the more she dressed, or undressed, under the bedclothes, or got her sister to stand guard while she was in the bathroom having a shower, the more irritated her father became.

West's anger showed itself in the way he talked about his daughter. When she was moody or morose, he would say it was because she was a lesbian, or a 'lemon', to use his favourite term. If she stood at the bottom of the garden on her own while the rest of the family were celebrating a birthday, it was because she was 'on' rather than because she was unhappy. If she refused to eat, it was because she needed a 'good sorting out' by a man, rather than that she was sickened by his relentless sexual advances. Frederick West tormented his daughter for refusing to have sex with him. But Heather West

253

shared her father's strength of character. She, too, was determined – not to give way.

'I hate my dad,' she confessed to more than one friend. The five-feet, four-inch-tall girl hardly knew what a father's love might mean, so relentless had been West's incestuous attentions. She had retaliated by becoming argumentative at school and morose and silent at home, and then developing an intense crush on one of her male teachers, which had eventually led to her father being summoned to see the headmaster. Frederick West politely told him that they had nothing to worry about. He would 'sort it out'. As one teacher recalled later, 'Mr West was very cooperative'. No one at Hucclecote School suspected child abuse.

The battle against her father's abuse had made Heather West a sometimes difficult, rebellious teenager. Although one teacher remembered her as 'very pleasant and willing to participate', another described her as a 'Jekyll and Hyde – one minute nice as pie, the next very aggressive', especially out of school in the company of older pupils. She had a reputation for bringing pornographic magazines to school, which had got her into trouble on a number of occasions, but she had taken eight CSE examinations, and kept up her attendance record throughout her final year. As her last term drew to a close in 1987, she was planning to put her long-fostered plan into action and leave Cromwell Street for ever. There were all sorts of possibilities, she told her girlfriends: joining the Army, working in a holiday camp, living in the Forest of Dean.

'But Heather was very wary of men and boys,' her younger sister Mae would recall. Her sister 'could be really hard towards us . . . She was very similar to Mum. You couldn't have cuddled her, she wasn't that sort of person.' Indeed, it is entirely possible that Frederick West was not alone in wanting to have sex with his daughter. Rosemary West, too, may have become increasingly attracted to the sixteen-year-old, egged on to be so by her husband. His daughters were his to do with as he chose, West had told his wife repeatedly during the fifteen years of their marriage, and the fact that he chose to allow his wife exactly the same rights was entirely his decision. The important thing was that his children should all be drawn completely into his incestuous circle.

His daughter refused point-blank. 'Heather and I had decided we would never give in and let him have sex with us,' Mae was to declare. She did not want to give in and join Frederick West's cycle of abuse. And she did everything in her power to fight her father off. She did not always succeed. Friends of the family recalled later hearing screams of 'Stop it, Daddy' and 'No, no, please, no' from the cellar of Cromwell Street while she was growing up. Rosemary West said that they were merely 'Heather having a nightmare'. But Heather confessed to one of her school friends that her father had forced her to have sex with him.

The spirited, dark-haired teenager had challenged her father and mother about the parentage of her three half-caste sisters. Her father

254

had been saying publicly that they were was 'a throw-back' to his 'gypsy past', but she claimed – quite correctly – that they were clearly the children of one of her mother's regular West Indian visitors. Heather West had even taken it on herself to confront one of the West Indian's daughters. As her stepsister Anne Marie was to recall eight years later: 'Rose and Fred were furious that Heather had been discussing their business outside the family, and she suffered a tremendous beating.'

At the family party to celebrate the third birthday of Frederick West's first grandchild, Anne Marie's daughter Michelle, on 17 June 1987, Heather West stood alone at the bottom of her stepsister's garden, just as she had done two years before. She even refused to pose for a family photograph with her younger brothers and sisters. The tensions at Cromwell Street were taking an ever-increasing toll. 'She wasn't talking to anyone and mostly kept her back turned to everyone else,' Anne Marie wrote later. But she also noticed that 'each time I tried to approach Heather and talk to her, my step-mother or my father would be there in an instant. It was as if they did not want me to be alone with Heather.'

Less than two days after this party Heather West disappeared. She was never seen again by her brothers or sisters. No birthday card or a Christmas present was ever received by her baby niece, her sister Mae, who had shared so many secrets with her over the past four years, or by anyone else. The troubled, spirited teenager vanished as completely as if she had been an assistant in an illusionist's act. One moment she was standing in the hallway of Cromwell Street, the next she was gone.

The children were baffled. So far as they knew, on the day after the party she had landed a job as a Yellow Coat at a holiday camp near Torquay. Then, at the last moment, the job had apparently fallen through. Her younger sister watched as she went 'to bed sobbing' and 'cried all through the night' in their shared bedroom in the cellar of Cromwell Street. 'I had never seen her like that before,' Mae West remembered eight years later.

The following morning, Friday 19 June 1987, Mae, along with the rest of the West children, went off to school, leaving Heather at home with her father, who was working on an outside building job and could not work that day 'because it was raining so hard'. By the time the children got back from school that afternoon Heather West had gone. 'And nearly all her stuff had gone too,' Mae West recalled. The explanation they were offered was plausible enough. 'Dad said the job was back on, and she had left with a girl in a Mini.' Stephen West was a little puzzled that his sister had not taken one of her most precious possessions, a book that she had been awarded as a school prize, but, like his sister, he thought little more about it.

In the weeks and months to come Frederick West kept up a pretence for his children that he and Heather were in contact – of a sort. He had 'seen her', or 'heard from her', although they 'hadn't had a chance to talk'. There were strange telephone calls that seemed

255

to be from Heather, but her sister and brother were never offered the opportunity to speak to her. It was all, of course, a charade put on to sustain the impression that Heather West was alive and well. The truth was the reverse. She was dead, and buried at the edge of the patio that Frederick West had so meticulously laid outside his house and on top of the bodies of Shirley Robinson and Alison Chambers a few years before – with his wife's help.

The timing of Heather West's disappearance was no accident. Like her half-sister Charmaine's before her, her murder had been deliberately postponed by her father until the end of the school year, although this time there would be no need to inform her teachers that she had 'moved to London'. There would be no need to tell them anything. Her school days were over, and to anyone who enquired where she was, both the Wests lied with their customary facility.

One friend and neighbour, Anne Knight, who looked after two of the nearby houses and had an office in Cromwell Street, was told by Rosemary West a couple of days after her daughter's disappearance: 'There was a hell of a barney here a couple of nights ago. We found out that she was going with a lesbian from Wales, and she has gone to Wales with her.' When another neighbour, Margaretta Dix, asked why she had not seen Heather for a couple of days, Rosemary West told her that her eldest daughter had decided to leave home, and, as there was nothing they could do about it, they had given her some money and she had gone off with a woman in a car. 'I'm not bothered if she's dead or alive,' Rosemary West told her neighbour bluntly. 'She's made her bed and she must lie on it.'

Shortly afterwards another friend of the family, Ronald Harrison, who had known the Wests since 1969 and whose own daughter was a friend of Heather's at Hucclecote School, asked where she had gone. Frederick West replied that Heather had been assaulting the younger children while she was babysitting, giving the younger children 'scratches' on their faces. As a result his wife had 'given her a good hiding' and a few days later Heather had 'run off'. But he told Harrison that Heather was alive and well and living in Brockworth in Gloucester, although he did not know exactly where. Both he and his wife also added the bare-faced lie, in response to any enquiry, that she 'always telephoned' to let them know she was 'all right'.

Yet another story emerged a few months later, when Rosemary West told the mother of one of Stephen's friends, Linda Tonks, that Heather had disappeared when 'she and Fred' had gone shopping one day and had taken 'all her belongings with her'. Frederick West confirmed this, explaining that their eldest daughter 'was a lesbian' while his wife nodded in agreement. Then Rosemary West told the window-cleaner Erwin Marschall, who knew Cromwell Street well, used to stay with Anne Marie, and had heard the screams one night several years before when staying in the house, that Heather was 'uncontrollable' and had 'run away from home' after 'taking all her belongings' – adding the further lie that she had called the police. She had, of course, done no such thing.

When Heather West's body was eventually recovered from beneath the patio at Cromwell Street it revealed a treatment identical in almost every respect to that suffered by the other victims. When the girl was unearthed, it was discovered that she had been decapitated, her body had been dismembered and disarticulated, a number of bones were missing, and those that remained were buried in a narrow two-feet-square shaft similar to that which had housed every other victim. Frederick West had abused his daughter precisely as he had his other victims, and for precisely the same reason – sexual gratification.

Two lengths of orange cord – twenty-two inches and fifteen inches long – were found with the body, the sort of cord that West admitted he carried on his van 'to tie ladders on to the roof', the sort of cord that could well have been used to tie her hands together, or to the beams of the cellar, or to bind her in some other way. When her remains were found the cord was entangled in what remained of her hair. But when Frederick West was confronted with the fact, he maintained only that it 'was what I tied the dustbin lid down with'.

When West was eventually confronted with a drawing of his daughter showing in detail which bones were missing from her body after it was recovered, he could barely bring himself to look at it. And when he was asked if there was any possibility that she may have been alive when the bones were removed, he broke one of his own rules and refused to offer an explanation. Instead, he said flatly: 'I've no comment on that.'

In fact, thirty-eight of Heather West's bones were missing from her remains, including her right kneecap, fifteen of her wrist and ankle bones from a total of thirty, and twenty-two finger and toe bones from a total of seventy-six. The mutilation did not end there. Not only had Heather West's legs been disarticulated from her pelvis with the aid of a sharp knife, leaving the familiar fine cuts on her bones, but her left thigh had also been smashed in two near her pelvis by a sharp-edged object, which Professor Bernard Knight, the forensic scientist who recovered her remains, believed had been done with a cleaver.

Frederick West eventually confessed in gruesome detail to the 'accidental' killing and dismemberment of his daughter, just as he had confessed to decapitating her. But he drew back from mentioning these other wounds to her body. To have done so would have been to reveal that there was far more to her death than a simple disagreement about her leaving home. He had seized the opportunity of his being at home with his daughter on that rainy morning in June 1987 to finally destroy her spirit by raping and humiliating her, and he had depended on some form of bondage to help him do so. When she refused to give in he had lost his temper, killing her as he had killed eight other young women in the past two decades.

Frederick West's rage made him 'like a madman', in the words of his son Stephen. But it was not a fury brought on by her desire to clean chalets at a holiday camp. It was inspired by her persistent rebellion against his authority and fuelled by his sexual lust. Had she been more submissive, Heather West might have survived. But that was not in her character, any more than it was in his.

With Heather's killing, West's depravity reached its lowest depth. He killed her, as he had killed Ann McFall, because he knew she was about to slip out of his control, and he could not tolerate the thought. And to rage was added fear: fear that once on her own she might complain that he had sexually abused her as a child, and, worse still, that she might voice her suspicions about the fate of some of the young women she had seen in Cromwell Street.

So he 'sorted her out' once and for all. He possessed her, then destroyed her, signing her death, as he signed the corpses of the earlier deaths, with his own unmistakable signature and in the place that was the focus of his fantasies and dreams, the basement of 25 Cromwell Street. In that sense, if in no other, this murder and its predecessors were ritual killings.

When the Wests' children came home from school on Friday 19 June 1987, Mae West remembered seven years later: 'Mum was quiet. She and Dad said they wanted a word downstairs, and said, "Oh, your sister has gone".' Only twenty months younger than Heather, and with the same dark looks, Mae had shared a bedroom with her for the past four years. 'Dad was really calm,' she recalled, 'when she told Stephen and me. I remember Mum standing and him leaning against the bedpost downstairs in the basement. Mum was quite upset. I thought it was because Heather had not said goodbye to her.'

In the weeks that followed, Frederick and Rosemary West together extended the patio at the back of their house. They laid a crossword pattern of vanilla and pink slabs that stretched to the very end of their small rear garden, and which their children would always refer to as 'two up and one across'. In doing so they put a concrete slab over the hole that West had so meticulously dug and covered in for their daughter Heather's body. They then constructed a barbecue opposite the site of her grave and put a pine table on the slab itself. All this came as something of a surprise to the Wests' children, who had been digging a hole themselves nearby to make a paddling-pool for the younger children, a hole that was suddenly filled in and covered over with concrete slabs.

Stephen West was equally surprised that neither he nor his sister Mae were ever invited to talk to Heather on the occasions when she was 'supposed to have rung up'. 'We didn't ask to speak to Heather, we knew that wouldn't be allowed anyway,' Stephen West wrote later. 'Knowing what I know now, I think they got somebody to ring up, so that if we had any suspicions it would calm us down.' In the years that followed, the Wests' older children filled in a Salvation Army form for a missing person, wrote to two television programmes about their sister, and even threatened to report her missing to the police. As soon as they did so, Frederick West 'sat us down and told us that

Heather was involved in credit card fraud and that if we went to the police we'd be dropping her in it', her younger sister remembered.

In the years after Heather West's disappearance, the Wests drew their familiar dark cloak around Cromwell Street once again, just as they had done in the past, and with very much the same success. In October 1987, for example, when Walter West came to visit them with his son Douglas and his wife, the Wests told him their eldest daughter 'had a job at a holiday camp with a friend'. Meanwhile, Frederick West went back to his old habits of picking up young women and offering them a lift, while Rosemary West returned to her life as a prostitute and went on to form a series of lesbian relationships.

But the veil that the Wests had always managed to draw over their activities could not last much longer. Their remaining eight children were growing older, less prepared to accept their parents' demands of silence, some of them less prepared to accept the abuse that they had suffered so persistently for so many years.

Something had changed for ever on that June morning in 1987. The evil love that he demanded of his children, like the love that he shared with his wife, was to prove West's undoing. Heather West brought the police to his door as surely as if she had walked into Gloucester police station and made a statement. Only it was to take almost seven years for her to do so.

Chapter Twenty

A father's right

'The act of evil brings others to follow,
young sins in its own likeness.'

Aeschylus, *Agamemnon*

Heather West was not forgotten in the months after her disappearance. Neighbours would enquire from time to time whether the Wests had heard from her, and Rosemary West would normally ignore the question or dismiss it truculently, telling a neighbour: 'I'm not bothered if she is alive or dead. She's made her bed.' Frederick West, on the other hand, would take just a little more care, explaining: 'She's phoned in the early hours of the morning and been abusive to Rose.' West would then conclude firmly: 'I've told her not to phone again.' As the months passed the questions began to die away.

West himself did not forget his daughter; he may even have mourned her in his own way. He took to standing on his new patio staring into space, or sweeping it aimlessly, 'as though he were thinking about something', as his daughter Mae remembered later. But her death taught him no lessons. West still could not control his obsession or desire. As time passed he turned his attention increasingly to her younger sister Mae, who by the spring of 1988 was almost sixteen herself. The girl knew that it was only a matter of time before her father forced her to have intercourse with him. 'He often talked about the right of a father to take his daughter's virginity,' she would recall seven years later.

For the moment West merely hinted at the strength of his own need. The spectre of his now dead daughter may, momentarily at least, have given him pause. But Mae West was also saved from the intensity of her father's desire for her by his own temporary departure from Cromwell Street. Since the closure of the Muir Hill Wagon Works he had been working for himself as a freelance builder, sometimes taking on small contracts to work away from Gloucester for a time. Late in 1987 he had gone to work in Weston-super-Mare and Bristol, returning home in the first months of 1988.

West next found himself a full-time job, working for Carson's, a firm of building contractors based in Stonehouse, just outside Gloucester, but he also kept up his part-time building work and odd jobbing for the landlords of the properties in Cromwell Street. His house and the street were still the focus of his life, the centre of his own alternative universe. It was there that he recruited participants for his amateur pornographic videos, there that he encouraged his wife to expand her list of clients, there that he would listen on the intercom system while she made love, or peep through the holes he had cut in the doors to watch, and there, too, that he would indulge his passion for perverted sexuality.

Everyone in Cromwell Street knew about Frederick West. One sixteen-year-old girl who moved in during 1988 remembered him and the street very clearly. Seven years later she would paint a portrait of West and his house, a portrait so vivid that it would bring this small street within five minutes' walk from the centre of Gloucester to life for anyone who read it. Her portrait also underlined West's particular and enduring charm.

Cromwell Street was, she began by explaining, 'a very rough, run-down area' where the majority of the houses were run as 'bed-and-breakfast businesses', which meant that the population was 'transient . . . with a lot of movement between the various establishments on the street'. This brought 'a large number of young, single people' to Cromwell Street.

'During the period I was resident there,' she explained, 'I would say only three of the houses in that street were occupied as family residences.' One of those, of course, was number 25. And it was no time at all before she was introduced to West, who was doing odd jobs for her landlord. By then, 'Fred West was known to me by reputation'. Her landlord had already told her cheerfully that he was 'kinky'.

The Wests' sexual reputation in Cromwell Street was well established. 'Apparently Fred would watch Rose having sex with other people,' the girl remembered, and was also 'very interested in group sex and in making pornographic videos.' It was also common knowledge among the young residents that 'Rose would have sexual relationships with people other than Fred, both male and female', and that the Wests would have 'sex parties which involved visitors to the home watching videos made by Fred featuring Rose and various partners, and then going on to have sexual intercourse themselves'.

But when the teenager actually encountered Frederick West in the early part of 1989, she, like so many other young women in the past, fell under his spell. 'When I first met Fred,' she remembered, 'my impression was that he was a very hard-working, caring man. Although I had initially been a little wary because of his reputation, I was quickly reassured by how kind and caring Fred appeared. When I met him, his main topics of conversation were his job, his family

261

and his house.' In no time West had invited her to look around 25 Cromwell Street.

By now aged seventeen, the young woman was very impressed. Some years later she was to recall West's conducted tour, especially around the two upstairs floors, which she remembered as being 'immaculate' and 'beautifully maintained – it was really smart'. On the first floor there was a sitting-room with a bar in it, plus a bathroom and a kitchen, while on the floor above there were two bedrooms, one of which had a video camera and microphones attached to the bed. There was a Yale lock at the foot of the staircase leading to the upper floors. 'Fred told me his children were not allowed in this part of the house.' And even though she was alone with him at the time, 'he didn't alarm me at all'.

West and the young woman became close friends. 'I felt towards him like a father or a brother,' she recalled, although she also admitted: 'Fred loved to talk about sex, and make sexualised comments.' She did not take them seriously. 'Even with all the sexual suggestion and innuendoes that Fred made, I still felt safe with him,' she remembered, safe enough to sit talking to him wearing 'only pants and a short T-shirt, or sometimes just a short towel and nothing else'.

At this stage she had not encountered Rosemary West. 'As with Fred, I had a bit of a preconceived opinion of Rose, because of all the gossip I had heard about her.' The gossip was that she loved sex and made love to anyone, man or woman. When they met, 'My first impression of Rose was that she was very stern, with no sense of humour. She appeared to be a private, withdrawn sort of person. Fred was always the one everybody knew, liked and talked to; Rose was quieter altogether.' As time went on, she realised that Rosemary West could also be a 'very moody person, unlike Fred who was very even-tempered', and that she 'would get bad-tempered for no reason', which meant that she would also become 'very nasty and vindictive'. Nevertheless, the two women 'quickly became very good friends'.

Now aged thirty-five, Rosemary West was in the middle of a long-standing lesbian relationship with a much younger woman, who had been a resident at Jordan's Brook Community Home. It had lasted for almost two years, and for a part of that time her lover had lived with her at Cromwell Street. But that had not prevented Rosemary West from having a series of sexual relationships with other young women, sometimes recorded on video, and neither had it prevented her from working as a prostitute in the local pubs.

Just as she had done for more than fifteen years, Rosemary West would visit a pub wearing a miniskirt, a see-through blouse and no underwear, and approach one of the older men to ask if he wanted a drink. If he accepted, she would then offer to have sex with him in Cromwell Street for £10 or £20, thereby undercutting the other local prostitutes who were charging £50. It was a technique she and her husband had refined over the years. Sometimes Frederick West would watch, and sometimes she would video the experience so that he could see it later.

But Rosemary West soon confessed to her new young friend in Cromwell Street that this was not her favourite sexual pastime. She preferred group sex and sado-masochism, especially when it was being video-recorded, and she particularly liked to 'punish people' by tying them up and spanking or beating them. She told her that she would regularly tie up and beat her lover from Jordan's Brook, just as they would sometimes approach other lesbians in bars and arrange for group sex sessions in Cromwell Street. And whenever possible Frederick West would video the proceedings. Indeed, he was regularly asking the young people he came into contact with in Cromwell Street if they knew 'anyone trustworthy' to take part in one of his pornographic videos.

West would invite young people from Cromwell Street to visit him, and play them one of his videos while they were having a drink. Sometimes this would become a prelude to some form of group sexual intercourse, but at other times he would simply offer to lend his guests one or more of the videos if they wanted to borrow it. They included his own amateur productions, often featuring his wife masturbating with a large dildo, or inserting a rolling-pin into her vagina, as well as commercial videotapes, which regularly included scenes of the bondage and humiliation of young women, often by an older man who appeared to be her 'teacher' or 'uncle'. West even offered to supply one of the local video stores. Most of the young residents of Cromwell Street considered this no more than 'just a bit of fun'.

Frederick West's employers saw him in very much the same light. 'Charming' was one description at the time; 'a pleasant man who would always pass the time of day', and 'obliging', 'never abusive and certainly not violent' were two others, while a third employer remembered West as 'never aggressive, honest and hard-working'. Just like the young men and women in his street, they, too, were seduced by West's carefully groomed image of himself, the image of the down-to-earth little man, a man who knows his place and yet is always prepared to oblige.

West's employers, like the residents of Cromwell Street, and the men who had worked alongside him in the light fabrication shop at Muir Hill, knew his smutty reputation, and recalled his leprechaun grin whenever a dirty joke was cracked or a sexual suggestion made, but they never appeared to sense the darker side that lay beneath. Perhaps they can be forgiven for that. How could they sense it? What cleverer scheme can the devil think up than to convince the world that the devil does not exist? Everything is permissible, nothing is ever too dangerous, providing 'you're among friends'.

West used the same technique within his own family. There was 'nothing wrong in violence and sexual abuse'; quite the reverse. They were 'completely normal' and 'nothing to worry about'. After all, they were a father's right. 'We didn't know anything different,' Mae

263

West would recall after her father's death. 'What was really confusing was that Mum was a really nice mum if she wasn't being nasty. And if Dad hadn't been abusing us, he would have been a really good dad.'

Mae West spoke for all her brothers and sisters when she explained: 'I couldn't ask him why he was doing this to us. There was no point in appealing to Mum. She knew about it, but she ignored it. She'd just say that Dad was playing, but she never really put it down to much. I think she thought that as he wasn't really hurting us, there was nothing to worry about.' To Frederick and Rosemary West, abuse was a normal part of family life, as familiar a part of their world as the string of young visitors who came and went night after night at Cromwell Street to watch pornographic videos or to have sex.

Kathryn Halliday, who was to be called as a witness for the prosecution at Rosemary West's trial, was among those who found themselves invited to join the motley flood of humanity washing through the elaborate iron gates at the entrance to 25 Cromwell Street. A divorcée, she had moved into 11 Cromwell Street in October 1988, along with her new lover, a lesbian. Halliday had hardly lived there a week when her ceiling started leaking, and she asked her landlord to recommend someone to help her to stop it. The landlord suggested Frederick West.

Ever helpful, West duly stopped the leak in the thirty-one-year-old woman's ceiling, engaging her as he did so in his inevitable sexual banter. When he discovered she was living with a lesbian partner, his eyes gleamed. 'If you see my missus – she'll sort you out,' he told her, adding by way of explanation: 'She likes a bit of both.' West then invited her to his house that evening, and Kathryn Halliday accepted the invitation.

When she arrived at 25 Cromwell Street, just a few doors down from her own house on the same side of the street, Halliday was immediately ushered upstairs to the sitting-room and bar on the first floor, where 'Fred asked me if I wanted to see any videos – pornographic videos. Anything I wanted he could put on for me.' The suggestion was that she could watch every kind of sexual perversion, including sex with animals and children. But the square-jawed woman simply asked if he had 'a straight video – showing ordinary sex', and West promptly put one on.

Moments later Rosemary West joined them. 'Rose came straight into the room and sat down beside me,' Kathryn Halliday remembered seven years later. She was wearing a miniskirt and a low-cut top. 'Nothing else. No underwear at all.' There were no niceties and no formalities. 'She began to undress me very quickly,' Halliday would recall. 'I must admit I was very taken aback. I'd never been in a situation like this. I was dragged upstairs to the front bedroom. It was very, very quick, very forceful. There were mirrors on the wardrobes and there was a double bed. I was pushed down on the bed, and Rose West joined me. She was quite aggressive. She proceeded to make love to me.' Frederick West, meanwhile, disappeared for ten minutes, then came back with a tray of drinks and a video camera. By now naked himself, he started to film the two women. 'It appeared that Rose was trying to get me sexually excited, and then Fred joined in. He made love to me while Rose was sitting astride me, on top of me.' But it did not last long. 'Mr West climaxed very quickly, and went downstairs to get another drink.'

Like many other young women before her, Kathryn Halliday had not bargained for the Wests' persistent and violent sexual desire. 'Rose became very aggressive. She held me down on the bed very hard. She gripped my wrists and began to taunt me. She was saying, "Are you woman enough to want to do all the things that we want to do to you?" ' Rosemary West wanted to use a variety of vibrators and dildos on Halliday, and then for Halliday to use them on her. The thirty-one-year-old tried, but 'couldn't use them all', even though 'the session went on until one o'clock or one-thirty in the morning'. Even then, Rosemary West was not anxious to bring it to an end. 'But Fred didn't join in again, after the first time.'

In spite of the aggression and the taunts, Kathryn Halliday embarked on a sexual relationship with Rosemary West after that first evening. The two women met 'about once a day, mostly during the day – but some evenings as well' for months. 'Rose would knock on the window at number 11 after taking the children to school,' Kathryn remembered, although she was told not to come to 25 Cromwell Street on Thursday mornings, because that was kept for male clients. During the day the two women would be alone, but in the evenings Frederick West would be there too.

Each time she went, Kathryn Halliday remembered, 'vibrators were there', to be used 'very very physically', along with 'dildos of different shapes and sizes'. One of the dildos was eighteen inches long and covered with nodules. Rosemary West liked to call it her Exocet, the name of a missile used during the Falklands conflict, but there were many others. Their meetings always started 'very gently and she was very persuasive. But once she had got you into the bedroom she wanted to make you vulnerable,' Kathryn Halliday was to confess to the jury at Rosemary West's trial for murder seven years later. 'When she got you into a vulnerable position physically and mentally, she would use that against your person.'

When Frederick West was there, he 'would often put on videos while we were having a drink, like most people would put on background music. They were all to do with bondage and sadism,' Halliday remembered. 'They were amateur videos. There was one of a girl in a black rubber suit having sex with a man. There were others with girls who were tied to a bed with chains and straps', and in one of them Kathryn even recognised the Wests' front bedroom. 'A girl with fair hair was being whipped and tied to the bed' by a man who might possibly have been West himself. 'She was forcibly being made love to – very, very forcefully.' A large dildo was being used, and the camera focused specifically on the young girl's distress.

During these evening sessions 'Fred would watch rather than take part', Kathryn Halliday would recall. 'He took part sometimes, but not very often at all.' On one occasion he ejaculated into his wife so quickly that she told him 'You needn't have bothered'. Indeed, if West took part at all, Halliday remembered, it was usually only when 'I had my hands and feet tied. Rose would sit across me. She would hold me down and Fred would make love to me. She was quite a big woman and very, very physically strong.' Frederick West made sure that the element of bondage increased steadily when he was present during the months that the thirty-one-year-old went to Cromwell Street: 'Most times I went in the evening, it would end up with me being tied up,' she remembered. On one occasion Frederick West even threatened to leave her tied up all night.

Inexorably, the Wests began to extend their sexual demands. 'She wanted orgasms all the time, like a machine,' Kathryn Halliday would recall. 'They wanted me to do more and more. They pushed me beyond my personal limits, and they hurt me. The first time was making love – the second time had become more forceful, more aggressive, more demanding. Rose West wanted me to do things to her which were very, very aggressive.' In her own words, Halliday had become 'like a moth to a flame'.

The Wests blindfolded their guest 'several times', and put a pillow over her head 'twice'. With the pillow over her victim's head, Rosemary West whispered: 'What does it feel like not to be able to see?' Then, after leaving the pillow in place for some time, she whispered again: 'Can't you breathe? Aren't you woman enough to take it?' Kathryn Halliday gradually came to understand that there was nothing the Wests enjoyed more than causing her pain, and that Rosemary West in particular 'had no limit to what she would do. They played with me and the idea that I was frightened. They got their thing from seeing other people frightened.'

Finally, the Wests took her to the top back bedroom at Cromwell Street. She was shown the four-poster bed, with two large wooden hooks in the pelmet, in the darkly decorated room, and then the contents of the wardrobe. Alongside a collection of short leather skirts and lingerie, there was a suitcase. Inside it: 'There were black rubberised masks and suits. There were all-in-one suits with slits for the nose.' But there were also masks with no nose or mouth holes, which Kathryn Halliday realised offered 'no physical means of being able to breathe'. But the masks and suits had obviously been worn, 'because they smelled of sweat'. When the Wests asked her if she would wear one of the suits: 'I said no and I edged out of the room. I was frightened. I never ever went back into that room.'

Even then, Kathryn Halliday did not break off her relationship with the Wests. They had become so close that Frederick West even tried to persuade her to move in with them, and bring her partner. She refused. But gradually, as their sexual relationship continued, they began to taunt her again about her inability to accept larger and larger sex aids, as Rosemary West could. They steadily increased the sexual pressure, showing her two large whips, a bullwhip and a cat-o'-nine-tails, and tying her to the bed more and more often. On one occasion West punched her in the face while his wife was holding her down, and on another she felt a sharp stabbing pain in her stomach which she discovered was a half-inch cut in her navel. 'Each time they pushed me a little further. They became more and more violent, physically and mentally. Fred would beat me around the head with his fists and Rose slapped me.' But gradually the Wests grew bored, 'because a lot of the time I couldn't take any more'. Finally, she accepted: 'I was getting way out of my depth. I realised just how dangerous things were getting. I never returned to Cromwell Street.'

In June 1989 Kathryn Halliday left Cromwell Street altogether. She was fortunate to escape. For had she not had a permanent lesbian partner living in the same street, there is every possibility that she would never have managed to. But like some of the other women who fell under the Wests' influence, Kathryn Halliday was unwary, to say the least. She had lived in the twilight world on the edge of the law, a vulnerable woman who had her own difficulties. It was this which had made her attractive to Frederick West in the first place, for he would have sensed that she was searching for affection and yet was also susceptible to domination, and threat, both by Rosemary and himself. Once again, West had chosen his target well. Kathryn Halliday made no complaint to the police, or to anyone else for that matter, after she left Cromwell Street.

Kathryn Halliday was not the only person driven out of Cromwell Street in 1989. Both Mae and Stephen West were forced out of their home by their parents. The previous summer, at the age of sixteen, Mae West had started to pretend that she was sleeping with her boyfriend Rob Williams so that her father would stop trying to abuse her. She knew that West was becoming ever more insistent, and that it would only be a matter of time before he forced her to have intercourse with him. But Frederick West responded by pushing her boyfriend into her room in the basement 'and making him stay the night'. West then took to asking him: 'How was she?' Early in 1989 she and her boyfriend took refuge from his leering attentions in a flat two streets away.

That summer Stephen West, then almost sixteen, also left Cromwell Street, getting a job as a motor mechanic shortly after leaving school. In March a teacher at Oxstall's Comprehensive School, where he was a pupil, had expressed concern that he might have been subjected to 'physical abuse', and the NSPCC had been invited to investigate. The Society contacted the Social Services Department in Gloucester, which had no record of the boy, and when he was interviewed he made no complaint about physical abuse at home, even though the NSPCC received a report in April that he had been hit with a mallet. The Society's records show only that he received a 'minor physical injury on the face' for which he gave 'a satisfactory explanation'.

In fact, between March and May 1989 the representatives of the Society held four meetings with Stephen West to explore the possibilities of abuse. In the end they decided to take no further action after Stephen himself decided that he did not want them to. Looking back six years later, the Society noted: 'On the evidence before it at the time . . . the NSPCC did not believe the case was a serious one.' Its case file was later to go missing, and there is certainly no record that Frederick West or his wife were ever questioned about the suggestions of abuse to their fifteen-year-old son. Not long afterwards the Wests themselves forced Stephen to move out of 25 Cromwell Street. They found him a bed-sitting-room not far away. It was not only a punishment. Frederick West was as determined as ever to preserve the privacy of his own bizarre world.

Cromwell Street was hardly left empty by the departures. Mo, as the Wests always called their first mixed race child Tara, was eleven, her younger sister Louise ten, and Barry nine, while the Wests' two other mixed race children, Rosemary and Babs, as Lucyanna was called, were seven and six. But for a time Frederick West was careful not to abuse his children. Though he had attacked his first daughter at the age of eight, they were, apparently, 'too young' for the time being. Instead he began to plan to have another child.

He may have wanted Rosemary West to make love to coloured men, and to have their children, but as he once told Howard Ogden: 'I am colour-prejudiced a lot.' This made him even more determined to have another child with his wife. Frederick West's desire to perpetuate the cycle of incest within his own family had not dimmed.

Not long after the two remaining elder children left home, the Wests decided to try to have another child together. First they visited a venereal diseases clinic in Cheltenham to ensure that they were suffering from no sexually transmitted diseases. They also wanted more information about the dangers of AIDS, but neither took a test to discover whether or not they were HIV-positive. 'But I knew we didn't have an ordinary sex life, like,' West admitted, 'That's why me and Rose went along in the first place.' And then, at the age of thirty-six, Rosemary West had her sterilisation operation reversed. At the age of forty-eight Frederick West set about becoming a father for the tenth time.

West's other principal interest at the time was his full-time job as a general maintenance man at a home for the autistic in Minchinhampton, seven miles south of Gloucester. Still working for the firm of Carson's Contractors, who had a contract to look after the home, West was on call 'twenty-four hours a day, seven days a week for odd jobs', as he put it, and for all sorts of minor tasks, including carpentry, plumbing and decorating. He never minded being called out, and would often disappear to the home at odd hours of the day or night in the red Vauxhall Astra van that he had recently been supplied with by the contractors. With thirty-two adult residents and sixty-one staff, Stroud Court was in the middle of a seventeen-acre country estate, where Frederick West had keys to all the buildings.

The main house itself had a series of rambling cellars, which one resident described as 'like a rabbit-warren', and where West was regularly to be found.

Frederick West clearly enjoyed working at Stroud Court, where he would engage the staff and residents in endless conversation: 'talkative as anything', as one would remember. And, as usual, West would take a particular pride in his sexual conquests and criminal connections, at one stage even boasting that he was 'involved in diamond smuggling'. Once again 'no one took him particularly seriously'; he was just a hard worker who seemed happy to do even the dirtiest jobs, like working on the cesspit. West would never complain. As he told the police proudly after his arrest: 'I mean, I got a good reputation with my work and everything else I do . . . If anybody was in trouble, I helped them out the best I could . . . with no bad intentions whatsoever . . . I like people to look upon me as somebody they can trust.'

Naturally, whenever West went to Stroud Court he seized the opportunity to pick up any female hitchhikers he came across on his way home, haunting the Stroud to Gloucester and the Cirencester to Gloucester roads just as he had done in the past. He would often drive between Stroud and Cirencester, stopping off at a small farm at Camp, near Painswick, where his employers had a workshop, before turning north again, back towards Cromwell Street. 'I've never done anything up the workshop,' West told the police after his arrest. 'I've never dug one hole up round that area.'

On Sunday afternoons he and Rosemary West would go out for drives in his van, and they would be 'gone for hours', as one of their daughters' school friends remembered later. Old habits died hard. It was nearly twenty years since the Wests had first started touring the area on the lookout for vulnerable young women. They saw no reason to stop now. The suspicion must be that they had also not stopped killing any young women unfortunate enough to fall into their hands. But that was a secret that neither Frederick West nor his wife was prepared to share with anyone.

At 25 Cromwell Street life continued much as it had before. One friend from the street recalled visiting the house 'almost daily' throughout 1990 and 1991 to find 'just the children downstairs'. When she asked where their mother was, the younger West children would explain politely that she had brought a man home and was upstairs with him. 'The intercom was always on, and it was switched to work both ways,' the woman remembered later. 'Consequently, on these occasions the children and I were able to hear Rose and her unknown male visitor having sex. Rose was very noisy, screaming and moaning, and it was very embarrassing for me in front of the children.' But, like so many other people who came into contact with the Wests, she did not feel the children's knowledge of their mother's sexual drive 'was particularly harmful or undesirable'. She simply concluded: 'Although my description of the Wests' family life probably sounds bizarre, at the time I accepted it as perfectly normal.'

Rosemary West's younger brother Graham Letts once approached his sister about her activities as a prostitute. 'What shocked me most was how casual she was about the whole thing,' he said later. 'She and Fred seemed to take pride in how slick the operation was.' Letts and his wife Barbara would often be there when the telephone rang, and 'Rose would disappear for half an hour'. But the Letts, too, did not think it dangerous. Even though they had been invited to watch pornographic videos, had seen the pictures of Rosemary West in the nude that decorated the bar upstairs, and had seen her take off all her clothes in front of them when she wanted to change – 'She wasn't wearing knickers. I don't think she ever did' – they thought life in Cromwell Street was normal enough. All Graham Letts could offer by way of explanation was: 'If I had known just how much deeper their perversion went I would have blown the whistle.'

Frederick West's sexual abuse of his own children finally resumed. In 1991, not long after one of his daughters had started at a local comprehensive school in Gloucester, West started to touch her indecently, just as he had touched Heather and Mae before her, taking her upstairs to the top bedroom in Cromwell Street, removing her clothes and telling her he was 'checking her over'. In the last months of 1991 he did so on four or five occasions, insisting on taking his daughter's clothes off himself. A year earlier, in her final months at her junior school, West had started making preliminary attempts to touch her developing breasts every few days. But he had not persevered. Now, he started making crude jokes about female anatomy.

Just as he had done with Anne Marie, Heather and Mae West before her, West would tell his daughter that it was perfectly 'all right for him' to touch her because she was his daughter 'and I produced you'. Her sister remained untouched by West, at least for the time time being but she, too, knew of his incestuous desire. She even confided to a friend at school that Heather 'had run away because of her father's abuse'. But that was a secret meant to be kept within the locked doors of Cromwell Street, guarded by Frederick and Rosemary West with meticulous care, and reinforced with violence. When she felt it was necessary, Rosemary West continued to punish her children viciously, beating one of her children with a wooden spoon or a leather belt, just as she had beaten Stephen. She would often wait to do it until her husband came home, so that the Wests could laugh about it together.

Not that Rosemary West was entirely in her husband's thrall. Late in March 1991 she rented a bed-sitting-room for herself in Stroud Road, not far from Cromwell Street, without telling her husband. Calling herself Mandy West, she explained to her landlord that she was 'a nanny' at Cromwell Street, who 'wanted to get away sometimes'. To prove the point she took her youngest daughter Lucyanna with her to meet him. The top-floor flat cost her a little over £100 a month, and she furnished it herself with considerable care. She rented it for more than six months, visiting it regularly during the day, and not leaving until late September. When she suddenly did so, she left all her newly acquired possessions, including a new hoover in its box.

After her sudden disappearance, the landlord at Stroud Road went to 25 Cromwell Street in search of 'Mandy' West and encountered Frederick West, who clearly knew nothing about his wife's arrangement. West told the man that there was no Mandy living there, but there were two Rosemary's: 'Did he want the older one or the younger one?' But at that moment Rosemary West emerged from the house to see who her husband was talking to. Flushed with embarrassment, she tried to deny that she had anything to do with the flat in Stroud Road. Ever keen to sense danger, West took charge immediately, saying he would 'clear the place out in a hour', and doing so. In his interviews with Howard Ogden three years later West would claim that 'Rose had flats all over Gloucester' that 'he knew nothing about', but it is far more likely that this represented her only attempt at independence. Rosemary West clearly wanted to keep some of her earnings and activities secret from her husband. But another reason may be that she had recently suffered a miscarriage.

In fact, Frederick West's carefully ordered life was about to fall apart, but the harbinger of his downfall was not his wife's small attempt at independence: it was the death of his father Walter. Now almost seventy-eight years of age, Walter West had been living in Much Marcle with West's younger brother Douglas and his wife for some years. But in the first months of 1992 his health had begun to deteriorate rapidly. Frederick's other brother John had called on him to visit their father in hospital, but Frederick categorically refused to do so, causing a rift between the two brothers which would never be healed. He was afraid of hospitals. He was also, probably, slightly afraid of his father, on whom he had once modelled himself, but whom he had now come to see as his rival as the dominant male in the West family.

But, characteristically, West managed to produce a romantic explanation for his failure to visit his father. 'I wanted to remember my father as I'd seen him the last time, that day in the garden,' he told Ogden two years later. 'That day I was sat in the garden with Dad under the plum tree, he said that he hadn't got long to go, and I felt really wonderful with him. Me and my father was close. Me and Dad always stuck together.' And he told the police: 'I set myself up round my father. I still am to this day trying to keep myself the way my father was. Me and him got on ace. He was my God, like. I wanted to be my father. I admired all he stood for.' Though West may have felt secretly that he could never live up to his father, he had spent his life trying to prove that he was worthy of his love, and using what he saw as Walter West's own sexual appetites as his archetype to do so.

Walter West died in Ledbury Cottage Hospital on 28 March 1992, less than four miles from the village that had been his home throughout the seventy-eight years of his life. Five days later he was buried in the parish church of St Bartholomew's, Much Marcle, where his eldest son had been christened and confirmed into the Anglican Church four decades earlier. Frederick West stood at the graveside, with his wife and his eldest daughter, Anne Marie. The wake was held at Moorcourt Cottage, now the home of his younger brother, Douglas, and the site of Walter West's own abuse of his eldest child.

Seven weeks later Frederick West took a further sordid step along the path that had begun in his father's cottage in Much Marcle. But this time it was a step that would eventually contribute to his downfall. Disregarding the risks inherent in the fact that his children were now growing up, ignoring the awareness that had begun to permeate every section of British society in the wake of Childline, overlooking the fact that publicity that had surrounded a number of sex-abuse cases – all of which had been reported on his own favourite news programmes – West calculatedly and repeatedly returned to the abuse of one of his own daughters. It was his right; why should he not exercise it? The family would always be loyal. They always had. Where was the danger?

One evening in late May 1992 West asked one of his daughters to help him to take some bags upstairs. Rosemary West had gone out, and the rest of the children were on the ground floor watching television, or in the basement. Frederick West ushered his daughter through the door leading to the top two floors of Cromwell Street, then locked it behind him as he followed the girl upstairs towards the bar room on the first floor. He wanted her to take a bag of wine bottles into the room.

Once they were both inside West told his young daughter to sit on the small sofa under the window. West then adjusted the video camera opposite them and pointed it towards her. He then took off his daughter's clothes and knelt down in front of her after unzipping his own trousers, telling her to 'look at the television'. West inserted his penis into her, after using some lubricant but without a condom. Then, even though she was plainly terrified, and shouting, 'Stop, Dad, it hurts', he turned the child over and abused her from behind, before turning her on her back again on the sofa and raping her a second time. The girl remembered afterwards the programme showing throughout her ordeal. It was *Just Good Friends*.

Downstairs, two of the other children had heard the shouts and had started banging on the locked door to their parents' part of the house. West shouted back, 'For fuck's sake', but otherwise took no notice. After he had finished he left the room and came back with a pad of toilet paper for the child to put into her knickers. Mascara was running down his daughter's face from the tears, but as he followed her back down towards the ground floor he told her only: 'Don't say anything.'

When they got back downstairs he warned her again: 'You mustn't say anything, you know, because I'll go to prison for five years. We'll all be split up, and you need a mum and dad at your stage of life.'

The girl did not reply, she simply went to bed and cried through the night.

She spent the rest of the week off school, as her father had encouraged her to in the first place, and he made no further approaches to her, beyond asking her if she was 'bigger' and whether she had 'put anything inside herself'. The girl told him that she had not. That weekend, while her father was out at work, she told her elder sister what had happened. But her ordeal did not end there.

One evening the following week West took his daughter to one side and told her that he 'would have to do it again', because 'there were two layers that needed breaking' and, as she herself recounted later, it 'could be dangerous if he didn't do it' as a 'man might hurt me in future'. The confused and terrified girl believed him, and later in the week he kept his promise, repeating the abuse in exactly the same way. The girl was in tears throughout the ordeal, begging her father to stop. His reply was: 'It'll be OK just this time. I won't need to do it again.'

This time, when his daughter went back downstairs she found that her mother had returned. The girl disappeared into the ground-floor bathroom, but both her parents followed her inside. West told his wife what he had done, and invited her to examine the girl. Rosemary West told her daughter to get off to bed.

Even that was not the end of the abuse. Before she went to bed her father told her that he wanted her to go with him the following day, a Saturday, to a warehouse he was painting near Reading. When they arrived at the deserted building the following morning, he raped his daughter for a third time, even though she was again shouting and trying to push him off. After he had finished, and they were sitting in his van, West patted her thigh and said: 'I'll leave it alone now.'

That weekend the girl told her sisters and her brother Barry what had happened. But none of them told anyone. They talked about calling Childline, and even discussed trying to find the video as evidence of the assault, but in the end, because the abuse stopped, they decided to do nothing. For all the West children, this was still their father, the head of their family, the man who gave them part of their definition of love.

In the days that followed the rape of his daughter at the warehouse, Frederick West took to collecting her from school even more diligently than he had in the past. He had to protect his world, and his family, from the suspicions of prying outsiders. Rosemary West, meanwhile, put a new lock on the front door to make sure that her children could not go out without her knowledge once they had come back from school. She kept the key on a piece of string around her neck.

Soon, through the voices of two of his children, one of them from beyond the grave, the secrets of Frederick West's nature would be exposed for the world to see.

273

Chapter Twenty-one

The root of all evil

'Human blood is heavy; the man that has shed it cannot run away.'

African proverb

Secrets will out. But they escape in the most unlikely ways. So it was in the case of West's latest assault on one of his daughers. The story of her rape and buggery at the hands of her father was not told at first by her, or even by a member of her family. It was told by a school friend to a passing policeman. The ugly world of Frederick West began gradually to come to light as the result of a chance remark to that most old-fashioned figure of authority in British society, a policeman on the beat.

Shortly after six o'clock on the evening of Sunday 2 August 1992, one of the girls from Beaufort Comprehensive School was joking with a uniformed police constable in Cromwell Street. One of a group of three twelve-year-olds talking to the officer suddenly asked him: 'What would you do if your friend was being assaulted?' The banter continued for a moment, and then the constable asked who was being assaulted. The girl told him that she was worried that her friend might have been 'mucked about with' by her father, who had taken a video while he was doing so. The officer did no more than make a note of the girl's story at the time, but the following morning he began to make enquiries.

Three days later, on Wednesday 5 August, the police formally alerted the Social Services Department in Gloucester, and then applied for a warrant to search 25 Cromwell Street for pornographic videotapes. Just before nine o'clock the following morning, a team of two detectives and four policewomen rang the bell and asked to speak to Frederick West. But West was not there. It was Rosemary West who opened the front door and asked what the officers wanted. As the women police-officers filed past her into the ground-floor living-room, where the children were still in their pyjamas watching television, one of the officers explained that they had come to search the premises for pornographic material following a serious allegation of child abuse.

Rosemary West immediately flew into a rage. While the first police-officer was still trying to explain what was happening, she started shouting abuse at the officers at the door, and then turned and ran into the downstairs living-room, where she screamed at her five children: 'You don't have to say anything.' Rosemary West then started to lash out at a woman police constable in the living-room, hitting her repeatedly, first with her fists and then her feet. Finally, one of the male constables grabbed her by the arm, twisting it behind her back, and arrested her for obstruction. Rosemary West's reply was succinct: 'Fuck off, you bastard.'

Immediately after her arrest she was taken to Gloucester police station, while the first search of her house was started by the three male detectives and the three remaining policewomen tried to comfort the West children. The police explained to Tara, Louise, Barry, Rosemary and Lucyanna why they had come, and gave them breakfast. Then they arranged for them to be taken to a local authority home nearby to be introduced to the team of social-workers who would be looking after them. By a strange irony the home they were taken to would have been known only too well to their father. It was part of the complex of buildings known as Jordan's Brook Community Home.

It was not until shortly after two o'clock that afternoon that the police finally located Frederick West. At two-fifteen he was arrested for rape in the small village of Bisley, a mile east of Stroud, and seven miles south of Gloucester. When he was cautioned, West replied fiercely: 'What – fucking hell, I know what this is – it's down to jealousy.' But he was then taken to Gloucester police station, where he was placed in the cells.

West was to be held on remand in prison and at a bail hostel for ten months before he would be allowed to return permanently to his own home, and by that time his five youngest children had all been taken into local authority care. The first chinks of light had begun to shine into the dark world of Cromwell Street. It was exactly a quarter of a century since West had murdered Ann McFall, and he had killed at least another eleven women in the intervening years. But he was still confident that he could escape from any charge. He had done so before. Why should he not do so again? When he was arrested for the assault on his daughter, he simply denied that it had ever taken place, calling the accusation 'Absolute rubbish' and 'Lies, all lies'.

He painted a picture of himself to the police as a straightforward, down-to-earth, working man who loved his wife and family but who had been subjected to foul and unfounded allegations. 'I left home this morning with a bloody family and a home,' he protested, 'and tonight I'm in prison and I ain't done nothing . . . I mean, we got what we want. We don't mess with our kids. We've got everything.' He went on to suggest that his daughter Mae had made up the charges to gain attention. 'I got no problems with my children at all. They think the world of their father as far as I know, all of them, I mean.'

But in spite of his confidence and bravado, the alternative universe that West had fought so hard to create, the incestuous world that he had sought to protect, was starting to disintegrate. And part of the reason for that lay in his own confidence. To the astonishment of the officers interviewing him, he began to reveal some extraordinarily bizarre details. He suddenly displayed an eerie knowledge of the times of his wife's and daughters' periods. 'Like my wife's on now,' he explained matter-of-factly to the two officers, adding, 'I think Louise is due because Louise is normally with her mother.' He also told them that his wife kept a note of all his family's menstrual cycles in a black notebook beside the telephone in the upstairs part of the house.

Slowly but surely he began to unfold his private life. After telling the two officers, 'Me and my wife leads an active sex life . . . We make love every night, I mean perhaps twice, it just depends on what happens', he went on, 'I mean, you'll find harnesses, you'll find bloody God knows what in my home that we make up and things we do. You'll find tapes where we've been out in the van, out in the lanes, making love, and we're not frightened to show it. We enjoy our sex life, but not with our children.' They also, he explained, had 'mates that come in and share our life with us . . . come in and sit with us, and perhaps make love with us, like'.

Then, at nine-thirty that evening, just as his second formal police interview drew to a close, he announced suddenly, and without being prompted: 'As far as I know, Tara, Louise, Rosemary and Babs should still be virgins. Nobody should ever have gone near them.' When he was told that one was suggesting that he had taken her virginity, he replied truculently: 'Well, prove it then, if she says that.' It was the first time he had ever allowed himself to lose his temper with a policeman.

On Friday 7 August 1992, the day after Frederick West's arrest, Emergency Protection Orders were made for his five youngest children at the Tewkesbury Family Proceedings Court. The children were to be placed in local authority care, and there was to be no contact between the Wests and their children. Indeed the children's whereabouts were not even to be disclosed to them. It was the first time in twenty-two years that there had been any official intervention in the life of Frederick West and his family. The five children under eighteen, now placed in care, were never to be looked after by Frederick and Rosemary West again

That same morning Anne Marie West broke her silence for the first time and made a long statement to the police describing the abuse she too had suffered at her father's hands throughout her childhood. Rosemary West was allowed to return to Cromwell Street that day on bail. From the time she found out about Anne Marie's statement, which mentioned Rosemary Wests's connivance in the abuse, Rosemary West never spoke to her stepdaughter again. The splits within the West family were widening. As Mae West, who returned home to stay with her mother at the time, was to record two years later: 'Anna was effectively kicked out of the family. Mum put the phone down on her whenever she rang up.'

Meanwhile, at Gloucester police station, Frederick West was being confronted with the details of his daughter's first twenty-five-page statement. 'Rubbish. Absolute lies,' he maintained fiercely. 'I never touched her.' West then went on to suggest that she had taken the detail of the statement from a book. 'It's all made up . . . She's copied it from somewhere . . . There ain't one blade of truth in it as far as I'm concerned.' He challenged the police to go to Cromwell Street. 'Knock on any door and they'll tell you those children are looked after.'

During his three police interviews on the day after his arrest, West wriggled and squirmed. He denied everything, condemning the children for 'ganging up on him' as it became ever more apparent that they were supporting the allegations. West tried to cast doubt on her story, portraying himself as the injured party. He suggested that two of his daughters may have wanted to 'go into care' and had dreamed up the story as a means of getting there. He suggested that his daughter was making the allegations because she was jealous that he was paying more attention to one of her younger sisters than to her. He suggested he had found her in bed with a boyfriend. He suggested she was angry with him for 'grounding her' after a gang of girls at school had threatened her with a knife because she had stolen one of their boyfriends. Each and every one of his explanations was noted, but he was still remanded in custody. He was finally charged on three counts of rape and one of buggery against his daughter.

Rosemary West, too, was interviewed by the police, and she insisted throughout that she had never sexually abused her children. Then she exercised her right to remain silent during the interrogations. Unlike her husband, she did not attempt to talk her way out of the charges. She left that to him – 'to sort it out'. Soon after eight o'clock on the morning of Tuesday 11 August she was arrested again and taken back to Gloucester police station, where she was interviewed a further ten times. Although she no longer exercised her right to silence, she strenuously denied every allegation made against her, and in the process contradicted each of her children's statements to the police.

When it was put to Rosemary West that her children had at various times been beaten in front of other men, had their bottoms painted with rude words, had photographs taken while they were naked, had been made to watch pornographic videos, had been put in boiling water, had had their trousers pulled down and been whipped, their mother called the allegations 'rubbish, absolute rubbish', exactly as her husband had done. When the police-officers asked her to explain the vast collection of rubber masks and suits, vibrators and dildos, and other sexual paraphernalia that they had recovered from Cromwell Street, she refused to discuss the matter. When they asked her about a video that had been found showing her being tied up in the back of a van and sexually assaulted, she declined to comment. When the officers asked her whether she had assisted her husband in the rape of his daughter, she denied it.

Rosemary West also told the police that she had no idea of the whereabouts of her eldest child, Heather. The girl had 'hung round the house for about six months and then left', she said. When she was asked where she was now, she replied, 'I don't know', and when she was asked whether she had ever had any contact with her daughter, she said bluntly, 'Not since she's left home, none'. The only explanation she could offer for her eldest daughter's disappearance was: 'I went out shopping one day, as per usual on a Friday, and come back home and she'd gone.' She was 'not sure' whether Heather had ever been reported as a missing person. 'As far as I'm concerned she hasn't just disappeared, she made a conscious decision to leave,' she said tartly in justification of her apparent uninterest.

Rosemary West then offered an explanation that had clearly been prepared in consultation with her husband. Their daughter was a lesbian and wanted her own life. Besides, even if they had wanted her to stay they were frightened that it might affect the other, younger children. 'Why I didn't pursue Heather to sort of stay home,' Rosemary West told the police, 'was Heather had told me, and certain things pointed to the fact, that Heather was a lesbian . . . and wanted a life of her own . . . And that was why she wanted to leave. She said it wasn't good for the rest of the children.'

But when she was asked, immediately afterwards, whether she, too, was a lesbian, she denied it point-blank. Instead, she simply elaborated on her earlier lies, telling the police: 'I know in my own mind that she's getting on with her own life . . . One of her friends told me.' She even maintained that she had heard from her daughter on the telephone 'a while ago', adding that 'She just rings to say she's all right', but that her husband might not be aware of it because 'she doesn't want to speak to him'.

In fact, the police did not pursue the issue of Heather West's sudden disappearance during the rest of Rosemary West's interviews concerning the alleged rape and buggery of her daughter. They told her simply that they were concerned that they could find no record of the girl having claimed any kind of Social Security benefit or having paid any income tax, or even any record of her having registered with a doctor in the five years since she had left Cromwell Street.

The fetid sexual world of Cromwell Street steadily began to emerge into view. A few days before Frederick West's confessions about his active sex life and the involvement of 'friends', Detective Constable Hazel Savage had taken a statement from Anne Marie, in which she had confirmed that she, too, had been abused by her father, with her stepmother's help, at the age of eight. But she had gone on to explain that she had also been the victim of a series of experiments involving the storage of semen in used condoms, which was then to be used by her father and stepmother for experiments in artificial insemination.

Just nine days later, Anne Marie retracted her statement completely, describing it as 'a figment of my imagination'. She would explain later that she was afraid that her parents would 'get at' her and her two young children. Three years later Anne Marie would confess: 'I left so much out. I felt uncomfortable about a lot of it because it sounded so unbelievable, and besides there were some things I couldn't imagine ever talking to anybody about . . . I recounted only what I thought might help the girl.' Detective Constable Savage did not believe Anne Marie's retraction. She was convinced the young woman's description of her abuse was true, just as she was convinced that Anne Marie's own search for her missing sister Heather concealed a mystery that demanded to be solved. Over the next twelve months this forty-nine-year-old officer with twenty-four years' experience was to devote herself to the task.

On Tuesday 11 August 1992 Rosemary West was formally charged with 'causing or encouraging the commission of unlawful sexual intercourse with a girl under the age of sixteen' and with 'cruelty to a child'. She first appeared before Gloucester magistrates the next morning after spending the night in the cells at Gloucester police station. She was granted bail on condition that she did not communicate with her younger children, her stepdaughter or her husband, and in the early afternoon of Wednesday 12 August in chastened mood Rosemary West returned alone to the now empty Cromwell Street. Allowed to communicate with only her two older children, Mae and Stephen, she started drinking, and that night took forty-eight Anadin tablets. She was found by the two children slumped on the sofa of her ground-floor living-room in Cromwell Street. And at 1.50 a.m. in the morning of Thursday 13 August she was admitted to Gloucester Royal Hospital, where her stomach was pumped. As her daughter Mae would recall: 'She looked old and frail, and nothing like Mum. It was as if all the energy had drained from her body.'

Neither Mae nor Stephen West told their father about his wife's suicide attempt, but 'he found out later'. The news clearly upset him, as did the order preventing her from having any contact with him until her next court appearance seven weeks later. No matter how their sexual promiscuity made it appear, Frederick and Rosemary West's relationship was a symbiosis. Neither was used to existing alone: they were linked by their dark imaginings.

West was by this time on remand in Gloucester Prison as a Rule 43 prisoner, a category reserved for sexual offenders who are segregated from the rest of the prison population. And like his wife, he, too, was suffering. When his two older children visited him, 'He started talking really strangely', Stephen West would recall later. 'He was crying and said that he'd done stupid things at night . . . the worst crime that we could ever imagine. He became all pathetic, and for the first time in our lives said "I love you". It was the first time I had seen him cry. He seemed scared to death.'

But West did not let his fear get the better of him during the police interviews that followed. No matter how frightened he may have been, he took elaborate pains to sustain his image as the hardworking man who was being unfairly accused. Even more significant, he also insisted that his wife was not responsible for anything that had happened in his house. 'I'm the boss and she follows,' he told Detective Constable Savage firmly on 18 August. 'We've always lived that way.' West went on to maintain that the sexual tone at Cromwell Street had always been set by him. 'I control Rose's sex life,' he insisted repeatedly. And when he was told that his wife had been charged with sex offences, West was clearly shocked, repeating the phrase 'This is crazy', and blaming his eldest daughter Anne Marie for 'trying to get her mum done as well'.

West also kept up this pretence of normality as the details of what the police had discovered in his house were put to him. It was no easy task, but made easier than it might have been by the fact that, although the two police searches of Cromwell Street on 6 August and 11 August had been extremely thorough, they had both failed signally to find a copy of the videotape that the police believed that her father had made of his daughter's abuse. One videotape was found smashed completely in a dustbin, and another thrown away in a waste-paper bin in the living-room.

But the police did make finds. They unearthed ninety-nine commercial and home-made videotapes, a vast collection of rubber underwear, a rice flail and a bullwhip, a suitcase containing a variety of straps and other whips, and a giant dildo kept in a metal box that had once housed a whisky bottle. They found photographs of the erect penises of a number of naked men, photographs of two of Frederick West's daughters naked or with very few clothes on, a photograph of Rosemary West sitting obscenely astride the gear stick of a car, as well as other photographs of her in a variety of sexual poses. The officers themselves described this haul as 'so disgusting and so vile and so difficult' to cope with that many people might find it impossible to talk about.

Frederick West made every effort to convince the police that there was nothing abnormal in his collection of pornography, or in his sexual relations with his wife. His sex life was 'perfectly normal'. But over a series of twelve interviews with the police between 18 August and 26 August 1992 it became ever more apparent that the sexual world he occupied was, in the words of one expert who interviewed him later, 'unique in our experience'. Another described Frederick West's amateur videos of his wife as 'of a most disgusting sexual character', showing as they did his wife in 'revolting sexual and lewd behaviour'.

West himself did not accept either description. His sex life was his own affair. When he was asked about the parentage of three of his younger children, he made no secret of the fact that his wife had a number of coloured lovers, or of the fact that he and his wife had been involved with 'a lot' of men. 'I mean, who's counting . . . There's probably dozens of them.' The men were 'selected by me and Rose, or by me at least'.

West then went on matter-of-factly: 'That's part of my enjoyment in my sex life, watching her with other men,' while 'the main kick is that she has sex with black men.' West saw nothing strange in taking a photograph of his naked wife exposing her vagina to the camera, having himself written the words 'black hole' across her stomach in lipstick, and keeping the photograph in an album. 'She was expecting a black child, that's why,' he said calmly.

In the midst of this defence of his sex life, Frederick West also offered his first version of the disappearance of his daughter Heather. He told the police that someone called 'Shirley' had come to pick her up. 'She went through the door laughing her head off, and she said: "Tell Mae and Stephen I'll get in touch with them or something." ' But when he was asked if she had indeed got in touch with them, he replied, 'I don't think so', but then added quickly that he had seen her himself 'about twelve months ago' in Gloucester, when she had been 'dealing in drugs' with Shirley, whose surname he 'had the vague idea was Robinson'.

No longer displaying the slightest sign of fear or guilt, he persistently challenged the police to take their case against him to court, claiming that the whole accusation was a fabrication that had 'damn near been rehearsed'. He insisted: 'I'll tell you what, this has got to go into court, and they have all got to stand up there and be counted on why these lies have come out like this, or who is instigating them.' He went on: 'I never thought my children would tell lies about me.' Finally, he blamed the whole case on their 'jealousy' of the better conditions of his 'flat upstairs' in Cromwell Street.

Frederick West would hardly have felt so confident had he not been well aware that he had already disposed of all incriminating videotapes. It is no surprise that when Rosemary West visited her husband at Gloucester Prison in the afternoon of Monday 10 August – the only occasion on which they were allowed to do so after his arrest on 6 August – one topic of whispered conversation between them concerned the whereabouts of the videotapes that West told his wife the police were looking for. Amid a discussion of whether Stephen West would be capable of a plumbing repair that seemed to be necessary on the top floor of Cromwell Street, there seemed to be the suggestion that some videotapes might need to be removed. Whatever they talked about, the tapes disappeared and their whereabouts have remained a mystery.

After a further court appearance in early October, when West was once again remanded in custody, he was sent from Gloucester Prison to a bail hostel, Carpenter House, in Edgbaston, Birmingham, where Rosemary West was at last allowed to visit him. Both were eager for these meetings. Rosemary travelled to Birmingham at least fourteen times in the following five months, and Frederick West himself was given a special dispensation to return to Cromwell Street for Christmas. The reason for his privileges has an all too familiar ring. West had persuaded the staff at Carpenter House, as he had persuaded so many other figures in authority in the past, that he was not in the least dangerous or threatening. They found him 'quiet and unassuming', well behaved and always anxious to please.

Life at Carpenter House was well ordered but hardly prison-like. The inmates were allowed to come and go as they pleased, provided that they were back in the hostel by eleven o'clock in the evening. West could receive visitors, and spend his time as he chose. In fact, he conducted himself while he was there as if he were still working. He went out after breakfast, usually carrying a black plastic bag. He would sometimes return briefly at lunch-time, and then go out again until late in the evening. In one sense he *was* still working. But not as a labourer: as a petty thief.

When Frederick West returned to the bail hostel every evening his plastic bag would often contain notes and coins. 'That was money I picked up on the streets during the day,' he would explain a year later, money he said that he collected 'near bus stops and telephones boxes, like'. He maintained that he could 'pick up £10 on a good day' and never failed to collect '£30 a week' throughout the period he was there. But the black plastic bag did not only contain money; it also contained credit cards which he said he 'found in wallets lying all over the place'. But not all his crimes were petty.

West was also seen talking to a number of young women during his time at the Birmingham bail hostel, one of whom he helped when her car broke down not far from Carpenter House. Though he would later tell the police that he 'stopped killing altogether after Heather', many of the people involved in his case are convinced that he committed at least one murder during his time there, in spite of the fact that the police were now clearly taking a far greater interest in him. If he did so, it would have been entirely in character. He would have disposed of the body in exactly the same way that he had disposed of all his victims' bodies: dismembered and shoved into a narrow two-feet-square shaft dug in an unlikely place. He had access to woodland and open ground, and could have stolen the necessary tools from sheds on people's allotments. Frederick West still believed he was invincible – that nothing and no one would ever stop him. Indeed, he may not have acted alone.

Whether or not he had, as he claimed, 'stopped all that girlfriend business' and 'never had no girlfriends up in Birmingham at all', there was still Rosemary West. She 'came up by train, two or three times a week', he told the police a year later. 'I had no worries.' He and his wife took to camping near Edgbaston reservoir, using a small blue igloo tent their son Stephen had given them, as well as a 'green sleeping-bag for a bit of a mattress'. 'It was for me and Rose to go and make love in the woods. It was the only place we had.'

After one visit she wrote to him: 'To my darling. Well, you really tired me out on Saturday, but it was a wonderful day . . . Remember I will love you always and everything will be alright. Goodnight sweetheart. Lots of love, Rose.' A large heart was drawn on the letter with an arrow through it. In the middle were the words: 'Fred and Rose.'

But Frederick West was also seen carrying the tent, together with the sleeping-bag, during his daily tours around the centre of Birmingham when his wife was not present, no doubt in the hope of persuading some other young woman to share it with him. It was just one of the pointers that convinced many observers of the case that he killed again during his period in the city.

But in the eyes of the bail hostel staff West was such a model inhabitant that in March 1993 he was allowed to move to the even more relaxed regime of a 'cluster house' (a more relaxed version of a bail hostel) in Handsworth. Here there was a minimum of supervision of the inmates. The house was subjected only to random checks. Here, too, his wife continued to visit him regularly, and here he was to stay for three months until his trial in June 1993. Once again he roamed the streets of Birmingham, but this time he did rather more: he took to slipping back to Gloucester and Cromwell Street without permission to see his wife. 'Dad would suddenly turn up out of the blue,' his daughter Mae would remember later, 'even though he wasn't supposed to.'

Throughout his time in Birmingham, West took pains to present himself to the psychologists and social-workers who came to interview him as a plain man 'wronged' by false accusations. He insisted he would contest the care proceedings against him 'to show the children that he cared about them', and he even prepared an explanation for his own and his wife's sexual exploits. He maintained to anyone who questioned him that he suffered from an 'inability to get an erection'. He first experimented with this explanation during his last police interview in Gloucester, explaining to detectives: 'I very rarely get an erection . . . because I got injured some years ago on a motor bike. I mean, it'll come up and suddenly it'll go boom . . . And that was how all this started with these men and that because Rose likes sex . . . I mean if I can get an erection once a month I'm bloody lucky, you know.'

Ever plausible, never argumentative, West would go on to explain that his children were simply the result of good fortune. 'It sort of caught at the right time and everything connected up right.' He suggested repeatedly that after he had come out of Leyhill Prison in the summer of 1971 he had 'got lucky' and managed to father Mae and Stephen but 'then it just died. There was nothing. I mean I never got an erection then for something like about four years, five years.' And this was the reason why he had encouraged his wife to take other lovers. 'As far as I'm concerned if I can't do it then I should help her to get someone else to do it.'

West refined this subtle but outrageous lie throughout his time on remand. Indeed, he planned that it should be the principal plank of his defence when his rape and buggery trial finally came to court, and he polished it meticulously. He told one psychologist that he had been injured 'in the genitals by an iron bar' while at work in 1973, and that since then he had experienced 'problems' in getting any form of erection. It was this that had driven him to find a family friend to help his wife become pregnant, and this that established that he had not engaged in any extra-marital affairs since the start of his relationship with Rose.

'I wish to clarify,' West insisted, 'in respect of our sex life, which I admit is not conventional, we have never involved the children . . . that is why we have separate living accommodation.' The pornographic videos, he explained, were only there in the hope of encouraging him to get an erection. Time after time, the professionals who interviewed or tested Frederick West described him as 'friendly and cooperative throughout'.

Sixteen months later, after his arrest in 1994, West would admit to the police that this picture of impotence was a complete fabrication: 'Because, I mean, I've never been injured, not sexually anyway.' He went on to explain that he had never suffered any injury whatever to his genitals, that he had never been struck by an iron bar or anything else, and that he had never had any sexual problems whatever (though that too, ironically, was probably a lie, in view of the speed of his own ejaculation in some instances).

West would also tell the police that at least one professional who interviewed him 'was a prat anyway', and that he could not understand some of the tests he had been given. 'They were all wrote on paper and you just had to tick and mark them . . . half of them I couldn't even read.' It was a mark of the contempt in which he secretly held many of those in authority, a contempt, however, which he took immense pains to conceal beneath his familiar mask of humility.

Throughout the autumn of 1992 Frederick and Rosemary West made a determined effort to persuade the local authority that they should be allowed to have their children back in their care. The children were theirs, and they loved them. The Wests continually presented themselves to the psychologists and the social-workers as a 'caring couple' who did not argue and 'discussed everything' and made all their decisions jointly. They also sought to cast doubt on the evidence of Anne Marie – who had withdrawn her statement accusing them of child abuse by this time – suggesting that she was 'living in her own fantasies' and that she had 'always rejected Rose as a mother'. West insisted that if his eldest child 'got a chance to back her into a corner and have a go at her she would'.

West told the police that 'Anna thought she was miles above Rose because Rose had half-caste children', and maintained that his daughter had been 'coerced into making these allegations' out of jealousy and her being 'vindictive towards us'. He went on to maintain that she 'had got in with the wrong crowd' and described her as 'an old baby who has always had a real mouth on her'. Returning time after time to his original explanation that she was 'jealous' of their flat upstairs, he insisted repeatedly that 'nothing whatever had happened'.

But these lies were to no avail. On 19 November 1992 Frederick and Rosemary West were committed for trial on the charges against them, and five days later, on 24 November, full Care Orders were made in respect of Tara, Louise, Barry, Rosemary and Lucyanna West at Bristol County Court. The Wests were denied contact with their five youngest children, unless the children themselves officially requested it. One factor that weighed against the Wests was the fact that their younger children seemed to have responded favourably to being away from Cromwell Street. Another was the photographs of the naked children found at the house, as well as the Wests' enormous collection of obscene videotapes.

Though no videotapes showing sexual abuse of the children were found, the obscenity of the tapes that were discovered threw an ugly light on life behind the iron gates that West had so meticulously crafted at the Muir Hill Wagon Works. It took one police-officer almost a fortnight to watch the pornographic tapes that West himself admitted that he kept in Cromwell Street, ranging as they did from commercial pornography to home videos made by West himself.

Among the commercial tapes were many examples of young women being 'instructed' in sexual matters by 'a master', as well as tapes of 'schoolgirls' having sex with several 'teachers' at the same time, often featuring anal intercourse, as well as others suggesting incest with 'an uncle', and many focusing on bondage and the participation of a voyeur. Among the home-made ones, all of which featured Rosemary West rather than her husband, either alone or with another partner (either male or female), many centred on her desire to urinate on herself in front of the camera. They also showed her inserting various large objects, including an orange, a pint beer glass and a beer can, into her vagina. 'I'd sooner watch ones of Rose,' West told the police after his arrest.

Significantly, the collection of home-made video-recordings also revealed that the Wests had updated their 'Rose's chocolates' system in the beginning of 1992. One videotape in particular, made between February and March 1992, featured timed and dated occasions in which Rosemary West first dressed to go out in front of the camera, and then returned later that evening, or the following morning, and undressed in front of the camera again to display the semen stains on her underwear. West himself was clearly the cameraman on each of these occasions, although only rarely did he allow more than an arm to appear in any shot, and he never spoke. West's desire to keep a record of Rosemary West's other sexual partners was thus clearly shown to be important to him. As for Rosemary West herself, she was still keen on marking her partners' sexual performances, on one occasion even going to the trouble of holding a small note up to the video camera along with her underwear indicating her score out of ten.

After the Care Orders had been placed on her five youngest children, Rosemary West returned the video camera to the Midlands Electricity Board, where it had been bought on hire-purchase, confessing to one friend 'it cost me my children'. From that time onwards she would never again allow herself to be videotaped in a sexual position. And much to Frederick West's annoyance, she would allow the police to destroy all the videotapes that had been recovered from Cromwell Street. When he found out, West insisted that they should 'start the collection again'. Gloucestershire County Council kept four of the videotapes, as proof of the Wests' unusual sexual activities. In 1994 they handed them to the police.

There is little doubt that Rosemary West felt the loss of her children far more sharply than did her husband. One social-worker who dealt with Frederick West at the time recalled later: 'Fred didn't seem too bothered. Perhaps because it meant that he could do what he wanted to when he was at home without worrying about the children, but Rose clearly minded a great deal. She missed them; without them there wasn't very much to do.'

Indeed, in the wake of the court's decision to grant the five Care Orders in respect of his youngest children, Frederick West became – for the first time in his relationship with the Social Services Department – non-cooperative, even a little truculent. Now, instead of addressing everyone he met as sir or madam, and deliberately going out of his way to appear helpful, he started to put on what his son Stephen later called 'his hard face'.

West knew that his wife was deeply upset that she was not being allowed access to the children unless the children requested it, and he resented the fact that now neither of them was to be allowed to see their children at any time without a social-worker present during a 'supervised' visit. 'For the first time, Fred shut down completely,' one social-worker remembered afterwards. 'He wanted to see his children alone, and that was all he wanted. He refused to compromise.' The reason was not only that he wanted to influence them, but also that he knew that that was what his wife wanted more than anything else.

The Wests did manage to see their five minor children after the Care Orders were placed on them. Rosemary West, in particular, saw them in the park at the end of Cromwell Street, and there were also occasions on which some of them found their way back to the house for short, unofficial visits. The seductive power of both Frederick West and his wife had not entirely disappeared, in spite of the intervention of the local authority. Indeed, in the months and years to come it would never disappear. Cromwell Street had been the family home, and, no matter the pain and suffering that may have been inflicted there, it still retained a powerful attraction to each and every member of the West family.

Throughout his period on remand in Carpenter House, and then in the 'cluster house' in Handsworth, Frederick West continued to protest his innocence. His daughter Mae, who had returned to Cromwell Street to live with her mother, remembered that her father had never lost confidence that he would be released. And once again, but for the last time, his confidence was to be justified.

On Monday 7 June 1993 the Wests appeared in the dock of Gloucester Crown Court before Judge Gabriel Hutton, the city's senior judge. Frederick West faced three counts of rape and one of buggery against his daughter, while his wife faced a count of encouraging the commission of unlawful sexual intercourse and another of cruelty to a child. But before the jury could be sworn in, counsel for the prosecution told the judge that two important witnesses were not prepared to testify.

The children had been told by prosecuting counsel that they might still have to give evidence directly in the court itself, even though video-links had been set up to allow them to give most of their evidence outside. And even though the children had been prepared for doing so by their social-workers, the prospect of actually giving evidence against their parents in open court proved too much. On the day itself the children refused to appear or to give evidence. In the circumstances, the prosecuting barrister informed the judge, 'We take the view that we cannot proceed, and accordingly we offer no evidence against the defendants.' The judge had no alternative. He returned formal verdicts of not guilty on all the charges.

In the dock, Frederick and Rosemary West threw their arms around each other in celebration. Twenty years after Carol Raine, they had again walked free from Gloucester Crown Court after facing serious charges. Thirty years after his original incest case, West had again seen evidence against him evaporate into thin air in minutes. West could not conceal the grin on his face. When he got back to Cromwell Street, he told Mae and Stephen that he had changed, and everything 'would be different'.

In a sense things already were. The younger children had gone, and Rosemary West had bought two dogs from a rescue centre for company. One was a small wire-haired terrier, the other a white mongrel. She had named them Benji and Oscar. She had also started to over-eat dramatically, cramming herself with chocolate eclairs and crisps while watching television. Without her children, Rosemary West's life had lost part of its meaning.

For his part, Frederick West did his best to convince Mae and Stephen that he had seen Heather West in Birmingham. He told them she had visited him, and 'would be home within a week', going on to insist that he had even seen her in a community centre in Gloucester since then. 'Mum just told him to shut up,' Mae West recalled later. The Wests' two elder children were beginning to wonder what exactly their father had been talking about when he had confessed during his time on remand in Gloucester Prison that he had done 'stupid things at night, when we were in bed'.

287

They had begun to wonder whether their elder sister Heather was alive or dead.

Not long afterwards, Mae and Stephen West set a trap for their parents. They arranged for them to watch a repeat of the television thriller *Prime Suspect 2*, which focused on the burial of a body under the patio of a house in a story that had its background in pornography. 'They just looked straight through it,' Stephen West would write two years later. 'They didn't pass any comment. They were staring at it, studying it . . . They went off afterwards and talked to each other.' Both of the elder West children were satisfied that 'there was nothing untoward going on. We thought that if there had been, they would have turned it straight off. Now we think maybe that would have been too obvious.' Not long afterwards, they repeated the experiment, this time by persuading their mother and father to watch the episodes of the television serial *Brookside* which dealt with a sexually abusive father who was buried under the patio. But once again there was no reaction. Once again it seemed as though the Wests could not know anything about the disappearance of their daughter.

After West was released from custody in June 1993 he returned to Cromwell Street and went back to work. Life in the house might be a little different now, with the younger children removed to care and the two elder ones visiting regularly, but that did not mean he could not enjoy himself. Working again for Carson's Contractors, and now driving a white Bedford Midi van, he went back to offering lifts to young female hitchhikers on travels around Gloucester. Frederick West picked up a 'new age traveller' who told him that she 'liked a bit of violence with her sex', as he admitted to the police a few months later. He also again offered rooms in Cromwell Street to young girls who might need a 'place to stay for a while'.

What he did not know was that the social-workers looking after his children had begun to hear about the 'family joke' that their elder daughter Heather was 'buried under the patio'. The remark had been made shortly after the five were first removed from Cromwell Street, but as the minor children had begun to settle into their new lives away from their parents so the repetitions became more frequent.

From the spring of 1993 the residential social-workers responsible for the children began to pick up more and more stories about the laying of the patio 'at the same time that Heather left home', and her being 'buried at nine down and three across'. At first the social-workers were unsure whether or not to treat the remarks seriously, but as the summer progressed they became convinced that the police should be informed.

In August 1993 Detective Constable Hazel Savage was detailed to find Heather Ann West, and in the months that followed, in the midst of her other duties, she made every effort to establish whether any trace could be found of the girl who would have been just about to celebrate her twenty-third birthday. DC Savage had already established that there had been no claims for unemployment benefit or sick pay, no registration with a doctor or a dentist, no hospital admissions, not even an application for a passport.

In the first weeks of 1994 she decided to take formal statements from the social-workers about the 'family joke' they kept hearing. The statements were to form the basis of an application for another warrant to search 25 Cromwell Street. Only this time the police were not going to be looking for pornographic videotapes or evidence of West's abuse of his daughter. This time the warrant would be to allow them to prove whether or not the family joke was true.

Chapter Twenty-two

Like pulling teeth

'The unrighteous are never really fortunate.'

Euripides, *Helen*

The final act in the tragedy that was Frederick West's life came to its climax on a damp day seven years after the murder of his daughter Heather. And, like the last act of any great drama, it came about as a result of its protagonist's own blind arrogance. For more than a quarter of a century West had literally got away with murder, and it had bred within him a confidence that knew no bounds, an utter certainty that he would always 'sort it out'.

Like a tragic hero, West had believed that he could do no wrong. He had failed to see that his abuse of his daughters, something that he regarded as 'a father's right', might finally bring the forces of law to his door. He saw his abuse as 'only natural', nothing even to comment on. Had he thought otherwise, there is every possibility that his other crimes would have gone unrecognised and undetected. For it was this appetite for the abuse of children, rather than his bestial murder of so many other innocent girls, that led to his downfall.

On the afternoon of Wednesday 23 February 1994, magistrates granted officers from the Gloucester Constabulary a search warrant under Section 8 of the Police and Criminal Evidence Act of 1984 to allow them to search 25 Cromwell Street for evidence 'as to the whereabouts of Heather Ann West'. The magistrates granted the warrant principally on the basis of the statements from the social-workers looking after the five younger West children and the 'family joke' about their missing sister. In the finest tradition of a Jacobean tragedy, West's downfall was occasioned by his own words.

No one can say for certain where the joke about Heather West being 'under the patio' started, but it bears all the hallmarks of a remark that Frederick West himself would have made. Behind the gates of Cromwell Street, within his own family, he would have felt so confident, and so comfortable, that he may well have implied that

290

he had the power of life and death, just as he had the power of 'breaking in' his daughters. It was the sort of grim joke that he would have delighted in telling his sons, for example, anxious to draw them into his own incestuous, masculine view of the world. Frederick West would have smirked when he said, in the privacy of Cromwell Street, 'You'd better be good or you'll end up under the patio.' But he did not dream that his own words might be repeated.

When the Gloucester police arrived at Cromwell Street shortly after one-thirty in the afternoon of Thursday 24 February 1994, while Rosemary West was watching *Neighbours* on the television in her ground-floor living-room, they were not aware that they were in pursuit of a serial killer. They were not even certain that they were in pursuit of a murderer. The police simply wanted to establish the whereabouts of Heather West, and by implication whether there was any truth in the sick joke they had heard was circulating.

At that moment hardly one single officer saw Frederick West as more than an ever amenable petty thief and occasional informant, with a 'bit of a reputation' for pornography and a wife who had worked as a part-time prostitute offering her services to men of all kinds. No officer could possibly have believed that he was to be revealed as one of the most extraordinary serial murderers in British history. How could he be?

West could barely read or write. He did not seem to have the intelligence to master anything complicated. There was nothing in the least threatening about him. He did not even seem mysterious. He seemed just a small, smutty little man with a gap-toothed grin.

As the five officers pushed past his daughter Mae into the living-room of Cromwell Street on that wet February afternoon in 1994, they certainly did not suspect that they were on the brink of unearthing a series of horrifying murders. There were even some in the Gloucester force who doubted whether their enquiries would bear any fruit at all, who even suspected that they were out on a wild-goose chase. There were certainly a handful who saw this investigation as the product of the obsession of a single female detective constable, who had first come into contact with Frederick West and his family almost thirty years before. Yet had it not been for this 'obsession', Frederick West's crimes might never have come to light. But now a new element of personal tension was introduced.

Rosemary West loathed the police. She blamed them for the loss of her five children; and she particularly loathed the bespectacled Detective Constable Hazel Savage, whom she referred to within the family as a 'bitch and an arsehole' who was 'waging a personal vendetta' against her husband and herself. And the moment she saw Savage walk into her living-room on that February afternoon in 1994, she once again lost her temper completely. She grabbed the search-warrant, looked at it, called it 'stupid' and then started to scream at the five officers.

At that moment her son Stephen arrived, and she told him to call her husband on his mobile phone. But Stephen West could not get his father to answer. He rang Frederick West's employer instead, and Rosemary West then told him: 'I don't care where he is, I want him home now.' That was shortly before one-fifty in the afternoon. By two o'clock West had left the house he was working on in Frampton Mansell, less than twelve miles away. But he did not reach Cromwell Street until twenty minutes to six that evening. Where he went in the intervening four hours remains a mystery, one of the many that still cloak his life, but there can be little doubt that he went to cover his tracks at another burial site or sites within an easy drive of Gloucester. One thing he did not do was run.

It was not until seven-fifty that evening that West gave his first formal interview to the police. At that stage he was so confident that the police investigation would come to nothing that he declined the offer of a solicitor. He had not been arrested, and was free to leave the interview room at any time. When he was asked if he could help 'trace' his daughter Heather, he replied simply: 'I've no idea where she is.' There was a pause. 'I think I've seen her quite a few times, actually,' West went on, although then he could not remember either the date or the year of her birth.

That night he stuck to the story that he had told his friends and neighbours in Cromwell Street for years, that Heather had been collected from his house by a woman in a red Mini – except it was not a car, but a skirt. It 'was just about to the bottom of her knickers . . . you know, if she bent, it lifted like that – you could see everything', he told the police with just the trace of a smirk. He informed Detective Constable Savage that she was 'into drugs . . . because she gave bloody drugs' to his son Barry when he was seven. 'He went up on the flipping church roof and thought he could fly.' He had seen his daughter the previous year in Birmingham, he added, 'in a Mercedes – I mean, she's into a load of crap'.

'I don't want any of my children to leave home,' he explained, adding some time afterwards that he had even been considering buying 23 Cromwell Street for Mae and Stephen West, now that his own mortgage was almost paid off. That, at least, was true. West had not wanted his daughter to leave him, or his control.

When Hazel Savage told him 'I cannot rest until I know Heather is safe and well . . . That's all I want', he replied at once, 'If I knew that I'd be the first one to tell you.'

But when it was suggested to him that it was a 'family joke' that Heather's body was under the patio, Frederick West laughed out loud. 'Oh, for God's sake. I mean you believe it . . . I think we better pack it up Hazel. We're talking rubbish, aren't we? . . . I mean, you're digging me place up. Carry on doing it.'

In his second interview that night, West repeated that Heather was 'bringing drugs from somewhere and taking them up to schools, recruiting school kids'. That was the reason he did not report her missing, he explained; he did not want to see her arrested. Digression followed digression as West suggested he had seen his daughter while on remand in Birmingham, that she had threatened his brother John with a piece of wood 'two by four' because he 'put his hand on her head', which he described 'as the reason I thought she was a lesbian', and his telephone conversations with her.

West clearly hoped that he might be able to persuade the police not to start excavating the garden of Cromwell Street, even going so far as to complain that they 'had no right' to rip it up. But as one officer explained to him, they were interested only in locating his daughter, and whether there was any truth in the family joke. 'Once that's sorted and checked, at least Hazel and the police will be able to say then, "Forget any of the rumours, we've checked that she's not there." '

Shortly before nine-thirty that evening, Frederick West left Gloucester police station for what was to be his last night of freedom. When he arrived home, he demanded a cup of tea, and then set about undoing his illegal rigging of the electricity meter in the kitchen at the back of the house without alerting the police constable sitting in the garden. Once he had done so, he 'took the dogs out for a walk' with his wife to the park at the end of Cromwell Street for three-quarters of an hour. As far as either Mae or Stephen West knew, it was the first time the Wests had ever taken their dogs out for a walk in the evening together. When they returned, West watched the late television news dressed only in his underpants, and shortly afterwards disappeared upstairs to bed with his wife.

No one except Rosemary West knows what she and her husband discussed that night. West said afterwards that he 'lay awake most of the night', thinking about what to do, while his wife said, 'We didn't just talk'. They almost certainly made love, as they had made love almost every night throughout their life together. West was to tell the police just a few days later: 'It was nothing for me and Rose to have it twice a night and then in the morning', adding 'Me and Rose probably only missed two days a month when we didn't have sex.' It was West's way of reaffirming and demonstrating his love for the woman with whom he had shared almost all his dark secrets.

Frederick West would also have told her that he would 'sort it out' with the police the following day, and that she 'had nothing to worry about', as he 'would take all the blame'. The pact in some form must certainly have been made in the early hours of the morning of Friday 25 February 1994. Though he would renege on it during his bleakest hours in prison, it was to bind him to her for the rest of his life.

West's greatest hope was that he would be able to protect his proudest possession – Cromwell Street itself – from being destroyed by the police. In the first instance he may even have believed that if he confessed to the killing of his daughter, the police would not even bother to excavate more than one single site in the garden, leaving the rest untouched. For he still cherished the hope that his younger children would be returned to their mother, and that family life would resume there.

West may also have believed that if he confessed to one killing, he was likely to serve only a comparatively short prison sentence and would then be free to return to Cromwell Street himself. For West sensed that the police were not certain whether they would find anything underneath the pink and cream patio slabs in his sixty-feet-long garden. During the early hours of Friday 26 February 1994, he decided to try to make sure they did no more than find the body of his daughter Heather. He did so by laying a false trail with what appeared to be a terrible confession, but was, in fact, one that concealed far more than it revealed.

When Detective Constable Savage returned to Cromwell Street the following morning and asked for the address of Rosemary West's mother, much to his wife's distress, West was already fully prepared. He had decided exactly what was necessary to preserve the world he had so carefully created in his home. He would make a sacrifice. He had existed in prison before, he could do so again. So he had packed what he called 'me prison lighter', together with his cigarette papers and tobacco to make a supply of roll-your-own cigarettes.

Shortly after eleven o'clock on the morning of Friday 25 February, and after spending less than a minute in private conversation with his wife, West walked out of his house and climbed into the unmarked police car. It was then, speaking to Hazel Savage, that he confessed to killing his daughter. It was the first of a series of calculated gambles to divert attention from the terrible truth of what actually lay beneath the patio, and the cellar, of his house.

'The thing I'd like to stress,' West told Hazel Savage just after five o'clock that afternoon, in his third official interview, 'Rose knew nothing at all.' Time after time in the weeks ahead, he would repeat the same words. West told the police that his exact words to his wife when he left Cromwell Street that morning were: 'I'll go and talk to Hazel and persuade her not to go up and see your mum.' And he went on to insist: 'Rose shouldn't be under stress, because she hasn't done anything.'

'Through the past eight years, there's quite a few times that I've actually decided I was going to come down to see you personally,' he told Detective Constable Savage. 'I mean, when I was in Birmingham my sole intention was to get back home, put my home all back together and then sort it out once and for all.' West specifically denied that he had told his family anything about his confession, or the murder of his daughter, just as he denied that he had told them anything about his dismemberment of the body.

West expanded upon his original story about Heather leaving with 'the girl in the red Mini'. Now he maintained that he had sent his wife out shopping, and then tried to convince his daughter to 'get a flat up the road'. 'She said, "If you don't fucking let me go I'll give all the kids acid and they'll all jump off the church roof and be dead on the floor." '

She stood there, and she had a smile and a sort of smirk on her face, like you try me and I'll do it. I lunged at her like that and grabbed her round the throat like that and I held for a minute.

How long I held her for I don't know. I can't remember . . . I can just remember lunging for her throat and the next minute she's gone blue. I looked at her and I mean I was shaking from head to foot. I mean, what the heck had gone wrong?

He insisted that he had not intended to kill his daughter. 'I mean, I just went to grab her, to shake her, and say take that stupid smirk off your face.' But then he had discovered that 'there was no way I could get any life back into her'.

West claimed that it was only then, when he knew that his daughter Heather was dead, that he decided to try to get her body into a dustbin, but could not manage to. Without hesitating, he said, then 'I cut her head off'. He then picked up a knife and 'cut her legs off with that . . . put her in the bin and put the lid on and rolled it down the bottom of the garden behind the Wendy house and covered it up and left it there.' Immediately afterwards, West told the police, he 'got all her stuff, which was by the door . . . all ready to go . . . and took it over and put it by the wall . . . in St Michael's Square'.

'Then Rose come back, must have been an hour or more later, and she said, "Oh, didn't you persuade Heather to stay?" or something, and I said, "No".' Frederick West stressed time after time: 'Rose knew nothing at all . . . She hasn't done anything.' Indeed, he embellished his story further by explaining that he had forgotten to remove his daughter's training shoes, which he had left in the hallway of Cromwell Street by mistake, and had been forced to lie to his wife, telling her: 'Oh, she's put her shoes on instead.' That night, West claimed, he had sent his wife out 'with the coloured bloke for the night', and it was then that he had dug a hole in the patio and buried his daughter.

Frederick West concluded his initial formal confession with the words: 'I want to get it sorted out. I mean, all right, me marriage has gone, me home's gone, but at least me home's done up that they'll get something to sell or keep.' The fate of number 25 Cromwell Street clearly concerned him far more than the fate of the sixteen-year-old girl whose body he had just confessed to dismembering into 'two legs, a head and a body'.

Shortly after seven o'clock that evening, while his wife was being detained in custody at Cheltenham police station, West accompanied Hazel Savage to Cromwell Street and showed her where Heather's body was buried. In his mind he was no doubt intent on minimising the damage the police might do to his beloved property. To his amazement, however, the police were clearly intent on excavating the whole of his garden. He had miscalculated badly.

By the beginning of the following afternoon, Saturday 26 February, the police had found no trace of the body of Heather West. Rain had been falling relentlessly in Gloucester for almost two days, and the fifteen officers in the search team at Cromwell Street were struggling against a sea of mud and sludge. They had brought in tarpaulins to cover the site, and a pump to help clear the excess water, but water seemed to be seeping up through the ground itself as well as falling from the sky. Progress was agonisingly slow. And, even though they were looking in the precise spot that Frederick West had told them the night before that his daughter's body was buried in, they could find no trace of her.

When he discovered this, West's attitude changed completely. He started to smirk. 'How many months will they carry on digging for?' he asked, then amending his question slightly. 'All right, how many weeks?' Shortly after two o'clock that afternoon, Frederick West retracted his earlier confession completely. He insisted that Heather was not in the garden of Cromwell Street at all, because she was 'possibly at this moment in Bahrain', where she 'works for a drugs cartel' as a 'drug runner'. In an extraordinary outburst he told the police:

Now, whether you believe it or not, that's entirely up to you. As far as I'm concerned I would like to see them all still stay out there digging in that garden because they tore my house apart eighteen months ago, and they weren't satisfied with that, they had to come back and rip my home apart. Then you came in yesterday and upset Rose over her mother and all that . . . That's the reason I made up that story . . . There ain't nothing in my garden. You can dig it for evermore. I've never harmed anybody in my life. You look on my records through life. I have never even punched anybody, 'cause I don't believe in it, hurting people.

West then condemned DC Savage for waging a 'personal vendetta' against him. 'Because you seem to want to get me for some unknown reason, well not me quite so much, but Rose. We've always had the feeling that you wanted to get me and Rose.' When Hazel Savage strongly denied this, West went on to claim that his daughter called him regularly on her mobile phone, and had even had lunch with him recently in Devizes in Wiltshire. He also insisted that she had 'bodyguards, a chauffeur and a new birth certificate'. And when he was asked, in the last minutes of the interview, whether his daughter was 'going to be under the patio', West said emphatically: 'No. They can dig there for evermore. Nobody or nothing's under the patio. I mean, I know Heather ain't in there. Nobody's in there. So what am I bothered about?' Finally, he called the whole matter 'a joke . . . it always have been'. It was now just after 2.45 p.m.

Eighty minutes later, at 4.05 p.m. on Saturday 26 February, the search team found Alison Chambers's thigh a little over two feet beneath the ground outside the rear extension bathroom West had constructed over the old garage at the back of Cromwell Street. The soil around it was waterlogged, 'semi-liquid mud' in the words of the forensic pathologist Professor Bernard Knight, who was called in to help the identification and recovery of the skeleton. The soil had been turned black and sticky as the tissue of the girl's body had decomposed in the ground, where it had lain for more than fifteen years. One discovery sparked another. Minutes later, the police found Heather West's skeleton on the left-hand side of the tiny rear garden, opposite the barbecue.

Had the police digging under the narrow patio that stretched from the back of Cromwell Street down towards St Michael's Square not found human remains that afternoon, Frederick West would certainly have retracted his first confession completely, and may even have walked out of Gloucester police station a free man once again. But in the growing dusk of that late February Saturday afternoon, the police realised that they were dealing with something, and someone, who was not at all what some of them had expected. For the very first time they were forced to confront the certainty that Frederick West was a significant criminal – not just a 'bit of a joke', not just 'flirty Fred', the man who sometimes called himself 'Fox' or 'Chief'. The man who had buried these bodies would, it began to dawn on them, turn out to be far removed from the ordinary 'domestic' crook whom some of them still privately believed him to be. Quite how far, both they and the watching world would discover in the weeks to come.

Predictably, the first person to change his tone in the light of the discoveries at Cromwell Street was West himself. Rumours of the finds in his garden reached him within twenty minutes, and, ever quick on his feet, when he walked back into the first-floor interview room at Gloucester police station shortly after four-thirty, the first thing he did was to apologise to Hazel Savage. 'I've got nothing personal against her at all,' he explained, blaming two tablets he had taken for making everything seem 'all weird'. West then added quickly: 'Heather's where I told you she is, and I mean they should have found her anyway by now, because she's there.' Moments later he was asked if there were any other bones in the garden. 'Well, that's a peculiar question to ask, ain't it?' he replied without hesitation.

Half an hour later Hazel Savage asked West who else was aware that Heather was buried under the patio, and West replied firmly: 'Nobody. That's a secret I've kept myself for eight years. I never told anybody.' Explaining this lie, he added with insistence: 'I love my wife . . . but I mean I don't want to destroy the love that I had there when I've destroyed one love already, you know . . . I mean, Heather's gone . . . Rose is not going to let me say to her "I've strangled Heather" without coming straight to the police.'

He then embarked on a long and elaborate reminiscence about his future father-in-law's attempts to prevent Rosemary Letts giving birth to their daughter 'because the parents said she had to have an abortion, right, and there's no way we wanted an abortion'. So great was his ability to divorce himself from his own actions, so little was his empathy for his own child, that he saw no contradiction between this rambling story and his admission – moments later – that he had placed her body in pieces on blue plastic bags in his garden. The

297

idea, he explained, was 'to keep fresh soil off the top of the ground' and disguise the fact that he had dug a fresh hole just two feet square and four feet deep in which to shove the jumbled remains of his and Rosemary West's first-born child.

It was not until seven-thirty that evening that Hazel Savage told Frederick West that they had found more than one bone under his patio. 'Fred, the question is, is there anybody else buried in your garden?' West paused. 'Only Heather.' Detective Constable Savage replied softly: 'You've never said to us that you scattered Heather all over the garden, and Heather didn't have three legs.' Once again West paused. Only this time he replied to a question from his solicitor's clerk: 'Have you any knowledge of where this other bone might have come from at all?' West's voice became a monotone: 'Yes. Shirley.' Hazel Savage asked: 'Shirley who?' 'Robinson, the girl who caused the problem.'

This was the moment at which Frederick West finally realised that he would never spend another night in Cromwell Street with the woman he loved. Seconds later, after being arrested for murder, he admitted that he had strangled Shirley Robinson. But then, yet again, he tried everything he could to put the police off the track and to protect his wife. He suggested that Heather and Shirley had been friends, and that Rosemary West had been in hospital when he had killed Shirley Robinson. Within half an hour he had admitted killing the girl, and told the police she was pregnant. After suggesting that Shirley Robinson had been only six months' pregnant when she died, he maintained: 'She was going to have the baby for another girl, in Bristol.' Then he offered a motive for the killing. 'Shirley was the one who was supplying the dope to Heather to take to the schools, and that was the reason we fell out.' Like almost every other statement in each of these first three confessions, this, too, was a lie.

At 9.15 p.m. after making a brief court appearance to allow the police to hold him for questioning for a further thirty-six hours, Frederick West went one step further and admitted that there were actually three bodies in the garden of Cromwell Street. He explained that the third one was 'Shirley's mate', who 'had turned up one night with a photograph of me and Shirley', and told him, 'As far as I can gather, you killed Shirley'. West then went on to expand on the lies that he had told earlier in the evening about his killing of Shirley Robinson. 'Shirley's mate', he explained, was about 'twelve months to two years later', and their bodies were 'by the bathroom window' and 'where the bins were' in his back garden.

No matter how open and collaborative he may have appeared, West was still concealing far more than he was admitting. Indeed, had he not seen for himself the full extent of the police excavations at Cromwell Street the previous evening, it is possible that he would not even have admitted the existence of the third body. Ever slippery, once again he took a calculated gamble. He hoped that if he admitted three murders it might persuade the police to leave the rest of Cromwell Street untouched, and convince them that the deaths were not part of a wider, even grimmer picture.

The following morning, Sunday 27 February, West went back to his house again to show Hazel Savage and the other officers precisely where Shirley Robinson and 'Shirley's mate' were buried. But back at Gloucester police station he maintained firmly that there was 'no question of anybody else', and in particular he denied that he knew anything about the whereabouts of his first wife and his stepdaughter. 'Now Rena and Charmaine, I have no idea where they went.' As far as he was concerned, he told the police, he was going to leave his house to 'Stephen, Mae and Rose'. Cromwell Street was still the single monument to his life. 'The rest gets nothing,' West said bluntly.

By one o'clock on that Sunday afternoon, Frederick West had been interviewed eleven times by detectives in the case, and had made just one brief court appearance. As far as the outside world was concerned, he was simply a father being questioned about the disappearance of his daughter Heather. The police had disclosed officially only that they were questioning a fifty-two-year-old man and a forty-year-old woman. Throughout many of his interviews, West had been accompanied by his solicitor, Howard Ogden, a local practitioner, who had represented him in the 1992 case, and whom West himself had requested should represent him again on the morning that he had first confessed to his daughter's murder.

The police had also suggested that he should be accompanied at each interview by a member of the local panel of 'appropriate adults', independent observers who were usually called on to be present during the interviews of children or the mentally unstable to ensure that the interests of those being interviewed were protected. Though there was no suggestion that West was unstable, the officer in charge of the Cromwell Street investigation, Detective Superintendent John Bennett, a bluff, square-jawed Gloucestershire man born in the nearby town of Stroud not long after West himself, had suggested after West's first confession that an 'appropriate adult' should sit in. The first choice would have been a member of the Social Services Department or the probation service, but all those available had already dealt with West over the care proceedings for his minor children, and were therefore disqualified. In the end the police had called on one of the panel of volunteers from a charity to fulfil the task. The name of the volunteer was Janet Leach.

So it was that shortly after lunch on Sunday 27 February, Frederick West, flanked by Howard Ogden and Janet Leach, explained in lurid, graphic detail exactly how he had killed and dismembered his daughter Heather seven years earlier. 'Janet turned green,' West claimed triumphantly to Ogden later. Her reaction was hardly surprising. But, equally, his version of events was hardly the entire truth. It, too, was another of his elaborate lies. He had deliberately made it shocking to conceal the even more revolting truth that lay behind it.

Clearly anxious to avoid any suggestion that sexual abuse might

299

have played any part in Heather's killing, West declared: 'She's still dressed. I hadn't touched her clothes, because there was no sexual motive in it at all. I mean, I wouldn't do nothing like that.' Equally determined to convince the police that there was 'no question of anybody else involved', West then claimed: 'The thing came into my mind that Rose could walk in on me at any minute, so I thought I've got to do something.'

It was only after he had failed to revive his daughter in the bath, West maintained, that he 'pulled her culottes off, because I mean it was all wringing wet', and only then that he had tied 'tights or something like that' around her neck. 'I know I put something round Heather's neck . . . I can see that knot . . . in the front of her neck.' Then West explained rapidly that he had found a knife. 'That's what I picked up the knife for, to cut whatever she had round her neck . . . 'cause I had no intention at the time of cutting Heather at all. I was just going to put Heather in the dustbin. And that was the whole idea.'

Throughout this confession he insisted that his wife 'knew nothing about it whatever'. She had been out shopping in Gloucester at the time of her daughter's death. He explained that he had to hide the body behind the Wendy house at the bottom of his garden in a dustbin because he was 'afraid Rose would come back at any moment'. He maintained that he had gone to considerable trouble to wash everything: 'There was no blood anywhere, no marks.' He claimed that he had taken his daughter's belongings, 'shoved them into black bags', and taken them to St Michael's Square, behind his house, 'for the dustman'. He even maintained that he had washed the urine stain out of the sitting-room carpet with 'a cloth in the sink', before Rosemary West returned. And that evening, he added, he had sent his wife out to 'stay with her boyfriend', because 'I knew she wouldn't be back until at least half-past seven in the morning'.

Just as he intended that it should, Frederick West's confession concealed far more than it revealed. For he went to elaborate pains to deny specifically four of the elements that habitually played their part in his crimes. West denied, without it even being suggested to him, that there was a sexual motive to his daughter's death. And he also denied that anyone else – particularly his wife – was involved, that bondage might have played a part in the killing, and that he had planned to mutilate the body. The truth, of course, is that all four played their part in the death of Heather West, just as they had done in the death of each one of his other victims.

The inescapable conclusion is that Heather West met her death precisely as so many of the other young women who found themselves in Cromwell Street with Frederick West met theirs. With Rosemary West's connivance, she was bound, abused, killed and finally mutilated. She had become as much a vehicle for her father's appetites as all the other young women whose lives he had snuffed out in the previous twenty years.

West tried to maintain that he was so overcome with grief at his

300

daughter's death that he had hardly been able to think. 'I mean,' he added, 'with Shirley and that it didn't matter. I wasn't that bothered whether they were dead or alive, you know. I mean, it was just to get rid of them.' He refused to admit, though it was certainly the fact, that exactly the same held true for his daughter.

Two hours after Frederick West completed this third formal confession of the murder of Heather West Gloucester Constabulary announced for the first time that they had charged a fifty-two-year-old man with her murder. Their official press release did not name West, but the following morning both the *Daily Telegraph* and the *Western Daily Press* proclaimed that he was the man due to appear in court that morning charged with her murder. As for Rosemary West, the police announced only that the 'forty-year-old Gloucester woman who was arrested on Friday in connection with Heather's disappearance' was 'still being questioned by officers in the city'. In fact, she was being questioned in Cheltenham, seven miles away.

West was still determined to keep any hint of suspicion away from his wife. On the Saturday evening, after his admission of the killing of Shirley Robinson, West had asked: 'Has Rose been told yet?' adding, 'How did she take it?' Then, to sustain the pretence of her innocence, he went on disingenuously: 'I expect she hates me now.' West asked specifically that his wife be told of his confession. The reason was clear. He wanted her to know that he was keeping to their pact, accepting the blame for everything, 'sorting it out' as he had promised he would.

Rosemary West kept her side of the pact too. After her initial police interview at Cromwell Street on the Thursday evening of 25 February, when she had refused to go to the police station – 'You'll have to arrest me,' she told the officers – she had stonewalled repeatedly when questioned about the disappearance of her eldest child. Then, after her husband's first confession on Friday morning, she had been arrested 'on suspicion of the murder of your daughter Heather', and later that day interviewed twice more herself.

Truculent, uncooperative and in stark contrast to her husband, she had answered the police reluctantly, her voice sharp with venom. All that she had talked about with her husband, she told them belligerently, on their last night together in Cromwell Street, was 'whether the patio would be put back' and that Heather 'must be around somewhere'. Rosemary West insisted that her husband had told her that he had seen Heather in Birmingham and that 'she looked rough'.

When Detective Sergeant Terry Onions told her that her husband had confessed to Heather's murder, her voice hardly changed. 'So you know where she is,' she said stiffly. 'So she's dead. Is that right?' There were no tears, no screams or wails, not even a break in her voice. It was not the reaction of a mother who suddenly realised that she had lost her first-born child. And when the detective sergeant went on to suggest 'That automatically implicates you', Rosemary West's tone turned harsh. She stared angrily across the interview room. 'Why does it automatically implicate me?' she rasped. 'It's a lie.'

Later that evening she stuck firmly to the story that she knew nothing about the death, or disappearance, of her eldest child. 'Fred just said she'd left', and he 'wouldn't tell her where she lived'. Unhelpful as ever, she maintained: 'I don't know anything about it. I was not aware of it.' The more the police suggested that there was no need for her to pretend any longer, that she could now admit the truth and make a clean breast of anything she knew, the less communicative she became. The only thing that she was prepared to admit was that her husband had been the dominant partner in their relationship 'in lots of ways'.

By the end of her second formal interview, Rosemary West had not budged an inch. 'Of course his moods go up and down,' she told the police, 'and, no, I didn't notice anything particular at the time. Like I say, he was at work a lot, and if I wasn't busy with the children, then I was out.' The pact was holding.

On the afternoon of Saturday 26 February, after the discovery of human remains at Cromwell Street, Rosemary West was again questioned by the police, and again she denied any knowledge of her daughter's death. 'I don't know nothing about it,' she told them, adding with barely a change in her tone: 'Why have we got to go through this again?' Asked about Rena and Charmaine, she replied flatly: 'Fred was sorting it out. It was their past, their children . . . I was only sixteen myself.' And when Detective Sergeant Onions told her that there might be the remains of another person in the garden, she merely sighed and replied: 'Oh, this is all getting too much.'

Nevertheless, Rosemary West's resentment of her eldest daughter was clear. She described Heather as 'a stubborn girl', who 'didn't want to do her own washing' and 'didn't want to move up off the seat', a girl who 'liked to be different to everybody else'. But when the detective sergeant brought the interview to a close by repeating that there was no need for her to 'protect Fred any longer' and asked her if there was anything she wanted to add, Rosemary West simply answered: 'No.'

The following morning, Sunday 27 February, Rosemary West was arrested on 'suspicion of the murder of Shirley Robinson and another as yet unknown female', but she refused to be interviewed immediately afterwards. When she did agree to the interview, in the early afternoon, she maintained: 'The only Shirley I knew used to come to the house when we had tenants.' She did not remember Shirley Robinson's pregnancy, she denied that the tenants ever paid their rent to her 'because they had drugs and that up there, so I didn't go near them', and she denied that she was covering up for her husband.

As the police interrogation went on, Rosemary West began to wilt. Her head dropped, and she turned away from the table to look at the floor, refusing to make eye contact with anyone. When Hazel Savage travelled from Gloucester to see her and tell her that her husband had specifically asked for her to be told about his confession, saying 'I know Rose will hate me', Rosemary West hardly acknowledged it. Her head remained bowed, looking down at the linoleum floor of the interview room in Cheltenham police station. A few moments later she denied again that she was covering up for her husband, and ended the interview by saying flatly: 'I told you what I know, and that's it.'

Rosemary West did not break the pact she had made with her husband. They were still bound together inexorably. She did not suddenly tell the police every detail of the crimes that she believed her husband had committed 'without her knowledge'. She 'kept her promise' to Frederick West: the promise of silence.

Throughout her two nights in custody she refused to eat anything, and she was examined by a doctor before being allowed to return home. Shortly after eight o'clock that evening she was released from custody on police bail and went back to Cromwell Street. When she got there she told Stephen and Mae: 'I'm spending one night here and then we're off, and we're never coming back to Cromwell Street again.'

In the months to come Rosemary West never once changed her story. At her trial for murder, she insisted that she knew nothing whatever about the fate of her first-born child. She told the court that her daughter had always intended to leave home 'as soon as was possible', and on this particular morning, though she had tried 'to persuade her to stay', Heather 'wouldn't listen to me'. After she had collected some money for her from the post office, her husband had told her: 'Don't bother with that, you'll only upset her again. You go and do your shopping and I'll talk to her.'

By the time she got back 'two or three hours later, something like that', her daughter had gone. She said she had wanted to say goodbye, but 'He just said he couldn't stop her'. Her husband had convinced her that 'She'd left with some woman in a Mini, who was going to give her a lift to this holiday camp.' And she had indeed gone 'round to a boyfriend's' that night.

Her husband was always saying, she told the court, that 'he had seen her here and seen her there'. Indeed, she went on, 'As far as I was concerned he loved Heather and made a fuss of her and called her his big girl. I couldn't ever believe he would hurt any of the children', although 'I wanted to know why he hadn't persuaded her to contact me.' The jury at her trial did not believe her. They believed that she knew very well that her daughter had been killed, and, in one of the first two verdicts they were to reach, found her guilty of her murder.

Only Rosemary West could tell the world, if she wished to do so, whether or not she was present when Heather West met her death. Throughout her police interviews she refused to offer any comment on her involvement in the killing. She declined to say whether Heather was going to make an official complaint about her sexual abuse at her father's hands, or whether West had been trying to 'break Heather in', as he had 'broken in' Anne Marie, perhaps with a view to making her a prostitute.

She also declined to comment on the suggestions that her daughter had called her a 'nigger-lover', that she 'liked inflicting pain during sex', and that she had once even denied to a neighbour that she had ever had a child called Heather. She refused to say whether or not her daughter had been tortured, or whether she had worked alongside her husband immediately after the girl's disappearance to complete the patio in their garden, thereby covering Heather's narrow shaft of a grave.

In spite of all these denials the jury had no doubts. They accepted that she had shown little or no interest in Heather's whereabouts after her 'disappearance' in 1987, that she had changed her story about the girl between two sets of interviews with the police, one in 1992, the other in 1994 – first saying that she spoke only to her, then only to her father – and, most damning of all, that, in his own confessions, Frederick West was protecting her. Specifically, they rejected her categorical statement that 'Fred is responsible for these murders, not me.'

The jury's verdict of guilty made clear their belief that Rosemary West certainly knew of her first-born child's death. And given her sadistic sexual tastes, and the vicious punishments that she regularly meted out to her children, it is impossible not to believe that she would not have participated in it in the most bestial way. She may well have wanted to seduce and then sexually torment her eldest daughter as much as her husband did. But she may have depended on Frederick West's disregard for human life to have gathered the courage to kill her.

Chapter Twenty-three

The perfect mother

'The cruellest lies are often told in silence.'

Robert Louis Stevenson, *Virginibus Puerisque*

On the morning of Monday 28 February Frederick West, his dark beard showing three days of growth, and still wearing the blue patterned jumper in which he had left Cromwell Street three days before, appeared before Gloucester magistrates charged with the murder of his daughter Heather. His solicitor Howard Ogden told the court that he was being 'cooperative' and assisting the police with two additional murder enquiries. Shortly after his appearance, Rosemary West left Cromwell Street for a police safe house in the small town of Dursley, thirteen miles south of Gloucester. West himself returned to the interview room at Gloucester police station to talk about Shirley Robinson.

Almost his first words were: 'I've got to be straight and honest with you. I've no idea when. I know Rose was carrying one of the half-caste children . . . We wanted a half-caste child . . . and it was planned. So, I mean, I was quite excited about it.' Minutes later he returned to his explanation for this second killing: that Shirley Robinson had 'caused a problem', she had threatened to upset his relationship with his wife. 'I looked at her and I thought, Gee, I've got to stop this bitch telling Rose, because Rose is the only thing that matters in my life, nothing else, not even my children.' He was certain that 'she's going to absolutely ruin my marriage'.

When Detective Constable Savage asked him if Shirley Robinson was the first person that he had killed, West replied quickly: 'Yeah, yeah, yeah, yeah. There's only three. There's no more.' He also insisted that he did not 'mutilate her' as such, just 'pushed her in with a spade'. Then, once again, West repeated: 'Rose had no suspicion I was doing anything apart from building the wash-room' while he was dismembering Shirley Robinson's naked and pregnant body, although he admitted: 'The ball joint makes a noise anyway . . . with the muscle and that pulling away.'

305

Shortly after five-twenty, the remains of 'Shirley's mate' were recovered from a narrow shaft beneath the bathroom window. And four hours later Shirley Robinson's remains were finally recovered from a similar narrow shaft by the back door, 'where the bins are', in West's own words. The complete remains of Shirley Robinson's unborn child were recovered at the same time. All the excavation work was now being supervised by one of the Home Office's most respected forensic pathologists, the stocky, bushy-eyebrowed Professor Knight of Cardiff University, who had once memorably called the human race 'a malignancy on the face of the earth'.

Throughout his interviews on Monday 28 February, Frederick West wove a crafty fabric of lies and half-truths. The tapestry included his reasons for killing Shirley Robinson ('She was threatening to tell Rose she was pregnant'), his explanation for the death of 'Shirley's mate', Alison Chambers ('She starts threatening about Shirley and if I give her money'), and his regret at killing his unborn child ('I mean the last thing I wanted to do was hurt a child of mine'). Throughout, West was confident, affable and relaxed. At one stage he even laughed when Hazel Savage called his collection of pornographic films 'all too vulgar'. At another, confiding that one of his greatest fears as a child was to be buried alive, he admitted 'That's why I strangled them, like . . . I wanted to make sure they were dead.'

The following morning, Tuesday 1 March, West insisted 'There's three in the garden and that's it' and denied that he may have become confused over the identity of 'Shirley's mate'. But then a little more of the detail of what had actually been discovered in the grave with the remains of 'Shirley's mate' began to emerge. There had been bindings. Detective Constable Savage did not go into detail, asking only 'What are they for?' West sidestepped quickly. He accepted that he may have 'put straps' around the girl's body to 'help him carry' her. And when Hazel Savage then suddenly asked him why she had a piece of belt tied around her skull, he still stuck to his story. He said instantly: 'Well, that probably had another piece through it. Holding her head forward.'

That afternoon the extent of just how economical Frederick West had been with the truth emerged even more clearly. He finally accepted that he had made admissions of his own guilt only when he had been trapped in a corner. When Hazel Savage pointed out that he had made his confession about three bodies only after he had seen the extent of the police excavations at Cromwell Street (and they had discovered a third femur), he muttered: 'Well.'

'What did you say to me when I was fingerprinting you?' Savage went on. 'You said, "Did you blame me for trying it on?" ' Frederick West replied sullenly: 'But when I realised they were going the whole way, then what's the point?' Hazel Savage leaned across the desk separating them. 'Right, so you haven't been totally cooperative, have you? It's been a bit like pulling teeth.' West did not flinch.

'Well, were you expecting it any other way?' he said coldly, his voice momentarily losing its familiar, affable burr.

In the weeks of interrogation to come, it became abundantly clear that no matter how cooperative West appeared, he would never admit to anything unless he was forced to do so. He responded to the interrogations with all the skill of a spy, committing his lies to memory and repeating them effortlessly, before carefully leading his questioners off into long digressions that confused or diluted their train of thought. West hid the motives for his actions behind a constantly moving series of glass screens that reflected what the detectives wanted to know, but which revealed none of the reality of his own thoughts.

At one level Frederick West was beginning to bask in the glory of his own notoriety. He was well aware that outside interest was mounting rapidly in the possibility that he might be a serial killer. But at another level West was still trying to conceal the truth about what lay beneath the cellar of his house. A certain amount of glamour appealed to him, but the ugly truth of what had gone on in the damp cave beneath his house was another matter. He had reluctantly admitted the killing of Shirley Robinson and her 'mate', but he had no intention of going any further. He kept insisting, 'That's all there is.'

In the late afternoon of Wednesday 2 March, Detective Superintendent John Bennett confirmed at a media briefing that West had been charged with the murder of two other women 'following the discovery of human remains in the garden of a house in Cromwell Street'. The team of investigating officers had expanded from fifteen to thirty, Bennett explained, and this was apart from the search teams still working at Cromwell Street. The police had also decided to empty the house entirely of its contents.

That same day Bennett had consulted the forensic psychologist Paul Britton, an academic who had provided the prototype for the television character Cracker, with a view to building up a psychological profile of West for the investigation. But the detective superintendent did not specifically announce this to the press.

Had Frederick West known, he would have been very flattered. But in his cell beneath Gloucester police station he was still intent on trying to maintain his image as an amiable little man who demanded to be underestimated, the disguise that had worked so well for him for more than twenty-five years. After a brief court appearance on the morning of Thursday 3 March, he was interviewed six times during the afternoon and evening, and his cooperative, relaxed air did not waver for a moment.

With police encouragement, he embarked on the story of his life. After giving an elaborate account of his early life, he bragged cheerfully about his sexual conquests, including having 'hundreds' of girls while he was in the Merchant Navy, and on several occasions being in bed with three or four girls at the same time and making love 'at least twice with each a night'. He talked about his first wife Rena and their life together in Glasgow, as well as her daughter

Charmaine. He explained that he disliked homosexuals – 'I mean, I couldn't kiss a man' – but felt that lesbians were a different matter – 'There's nothing dirty about two women being attracted to each other, is there?' He told the officers interviewing him that he liked to watch his wife with other men – 'It's a turn-on' – and that 'It was important to keep our sex life alive and changing'. But he still insisted 'I haven't touched other girls since Shirley, because it was causing slight problems with Rose.'

Finally, on the evening of Thursday 3 March West was asked if he could remember some of the residents of Cromwell Street, whose names the police had discovered. He embarked on the task gleefully, managing to remember many many young people – except a girl named Lynda Gough: 'Don't ring a bell,' he said. 'I mean, there was dozens of girls staying there that shouldn't have been there. They were using the address.' When he was told that her parents had even come to look for her after she had stayed at Cromwell Street, he replied cheerfully: 'I . . . we had hundreds of parents coming asking . . . Hazel [Savage] was there very often, fetching girls from there.' When Detective Constable Savage suggested that Lynda Gough could be the third girl in the garden, Frederick West said only: 'Wouldn't have thought so.'

By early the following afternoon, however, West's memory had improved. He had decided overnight that it would be better to acknowledge that he knew the girl. Yes, Lynda Gough had been seeing one of the lodgers, he explained, and had then asked if she could move in. 'The room by the bathroom was empty, so I said yes,' he explained politely. He even admitted that he and his wife had gone to pick up Lynda's belongings from her parents' house. But he then maintained that she had been involved with a lodger called Terry who had 'smashed me straight on the top of the head' with an ashtray when he had asked him about her, injuring him so badly that he had 'to go to hospital for stitches'. After that Terry and Lynda had left for Weston-super-Mare, 'as far as I know'.

What Frederick West did not know was that at that very moment the police were using a new ground-probing radar device on the floor of the bathroom at the back of the ground floor of his house at Cromwell Street. Acting on their own instincts, and on the advice of Paul Britton that West was likely to have killed more than the three people buried in his garden, they had decided to embark on a far more detailed study of the house. Within an hour the ground-probing radar had indicated that a body might be buried underneath the bathroom. West's disingenuous description of Lynda Gough had come too late. The police were now determined to excavate the rest of the house.

At three-seventeen on the afternoon of Friday 4 March, Hazel Savage informed Frederick West formally that the police intended to 'dig up the whole of the basement'. He did not blink, and returned to his cell, where he talked for a time to Janet Leach. Less than three hours later he asked for a meeting with his solicitor, who in turn handed a message to Detective Superintendent Bennett. Written out by his solicitor, and signed by West, it stated simply: 'I, Frederick West, authorise my solicitor Howard Ogden to advise Superintendent Bennett that I wish to admit to a further (approx.) nine killings, expressly, Charmaine, Rena and others to be identified.'

When it was read out in a formal interview, which began at six-ten that evening, Detective Constable Savage asked West how many bodies there were in Cromwell Street. He replied calmly: 'That's the ones I can remember.' Frederick West was no longer an ordinary domestic murderer.

'I got it in me mind in a certain way,' West explained confidently in the first minutes of the interview, 'and I don't want to change that if I can help it.' He told the officers first that Lynda Gough was under the bathroom, 'quite deep . . . 'cause there was a big cellar underneath originally'. Then West told the police that they needed to move on to the cellar. He explained that they needed to look for a series of graves, adding: 'Now these, I'm not a hundred per cent sure on some of these.'

Nevertheless, West identified the first body as being buried by the false fireplace he had put in the front cellar room: 'I think she was Dutch or summat.' Another girl in the cellar was from Newent, but he could not remember her name. But he could remember that another was called Lucy Partington, although he was not sure exactly which of the graves contained her body.

In a soft, confidential voice, West went on to explain that he had got his first wife Rena 'absolutely paralytic', then taken her out to Dymock, 'where I know, and strangled and buried her there'. The same evening he had strangled his stepdaughter Charmaine, 'who was asleep in the back of the car', taken her back to 25 Midland Road, and put her in the back basement extension and buried her in the coal. Were all the bodies dismembered? 'To my memory, yes,' came the reply.

When Hazel Savage asked shortly before seven o'clock that evening, 'Is there anybody else involved with you?', Frederick West replied at once, 'Nobody at all.'

Later that evening West went back to Cromwell Street, and, using an aerosol paint spray can, marked the floor of his own cellar with neat eighteen-inch squares to indicate where he remembered four of the bodies were buried.

By the following morning, Saturday 5 March, West had also prepared a sketch plan of the different rooms in the cellar with the help of the 'appropriate adult', Janet Leach, and, when his formal interviews resumed shortly before lunch, he took the detectives through it. At the same time he also gave his first full account of the death of his stepdaughter Charmaine. But again he began to lie. 'She was fully clothed and everything,' West claimed. 'There was no clothes taken off her or nothing.' He went on to maintain: 'She wasn't dismembered at all.' He had killed her 'about a week' after he had been released from Leyhill Prison in June 1971.

During the afternoon, as the police started to excavate the cramped cellar of Cromwell Street, West began calmly to give a detailed description of the girls he thought they were about to unearth. Among them were 'the Dutch girl' with a 'nice figure' whom he had 'picked up in Tewkesbury'; the 'Worcester girl' who had 'scars on one of her arms or her hands from a firework accident'; and the 'Newent girl' who used to 'come to visit'. West explained that he did not know their names because he 'gave them all nicknames' in case he ever 'shouted out their names while he was making love to Rose'. Shirley Robinson, he told the officers, was known to him only as 'Bones'. This, too, was a lie.

By nine o'clock on that Saturday evening in March, West had embroidered his story a little more, claiming that there were two 'Worcester girls' in the cellar, as well as Lynda Gough in the 'inspection pit' beneath his bathroom extension, bringing the total of bodies under the house to six, and the total in Cromwell Street to nine. 'I don't think any of them were cut up,' he announced, but adding: 'I ain't sure, I wouldn't be one hundred per cent on that, mind.' It was another lie.

Next morning the *Sunday Mirror* front page bore the headline 'House of Horrors'. The legend that was to become Cromwell Street had begun. At seven-thirty the previous evening Detective Superintendent Bennett had announced to a packed press conference that during the afternoon the police had found what appeared to be the remains of 'two further human beings'. They were the skeletons of Thérèse Siegenthaler and Shirley Hubbard. In the three days that followed, the police search team uncovered four more sets of remains – those of Lucy Partington and Juanita Mott on Sunday 6 March, Lynda Gough on Monday 7 March, and Carol Ann Cooper on Tuesday 8 March. By then the nine bodies in Cromwell Street had all been recovered.

It was to be eight weeks before Charmaine West's remains were to be unearthed from beneath the concrete floor over the old coal cellar at Midland Road, a month after her mother, Rena West, was recovered from Letterbox Field in Kempley at 3.45 p.m. on 10 April. West himself was formally charged with her murder four days later. It would then be a further four weeks before Ann McFall's remains were discovered in Fingerpost Field in Kempley, just a few hundred yards from West's family home at Much Marcle. And throughout each and every of one of those weeks, Frederick West cheerfully continued to talk to the police. But getting the truth out of him was still like pulling teeth.

By the time the body of Carol Ann Cooper had been unearthed from beneath the cellar floor at Cromwell Street, it had become clear to the police that Frederick West was still concealing far more than he was prepared to admit about the killings. He was attempting to conceal, for example, that bondage might have played some part in the deaths. Indeed, it was not until he knew for certain that the police had discovered bindings with some of the remains that he suddenly admitted, on the afternoon of Tuesday 8 March, that the girls had been tied up.

An exasperated Hazel Savage put it to her fellow officer during an interview: 'He didn't want to talk about bondage in the beginning. We've been here for days. He's never talked about it . . . He is now saying "I'd better think up this story that she hung herself".' Frederick West's demeanour did not change; he just smiled his naughty boy's smile, his confidence unshaken. At the end of that evening he told the police confidently: 'I mean, every girl I picked up I didn't put in the basement.'

When he was asked where he did put them West laughed out loud, and replied: 'I dropped them off where they wanted to go.' He was still one step ahead. The other victims were still his to control, his to know where they were, his to tell the police about when – and if – he decided to. They were his trophies, proof of his power over the world.

As the days passed West continued to play cat and mouse with the police, telling them repeatedly: 'There is certainly nobody else to my knowledge that you will find dead, nobody.' In particular, he insisted that he had not killed Ann McFall: 'She was a saint as far as I was concerned.' But then West returned to hinting, tantalisingly, 'Well, if there's some more I'll try and think who they are', before suddenly reverting to his original story: 'No, you've got all that I had anything to do with.'

West's rambling explanations contradicted themselves time after time. In a description of his first meeting with Carol Ann Cooper, for example, he insisted that he had 'picked her up in a lorry', even though he had stopped driving lorries two years before her disappearance in 1973. He then unexpectedly admitted that he would 'probably have buried her on the way back somewhere . . . I wouldn't have taken the risk of bringing her back if I'd had something to bury her with'. The possibility that West was actually describing the abduction of quite another young woman – whose body had indeed been buried somewhere on the road – prompted the police to ask if he had been able to bury somebody else somewhere else. 'No, No,' West replied hastily, adding with equal suddenness, 'Can I have a smoke?'

'See, I had affairs with so many different girls. I mean, you're not talking one or two,' West told the police repeatedly, 'and . . . everyone didn't end up in disaster, by no means.' And when he was asked why he had not killed in the last years of his life, West replied, as smoothly and persuasively as ever: 'Why did I stop for eight years and not do any more? There's a simple answer for that. When I attacked Heather I got such a shock that I didn't know how the hell to get over it . . . Then I sorted it out, what the problem was, and it was messing about with other girls, with the fear of Rose catching me.'

His self-confidence never wavered. He toyed with the police throughout his interviews, daring them to prove that he was a liar. 'I tell you what,' he announced suddenly on Friday 18 March, 'I can't remember half the places I've been laying concrete and patios. It's an everyday thing for me.' And he burst out in a fit of laughter. 'I mean, when they talk about going through places that I've been, I mean you're going to be here for a month . . . Every day's a different place, and two or three places a day, like. Asda stores, Gateway stores, offices all over England.' He had been in Reading and Leicester, Nottinghamshire and Newmarket, he told them with a grin on his face. 'I shall have done me life sentence and back out or buried or something by the time you got round to it.'

They were not the only red herrings West fed to his interrogators. On Sunday 20 March West was taken to 25 Midland Road to show the police the site in which he claimed he had buried Charmaine West. But no sooner had he returned to Gloucester police station than he started to insist that his stepdaughter's body could not be there, as she must have been taken away 'during the demolition'. 'They can go and dig the whole of Midland Road up, but they won't find nothing there, because there's nothing there.'

The next day, West explained: 'Charmaine was wrapped up in a lot of blankets, 'cause she wasn't cut up or nothing, she was just as she was.' On 12 April West changed his story completely, telling the police instead: 'Charmaine is not dead. Charmaine is well, and that I can assure you of . . . I never touched Charmaine.' And when he was told that Midland Road was about to be excavated, he replied: 'I can state this on my life that they will not find anything at Midland Road at all. And I would like that to go on the record as said.'

The reason for Frederick West's decision to lie about his step-daughter's death was not only that he was anxious to prevent the discovery of her naked and dismembered body. It was also to distance his wife from any suggestion that she may have played a part in her killing. West knew that she had lived there with Charmaine while he was in Leyhill Prison, and he did not want there to be any suspicion that she might have acted alone.

The pact that he and Rosemary West had made on the Thursday evening of 24 February 1994 depended upon his taking 'all the blame' for every action. It was his gift to a woman whom he adored. And as the weeks of his police interviews dragged on, it became ever more apparent how great West's love was for his wife. Frederick West saw the drama of his life as a love-story as well as a tragedy.

'I make sure nobody harms Rose,' he confided to the police on 21 March. 'I worship that girl, my wife. We've got a very special thing in our own minds . . . it's got stronger.' Indeed, West's determination to cast his wife as blameless knew no bounds. The next day he denied that she ever 'had any sexual relations with any girls, 'cause I would have known that', and the next added that 'Rose was not a lesbian. I've tried several times to get her into it, but without success'. Three days after that, he tried to convince the police that his wife did not even enjoy her relationships with other men. 'She was just doing it, because I wanted her to.' On the same day he claimed she would have 'turned me in' if she had known about the killings. 'I mean, as much as she loved me and that . . . I mean, Rose would not harm anybody . . . Rose didn't have a violent nature at all.'

West told the police repeatedly that he and his wife were 'mentally locked into each other in a big way, and we still are at this moment', and that this was the sole reason for his killing. 'I always told the girls that no way would I ever leave my wife. That was always made quite clear to every girl I had an affair with, that there was no way that I would ever swap Rose for any other woman in the world.' For once West was telling at least part of the truth: for though his explanations were designed to protect his wife, they were also based firmly in his love for her. Using his curious and revealing phrase, he insisted: 'I mean we're not evilly locked together at all.' And he went on: 'I mean, Rose might look a bit hard faced and that, but Rose is soft as a kitten and I mean I know that because I've lived with her so long, and controlled her life for so long . . . I've been tempted over the years to tell Rose, I must admit, but I never ever did. I backed off it'.

When Detective Constable Savage confronted West, telling him that she could not understand how his wife, 'the lady of the house', could have nine bodies buried in her house and not have 'a clue' they were there, West did not budge. 'Well, that's the truth,' he told her. And when she suggested that she found that hard to believe in the light of their joint attack on Carol Raine in 1972, West insisted: 'I set Rose up to do that, that was my fault,' adding defensively, 'Rose was pregnant practically all the time . . . She had more to do than to bother with that sort of thing.'

The tension between Hazel Savage and Rosemary West, which had rumbled on in the background throughout West's interrogations, finally surfaced on 28 March. Savage told Frederick West bluntly that she found it unbelievable – and so did the experts the police had consulted – that he had stopped killing for two periods of six years: between 1967 and 1973, and then between 1987 and 1994. She added that the only reason she suspected he was claiming this was his fear of implicating his wife in any killing.

Breaking the confidential tone he had used throughout almost every one of his interviews, West screamed at his interrogator: 'Rubbish. Because Rose had nothing to do with it at all . . . Rose knew nothing of what I was doing at all, ever.'

Four full weeks after the recovery of the first body from Cromwell Street, and after more than a hundred police interviews, Frederick West was still insisting: 'All Rose wants to be is a mother, and that's all she's ever been . . . an absolutely perfect mother.'

Chapter Twenty-four

An evil love

'The world is still deceived by ornament.
In law, what plea so tainted and corrupt
But, being season'd with a gracious voice,
Obscures the show of evil?'

Shakespeare, *The Merchant of Venice*

In the alternative universe created by Frederick and Rosemary West at 25 Cromwell Street one emotion was paramount above all others – love. No matter how terrible the pain or unremitting the suffering they inflicted on others, they remained tenaciously in love. Their distorted version of love lay at the heart of their being. They had used it as their justification for murder and for the abuse of their children. Both had started their lives searching for love, longing for it to be reciprocated, and both had finally found it with each other. Each satisfied the other's need. Frederick West quite simply 'adored his wife', in the words of one friend, and 'would do anything in the world for her', while Rosemary West would stop at nothing to please her husband.

The clearest proof of the Wests' devotion to one another lies among the videotapes seized by the police during their child-abuse investigation in 1992. One of the tapes was made by Frederick West of his wife during February and March of that year. The first part was no more than West's updated version of 'Rose's chocolates' whereby, instead of putting her used knickers in a jar, he asked his wife to hold them up for the camera. On each occasion her husband would zoom in on the stains made by another man's semen.

There was no aspect of sexual depravity that Rosemary West would not explore for her husband, and few that he had not asked her to. Each had demanded that the other prove their love by means that were almost beyond contemplation. They had proved it in the terrible humiliation and torture of innocent young women, in the killing of their eldest child and their eight-year-old stepdaughter, and in the abuse of their remaining children. Neither had baulked at these murderous actions, seeing them rather as proof of their evil love. Their relationship, born in sexual desire and fostered in perversion, had reached its zenith.

Neither Frederick nor Rosemary West cared to distinguish between the spiritual expression of love and its ugliest manifestation in sexual perversion. For them both, the two were inextricably mixed. Neither saw any contradiction between the depraved exhibition of sexual promiscuity for their home video camera and their private protestation of a far more romantic love. Their love for one another was their justification for their every action, and their killings. And the two loves existed side by side, just as they did on the videotape made by Frederick West in the spring of 1992.

For immediately after his new version of 'Rose's chocolates', and a sequence showing Rosemary West urinating on a teatowel in her kitchen in Cromwell Street, with which she proceeded to wipe her naked body, Frederick West's videotape jumped to a carefully selected section of the 1943 film version of Charlotte Brontë's novel *Jane Eyre*. The sequence West had so painstakingly added to the videotape was the one in which Orson Welles, as Edward Rochester, finally declares his love for his daughter's governness, played by Joan Fontaine. The juxtaposition of these two starkly different video images, which had obviously been made quite deliberately, is so swift and so striking that there could hardly be stronger proof of the extent or nature of their depraved mutual love.

Frederick West's extract from the Twentieth-Century–Fox black and white film began exactly as Orson Welles explains to Joan Fontaine in the garden of Thornfield, Rochester's house in Yorkshire: 'It is as if I had a string somewhere under my left rib, tightly and inextricably knotted to a similar string situated in the corresponding quarter of your little frame.' Jane Eyre replies that to leave him 'is like looking on the necessity of death'. And when Rochester pleads with her to marry him, even though he is already married, she finally agrees, and they embrace as a fork of lightning hits a nearby tree. 'I love and I was loved,' Jane Eyre concludes, as the gathering storm envelopes them both.

The Wests clearly saw a parallel with their own lives. For the extract of the film that they took such pains to keep goes on to reveal that Rochester cannot marry because he is already married, just as Frederick West himself was when he met the young Rosemary Letts, the 'nanny' whom he had found for his own children. Even the battle that Rosemary Letts then waged to be allowed to live with West and bear his child seems to be reflected in their chosen extract, as Jane finally returns to the ruined Thornfield and the blinded, disabled man she loved.

Because of this love, on the night of 24 February 1994 Frederick West told Rosemary to 'blame him' for everything. He believed that if he took the blame, his wife would be left alone, untouched, and still the mistress of Cromwell Street. But, misled by his earlier contacts with the Gloucester police, he had underestimated the tenacity of Detective Constable Savage and the other officers now involved. By the end of March 1994 the police were convinced that he could not have acted alone. Indeed, they were in no doubt that not only must Rosemary West have been fully aware of his every action, but that she must also have been a participant.

On Wednesday 20 April 1994, eight weeks after the police first arrived at Cromwell Street with a warrant to search for Heather, Rosemary West was arrested and taken to Cheltenham police station. At first she was questioned only about allegations of child abuse and of acting as a prostitute at Cromwell Street, and throughout four official interviews that day she answered the police's questions evasively rather than aggressively.

The next morning, Thursday 21 April, she declined to answer any further questions. For thirteen minutes she refused even to agree that her name was Rosemary West, admitting only: 'I've just got nothing to say.' It was a decision that she would stick to rigidly throughout the rest of her time in custody. Indeed, it was to be seventeen months later, when she walked into the witness-box at her trial on ten counts of murder, before she would agree to answer any further questions about the case.

On the same day, seven miles away at Gloucester police station, Frederick West was explaining that his wife had started to have sex with other men only 'as a turn-on for me and herself', but that he made sure always to make love to her either before she went out with another man or when she came back. As for the deaths, 'it had been a long secret, longer than I believed', West confessed. As far as he knew his scheme was working. There was at least the chance that she would return to Cromwell Street and be reunited with her children.

At three-forty on the afternoon of Saturday 23 April 1994, Frederick West's plan began to break down when his wife was 'arrested on suspicion of the murder of a girl called Lynda Gough'. Throughout three police interviews that afternoon, she continued to exercise her right to remain silent. She answered each and every question, including those that suggested she might have tortured or been involved in sexual acts with the nineteen-year-old girl before she was killed, with 'No comment'. At six-fifteen the following afternoon she was charged formally with Lynda Gough's murder. Her reply was straightforward: 'I'm innocent.'

Time after time in the weeks to come, officers from the Gloucester Constabulary offered Rosemary West the opportunity to repudiate her husband, and to admit that she had been 'forced' to act against Lynda Gough and the other young women whose bodies had been discovered in her house in Cromwell Street. But just as she had done in February, she declined each offer, saying only 'No comment'. She was still honouring her part in the pact she had made with her husband, 'keeping her promise' to him.

Steadily, as the last days of April ebbed into May, Rosemary West was charged with a total of nine murders, culminating with that of her own first born-child Heather West. To each charge, bar one – to which she made no reply whatever – she answered: 'I'm innocent.' But the charges began to make a subtle difference to her attitude to the case, and to her husband. She started to cast herself not only in the role of a doomed lover, Jane Eyre unable to marry her own Rochester, but also in the quite separate role of a naive victim, a woman who had suffered at the hands of an evil and manipulative madman.

She had realised that their original pact, in which her husband had told her to let him 'sort it out', allowed her to portray herself as completely innocent of any knowledge of the girls whose murders she was now being charged with – without breaking her promise. She could indeed deny all knowledge of the victims and remain loyal. But she also added her own subtle variation. She decided to make a public show of rejecting her husband.

On Monday 25 April the police began preparations to excavate the basement of 25 Midland Road. They actually started digging at eleven o'clock the next morning. As they did so, Frederick West was explaining proudly to Detective Constable Savage his plans for having his children 'baptised together', and how his wife had written to him when she was a young woman of fifteen, telling him to meet her in Pittville Park in Cheltenham on a Sunday afternoon to make love, and finishing her letter: 'Keep saying your prayers and remember I'll always love you. Lots of love, Rose.'

West could not conceal the smile on his face. When Hazel Savage suggested to him that he seemed to be enjoying the questioning, he replied: 'Yeah, why not?'

'I don't know,' the detective answered. 'I don't understand it really.'

'You will in the end,' West replied.

'Will I? When will I understand it?'

'I don't know. At the end, whenever that is,' West told her.

Then he added, with another grin: 'You're the love of my life, Hazel. I can't even remember Gloucester police station without Hazel.'

At that moment, as far as Frederick West knew, everything was still proceeding according to his private plan. The banter with Hazel Savage was no more than to keep himself amused.

Shortly before lunch on Wednesday 27 April Hazel Savage broke the news to West that his wife had been charged formally with the murders of Lynda Gough and Carol Ann Cooper. In an instant, and without warning, his demeanour changed completely. Now he was afraid for his wife.

The next day Frederick West asked for time to consult his lawyers, and at 9.38 a.m. on Friday 29 April, he retracted every one of his confessions. He first asked Howard Ogden to write out another note, a counterpart to his 4 March confession of nine murders. Then, in a two-minute interview, West put the note into his own words, telling the police: 'Well, I have not, and still not, told you the whole truth about these matters. The reason for this is that from the very first day of this enquiry my main concern has been to protect other person or persons, and there is nothing else I wish to say at this time.'

As soon as West had finished, Hazel Savage asked him if he was feeling all right. 'Yeah, perfect,' he replied. 'That's what the doctor just said.' In the weeks to come he was to refuse repeatedly to identify which 'person or persons' he was protecting, even though the police persistently attempted to persuade him to do so. It was, in fact, Frederick West's last attempt to throw his pursuers off the scent, his last effort at subterfuge. For though it may have appeared so at first sight, West was not now simply acknowledging that his plan to save his wife had failed, and that he was now content to shift the blame to her. It was, as always with him, considerably more complicated than that.

At one level Frederick West wanted to confuse the issue, and in the process give himself a chance to think. At another he wanted to fight the battle alongside his wife. If Rosemary West was to be charged alongside him with at least ten counts of murder, then he would provide her with another alibi altogether and blame someone else entirely. West's mind was fertile enough to think of other potential assailants whom he could hint might be guilty of the crimes.

At yet another level West was also thinking that the charges against his wife might enable him to escape. He did not intend to break their pact, but if that was how a jury decided then he would not object. For West was only too aware that he would be far less capable of tolerating a long period of imprisonment than she would. 'Rose is a creature of habit,' he once told the police admiringly. West suspected that the habit and routine of prison life would be far easier for her to accept than for him.

In the ensuing five days Frederick West gave just one brief interview to the police, one in which he hardly made any comment. But then events intervened to force him to react. At 7.10 p.m. on Wednesday 4 May, an officer excavating beneath the kitchen floor of the ground floor of 25 Midland Road found what appeared to be human remains. It was the most terrible discovery of the entire police investigation, for the eight-year-old's body had been brutally destroyed. The single piece of evidence that West had prayed would never come to light was lifted from the concrete floor of the tiny villa on the edge of Gloucester to haunt him.

In an interview just after two o'clock on the following afternoon, Frederick West was told that they had found what seemed to be the remains of Charmaine. The child's body was not wrapped in blankets, as West had once insisted that it was; nor was it clothed, as he had also maintained; nor was it in one piece in the tiny hole in the ground into which it had been stuffed. For the first time in his police interviews, Frederick West began to cry. Almost the only words he could bring himself to say were: 'I mean, I'm the only dad she's had.'

It was to be another five days before West was interviewed again. And when the interviews resumed, on 10 May, he refused to explain anything whatever about the death of his stepdaughter Charmaine.

He was charged with her murder on the following day but refused to say anything in reply, just as then he refused to return to Fingerpost Field to assist the police search for the body of Ann McFall. Her body, too, was one that he now prayed would never be found.

The remorse that West may have felt for the killing of Ann McFall – the only murder that he was never to confess to – may have been the reason for his initial decision to tell the police where he had buried her body. But the fact that they had failed to find it convinced him that they might never do so. In fact, it was to be almost another month before McFall's body was unearthed in Fingerpost Field near Dymock. By that time the Gloucester police were on the very brink of giving up the search entirely after excavating a hole almost the size of an Olympic swimming-pool, twenty metres by thirty to a depth of two metres.

In the meantime Frederick West had gone into denial. He, too, had begun to refuse to comment as a team of officers questioned him repeatedly about the missing bones, the masks, gags and bindings, and the cuts in the bones found on the victims. Now he remained silent and uncommunicative as two officers asked him whether he had attacked the young women found beneath his house and garden at Cromwell Street before or after their deaths.

When West was asked if there was anything specific he wanted to say, he replied: 'Yeah, I had nothing to do with these girls' deaths at all. I have lied through the statements and at this moment I am not prepared to change that . . . I am not prepared to say who I am protecting in this case.' A little later he added: 'I am not so worried for myself, probably, but I have eight children out there.' Then, when he was asked if his reply meant that he thought the 'person or persons' he was referring to might harm his children he replied: 'I suppose.'

Finally, at 12.40 p.m. on Friday 13 May, West ended his hundred-and-thirty-second interview at Gloucester police station with the words: 'Nobody spares a thought for what I've lost in this. I've lost more than anybody else. Couldn't we end this?' '

Frederick West was sent to Her Majesty's Prison at Winson Green in Birmingham as a remand prisoner while the police continued to question and then charge his wife with the murder of the nine victims found in Cromwell Street. On Thursday 2 June he returned to Gloucester briefly to appear before the magistrates' court, and was once again remanded in custody. The following day Rosemary West, too, was remanded in custody there, and her interrogation at Cheltenham police station brought to an end. She was sent to the nearby Pucklechurch remand centre. The Wests had neither seen nor spoken to each other since their last night together in Cromwell Street.

The starker, less familiar conditions of Winson Green prison in Birmingham had a dramatic effect on Frederick West. Though he would try to insist that he was 'a hero in here, a saint, everyone's after me signature', he became increasingly frightened and withdrawn as the weeks passed. Almost his only consolation was a continuing series of interviews with Howard Ogden, who travelled up to see him regularly from his small office in Cheltenham from the middle of May until the end of July. His only other regular visitor was his eldest son Stephen.

Ogden tape-recorded his conversations with Frederick West. Although they were designed as the first steps in the preparation of West's defence, Ogden also did so with a view to offering them for sale, an action that would eventually bring him into conflict with the Law Society, and see him lose the right to practise as a solicitor for a period of one year. Passing preliminary judgement on his actions, Mr Justice Lightman told the High Court: 'I can think of nothing more calculated to bring the legal profession into disrepute and destroy public confidence.' Ogden was then ordered to hand over the tapes.

West's conversations with Ogden were a bizarre mixture of lies, fantasy and half-truth, which reflected West's fear and mental deterioration in prison. In more than twenty hours of interviews, West sought to deny any wrongdoing whatever on his part, casting himself for the first time as the innocent bystander, caught up in his wife's wickedness. In that respect the interviews are ludicrous. But they offer an insight into the Wests' alternative universe. And they were the only occasion on which Frederick West broke the pact he had made with his wife on that February night in Cromwell Street three months before. In his desperation he sought a scapegoat, and that scapegoat was his wife.

In every one of his fifteen conversations with Ogden at Winson Green, West returned to his familiar lengthy, rambling style of story-telling, heaping detail on detail, reminiscence on reminiscence, repeating some things endlessly, then suddenly revealing something unexpected. But the pressure of his time on remand, and the realisation that he would now almost certainly spend the rest of his natural life in prison, had unhinged him. His mind was wandering, confusing fact and fantasy, trying to reconcile the reality of his killings with the need to deny them. West began to dissemble.

In West's first interview with Ogden, on Wednesday 18 May five days after his last police interview, he did not start by incriminating Rosemary West. At that moment his mind was still strong enough to sustain their pact. Ceaselessly rolling hand-made cigarettes in his short fingers, West set about describing his first meeting with his wife, and how she had 'taken over from Rena', who 'kept disappearing for a week or fortnight at a time – after she'd had Charmaine'.

In what may have borne some resemblance to the truth, West told Ogden that Rena had been 'supplying girls for these parties' given by Rolf, at which girls were used for immoral purposes. West claimed that he had known Rolf first, and had then introduced him to Rena, who began to use him as her pimp before they went back to Scotland together. 'Rena always looked after me,' West explained. 'She was never unkind to me in any way.' And he went on to deny that he had killed her. But then he specifically accused Rena West of killing his

320

'angel', Ann McFall, and went on to claim – quite suddenly – that Rolf had 'recruited Rose' to 'get' his first wife.

'I am not lying to you in any way,' West assured his solicitor. 'Anything I say to you can be backed up. What I tell you is the gospel truth.'

By the time Ogden returned to Winson Green a week later, West had prepared his new sanitised version of events. He began by trying to spread the guilt for the killing of the young women in Cromwell Street as far as he could, and maintaining that the accounts of his own sexual appetite were 'fantasy'. Claiming that Rosemary West, not he, was guilty of the killings, he also implied that his younger brother John had been involved, "cause John was shagging Rose for fucking years . . . I knew that'. West blamed his wife's sadistic sexual nature for the murders, and insisted that he had 'deliberately mixed things up' for the police.

Throughout, Frederick West set out to cast himself as the innocent. He denied that he had any kind of sex life with his wife. 'I hated it. I hated the smell of her at times as well.' He denied that he liked bondage: 'I put it on Rose once, and even then I didn't like the idea of it, and I didn't ever have anything to do with it.' He denied any attack on his other daughter: 'All I did was kick her in the fucking arse at the gate, a few nights before, for being with a drug addict.' He denied any attacks on either Anne Marie or Mae. He denied that Heather West was his daughter. He denied that he had attacked Carol Raine: 'That was Rose attacked her, not me.' He denied that the cellar at Cromwell Street had been kept locked: 'The basement was always wide open. Anybody who wanted to go down there could.' He denied that 'it was kitted out for sex games'. He denied that he was interested in pornographic films. He denied that he ever knew that his wife advertised in contact magazines, and he denied that he had ever encouraged her to have sex with any other man.

'Rose fucking ruled me, I didn't rule Rose. Everybody knows that,' West told Ogden. 'Every penny I earned she had. She searched my clothes to make sure I didn't have any money.' West accused her of having 'new clothes all the time', when 'most of my clothes was off building sites'. West claimed that his wife 'laid roofs' and 'could mix plaster all right. She dug holes and everything'. She was also 'a brilliant cook', but 'had special food of her own, kept the best of everything for herself'. Most of all, he insisted, 'Rose must be cool, calm and collected'.

To demonstrate exactly how cool, calm and collected his wife could be, Frederick West proceeded to try to convince his solicitor that he knew nothing about the killings in Cromwell Street until the evening of 24 February 1994. 'When Rose told me where the bodies were and everything, I died at that moment. Every feeling dropped out of me body.' West claimed 'I didn't suspect Rose of anything', and went on, 'I was quite prepared to take it. It was my fault that these girls got too vulnerable. I should have checked on my own home more.'

Careful to sustain the fiction that he 'fell asleep' in a lay-by for 'two to three hours' on his way back to Cromwell Street that afternoon, West remembered: 'Rose was in some kind of state. She was crying and shaking and God knows what, and that ain't Rose, believe me. She's a hard case, no messing with her.' West went on to tell Ogden that he 'couldn't quite catch on why' she was so upset, but that he had gone to the police station to tell 'Hazel Savage about Heather – what I knew'. When he returned home again West maintained that he caught up with his wife in the bar room on the first floor and told her: 'There's piss-all out there. What are you worrying about?' In this version of events, Rosemary West told him: 'Oh, yes there is.' And he replied: 'What the hell do you mean? She said, "Heather's out there." '

Then West offered what may have been part of the truth. 'I shall have to take it,' Frederick West said he told his wife. 'You say nothing.' But 'I wanted to get out of the house there and then. It seemed as though my whole life stopped there, finished . . . I drank my tea, took a couple of Paracetamol and I said: "Right, what happened, then?" She wouldn't tell me no more, nothing. I said: "Is that it?" She said: "Oh no. There's Shirley and Shirley's mate." '

West said that he had then asked his wife: ' "How many is there?" She says: "I don't know, seven, or eight, or nine, something like that." ' According to West, his wife then pointed out to him where each of the bodies was buried, and 'she named them all'. She also told him that 'Charmaine's in the cellar at the back of Midland Road', and 'Rena's out at her beauty-spot'.

West told his solicitor that Rosemary West's explanations for the deaths were 'sex acts that went wrong, bondage that went wrong'. That night he lay on the bed, 'I was in a trance, in limbo, like', but he was sure that the police would 'just dig the bodies up and leave Rose, Mae and Stephen' living there in peace. It was one of the few honest remarks in Frederick West's entire fabrication, along with his remark a few days later: 'What I did all the time, and I'm still trying to do it now, is cover up for Rose.'

'Everything was so blatantly cruel,' West confessed on 31 May. 'The main problem I've had is that I swore on the kids' lives that I wouldn't shop Rose for what she did. That's the only way I could get her to tell me what she done to Heather, 'cause she wouldn't tell me what she'd done to her.' He was afraid that his wife had 'tortured her', and hoped 'that she hadn't been sent to the niggers in Bristol', concluding: 'At this time I knew nothing about any other girls. Nothing. Only Heather.'

Cromwell Street, he said, 'was more secure on secrets than GCHQ is . . . She never told me nothing. That was her policy in life. She told nobody nothing.' And his wife had threatened him by saying: 'If you drop me in it, you won't last long, and they'll make sure you die a horrible death.' West claimed to Ogden that when he suggested to his wife that she could not have acted alone, and there must be

322

'somebody else mixed up in it', she had told him: 'You don't need to know that.'

Throughout this litany of fantasy and falsehood, which rambled on throughout June, Frederick West denied playing any part in the killings. The day after the discovery of Ann McFall's remains in Fingerpost Field shortly after six o'clock on the evening of Tuesday 7 June, he told Ogden that his first wife Rena had killed her 'and Rena must have told Rose that she was in the pond'. Rosemary West had 'no feelings at all', he maintained.

On rare occasions reality would intrude into the fantasy. When Ogden asked West why he thought his wife 'stopped after Heather', West paused before replying: 'Did she stop?' He then went on: 'There's a farm somewhere that Rose had a lot to do with.' A few minutes later he told Ogden: 'I don't even know if they got them all.'

'I knew that you wouldn't get anything out of Rose,' West said. 'If she went down that police station, they'd never have found any of 'em, if I hadn't got it off her, 'cause she'd never have said a word. She can just shut herself off, and you can carry on for evermore.' He insisted to Ogden: 'Rose is the only person who knows the names of the people, what went on, what it was, what she was getting these girls for, and everything.' But West also told his solicitor that he still thought 'the world of Rose', even though 'these things have happened'.

Then, on Thursday 30 June, in the midst of his interviews with Ogden, Frederick West was briefly reunited with his wife, in the dock at Gloucester magistrates' court. It was their first appearance together. He was charged with eleven counts of murder, she with nine, as well as other sexual offences.

In the dock West made every effort to touch Rosemary West, to establish some form of contact with her. At one point he even stretched over to stroke the nape of her neck, and whispered in her ear, but she stared straight ahead, no longer the woman who had hugged him so enthusiastically just one year earlier as the child-abuse case had collapsed. Now she seemed to shrink back from him, playing her role as his innocent partner, trapped by his evil ways, to its own perfection. West looked crestfallen. It was not what he had expected. The possibility that he might now be isolated from the woman he loved, who might even go free, began to consume him.

The police seized the opportunity of West's return to Gloucester to arrest him for the murder of Ann McFall. Over the next three days he was questioned repeatedly about the disappearance of the Scottish girl who had become his nanny, and then become pregnant by him. And throughout he maintained his innocence. 'I don't know what happened to Ann,' he told the police. 'All I know, I thought the world of her, look . . . No way would I have anybody touch her.' Nevertheless, shortly after seven o'clock on the evening of Sunday 3 July, West was charged with her murder.

It was in the wake of that final charge that West began work on his memoir of the Scottish girl. It was almost certainly the only way he could find to convince himself that he had not killed her, an attempt to deny what may have been – for him – the one significant killing in his career, the one death which, in retrospect, he may have regretted. Shortly after he returned to Winson Green prison, he began to write, and to tell his solicitor again, that his first wife Rena was responsible, although he also told Ogden: 'I don't think Rena would have done it absolutely deliberate. I think she was so drugged out of her brains and everything else, drink and everything else, that she stabbed Ann.' They were West's own lies, devised for himself, his flimsy protection against the evil of his own actions.

By the middle of July West had decided that he had to 'tell the truth'. 'If I'm to have any chance in this case at all,' he confided to Ogden in an interview, 'I gotta go back to the police and tell the truth. I know exactly what the truth is . . . What was killing it before was that I wasn't prepared to admit knowing about Ann.' West's private despair at his wife's coldness then came tumbling out, as he blamed her and her father for the deaths in Cromwell Street. 'Why should I take the rap?' he demanded suddenly. 'Rose broke every promise she made to me.'

Frederick West then proceeded to admit, for the first time, the depraved sexual element in the killings, adding, 'I don't know if the girls were cut up at Cromwell Street, or somewhere else'. West suspected, he told his solicitor, that it was 'somewhere else', and he denied flatly that he had ever buried anyone at his house. 'I didn't know anything about any of the girls in Cromwell Street.' Minutes afterwards he contradicted himself completely, explaining: 'All the girls I got on great with. But there was never any sexual relationship with them . . . I used to talk fucking dirty to them and they'd talk dirty back.'

But he insisted that he had never even met Lucy Partington or 'the Dutch girl', suggesting that 'Rose's father' must have picked them up on his way home.

In the past Frederick West had never told the police that his wife played any part in the killing of his daughter Heather, beyond once dropping the remark: 'I ain't in this on me own, you know.' Throughout his police interviews, until he retracted every confession, he had stuck firmly to the story: 'Heather was sheer accident – her, you know, just happened at that moment . . . Heather just stood there with her hands in her pockets flipping her trousers like that and laughing at me . . . that was the end of everything.'

Now West transformed totally this version of events. In his interviews with Howard Ogden at Winson Green, he specifically blamed Rosemary West for Heather's murder, claiming that his wife had confessed to him on their last night together in Cromwell Street that she alone had been responsible. 'I didn't ask any details,' he said, because 'I didn't want to know what had happened. I thought the world of her. The main problem I've had,' West went on, anxious as always to cast himself in the most favourable light, 'is that I swore on the kids' lives that I wouldn't shop Rose for what she did.'

Rose always had this thing against Heather, that Heather smelled. She always used to say: 'You can smell that little bitch, that dirty bitch.' . . . Rose hated Heather, right from an early age . . . She didn't kill her on the spur of the moment, that's obvious, because she moved her out of the house. She did exactly the same with Stephen, after she attacked him, moved him out without me knowing.

But on the night before the police started to excavate their garden, Rosemary West had told him: ' "That thing's out in the garden." . . . I said: "What do you mean?" She said: "Heather, I killed her." '

Well, I must have sat there for ten minutes, absolutely shocked, gone. I couldn't even think. I couldn't speak. I couldn't think of a thing to say. Me mind had gone . . . I thought Rose was just going to say: 'I strangled her and buried her in the garden, fully clothed, dressed, everything.' Then she says: 'Oh, she's cut up. Her head's cut off.' I give a few deep breaths and said: 'What do you mean?' She said: 'I had to cut her up to get her back home in a dustbin . . . I brought her home in a pushchair.' That was the trolley she used for shopping.

This time West explained that Heather had left Cromwell Street with a girl 'with a red mini skirt on'. But 'What I didn't know was that Rose had offered Heather £600 to go away', but that Heather had rung him a week later 'because the money hadn't arrived'. In this version West claimed that it was only then that 'Heather was killed somewhere else'. In this version he insisted that it was his wife – and not he – who had been in contact with Heather after she left Cromwell Street, and that she had told him to tell the children, and anyone else who asked, that he had seen the sixteen-year-old regularly over the years. 'I just followed through what Rose told me,' he claimed.

Like so many of Frederick West's other versions of events this, too, was a tissue of lies. But it did contain some grains of truth. In particular, West maintained to Ogden that his daughter was a lesbian. 'Heather hated men. There was no doubt about that. She made it quite clear to me, she hated men near her. I had nothing against Heather being a lesbian, if that's what she chose to be,' he went on. 'She was floating between one and the other all the time, and I always said if you get a good man it'll settle you down . . . 'cause all Heather said when I picked her up from school was what knickers the teachers had on.' Significantly, West also told Ogden that he 'always suspected' that Heather West was not his child, 'and that Rose was already pregnant when she came to me at Lake House. That's why she was in such a hurry and that.'

These last assertions are significant. For there is no doubt that Frederick West excused himself from guilt about killing the sixteen-year-old both by telling himself that she was not his child in the first place, and at the same time consoling himself with the thought that it was 'a father's right' to sexually initiate his daughter. Taken together with his claim that his wife was responsible for Heather West's killing, they lead to the inescapable conclusion that he and his wife together attacked and murdered their first-born child on that wet June morning seven years before.

As July wore on, West became more and more voluble about his wife's sadistic sexuality and her rapacious appetite. 'It would be easier if people asked me who Rose didn't have sex with, not who she did. I mean, there were so many', explaining: 'This making love to her after every nigger. Load of fucking rubbish. I had less sex with Rose than anybody, because she was at it all day with different blokes, at it all night with different blokes. When I did join the queue . . . Rose provoked me all the time. If I'd attacked anybody it would have been Rose . . . It never stopped. It didn't stop at all.'

By the third week of July West's desperation was becoming ever more evident. 'I don't put in to see nobody,' he told Ogden. 'I don't want to see nobody. I've got nothing to say to nobody.' He did not know anything about the killings. He had made it all up to protect his wife, and now she had abandoned him.

All that was preoccupying West now was his new vision of his wife. 'All I am worried about is Rose getting out, because if Rose is out, Rose is gone, and they ain't gonna find her. What she thought is that they'd have left her at the house, and she'd have just vanished.' West was also convinced, he claimed, that she would kill again. 'She can't stop.'

Now West knew nothing about the dismemberment of the bodies, nothing about the abuse of his children, nothing about incest. 'You didn't put a bull to a calf that was his child and all that,' he told Ogden. 'To touch your own kids, your own daughters, it was disgusting.' West denied attacking Anne Marie, and maintained that the attack on his other daughter had been carried out by his wife with a vibrator. 'Rose tried to break her in. Got too close to me coming home. Walked out and left her there in disgust.' It was another tissue of lies, but in revealing the depths of his wife's depravity West was also revealing his own.

'Rose knows the answer to it all,' he told Ogden on 22 July. 'Even the police don't think I done it on me own.' Flatly denying that he knew anything at all about ritual killing – 'never had anything to do with it' – West went on to explain: 'There's no video of Rose touching a girl, for a simple bloody reason – 'cause Rose didn't want to show the bloody cruelty of what she was doing to these girls.' His wife kept a green hardback diary behind the meter box in which she kept a sheet of paper which marked where the girls were buried. 'Rose wanted it wrote down, she enjoyed this. Rose wrote everything down, always.' There was also, West insisted, an audiotape attached to the back of the dairy 'for her ears only'.

On Wednesday 27 July, the day before he was due to make his next court appearance with his wife, West gave Ogden his last interview, the fifteenth in the series that had begun ten weeks before. They discussed, as they had on many occasions, some of the witness statements made to the police during the case, and West told Ogden that he could not 'see anything in rape'. Nevertheless, he went on to confess: 'If a girl says no, the only thing I had out of it was more of a challenge to get her.' Then, quite suddenly, he paused in the middle of the interview and said: 'Fuck me, I should go to hell for what I've done.'

A few days after his court appearance on Thursday 28 July, Frederick West dispensed with the services of Howard Ogden as his solicitor and replaced him with the Bristol firm of Bobbetts Mackan. West had discovered that Ogden was offering the contents of their taped conversations for publication, and he was concerned that his confidences had been broken.

More important still, he had no wish for his rejection of his wife to reach her ears. No matter what he might have said in private, in a confidential conversation with his solicitor, including that he 'would give evidence against her', West did not wish to say so publicly. Part of him still hoped for a reconciliation; in part of Frederick West's mind, at least, his wife was still Jane Eyre.

Typically though, Rosemary West was not the only woman in Frederick West's thoughts. Janet Leach, the thirty-eight-year-old independent observer who had been present for eighty of his interviews with the police, had been almost the only woman – apart from Detective Constable Savage – with whom West had been in regular contact during his months in Gloucester police station. Though she had eventually been replaced as the 'appropriate adult', she had sat alone with West in his cell many times during his police interrogations. West had confessed to her that he was 'protecting' his wife, and 'that he would do anything' for her. 'They'd made a pact that he would take the blame for everything,' Leach recalled seventeen months afterwards. 'And Rose would never say anything.'

Janet Leach may have come closer to glimpsing the real nature of Frederick West than many other people. He had confessed to her that he 'wasn't very good at sex but that she was very demanding and he would do anything for her'; and Leach saw at first hand how upset West had become when his wife had been arrested and charged in April. 'He just said that the police were getting too close and they would find out that Rose was involved.' West admitted to her that the dead girls in the cellar of Cromwell Street were 'some of Rose's mistakes. It was all sexual. It wasn't meant to happen.' He had gone on to claim that his younger brother John had been involved 'a lot' in the abductions and murders – indeed that he and Rena West had killed Ann McFall, that there were 'another twenty' victims, including Mary Bastholm, whose remains were 'on the farm'.

After she had ceased to be the 'appropriate adult' during his interviews, on 7 May, Janet Leach had kept in touch with West by letter. 'Fred asked me to keep in touch – about the other bodies,' she would explain later. After his transfer to Winson Green prison, Leach went to visit every week. And as the months wore on he took to telephoning her three nights a week and 'sometimes every night'. Leach believed that West would confide in her. 'He said he would disclose to me where the other bodies were buried.' But he never did so.

In the absence of his wife, Frederick West had set about grooming Janet Leach exactly as he had groomed so many other women throughout his life. He carefully seduced her into his own world with his subtle mixture of confidences and flattery, making the mother of five feel that she alone understood him, and that she alone was capable of helping him. The strain of her involvement with him was to bring about a stroke a month after she stopped seeing him at Gloucester police station, but she had recovered sufficiently to start visiting him in Birmingham in July. 'I think he thought I reminded him of someone,' she was to remember. That is exactly what West told her, as he had told more than one other woman in the past – that she reminded him of Ann McFall.

West was steadily becoming more and more distressed. And on Monday 1 August, he was visited by Dr James McMasters, the Winson Green prison medical officer and psychiatrist. 'He said he felt his solicitor had manipulated him,' Dr McMasters was to recall more than a year later. 'He felt uncertain as to how he was going to cope with the court case,' and 'protested his innocence,' claiming that 'he had been telling lies to the police and not giving them full information about who he suspected was involved.' As the interview wore on, Dr McMasters watched West become 'calm and quite rational'. West had resumed his favourite trick of presenting a sane face to the world. Dr McMasters, who was to visit Frederick West thirty-nine times during the next five months, was to reach the conclusion that 'he was not mentally ill, and was not at risk of harming himself'.

That opinion was not shared by West's eldest son Stephen, who insisted later that he had 'told anybody that would listen that Dad was going to kill himself'. West may have been more honest with his son than with anyone. In the first weeks after his arrest, he had confessed to Stephen that he had killed all the victims, but warned him: 'When they start telling you that snuff movies are involved, don't believe them. It was not quite like that.' But West admitted to necrophilia, telling him: 'I only made love to them when I thought they were dead.' West never explained why he did it, claiming only: 'I've done it all.' As Stephen West was to write after his father's death: 'I believe that what he told me then was the truth.'

One other fact that was increasingly preying on Frederick West's mind was the deaths of many other young women. In mid-July, West had intimated to a prison officer and a probation officer that he had killed more than the dozen victims, more than the dozen for whose murder he was awaiting trial. He had hinted that there might be eight 'extra' girls, and had rambled on about his wife wrapping their bodies in white plastic mackintoshes. West suggested that although some were in Gloucester and Cheltenham, others were further afield, in places where he and his wife had been on holiday, including Snowdonia.

West told his son, too, that he had killed 'many' more young women, suggesting that he did indeed have a 'farm' twenty-five minutes' drive from Cromwell Street. He also hinted to others that he had killed while on trips away from Gloucester on his own. But he steadfastly refused to tell the police. West still liked to surround himself with secrets. 'There's only one person who's going to tell them about it, and that's me,' he told Stephen.

In Winson Green prison Stephen West watched his father gradually deteriorate. 'The second time I went to see Dad in prison,' the twenty-one-year-old was to write later, 'he told me bluntly: "If they take their eyes off me, I'll be gone." I told him he shouldn't do anything like that, but every time I went to see him he used to cry for the first twenty minutes.' In his son's mind, Frederick West had recognised that he would spend the rest of his life in prison, and could not face it, any more than he could face being separated from his wife and his house. 'I don't think he could accept that life as it was in Cromwell Street was over,' his son was to explain. 'He said he loved Rose and missed her.'

For four months Frederick West kept the worst of his growing depression at bay by devoting his time and energy to the task of completing his memoir of Ann McFall. *I Was Loved by an Angel*, this began, though he had given it no title. In the weeks after his fifty-third birthday in September he laboured to write out a fair copy in longhand, after painstakingly making a rough copy first. Over and over again West wrote: 'Our love, it was so true and faithful and would last for ever . . . The girls were my treasures, and now I had Anna. What a gold-mine. All I had to do was to get a house and love them. It was so easy . . . Anna and I had no secrets from each other.'

In the last months of his life Frederick West was gripped by the passionate desire to prove to himself and to the world that he could not have killed the one woman who had truly loved him, even though he had told his son that he had killed her 'because he loved her and couldn't have her'.

Now casting himself as a doomed lover in a romantic tragedy, West wrote that shortly after Ann McFall had discovered that she was pregnant with his child they had returned together to 'the same spot where Anna became pregnant'. 'Just then a shooting star went across the sky,' West wrote. 'I said to Anna: "Make a wish." Anna looked at me. Anna said: "I have no need to make a wish upon a star . . . I have you." ' Struggling to convey his sense of loss, he went on: 'Anna's hair and eyes shone in the moonlight. She was so beautiful and so in love with me and our baby, and I was so in love with them: both of them.'

West was re-inventing his alternative universe, re-drawing his internal mental map, in an effort to give himself some peace. And as Anna McFall's story began to draw to its close, so, too, did his life. On the final page of his memoir, West did not describe the young Scottish woman's death, however. Instead, he chose to conceal the truth once more, taking refuge again in romanticisation. He brought his 30,000-word manuscript towards its close with the words: 'Anna gave her life for me without thought for her own life. Her love was so strong for her baby and me. I have no idea how Anna died, but all I do know is Anna died loving me. And Anna knew that I loved her more than words can say.'

This, too, was another jumbled version of the truth. For Frederick West left another document with his memoir which hinted at yet another explanation of Ann McFall's death. 'The end of this story,' he wrote on a single sheet of lined paper from a prison exercise book, 'is in my heart. All I can say is, I never harmed Anna, and Anna gave her life for me to stop a man from making love to her . . . The man who killed Anna will live in hell on earth for a long time.'

In fact, it was Frederick West himself who wanted to escape that hell on earth. By the end of November the balance of his mind was wavering fatally. His description of the death of Ann McFall seemed to allow West to contemplate his own death, and he did so in a lengthy inner conversation with himself, some of which he jotted down.

In one fragment he explained to Janet Leach the reasons for his impending suicide. 'I have gone to Anna, Heather, Charmaine, Rena, Shirley and my two unborn children who never had a chance to see life or I to see them or hold them . . . I know how the families of the girls feel. I lost 5 in this tragedy.' He ended the note: 'I wish to thank Janet for all she did for me . . . Janet looked so much like Anna it was hard not to love her, but it was not right.'

But even though Janet Leach had become an important part of West's re-drawn world in Winson Green, she could never replace Rosemary West. On his wife's forty-first birthday in November 1994, West wrote to her, proclaimed his undying love for her. 'We will always be in love,' he told her. 'The most wonderful thing in my life is that I met you. How our love was special to us. So love, keep your promises to me. You know what they are.'

Then, after telling his wife that he wanted to be buried beside her, and asking 'Lay Heather by us, we loved Heather', West concluded: 'Well Rose, you will be Mrs West all over the world. That's wonderful for me and you. I have not got you a present, but all I have is my life. I will give it to you my darling. When you are ready, come to me. I will be waiting for you.' At the foot of the letter West had drawn a gravestone with the inscription: 'Fred West and Rose West. Rest in peace where no shadow falls. In perfect peace, he waits for Rose, his wife.' But the letter was never posted.

A fortnight later, on Monday 12 December, the day before his sixth court appearance alongside his wife, he wrote to her again: 'To

Rose, as in life and as in death, our love will never die. Rose and I will love for ever in heaven. I will wait for you darling so please come to me.' West ended his letter with the words: 'You know I love you only and you love me only. Well the world knows you are my wife and I am your husband, and always will be. You will become a widow. I love you darling, Fred West.' But that letter, too, went unposted. West was preserving in his mind a romantic image of his wife, an image that could never match the reality.

That became only too clear to West the following morning, Tuesday 13 December, when he saw Rosemary West for the last time. She stood alongside him in the dock at Gloucester magistrates' court, separated from him by two women prison officers. Stone-faced and looking straight at the bench, she ignored him, just as she had done on the five previous occasions. Rosemary West had even asked the officers to tell him that she did not wish to speak to him.

Frederick West kept stealing glances at her, as the details of the twelve charges of murder against him were read out to the court. She did not turn to smile, or even to acknowledge him. She had taken to the role that he himself had given her so completely that she now believed it. She was still the woman to whom he was 'inextricably knotted' by a string somewhere beneath his left rib, but now there was apparently no room for him.

Trapped in Cell 8 on D3 landing at Winson Green, West's whole purpose, his entire way of being, had been destroyed. There was no opportunity to 'shoot round' anywhere, no chance for 'a bit of fun', no opportunity to visit 'bunny land', no prospect of the poacher's life. Suicide offered an escape from an intolerable captivity, but it also offered what West saw as three other, more subtle attractions. It meant that he would take with him to his grave the details of his other victims and the sites of their graves; it would mean that no one would ever forget him. And, finally, it would offer his wife – so he believed – the chance to get off.

It was this thought, above all others, that convinced West to kill himself. He told his son Stephen so in the last month of his life. 'He was worried that he would never be with Mum again, and he said that he would give up his life for Mum so that she could live a normal life and be out.' It was the last gift that he could give the woman who had set out in their life together as the 'nanny' for his two children in a grubby caravan in Bishop's Cleeve. 'I'll give my life up,' West told his son, 'so she can have that.'

In the last days of December West confirmed it. He wrote a final note to his wife. 'To Rose. I loved you for ever. I made mistakes. I am so upset about you being in prison. Please keep your promise to me. I have kept mine.' The letter ended: 'I can't tell what I know. You are all free to go on with whatever you want to, but think of all I did for you all, and never complain. I love all of my children. They were all mine.' He signed it: 'All my love and kisses to you darling, Fred.'

Frederick West then set about planning his death with all the care he had taken in planning the deaths of so many innocent young women. And there would have been the same sly, ugly grin on his face as he did so. For suicide represented West's final victory over the world, proof that he was no 'ordinary domestic murderer', that he was far more than the smelly, flirty little man that the police had seen him as for so long. In his mind his death would ensure that he would for ever remain shrouded in mystery, a man who took his secrets to the grave, a man who may have killed many, many more women than even the darkest imagination could conceive. His suicide was designed to set him apart, to underline his celebrity. Death was not defeat for West, but the only sure guarantee of his perpetual notoriety. He did not intend to have that denied him.

On the morning of Sunday 1 January 1995 West woke in his small cream-painted cell in Winson Green, and, after washing in the corner sink, dressed in the prison issue clothing of brown jeans and a blue and white shirt. The clothes did not fit particularly well. He had lost weight in the seven months he had been in prison, and his hearing had deteriorated so much that he had been fitted with a hearing aid. After breakfast he was allowed out into the prison's exercise yard, where he took care, as he always did, to be polite to anyone he encountered. The shouts when he passed of 'Build us a patio, Fred' and 'Are the kids getting under your feet?' had diminished as the months had slipped by, but he still took care never to cause trouble, never to confront anyone.

Back in his cell, West wrote a brief note: 'To Rose West, Happy New Year darling. All my love Fred West. All my love for ever and ever.' In just four weeks' time they would have been married for twenty-three years. Then, shortly after eleven-thirty, he collected his 'special' meal of soup and pork chops and went back to his cell. West knew that he would be left alone for at least an hour to eat, but he did not do so. Instead he retrieved a seven-foot-long rope he had made himself, by sewing a prison blanket, then attached it to the severed handles of a prison laundry bag with needle and cotton, plaiting the strips into a cotton strand, a ligature that a poacher would have been proud of.

Balancing on the linen laundry bag, Frederick West then threaded the plaited cotton handles through the bars of the ventilation shaft directly above the door of his cell, tying it as tightly as he always did. Making a noose from the thicker rope, he slipped it over his head and around his neck, then kicked the bag silently away from beneath him. But West did not die at once, as he probably knew that he would not. Instead, he strangled himself 'for a minute or two', hanging just a few feet above the floor of his cramped cell. He had chosen to die, and he had chosen how he would die – in a bizarre if unconscious salute to the young women whom he had caused to suffer a similar fate.

Just before 1.05 p.m. a prison officer returned to Frederick West's cell but could not open the door. The dead weight of his body was holding it shut. When two officers finally managed to push the door open, and cut West down, there was no chance of reviving him. By the time the prison doctor on duty arrived at one-forty, there was nothing to do but pronounce him dead.

One of the letters left in his cell was to his daughter Anne Marie. It ended: 'When you read this remember me and bear me in your mind, and let the world say what they will. But speak of me as you found me.' West, once again, outwitted the law. On the wall of his cell he scratched his own proud epitaph. It read: 'Freddy, the mass murderer from Gloucester'.

West offered no atonement for his wickedness, no apology for the dreadful suffering and humiliation that he had brought on so many young women and their families. The man who had snuffed out the lives of the innocent killed himself not out of despair, or even out of desperation, but out of vanity, a desire to remain mysterious and always to be remembered.

In this, at least, he achieved success, for just as he had predicted to himself that it would, the news of his death made headlines. In the months and years to come, no one was likely to forget that Frederick West had killed himself on New Year's Day.

Chapter Twenty-five

The last gamble

'For behind the wooden wainscots of all the old houses in Gloucester, there were little mouse staircases and secret trapdoors; and the mice run from house to house through those long narrow passages; they can run all over the town without going into the streets.'

Beatrix Potter, *The Tailor of Gloucester*

In the last years of his life Frederick West kept his keys on a ring with a small tag. The tag bore a simple message: 'Heaven doesn't want me and Hell is afraid I'll take over.' And it was not a joke. It was the vainglorious remark of a man who took a terrible pride in his own evil. It is the clearest indication there could be that West killed for pleasure, and that he did so in full command of his senses.

Behind that obsequious little grin lay an intensely vain man who was convinced that he could do whatever he wanted, regardless of the cost in pain and suffering, regardless of the law, regardless of morality. West saw nothing wrong in soiling the world around him with his own lust, or in defacing the lives of vulnerable and naive young women whom fate threw into his path. He viewed such things as his right.

The stain of West's murderous vanity consumed his own family. It was there that the killing began. Lest anyone forget, his children's nanny and her unborn child, his first wife and her first child, the young woman who mistakenly thought she might become his third wife and her unborn child, and his eldest child by his second wife, all died at his hands. 'The ferocity of the assaults will tend to be greater for pre-existing relationships,' according to the criminal psychologist David Canter. This was certainly so in West's case.

West killed not only for pleasure. He also killed for convenience. If a young woman who fell into his hands threatened to cause him or his wife a problem, he killed her without hesitation – 'to sort it out'. Like the jobbing builder that he was, he then treated his victims as if they were no more than a piece of sewage pipe, there to be used and

334

buried. The girl had served her purpose. She deserved nothing more. Then, after his pure and protracted sadism, he killed as he lived – in haste. On such occasions the body was just another 'job' to be finished off as quickly as possible, before he nipped home, or back upstairs, for a mug of tea.

But whatever form his murderous activities took, he concealed them in the subtlest way – by donning the mask of the simple-minded ordinary man, anxious to help, never to be feared. He stealthily persuaded the professional social-workers, doctors, teachers and policemen who knew him that he could be ignored. 'Fred had the entire community eating out of his hand,' in the words of consultant child and adolescent psychiatrist Dr Eileen Vizard, FRCPsych. 'He had groomed every professional he had ever encountered into trusting him. There is a great deal of skill involved in that.'

For also present was an element of perverse sincerity, which cast a spell over almost everyone he met. It was a spell so strong that even his children have remained subject to it. When his first-born child, Anne Marie, was called to identify his body in the mortuary after his suicide on 1 January 1995, she trembled, and wrote later: 'He wasn't the dad I knew, the one who I remembered from my early childhood who used to ruffle my hair and tell me that he loved me.' Another daughter, Mae, wrote: 'I tried to hate him, but I don't think I can . . . I just forgave him. Despite everything I still loved him.' His eldest son Stephen added: 'When I looked at him lying there on a table at the Coroner's Court, I said a prayer in my mind. I just said how much I cared for him and how much I wanted to stick by him.'

Frederick West's youngest children see their father in this same light. Talking about him for the first time, Louise West remembered: 'He kissed me good night as any other father.' For her, 'he was just my dad and I loved him'. Aged eighteen in November 1996, she explains: 'His bad side was a bit extreme, as in what I know now from the press, not as how I knew him then. On his good side, he was good and nice because he was my dad. If he gave you anything you treasured it.'

The memory of her father that Louise West treasures most was 'the funny side'. He 'was rude and morbid, but always had a sense of humour', she recalls, with jokes that he 'used to kick in when you were beginning to think he was getting serious'. She does not recall ever feeling 'sad or depressed around him', remembering instead that he used to sing 'I Want to be Bobby's Girl', and used to 'take the piss out of people'. Most of all she recalled her father as a man who was 'always doing something'. 'When he was at work we were at school, and when we were at home he was always at work.'

In fact, Louise West remembers her childhood as 'very up and down. Dad wasn't around all the time. He had to go out late and earn money. He was the bread-winner, and therefore demanded respect. He was rather old-fashioned.' But she also acknowledges that 'things could change drastically at times, up and down, depending on the money situation'. The Wests 'signed her birthday cards together – although they were written by Mum'. Her parents argued, but even though 'they had fights, they got on. They argued like parents and they kissed like parents. They loved each other.'

West's daughter Rosemary, now fourteen and, like Louise, speaking for the first time about her family, also remembers 'some happy times and some bad', although she adds, 'but doesn't every family have bad times?' None of the Wests' youngest children see their parents only in a bad light. Even though West was not her natural father, Rosemary speaks of him as if he were and says, 'I felt my father loved me. He cuddled me, cared for me and looked after me.' Now, four years after being separated from him, she adds: 'I can remember his face and smile. When he gave me money for all of us to get some sweets down the shop.'

Coping with the knowledge of their father's crimes has not been easy for any of the Wests' five youngest children. Rosemary West, for example, accepts that she 'didn't really know my dad' when she thinks about it now. 'I thought I did, but no. I don't really know what to think. He was my dad, and what I knew of him was good. Then I hear what he had done, and I'm not so sure.' Nevertheless, the capacity for mercy and forgiveness among the Wests' youngest children is striking. 'I think my mum and dad did love each other,' Rosemary concludes. 'I suppose they had bad times as well.'

One of the team of residential social-workers who looked after the Wests' youngest children for two years after the Care Orders in 1992, and throughout the revelations of Cromwell Street, wrote afterwards: 'The children's fortitude and desire to be ordinary in the face of all that was happening in their lives was an inspiration to those who worked with them.' And this was in spite of the fact that 'we heard things and had to tell them things that no kids should ever have to hear, let alone experience'.

Another of the social-workers who dealt with the Wests after the 1992 case, and during their arrest in 1994, even pays tribute to the Wests as parents, saying: 'Despite the atrocities, Mr and Mrs West must have got certain aspects of child care and family life correct, as their younger children are charming, and remarkably normal on the surface, in spite of their experiences.'

The Wests' youngest child, Lucyanna, thirteen in July 1996, is clear proof of that. She remembers her childhood as a 'mixture of happy and unhappy times', although she is less sure whether Frederick West loved her. 'I wasn't his best daughter, like Rose or Tara. He didn't really show if he loved me, or I can't remember.' She, too, remembers her parents' arguments. 'I suppose they must have loved each other at least a little bit, but I'm not sure how much,' she adds, but concludes firmly: 'I think it is obvious he wasn't a good man.'

West's youngest children no longer live in Gloucester, or Gloucestershire, and have been given fresh identities to allow them to restart their lives away from the pressures surrounding their father's death and their mother's imprisonment. It is just as well, for even in death Frederick West was still bathed in the macabre.

In March 1995, shortly after his wife had been formally committed for trial on ten counts of murder – having been charged with the murder of her stepdaughter Charmaine in addition to the nine original charges – Frederick West's body was released for burial. And now two final twists took place in the story of his life.

At ten o'clock in the morning of Wednesday 29 March 1995, West was cremated at Cranley Crematorium in Coventry while a fist-fight raged between reporters and photographers from two rival news-papers. Only Stephen, Mae and Tara West were present to represent the family, although Anne Marie arrived some time after the service. Then, on Friday 3 November, on the very day that four extracts from their father's interviews with the police were played to the jury at their mother's trial, Stephen West decided to carry out his father's wishes and scatter his ashes on the graves of Walter and Daisy West in the churchyard at Much Marcle. In the early hours of the following morning, in an effort to avoid the attentions of the press, he set off with Anne Marie for the Herefordshire village where his father's life had begun.

There, in the still darkness of a winter's night, the final drama of West's life was played out between two of his children. On the way to Much Marcle, Anne Marie told her stepbrother to stop the car, she then grabbed the urn containing her father's ashes from the back seat and ran off into the darkness. (She later claimed that she wanted to pour her father's ashes into the same urn that contained the ashes of her mother Rena and stepsister Charmaine.) Stephen West gave chase, and tried unsuccessfully to locate her in the darkness. Finally, he called the police, and a police helicopter found his stepsister in the countryside. His father's ashes were returned to him, and once again he set off with his stepsister for Much Marcle churchyard. On the way, she seized the urn for a second time and once more disappeared into the darkness. But this time she did not return. Stephen West wrote later: 'She said she's got this little room in the house with a low-wattage bulb and she's got the ashes in a corner with other memorabilia.'

Secrets at the dead of night, mysteries to fog the imagination – even in death they were still the stuff of Frederick West's life. He had taken with him to his grave the secrets of the deaths of so many young women. One of the most disquieting was the fifteen-year-old waitress Mary Bastholm, who went missing at the beginning of 1968. Throughout his initial police interviews West insisted, 'I have never known the girl, never spoke to the girl in me life', even though there is considerable evidence that not only was she an acquaintance of Ann McFall, who used to spend time with her at the Pop-In café in Gloucester before her own disappearance in 1967, but she was repeatedly seen with West himself. 'I'm telling you straight, there ain't no messing, I never knew Mary,' he continued to protest. It was a tooth that he did not intend to have pulled by the team of investigating officers until he was good and ready.

In the last months of his life the knowledge that there were other

337

crimes that he might or might not admit to having committed bolstered his sense of power and self-importance, sustaining him through the painful process of writing his memoir of Ann McFall. There was always a strain of pride in his voice when he told the police: 'I'm not in a counting match . . . To try and get as many as I can.' It was one of the last controls West had. In fact, as his son Stephen puts it, West knew and the police knew 'there are more bodies, a lot more', but 'no one knows exactly how many'. One reason for his silence was, of course, his relationship with his wife. But that had become less straightforward since the 1992 abuse case.

The case itself was an 'unpleasant, but rather typical child-abuse case', in the words of one of the social-workers directly involved. They had certainly 'encountered far worse cases'. At the outset the Wests' reactions 'were not unusual from other cases in that they completely denied the allegations'. They took care to cast themselves as they always had, as ordinary, straightforward, working people, and the united and unthreatening front they had presented so successfully for more than twenty years still carried conviction.

Neither Frederick nor Rosemary West struck the social-workers as 'at all challenging', and neither 'sought to seriously challenge the care proceedings'. Their attitude depended on the circumstances. They were 'always respectful, even timid in the face of the court' – though the social-workers now recognise that they had no compunction about breaching the 'no contact' order and seeing their children. The Wests, say the social-workers, were 'very skilled at controlling, even manipulating the situation' by portraying themselves as 'vulnerable, timid individuals who were being bullied by the Social Services'. One social-worker remembered afterwards this even went 'to the extent that you could feel sorry for them (if the abuse was put to one side)'.

Frederick West took care to treat every figure in authority (or who appeared to be in authority) with an exaggerated subservience. 'Anyone wearing a suit was greeted with overwhelming respect', in the words of one social-worker, although there were rare occasions when his dark side surfaced. On the day in December 1992 when the final Care Orders were granted in respect of their five youngest children, he walked up to one of the two female social-workers and stood very close to her, looking her straight in the eye. He congratulated her on gaining the Order – and the children – but he did it in such a way that 'it was difficult to determine if he was being sarcastic or threatening'.

On another occasion during the proceedings he said of one of the female social-workers: 'I have never seen such an evil person; she is divorced with no children and possibly a man-hater.' Looking back, the social-workers accept that he was 'astute at identifying those professionals whom he could manipulate and those he could not'. Indeed, they recall one meeting where he confronted both a male and female worker, and although the man asked all the questions,

'Mr West never took his eyes off and directed all his answers to the female'. If he chose to do so, he could make any social-worker feel uncomfortable – 'which was not the case with Mrs West'.

It was Frederick West who acted as the spokesperson for the couple, but although he always appeared to be in control of the relationship, the social-workers suspected that, beneath the surface, 'Mrs West was perhaps a much more dominant, stronger character than she appeared to be'. But they recognise that it was West who drove the relationship, he who had ensured that their abuse would never surface, he who had orchestrated their lives. They now insist: 'Anyone with the cunning and adroit character of Fred West could operate in the modern era undetected.'

Throughout the 1992 case the Wests were at pains to present a united front. The social-workers dealing with their case cannot remember a single occasion when they did not appear together, 'being as one in all respects', and embracing in the dock when the case against them collapsed in June 1993. But in the aftermath of the case strains began to appear in the Wests' relationship.

Frederick West had always treated each of his children as though they were his possessions, and decided that if he could not see them without being supervised by someone from the local authority, he did not want to see them at all. Rosemary West, by contrast, was anxious to keep in contact with her children, no matter what conditions might be imposed by the Social Services Department responsible for them. But, as always, she bowed to her husband's wishes and agreed not to see them at all. It was the first true breach in the intricate tapestry of shared lust and desire that had bound husband and wife together for two decades.

Their daughter Mae insists now that her mother, in the wake of the case, even contemplated leaving her father. 'She went upstairs and packed one day after he came home, but he crept upstairs to listen outside the door – as he always did – and persuaded her not to.' West had not lost his ultimate control over his wife. Indeed, he would not finally do so until she was removed from his care entirely by his imprisonment after their last night together in February 1994.

From that moment onwards Frederick West, the man who liked to be called 'Fox' – ''cause no one can ever work me out' – accepted his fate, and accepted it completely. Throughout the hours of police interrogations, he never once incriminated the woman whom he insisted 'would not harm anybody . . . I mean, Rose didn't have a violent nature at all'. Even when he privately retracted his initial confessions, telling Howard Ogden that she had been responsible, he then changed his mind again, wrapping himself once more in his own inner narrative of their love-story. 'I was so locked up in Rose, for what reason I still don't know,' he told the police; 'we were mentally locked into each other in a big way . . . And we still are at this moment.'

Frederick West's calculation had been that his suicide would ensure his wife's release. Rosemary West seized upon the idea and did everything in her power to convince the world that this was true. His suicide was his last bit of 'sorting out', his last gift. And when she reached her trial for murder at Winchester Crown Court on Tuesday 3 October 1995, part of her was still convinced that his plan to save her would work.

Sixteen days after her trial began, when she gave evidence in her own defence from the witness-box, in which she denied meeting many of the innocent young women who met their deaths at her hands, she was still clinging to that conviction. She had not budged four days later, when the jury heard her husband's tape-recorded confessions to the police, all of which specifically excluded her. In her mind, she believed the confessions meant that there had to be 'a shadow of doubt in the jury's mind', a doubt that would ensure her acquittal. In fact, it was her, and her husband's, last miscalculation.

Ironically, Rosemary West was betrayed by another woman. The doubt on which she and her husband depended was cast from the jury's mind, in part at least, by the last woman to play a significant role in Frederick West's life – Janet Leach, the 'appropriate adult' during eighty of his police interviews. It was her evidence, suggesting that there had been a pact between the Wests, a plan that he should take the blame, which finally convinced the jury that Rosemary had been involved in the killings. West's fascination with women, his inability to resist the possibility of a seduction, even when he was in prison and charged with murder, tipped the scales. In that sense Rosemary West was convicted by reason of Frederick West's own lust.

At Winchester Crown Court on the afternoon of Tuesday 21 November 1995, the jury of seven men and four women (one juror having been stood down during the trial) reached unanimous verdicts that Rosemary West had killed her first-born child Heather, her husband's stepdaughter Charmaine, and Shirley Robinson. Shortly before lunch on the following day they announced precisely the same verdicts on her guilt in the cases of the seven other young women whose dismembered and mutilated bodies had been recovered from her small semi-detached Edwardian villa in Cromwell Street. Common sense, in the jury's opinion, dictated that 'she must have known'. The trial judge, the Honourable Mr Justice Mantell, sentencing her to ten life sentences, concluded with the words: 'If attention is paid to what I think, you will never be released.'

Four months later, on Tuesday 19 March 1996, the Court of Appeal in London agreed with the jury's decision, and refused Rosemary West's application to appeal against her verdict. The Lord Chief Justice, Lord Taylor of Gosforth, Mr Justice Mitchell and Mr Justice Newman concluded their formal judgement, delivered less than a fortnight later, with the words: 'The applicant and Fred were in the habit of sexually and sadistically abusing young girls in the cellar of their house for their joint pleasure.' They ended: 'The jury had the advantage of hearing and seeing the applicant give evidence and be cross-examined. Clearly they rejected her evidence. We fully understand their doing so. The concept of all these murders and burials taking place at the applicant's home and concurrently grave sexual abuse of other young girls being committed by both husband and wife together, without the latter being party to the killings is, in our view, clearly one the jury were entitled to reject. The evidence in its totality was overwhelming.'

Chapter Twenty-six

An ideal husband

'The imagination of man's heart is evil from his youth.'

Genesis, viii, 21

To examine evil is neither to excuse it nor to condone it. To turn away from the dark realities of life simply because they may be uncomfortable is to hide from the world. Worse still, it is to risk allowing evil to run unchecked. If we are to understand ourselves, we must understand every element of human life, good or bad, sublime or vile, no matter how foul some of those elements may be. To confront the actions of a man who rejected the moral conventions of the 'normal' world can help to throw light on the darkest corners of the human psyche. It can also help us to draw a little closer to answering a question that has always haunted the world: where does evil begin?

What is to be made of the life of the late Frederick Walter Stephen West? Was he an irredeemably evil man who tainted all around him? Was he one of the most extraordinary murderers to have surfaced in Britain in the twentieth century? How do his crimes compare with those of other murderers? What parts do his genetic background, his upbringing and his personality play in helping to explain his heinous actions? Does he prove that there is an element of evil inherent in mankind? What does West's relationship with his wife tell us about his world? Indeed, would she now stand condemned to a lifetime's imprisonment had she not encountered him? And, finally, does the life of Frederick West have anything to say about the nature of British society in the last years of the millennium?

Frederick West once told the police with a slight smile and without a shadow of irony in his voice: 'Nobody went through hell. Enjoyment turned to disaster. That's what happened on all of it . . . well, most of it anyway.' That remark alone confirms one truth about him. He *was* one of the most extraordinary of murderers: a killing machine without an ounce of contrition or regret. He violated every accepted rule of human conduct. He showed no conscience about causing unimaginable pain and suffering to his victims before killing them. And he killed repeatedly for no reason beyond a desire for pleasure and amusement, and to evoke that same pleasure and amusement in his wife. There is a moral depravity to his crimes that cannot be described by any other word than evil.

As Richard Ferguson QC, Rosemary West's defence counsel, declared at her trial, Frederick West was 'a man devoid of compassion, consumed with sexual lust, a sadistic killer, someone who had opted out of the human race and, you may think, someone who was the very epitome of evil'. The world will never know for certain how many women met their deaths at his hands, but the number is certainly far more than a dozen, and indeed could well be five times that number. For West killed with a terrible regularity – three girls a year in the early 1970s – and if he continued that carnage over the succeeding two decades then the figure of sixty victims becomes all too possible.

Frederick West was not mad. His was no world of strange imaginings, of voices that whispered to him in the night, or visions that sprang up to haunt his every waking moment. He was a voyeur and possibly a sexual inadequate, but he was neither schizophrenic nor paranoid. Hard though it may be for some to accept, he lived in the everyday world, on the surface at least, a competent, even balanced member of society. Indeed, in a rare display of emotion, he once told the police angrily: 'What do you want fantasy for? I don't believe in fantasy worlds. I live in this world.' Four months later he was to tell his solicitor: 'I don't know nothing about bloody serial killers. I didn't read fucking murder stories.' In his perverted but still rational vocabulary, he was doing his victims 'a favour' by subjecting them to sexual bondage, ''cause it was what they wanted'. In fact, it was not what they wanted but what he wanted that was the motive behind his actions, and what he wanted was a sense of their terror.

As the American writer Clancy Sigal has put it in another context, to inflict pain can bring the perpetrator 'a fiery incandescence, an existential flowering', and this, though he could never have expressed it, was West's aim.

West was well aware of the celebrity his murders would bring him in the last decade of the century. He told his eldest children to 'make what they can' out of his life, just as he urged Janet Leach to write his story. Notoriety became his passion. 'You'll always be Mrs West' in the eyes of the world, he wrote to his wife in the last days of his life. Once out of the way of committing further crimes, it was this desire to be remembered, never to be dismissed or forgotten, that became his ultimate objective.

But where did this, and the rest of West's motivation, spring from? Steve Jones, Galton Professor of Genetics at University College, London, among others, has drawn attention to the fact that some serial killers have carried the gene Dopamine D2 receptor A1, the now famous 'criminal gene'. Indeed, the convicted American murderer Stephen Mobley, now on Death Row in the state of Georgia, has even launched a defence based on the fact that the gene may have given him an 'inherited predisposition to crime'. And it is entirely possible that West possessed the gene, although, tragically, no attempt was ever made to establish whether this was the case, either during his period of imprisonment or at the autopsy after his death.

In fact, as many as one in five of the world's population may carry this 'reward gene' which favours instant gratification. In Professor Jones's words, 'It is said to be frequent among cocaine addicts, among autistic children, and even in people with withdrawn personalities', although he cautions, 'Most geneticists question whether a single gene could have such diverse effects', adding, 'With the new genetics, it is becoming easier to blame all bad conduct on DNA. Acts once thought of as the result of poor upbringing are more and more ascribed to inborn weakness.'

In Holland a team led by Professor Hans Brunner has also identified a gene defect which may increase aggressiveness among those who have inherited it. The defect to the gene responsible for the enzyme monoamine oxidase-A has also been demonstrated by scientists in France and the United States as encouraging aggression. But once again, no research was undertaken to discover whether this defect was present in the make-up of Frederick West.

Genetics is by no means the only scientific discipline to suggest that part of the motivation for criminal behaviour may lie within the chemistry of the human body. Adrian Raine, a British psychology professor, among others, has pointed out that the lack of 'inhibition' in the frontal lobe of the brain can create a predisposition to criminal behaviour. That could be brought about by a severe bang on the head as a young man, like the one West suffered in a motor-cycle accident at the age of seventeen. It can alter the chemical balance in the brain in such a way that the individual finds difficulty in restraining his aggressive instincts.

But an aberrant or defective gene, or a severe blow to the head, are not enough in themselves to explain the actions of a man who took an intense and gratuitous pleasure in torture, mutilation and death. Professor Sir Michael Rutter, Britain's leading child psychiatrist, has concluded: 'Genes do not lead people directly to commit criminal acts. There may be a propensity to aggression or anti-social behaviour, but whether or not the individual actually commits some criminal act will also be dependent on environmental facts.'

The Commission on Children and Violence, which was set up in the wake of the murder of two-year-old James Bulger in Liverpool in 1993, supported the view that environment was more important than genetics in turning a child to crime. 'That an individual child becomes violent is never inevitable,' the report concluded. 'Families can and often do provide the security and love necessary to protect children – even high-risk children – from becoming violent.'

So did Frederick West's childhood and early upbringing precipitate his later crimes? They offered no security or love to protect him:

344

quite the reverse. They offered him an example of incest and violence that was to remain part of his character throughout the fifty-three years of his life. The point is not simply that he may have been seduced by his mother Daisy at the age of twelve. His father, too, played a significant, indeed probably central role. In the words of Dr Eileen Vizard, discussing the case in detail for the first time: 'In families like the Wests, with such a strong history of abuse, it is very likely that parents or carers have been involved in abusing.'

West learned the facts of child abuse at Moorcourt Cottage, just as he learned how to cut a pig's throat or steal a pheasant. And that in turn led him to 'identify with his aggressors', as Dr Vizard puts it, thereby adding this unconscious motivation to his own, often repeated determination to 'set myself up like my father'. 'You see it in concentration camps, and conditions of terrible savagery,' Dr Vizard explains. 'For the purposes of self-protection the victim starts to idealise the abuser.'

Walter and Daisy West shaped Frederick West's life. He persuaded his son that what they were doing was right, and, worse still, that he was 'enjoying it', and was therefore 'just as bad'. 'In cases like this that's where the moral corruption comes in,' Dr Vizard says, 'because the child hasn't got the brain power, the capacity, to say, "Oh no, you're a bigger person, you should know better." ' In her view 'The abuser scrambles the brains and the thinking processes of children. If you have someone telling you that black is white, that the pain you are feeling is good, and the person in charge of you is saying, "No, that actually means you love it, and anyway you must love it otherwise you wouldn't have let me do it", it is almost impossible to resist. To a child of five or six that is insurmountable logic, and therefore taken inside their heads as the way people think.'

Once established, the cycle of incest repeats itself. So it did in the case of Frederick West. The stain of child abuse ran through his life like a dark river, leading him inevitably to seek it out in his wife. Indeed, Dr Vizard sees the genesis of their relationship in sexual abuse. Rosemary West, too, was the daughter of a dominant and abusive father, a man whose actions she also idealised. 'It is very likely that Rose would have had in her head a working model of a man like that,' Dr Vizard maintains. ' Rose stood out a mile to Frederick West because of her own vulnerability.'

Dr Vizard believes that 'it is likely that when they met, Rosemary West was already corrupted'. West sensed that, and seized on it. She would have taken no persuading, seeing in West the pattern of her father. She 'would have been easily sexually aroused', according to Dr Vizard, 'for that is one of the paradoxes of sexual abuse'. Rosemary West 'like many incest victims probably couldn't think clearly for herself, and was ready to be taken further'.

West's 'first step (like all abusers) would have been to try the big romantic number, to try and impress her. She's a very vulnerable girl. She feels flattered by the attentions of this vivacious jack the lad,' Dr Vizard explains. 'She may have been the classic incest victim.

345

She may have had low self-esteem, and learning difficulties. And very soon after she had been swept off her feet, West may have introduced her to more perverse sexual practices, as an exciting thing to do. It may not have been long before he tried out the bondage and the sado-masochist side of things.'

In that respect Rosemary West was one of her husband's earliest victims. 'Had she fallen in with a non-abuser, I would not have thought she would have ended up killing, but I would have thought she would have ended up an absolutely hopeless, violent mother because I think she has obviously got major impulse control problems.'

What may have moved her on from remaining a victim, Dr Vizard suggests, based on her experience of many other cases of serious abuse, may have been her experiences with her father, and her 'identification with the violence and excitement of her father's behaviour', even though 'she does not even know that she identifies with aggressors in this way'. It was Frederick West who first recognised this and capitalised on it. 'He picked out within her this cruel sadistic streak, this identification with the aggressor, and he shaped it.'

In Dr Vizard's opinion, West may have selected his second wife carefully, and rapidly proceeded 'to sexualise her'. Her clinical experience with abusers suggests that Rosemary West would have been expected 'to produce babies for abuse', and would herself 'have become so excited and aroused by the prospect of having a child in her power that the whole process of child rearing was sexualised.' The possibility that she might also have a young woman, no older than herself, within her power to abuse sexually may also have increased the 'crescendo of excitement, after which she feels able and justified, and strong enough, to kill'. Dr Vizard maintains:

> Once you link up serious sadistic physical violence with sexual excitement it's a heady combination. It's often rehearsed through masturbation and fantasies, and you can't reverse it once you've started. By the time sadistic abuse had got under way, the level of sexual arousal and bloodlust was so high that I do not believe that self-control was on the agenda.

The fact that Ann McFall refused to go down the same path as Rosemary West led West to kill her and to replace her soon afterwards with a young woman who did not threaten to leave him, or disagree with him. His own success then led to the sixteen-year-old Rosemary Letts rapidly ceasing to be his 'apprentice', becoming instead his partner in every sense. 'It seems likely that Rosemary West was inducted into a partnership quite quickly,' Dr Vizard concludes. She is convinced 'West was a master abuser'.

But child abuse, though part of Frederick West's motivation, cannot be its excuse. While child abuse is an ever-increasing fact of British life, now estimated to afflict one family in every twelve, not every abused child goes on to kill.

'Anger with himself and the fates that have led him to his desolate situation' is another theme of 'such men's stories', according to David Canter, Professor of Investigative Psychology at Liverpool University, and one of Britain's principal criminal psychologists. According to Canter, West and other killers like him see their victims as 'vehicles' for their desires, who cast themselves 'in the role of tragic hero, living out in their assaults the sense of power and freedom that they feel is absent in the other stories they are forced to live'.

'Their ability to express themselves and to make contact with women is at the heart of their crimes,' Professor Canter writes in his study *Criminal Shadows*. 'These are offenders whose native intelligence and life opportunities have enabled them to learn how to present a sociable face to the world.' They know what 'the story of human relationships ought to be, but this always appears to be a part they play, not a role with which they are at one. They can recognise what empathy may mean but they never feel it.' Canter is convinced that 'these are the criminals who come nearest to exhibiting pure evil'.

Canter sees men like West as 'sane but remorseless' who have 'never fully developed the capacity to see the world as others do', and therefore 'feel no blame or guilt' for the consequences of their actions. For these men, he goes on: 'The locations they choose as central to their drama will be far from arbitrary and go beyond opportunism. These locations will carry some meaning, a special significance for the offender.' Killers like West, who see their victims as vehicles for their emotions, will have more social contact with them, but 'it will be an interaction in which the victim has to be harnessed to the offender's will. It is not enough for them just to be used; they must be exploited.' Professor Canter concludes: 'Their lives are littered with people who thought that it was possible to share their feelings, only to find themselves used and abused.' There could hardly be a more precise description of West's friendships.

One person alone who shared his life threw off the shackles and became mistress of her own fate – Rosemary West. She became his partner in the fullest sense, first led into and then in turn participating in his sadistic crimes, until she became almost his mirror image. Each spurred the other on, each anxious to excite and control the other, each prepared to go to any lengths to do so. West may have started as the engine of their relationship, urging the young Rosemary Letts to explore ever more dangerous depravities, but she steadily became a creative, imaginative force within it, the woman whom he came to treasure above any other – the only person who 'fully understood' him. His sexual lust was fired and inspired by hers, both ever more determined to go to greater and greater lengths to satisfy their addiction. And, as they did so, so their crimes grew ever more terrible.

'Rose became a heroine to him,' Professor Canter explains. 'They exploited each other, although I don't believe that they knew what

347

love truly meant. I don't think there was any genuine feeling between them, only their distorted version of the emotion, although that will have its own force.' Cromwell Street was the Wests' 'other world', and 'West may even have felt he was giving the girls who became his victims a form of love and care – representing his confused understanding of what love and care were'. Canter believes:

> The murders may have occurred out of rage, or to hide a guilty secret, or to keep control of them in some way, or for some banal reason, like he wanted to 'sort it out', but they were not solely lustful. They arose out of a determination to control, or coerce, but they were also part of his disorganisation. 'Sorting out' is such a benign phrase that it made the weird world he had created for himself seem acceptable. In his terminology, 'sorting out' is the equivalent of ethnic cleansing.

Certainly, Professor Canter agrees with Dr Vizard that West's attitude 'partly derives from his experience of love as a child – and he passed that on to his children, giving them a confused understanding of what love is. Incestuous individuals think they have a right to discipline their children violently and to sexualise them. In West's case the incest takes place against the background of his mercurial emotions.' Canter explains:

> He was re-interpreting the world to allow himself the role of paterfamilias, and in doing so he became, in many ways, the 'ideal husband'. He did all the work, looked after everyone, and kept the family together. He may even have felt what one psychologist had termed 'appropriate indignation' against his children and his victims – that they ought to allow him to do what he wants to them.

Frederick West's language and patterns of conversation convince Professor Canter that he was not at all mad. 'His speech is not schizoid, nor is it that of a psychopath. He creates stories on the hoof – even when he cannot truly remember the details – and then tells himself to remember the ones that he thinks work. The direct speech he so often uses was designed to give what he says credibility, and he was well aware of that. His charm, that sort of wide-eyed innocence, was quite deliberate, a technique like the television detective Columbo. He was an expert con-man.'

West's verbal ability was vital to his success over so many years. The neuro-linguistic programming (NLP) consultant Jane Mathison believes that West depended on the 'hypnotic language patterns'. An approach to understanding how human beings process information, which was pioneered in California in the 1970s, NLP seeks to establish how 'the inner worlds' of its subjects work. Mathison believes that West's language 'is the art of seduction and persuasion, painting vivid portraits in words, evoking sounds and smells, bringing a sense of movement, all of which helps to draw the listener into his world'.

It was a verbal skill that almost certainly helped West to persuade so many young women to place their trust in him, just as it managed to convince so many people in authority that there was no need to take him seriously. He could control the pace and rhythm of a conversation in a way that was 'literally seductive', in Jane Mathison's opinion. Mathison explains:

West used a whole range of hypnotic tricks in the way he spoke. He uses his voice very much as a hypnotist uses his. He used words that a hypnotist uses. He asked rhetorical questions, started sentences which went on for ever, repeated himself carefully, employed abstractions like 'I'm wondering', all as a means to allow him to entrance the person he was talking to.

Both for his victims and for the police interviewing him West wove a spell with words, according to Mathison. The women who came into contact with him probably 'never doubted that he was in control, because he threw a net over the relationship with words'. She suggests that he was careful to 'elicit non-verbal cues of agreement' from those he came across, often by using the word 'see?' in his sentences. Both conclusions underline that West was a great deal more acute in his understanding, and in his use of language, than he may have appeared.

He even managed to use language to help him avoid a sense of guilt for his actions. Mathison, like Professor Canter, suggests that West deliberately employed benign phrases – like 'helping out' or 'sorting out' – to make his behaviour acceptable to himself and to those around him. Both see it as no accident that West should use such common or garden phrases, and both draw parallels with the Mafia's 'offer he cannot refuse', Hitler's 'final solution' and the 'surgical strike' of modern weapons technology as phrases that can make 'the unthinkable palatable'.

Dr Bryan Tully, a clinical and forensic psychologist who regularly gives expert evidence in criminal cases, maintains that some criminals, including confidence tricksters – 'and perhaps West too' – live in a 'linguistic world where speech is almost more important than reality'. For West: 'It is as if he is tuning in to his own commentary on himself.' Dr Tully explains:

One of the things that seems to be quite common among serial killers in the States is that they are engaged in a very rich imaginative world. They are having conversations with themselves. The victim may come into it, but really that's almost accidental. So if they do something dreadful to someone, it's really no more than an extension of the imagination, and it does not require them to have any feelings.

One American serial killer who could be compared to West is John

Wayne Gacy, who was arrested in 1978 after police recovered a dead body from underneath his cellar floor. By the time their excavation was completed they had unearthed a total of twenty-seven bodies, most of them from under the house, although Gacy also buried some in the yard of his house and others in the river. He was finally charged with the murder of thirty-three young men, and the police believe the killings began in 1972. Gacy managed a Kentucky Fried Chicken restaurant, and spent a great deal of his spare time entertaining at children's parties dressed as Pogo the Clown. When he was first arrested he confessed to the killings, then retracted, then claimed that he killed the first victim in 'self-defence'. Gacy never apologised for his actions. But he was, the police reported after his execution in 1992, 'extremely popular' and 'chatty' with his prison guards.

Dr Tully suggests that West 'operated in the present brilliantly', which meant that he did not have any remorse, 'because for remorse you have to have some emotional attachment to what you think you are, or the way things ought to be, and then be aware of your departure from that'. West's mind did not work in that way: 'And if you don't have that, killing is just a practical issue.'

This psychological approach contradicts the lurid 'Dr Jekyll and Mr Hyde' theories about West, which demonise him as a serial killer and suggest that he must have been mentally unbalanced to commit such appalling crimes. But, like the theories about his genes and his upbringing, it does not and cannot excuse him. This psychological analysis is helpful, but it alone is not the answer. There remains something intrinsically evil, a quality of depravity, which no psychological explanation can eradicate.

John Douglas, who worked for the Federal Bureau of Investigation for twenty years, specialising in hunting serial killers, and who became the prototype for the FBI agent in the thriller *The Silence of the Lambs*, believes that such people remain soulless, irredeemable villains. 'I have interviewed so many of them,' Douglas says, 'that I can see in their eyes how they can turn on you in a second. They can seem nice and friendly on the outside, but they're chameleons. They change at a moment's notice.'

Douglas was chief of the serial killer unit at the FBI Academy in Quantico, Virginia, which interviewed more than a hundred serial killers. He believes that one of the fundamental keys to understanding lies in their personality. Such a person 'is usually an inadequate nobody, but when he is killing he feels that for once in his life he can be in control'. Douglas also suggests that such criminals are often 'on the prowl', usually in a 'commercial van with few windows' and often take with them a 'kit' which includes 'duct tape' and handcuffs.

But what sets Frederick West apart from this pattern of serial killers is the involvement of his wife, although even here the current scientific research helps to shed some light. 'There are two classes of women in sadistic and violent crimes, the research shows,' Dr Bryan Tully explains. 'One group is very abused and disadvantaged. But the other, the ones who are involved in serial or multiple cases, are always involved with a man, and they have a very powerful relationship. In that respect Rose fits what has become a clear pattern in the English-speaking world: she has been in partnership with a man with whom she has a very powerful relationship. But without the man it does not happen.'

Together, Frederick and Rosemary West were even more dangerous than West would have been alone. He would certainly have killed without her. He certainly killed Ann McFall before he knew her, just as he may have then set out to 'rebuild' that 'broken relationship', to use Professor Canter's phrase, thereby making it 'central to his personal mission'. West may even have continued to kill without his wife's help throughout their years together, burying the bodies of his sole victims in another site entirely, one that she may not have been aware of. But Rosemary West brought an extra ingredient to his killing, a violent imagination that would not have been present without her. She participated in his world with a devilish enthusiasm.

West worshipped his wife. Their amateur videos underline that clearly. As Professor Canter explains: 'They [the videos] were probably to create some kind of account of themselves, and therefore were very important. They created a reality for the Wests.' Rosemary became his most perfect creation, the woman who would do everything he asked, and whose appetites came to rival his own. He brought her victims as sacrificial offerings, just as she brought him young women to abuse. They heightened each other's sexual awareness and desire, and they did so consistently throughout their time together. Neither dominated the other totally; each contributed a particular element to the chemistry of their mutual love.

Only in the last few months of his life did Rosemary West turn against her husband, and she did so only after he had specifically told her that she should. In the last few months of his life West realised that he would never be reunited with his wife, and recognised that he would never survive in prison. As Dr Bryan Tully puts it: 'For a person like that, incarceration would be hard to manage. It's unbearable. You can't talk to the walls, you can't sort anything out.' Suicide was the only logical response, the only action that would bring his inner narrative, in which he figured as a doomed and tragic romantic hero, to a fitting and satisfying end.

Yet even these personal reasons are not enough to explain Frederick West completely. There is a cultural dimension to his life and crimes which also cannot be ignored. West lived and explored a world beyond the 'top-shelf' magazines of soft-core pornography. The magazines and videos that he obtained, or made, were extreme versions of the 'Readers' Letters' and 'Readers' Wives' familiar in every high street newsagent and video store. But West did not demonstrate embarrassment in this world; he revelled in it, and in doing so touched a nerve in the society in which he lived. He existed in a culture that is uncomfortable with its own sexuality, uncertain how to express it or channel it. And he instinctively exploited that uncertainty, channelling it into extreme violence.

Sexual experiment is one of the unspoken themes of contemporary Britain. It is nevertheless much practised in private. And there is a hypocrisy towards this sexual freedom which West revelled in. The contact magazines in which he and his wife used to find partners are available freely throughout Britain, just as familiar a part of British life as parties to sell underwear. Some of the respectable broadsheet newspapers, as well as the tabloids, regularly contain small ads for catalogues that offer the most elaborate range of sexual aids and harnesses, many of which offend the more reticent of their readers. West seized upon this unspoken theme, as well as the current fascination with bondage and sado-masochism, and through it satiated his most perverted desires. His crimes reveal the sexual decay that can lie beneath the apparently calm surface of a comfortable English county town.

Exactly half a century ago George Orwell suggested that the classic English murder was usually a 'domestic poisoning', in which, although 'sex was a powerful motive . . . the desire to gain a social position' or at least 'not to forfeit one's social position' was far more important. In his essay *The Decline of the English Murder*, he concluded that no other English killing 'would be so long remembered as the old domestic poisoning dramas, product of a stable society where the all-prevailing hypocrisy did at least ensure that crimes as serious as murder should have strong emotions behind them'.

Orwell contrasted the class basis of the English murder with the world of the 'false values of the American film', then epitomised by the so-called 'Cleft Chin Murder' committed by the eighteen-year-old English waitress Elizabeth Jones and her American boyfriend, the Army deserter Karl Hulten. 'The whole meaningless story,' he wrote, 'with its atmosphere of dance-halls, movie-palaces, cheap perfume, false names and stolen cars, belongs essentially to a war period.' West proves emphatically just how much English society has changed over the past fifty years, and English murder with it.

But one thing that has not changed is the abuse of children. That remains one of Britain's unspoken tragedies, a crime often cruelly concealed behind a mask of respectability – just as it was with West. To understand that is to understand something of his nature, and the genesis of his dreadful crimes.

The life of Frederick West poses an age-old question. Must the sins of the fathers continue to be visited upon their children? Or can we, by examining his case with intelligence and with charity, and then by acting with charity too, begin to help all abused children, including his own, to free themselves from the burden of their childhood?

None of this is to excuse West for one moment. There can be no excuse. The analysis of what may have lain behind his crimes is not to lessen their enormity, nor to diminish their horror. He was an evil man, bred by – and breeding – an evil love.

Epilogue

Gone to the devil

'When all the blandishments of life are gone
The coward sneaks away to death, the brave live on.'

Martial, *Epigrams*

The life of Frederick Walter Stephen West came officially to its end
on Friday 12 July 1996 in the unlikely Gothic splendour of the
Birmingham Victoria Law Courts, once the site of the city's assizes.
A jury of six men and three women, sitting before the Coroner Dr
Richard Whittington, formally decided – by a majority of eight to
one – that West had indeed killed himself just before one o'clock on
New Year's Day 1995, in his cell at Winson Green Prison.

Over two days, the jury had heard the 'infinite pains' West had
gone to in his determination to take his life. He had volunteered to
mend his fellow prisoners' shirts, thereby giving him access to a
needle and thread. He had secretly sewn a thick eighty-eight-inch
long rope from the hem of a green prison blanket and then
attached that rope to plaited loops made from the handles of the
laundry bags the shirts for repair had come in using his poacher's
knots.

The stealth West had brought to his life, he brought to his death.
Slipping the noose around his neck – moments after a prison officer
had glanced into his cell – he had not risked standing on a chair. The
noise of his kicking it away might have attracted attention – seen an
officer come to save his life. Instead, he had climbed on to the
laundry bag full of shirts, tied the thin white strips attached to his
thicker, sewn rope to a ventilation grille above his cell door, and
silently pushed the bag away from beneath his feet, leaving his body
suspended two feet above the floor of his cell.

In the words of the pathologist Dr Peter Acland, Frederick West
was 'dead almost instantaneously,' certainly 'within one or two
minutes,' the supply of blood and oxygen to his brain fatally cut off
causing cerebral anoxyia. He would have known exactly how long it
would take to die. He had seen so many innocent young people die.

And, as his son Stephen put it after the verdict, he knew 'how to cheat the law'.

Like a thief in the night, Frederick West stole away from life.

There was no suicide note, just a cardboard box on the small table in his cell containing a few papers. There was his memoir, jumbled with notes to himself, and letters – to Janet Leach, to his children and his grandchildren, and most important of all, to his wife Rosemary West.

'Our love will never die,' West had written, 'Rose and I will love for ever in heaven. I will wait for you darling. So please come to me.'

On another, meant for her forty-first birthday, West had written, 'I have not got you a present, but all I have is my life. I will give it to you my darling. When you are ready to come to me I will be waiting for you.'

At the foot of the letter to his wife he had drawn a simple gravestone. It bore the inscription: 'In loving memory Fred West, Rose West'. Underneath was printed in capital letters: 'Rest in peace where no shadow falls. In perfect peace he waits for Rose his wife.'

The life of Frederick West

29 September 1941 – Frederick West born in Much Marcle, Herefordshire.

14 April 1944 – Catherine 'Rena' Costello born in Coatbridge, Scotland.

8 April 1949 – Ann McFall born in Glasgow, Scotland.

29 November 1953 – Rosemary Pauline Letts born in Northam, Devon.

28 November 1958 – Frederick West has a serious motor-cycle accident.

9 November 1961 – Frederick West's trial for alleged incest halted at Hereford Assizes.

17 November 1962 – Frederick West marries Rena Costello at Ledbury Register Office, Herefordshire.

28 November 1962 – Frederick and Rena West move to Coatbridge, Scotland.

22 March 1963 – Charmaine Carol May West born in Coatbridge, Scotland to Rena West.

July 1963 – Frederick and Rena West move to Glasgow from Coatbridge.

6 July 1964 – Anna-Marie (later Anne Marie) West born to Frederick and Rena West in Glasgow.

July 1964 – William and Daisy Letts and their family move to Bishop's Cleeve, Gloucestershire.

December 1965 – Frederick West leaves Glasgow and returns to Much Marcle with Charmaine and Anna-Marie, but without Rena West.

December 1965 – Frederick West asks Hereford Social Services to take his two children into care.

February 1966 – Frederick and Rena West are re-united and move to The Willows caravan site, Sandhurst Lane, Gloucester. Their two children join them.

July 1966 – Charmaine and Anna-Marie West placed in care again.

August 1966 – Charmaine and Anna-Marie returned to the Wests at The Willows caravan site. Ann McFall is now living with Frederick and Rena West.

September 1966 – Frederick West and Ann McFall, together with Charmaine and Anna-Marie West, move to Watermead caravan site near Brockworth, Gloucester. Rena West is not with them.

March 1967 – The body of teenager Robin Holt is found hanged near The Willows caravan site.

July 1967 – Rena West returns to Gloucester and moves back in with her husband at Watermead caravan site. Ann McFall moves out, first to a friend's caravan on Watermead, then to a smaller caravan back at The Willows, Sandhurst Lane.

August 1967 – Ann McFall disappears from The Willows caravan site, Sandhurst Lane, Gloucester. She is nearly seven months' pregnant. Her remains, together with the remains of her unborn child, were recovered from Fingerpost Field, Kempley, on 7 June 1994.

September 1967 – Frederick and Rena West move to Lake House caravan site at Bishop's Cleeve.

6 January 1968 – Mary Bastholm, aged 15, disappears from a bus stop on Bristol Road in Gloucester. She is never seen again.

6 February 1968 – Daisy West dies suddenly, at the age of 44, in Hereford Hospital.

December 1968 – Rosemary Letts leaves school, and goes to work in Cheltenham.

October 1969 – Rena West leaves her husband again. Rosemary Letts starts to act as the nanny to Charmaine and Anna-Marie West at Lake House caravan site in Bishop's Cleeve.

18 November 1969 – Frederick West is imprisoned for three days for non-payment of fines. Charmaine and Anna-Marie West placed in care.

21 November 1969 – Rena West returns to her husband at Lake House caravan site, and her children are returned from local authority care, but she leaves again within three days.

28 November 1969 – Charmaine and Anna-Marie placed in care again.

29 November 1969 – Rosemary Letts is 16.

February 1970 – Rosemary Letts is now pregnant by Frederick West.

March 1970 – Rosemary Letts placed briefly in care by her father William Letts. She then leaves her parents' home and goes to live with Frederick West at 9 Clarence Road, Cheltenham.

March 1970 – Charmaine and Anna-Marie West are returned to their father's care. Frederick West tells the local authority that Rena West has returned home, and that Rosemary Letts is also present to help them look after the children.

April 1970 – Frederick West and Rosemary Letts move to 10 Midland Road, Gloucester, apparently without Rena West. They move shortly afterwards to 4 Park End Road, Gloucester.

July 1970 – Frederick West and Rosemary Letts move for a third time, to 25 Midland Road, Gloucester.

17 October 1970 – Heather Ann West born at Gloucester Royal Hospital to Rosemary Letts.

4 December 1970 – Frederick West imprisoned for nine months for dishonesty and theft, a further one month's sentence is imposed upon him four weeks later.

January 1971 – Frederick West is transferred from Her Majesty's Prison Gloucester to Leyhill Open Prison, Wotton-under-Edge, Gloucestershire.

24 June 1971 – Frederick West is released from prison.

June 1971 – Charmaine West, then aged eight, disappears. Her school records suggest she has 'moved to London'. Her remains are recovered from beneath the kitchen floor at 25 Midland Road on 5 May 1994.

August 1971 – Rena West disappears. Her remains are recovered from Letterbox Field, Kempley, on 11 April 1994.

29 January 1972 – Frederick West marries Rosemary Letts at Gloucester Register Office. He describes himself on the marriage certificate, signed by both him and his new wife, as a bachelor.

1 June 1972 – May June West born to the Wests. She later changes her name to Mae.

September 1972 – The Wests move into 25 Cromwell Street, Gloucester.

October 1972 – Carol Raine goes to work for the Wests as a nanny to Anna-Marie, Heather and Mae West.

November 1972 – Carol Raine leaves the Wests.

4 December 1972 – Carol Raine is abducted, beaten, and indecently assaulted by Frederick and Rosemary West.

12 January 1973 – The Wests plead guilty to charges of occasioning actual bodily harm and indecent assault on Carol Raine. They are fined a total of £50 each.

19 April 1973 – Lynda Gough, a 19-year-old seamstress, disappears. She had been a regular visitor at 25 Cromwell Street. She is reported missing to a local police-officer. Her remains are recovered beneath the rear bathroom extension of the house on 7 March 1994.

19 August 1973 – Stephen West, the Wests' first son, is born.

10 November 1973 – Carol Ann Cooper, a 15-year-old resident of the Pines Children's Home in Worcester, disappears after getting on a bus in Tewkesbury. She is reported missing to the police. Her remains are recovered from beneath the cellar floor at 25 Cromwell Street on 8 March 1994.

27 December 1973 – Lucy Partington, a 21-year-old third-year undergraduate at Exeter University, disappears on her way to a bus stop in Cheltenham. She is reported missing to the police. Her remains are recovered from beneath the cellar floor at 25 Cromwell Street on 6 March 1994.

16 April 1974 – Thérèse Siegenthaler, a 21-year-old sociology student in London, last seen leaving London for a hitchhiking trip to

Ireland, is reported missing to the police. Her remains are recovered from the beneath the cellar floor at 25 Cromwell Street on 5 March 1994.

14 November 1974 – Shirley Hubbard, a 15-year-old on work experience at a Worcester store, runs away from her foster-parents' house in Droitwich, and is never seen alive again. She is reported missing to the police. Her remains are recovered from beneath the cellar floor of Cromwell Street on 5 March 1994.

11 April 1975 – Juanita Mott, then aged 18, who had visited Cromwell Street regularly, disappears after setting out to hitchhike to Gloucester from Newent. She is not reported missing to the police. Her remains are recovered from beneath the cellar floor of Cromwell Street on 6 March 1994.

April 1977 – Shirley Robinson, then 17, comes to live at 25 Cromwell Street as a lodger.

October 1977 – Shirley Robinson becomes pregnant by Frederick West.

9 December 1977 – Rosemary West gives birth to Tara Jayne West, always known as 'Mo'. Her father is not Frederick West.

May 1978 – Bill Letts dies at the age of 58.

June 1978 – Shirley Robinson disappears when eight-and-a-half months' pregnant. Her disappearance is not reported to the police. Her remains are recovered from the rear garden at 25 Cromwell Street on 28 February 1994.

17 November 1978 – Louise West, the fourth child of Frederick and Rosemary West together, is born in Gloucester.

September 1979 – Alison Chambers, then aged 17 and recently released from care, who has been a frequent visitor to Cromwell Street, writes to her mother to tell her that she is working for a family as a nanny. She is not seen or heard of again, until her remains are recovered from the rear garden of 25 Cromwell Street on 28 February 1994.

16 June 1980 – Barry West, the second son of Frederick and Rosemary West, is born in Gloucester.

October 1980 – Frederick West convicted of receiving stolen goods. He is sentenced to nine months' imprisonment, suspended for two years. The jury hears of his recording sexual relations with his wife in his van on audiotapes.

13 April 1982 – Rosemary West gives birth to Rosemary West Junior. Her father is not Frederick West.

16 July 1983 – Rosemary West gives birth to Lucyanna West, always known as 'Babs'. Her father is not Frederick West. Rosemary West is sterilised after the birth.

19 June 1987 – Heather West, by now aged 16, disappears from 25 Cromwell Street. She is not reported missing to the police. Her whereabouts remain a mystery until her remains are recovered from beneath the patio in the rear garden of 25 Cromwell Street on 26 February 1994.

28 March 1992 – Walter West dies at Ledbury Cottage Hospital, aged 78.

6 August 1992 – Frederick West is arrested, and subsequently charged, on three counts of rape and one of buggery against one of his daughters. He is remanded in custody.

11 August 1992 – Rosemary West is charged with cruelty and 'causing or encouraging the commission of unlawful sexual intercourse with a child', one of her daughters. She is released on bail.

12 August 1992 – Rosemary West attempts suicide at 25 Cromwell Street and is admitted to Gloucester Royal Infirmary at one-fifty the following morning, where her stomach is pumped out.

September 1992 – Frederick West is sent to a bail hostel in Birmingham to await trial.

September 1992 – Mae West moves back into 25 Cromwell Street to keep her mother company after Rosemary West's suicide attempt.

7 June 1993 – Frederick and Rosemary West face trial in Gloucester. Two witnesses refuse to give evidence against them, and Judge Gabriel Hutton enters formal verdicts of not guilty. The Wests embrace each other in the dock.

24 February 1994 – The police arrive at 25 Cromwell Street with a search warrant for the garden 'in connection with the disappearance' of Heather West. The Cromwell Street investigation officially begins.

25 February 1994 – Frederick West is arrested and confesses to the murder of his daughter Heather for the first time. While Rosemary West is detained at Cheltenham police station, he is taken by the

police to the garden of 25 Cromwell Street, where he tells them they are 'digging in the wrong place'.

26 February 1994 – The remains of Heather West are recovered, as well as another human thigh bone. Frederick West again confesses to her killing, as well as to the killings of Shirley Robinson and Alison Chambers.

27 February 1994 – Frederick West is taken back to 25 Cromwell Street by the police, where he is asked to identify the sites of the remains of Shirley Robinson and Alison Chambers. Rosemary West is released on bail pending further enquiries. She returns to Cromwell Street.

28 February 1994 – The remains of both Shirley Robinson and Alison Chambers are recovered from 25 Cromwell Street. Frederick West appears at Gloucester magistrates' court charged with the murder of his daughter Heather.

2 March 1994 – Frederick West is formally charged with the murders of Shirley Robinson and Alison Chambers.

3 March 1994 – Frederick West collapses during a court appearance at Gloucester magistrates' court.

4 March 1994 – Frederick West admits to nine further killings, including that of his first wife Rena West and his stepdaughter Charmaine West, as well as Lynda Gough 'and others to be identified'. Frederick West is taken back to 25 Cromwell Street by the police to mark where the bodies are buried.

5 March 1994 – Frederick West is taken to Letterbox Field, where he points out the area in which he buried his first wife Rena. The remains of Thérèse Siegenthaler and Shirley Hubbard are recovered from 25 Cromwell Street.

6 March 1994 – The remains of Lucy Partington and Juanita Mott are recovered from 25 Cromwell Street.

7 March 1994 – The remains of Lynda Gough are recovered from 25 Cromwell Street. Frederick West is taken to Fingerpost Field, Kempley, and points out the position that he believes Ann McFall may be buried. He denies killing her.

8 March 1994 – The remains of Carol Ann Cooper are recovered from 25 Cromwell Street, bringing the total number of bodies recovered there to nine. No further bodies are to be recovered from the house.

11 March 1994 – Frederick West appears at Gloucester magistrates' court on eight separate charges of murder, a ninth, that of Carol Cooper is laid against him six days later.

17 March 1994 – Frederick West is charged with the murder of Alison Chambers, one of the first victims to be recovered from the garden of 25 Cromwell Street. It has previously proved difficult for the police to identify her.

20 March 1994 – Frederick West is taken to visit 25 Midland Road, and insists 'You won't find nothing there'. He also denies any knowledge of the disappearance of Mary Bastholm, although he is taken to Bristol Road, Gloucester by the police.

29 March 1994 – Excavations begin at Letterbox Field, Kempley.

6 April 1994 – Frederick West is taken to the site in Letterbox Field, where he indicated that he had buried the remains of Rena West.

10 April 1994 – The remains of Rena West are discovered at Letterbox Field.

13 April 1994 – Excavations begin in Fingerpost Field, Kempley, the site which Frederick West suggested contained the remains of Ann McFall.

21 April 1994 – Rosemary West appears before Gloucester magistrates' court charged with another matter, and is remanded in custody. These proceedings are later dropped.

24 April 1994 – Rosemary West is charged with the murder of Lynda Gough, the first of nine murder charges brought against her in the eight weeks to come.

25 April 1994 – Rosemary West is again remanded in custody.

26 April 1994 – Excavations begin at 25 Midland Road, Gloucester.

29 April 1994 – Frederick West retracts his confessions: 'I have not and still cannot tell you the whole truth . . . from the very first day of this enquiry my main concern has been to protect another person or persons.'

4 May 1994 – The remains of Charmaine West are recovered from below the kitchen area at 25 Midland Road.

11 May 1994 – Frederick West is charged with the murder of Charmaine West.

13 May 1994 – Frederick West's 132nd and final interview in the first series at Gloucester police station.

2 June 1994 – Nine of Frederick West's eleven murder charges are amended to joint charges with his wife Rosemary at Gloucester magistrates' court.

3 June 1994 – Rosemary West appears at Gloucester magistrates' court, where her nine murder charges are amended to joint charges with her husband.

7 June 1994 – The remains of Ann McFall are discovered in Fingerpost Field. She is the last known victim to be recovered.

30 June 1994 – Frederick and Rosemary West appear together for the first time at Gloucester magistrates' court. He is charged with eleven counts of murder, she with nine.

3 July 1994 – Frederick West charged with the murder of Ann McFall, bringing the total number of murder charges against him to twelve.

1 January 1995 – Frederick West is found hanged in his cell at HM Prison Winson Green shortly before 1 p.m.

13 January 1995 – Rosemary West is charged with the murder of Charmaine West. It is the tenth murder charge laid against her.

14 February 1995 – Rosemary West is committed for trial on ten charges of murder.

29 March 1995 – Frederick West is cremated at Cranley Crematorium, near Coventry.

3 October 1995 – The trial of Rosemary West on ten murder charges begins at Winchester Crown Court.

21 November 1995 – The jury unanimously returns three verdicts of guilty, and retires again to consider the remaining seven charges.

22 November 1995 – The jury unanimously returns a further seven guilty verdicts. The judge recommends that Rosemary West should never be released.

19 March 1996 – The Court of Appeal refuse Rosemary West permission to appeal against her conviction.

12 July 1996 – A jury at the inquest into his death decides that Frederick West killed himself. His life officially comes to an end.

Index

buggery, charges of 274, 277–8, 284, 287

Bulger, James 344

burial of bodies *see* murder victims (*subheadings for* death *under individual entries*)

Canter, David (Professor) 160, 179, 190, 195, 334, 347–9, 351

caravan sites in Gloucester 53, 55–63, 65–8, 75

care orders for FW and RW's children 285–6, 336, 338

Carpenter House 281–3, 286

Carson's Contractors 268

cellar at Cromwell Street 120–2, 124, 133–4, 142, 215, 310

Chambers, Alison (or Al or Ali) 227–35, 247, 256, 296, 306
  death of 231–5, 241

Childline 272–3

children of FW
  claimed number of 32, 153, 168
  see also daughters; sons

children's homes 154–5; *see also* Jordan's Brook

church-going 20, 23, 25, 42, 149, 272, 317

Clarence Road (Cheltenham), flat in 97, 102, 109

Cleft Chin Murder, the 352

clothing, FW's *see* dress

colour prejudice, FW's 268

Commission on Children and Violence 344

condoms, use of 224

confessions and retractions, FW's 9–11, 13, 16, 105–7, 111, 114, 141–4, 156–8, 166–8, 175–8, 187–90, 193–5, 212, 218–22, 231–4, 293–6, 299–301, 303, 307–9, 317, 319, 324, 340

contact magazines 198, 246, 252, 321, 353

contraception 59

convictions, criminal, FW's
  for larceny as a servant (April 1961) 34
  for theft and deception (June 1968) 82
  for motoring offences (June 1969) 90
  for theft (August 1969) 90
  for theft (March 1975) 191
  for receiving (November 1975) 200
  for receiving (October 1980) 237

Cooper, Carol (Caz) 154–60, 162, 171, 174, 186–7, 310–11, 317
  death of 157–60

Costello, Catherine (Rena) *see* West, Rena

Cotswold Tyres 95–6, 98, 100

countryside, influence on FW of 1–3, 17, 21, 23–5, 30, 75, 112

Court of Appeal 340

cowardice, FW's *see* fighting with men

cremation, FW's 337

Crick, Terry 94–5

criminal contacts, FW's 227, 268

'criminal gene' 343–4

Cromwell Street (Gloucester), house in
  purchase of 120
  reputation of 228, 261–2
  structural alterations to 148, 247

Daily Telegraph 301

Daisy Cottage 34, 37

daughters of FW *see* West, Anna-Marie; West, Heather; West, Louise; West, Lucyanna; West, Mae; West, Rosemary; West, Tara

Davies, Alan (Caz Cooper's sometime boyfriend) 186

Davies, Chris 250

Davies, Dan 186

Davis, Alan 'Dapper' (lodger at Cromwell Street) 125, 127, 140

death of FW *see* suicide

declarations signed by RW 240, 244–5

Department of Health and Social Security 149, 223

deviance, sexual, FW's 39–40, 64–6, 79, 91, 93, 113

diary, sexual
  FW's 26
  RW's 242, 248, 326

dildos 242–3, 265, 277, 280

dirtiness of FW 1, 21, 23, 29, 33, 92, 164, 269

disappearances of FW 5–6, 29, 97, 292

dismemberment and disposal of bodies 71, 309, 326; *see also* murder victims (*subheadings for* death *under individual entries*)

divorce from Rena West, FW's 61

Dix, Margaretta 256

Dobbs, Arthur 252

dress, FW's 1, 8, 21, 25–6, 30, 35, 94

drinking, FW's 32, 41, 44, 94

drugs 94, 116, 127, 139, 153, 197, 292, 294, 296, 298, 302, 321

drugs raids 146–7, 182

education, FW's 21, 23

electricity meter, tampering with 8, 293

Emergency Protection Orders 276

emotion shown during questioning by FW 195, 313, 318, 343

368

Savage, Hazel (Detective Constable) 6,
    9–12, 16, 62, 181, 278–80, 288–9,
    291–9, 302, 305–6, 308–9, 311,
    313, 316–18, 322, 327
scapegoat, RW as 320–6
Scarface 54
scoring of sexual partners, RW's 285–6
Scorpions, the 139, 154
searches for missing persons 173–4
secretiveness of FW 161, 329, 332,
    337–8
seduction of local girls, young FW's
    26–7, 32–3, 38, 52
serial killers 343, 349–51
sewer system, use of 235
sex parties 64–5, 74, 81–2, 134, 194,
    261, 320
sexual abuse
    of Carol Raine 129–33
    of FW and RW as children 24–5,
        96
    of FW and RW's children 134–7,
        150, 199–201, 258–9, 270, 272–7,
        290, 300, 326
    of 'Miss A' 207–9
    of murder victims 324; see also
        murder victims (subheadings for
        death under individual entries)
sexual aids 265–7, 276–8, 280, 352
sexual appetites of FW and RW 22–7,
    32–5, 38–9, 42–5, 62–8, 74, 82–3,
    101, 125–6, 130, 137–8, 153,
    160–1, 205, 240, 243, 352
sexual barter 101, 125
sexual harness 177–8, 195, 276
sexual inadequacy, FW's 242, 244–5,
    283–4, 327, 343
Sheward, Conrad 132
shipping, FW's jobs in 32–3
Siegenthaler, Thérèse 174–80, 189–90,
    193, 310
    death of 175–9
Sigal, Clancy 343
silence after arrest, RW's 316
Simon Gloster SARO 115, 118
sisters of FW see West, Kathleen
    (Kitty); West, Gwendoline (Gwen);
    West, Daisy ('Little Daisy')
Skulls, the 48, 50
Small, Father 42
Smith, John 132
snuff movies 171, 234, 328
sociability, FW's 347; see also affability
social workers, views of 336, 338–9
sons of FW see West, Stephen; West,
    Barry
Stanniland, Ben 125, 127, 130–1,
    140
starvation of murder victims 188

sterilisation, RW's 249, 269
strength, physical
    FW's 240
    RW's 158, 266
strength of character, FW's 240
Stroud Court 268–9
Stroud Road, room at 270–1
suicide, FW's 49, 330–2, 352
suicide attempt, RW's 279
Sunday Mirror 310

talker, FW as 2–3, 27, 34, 61, 81, 116,
    133, 183, 348–9
Taylor of Gosforth, Lord 340
television 174, 287–8, 291, 293
thefts by FW 34, 82, 90, 144–5, 150,
    191, 198, 200, 227, 282
Thorneybrook, Mick 117
Tonks, Linda 256
torture of murder victims 322; see also
    murder victims (subheadings for
    death under individual entries)
trials
    of FW for incest (1961) 34–7, 287
    of FW and RW for sex offences
        (1992) 285–7, 338–9
    of RW for murder (1995) 340
trophies 72, 90, 144, 160, 222, 235,
    245, 311
Trotter, John 47–8, 56
Tully, Bryan 349–50, 352
Tyler, Glenys (née Letts) 85, 88,
    205
Tyler, Jim 88, 205

urination 242–3, 285, 315

vanity of FW 334
venereal diseases 33, 268
verbal ability, FW's see talker
Vestey, Robert (Detective Constable) 6
vibrators 135, 199, 207, 240–3, 265,
    277, 326
victims, FW's methods of targeting and
    luring 45, 52, 78, 115–16, 153–4,
    169–70, 267
Victoria café 46–7, 55
videotapes see pornographic videos
violence, physical
    of FW 68, 41–9, 55–6, 65, 82–3, 90,
        101, 200–1, 239–40, 251, 263,
        345
    of RW 99, 103–4, 123–4, 150, 162,
        184–5, 201, 215, 239–40, 249,
        270, 275, 304, 313, 339, 346
    towards FW and RW in childhood
        19–21, 33, 85–7, 93
Vizard, Eileen (Dr) 147, 335, 345–6,
    348